Perfect Moderns
A History of
the Camden Town Group

FOR SUSANNAH

Wendy Baron

Perfect Moderns

A History of the Camden Town Group

ASHGATE

Published by
Ashgate Publishing Limited
Gower House
Croft Road
Aldershot
Hants GU11 3HR
England

Ashgate Publishing Company
Old Post Road
Brookfield
Vermont 05036-9704
USA

British Library Cataloguing-in-Publication data
Baron, Wendy
Perfect moderns : a history of the Camden Town Group
1. Camden Town Group – History 2. Painting, Modern – 20th century – England – London 3. Painters – England – London – Biography
I. Title
759.2'142

ISBN 1 84014 291 X

Library of Congress Cataloging-Publication data
Baron, Wendy.
Perfect moderns : a history of the Camden Town Group / Wendy Baron.
    p.   cm.
Includes bibliographical references.
ISBN 1–84014–291–X (alk. paper)
1. Camden Town Group. 2. Painting, Modern–20th century –Great Britain. 3. Painters–Great Britain–Biography. I. Title.
ND468.5.C35B3724 2000
759.2'142—dc21
99–36706

CIP

ISBN 1 84014 291 X

Printed on acid-free paper
Typeset in Plantin Light by Bournemouth Colour Press, Parkstone. Printed in Singapore.

Contents

Acknowledgements

My earlier book on the Camden Town Group was published exactly twenty years ago. It is now out of print and, inevitably, out of date. I had expected that by the close of the twentieth century a clutch of monographs would have been published on the lives and work of some of the best British painters of the early 1900s. This would have made much of the present book, in particular the 'Catalogue of works in public collections by members of the Camden Town Group', redundant. There have been some developments: the welcome research on John Doman Turner by James Robertson and the publication of Anne Thorold's impressive catalogue of the paintings of Lucien Pissarro. I hope that this new book, with its expanded catalogue, will be a spur to further research into the work of these artists.

It would have been impossible to compile a catalogue of paintings in public collections by sixteen artists without the generous co-operation of staff in galleries and museums worldwide. Those who responded to my letters are listed below. A few curators were so exceptionally helpful I must thank them specifically and individually. Angus Trumble of the National Gallery of South Australia negotiated on my behalf with private collectors in and around Adelaide, obtained photographs for me and most importantly suggested structural changes to make this book a more useful work of reference than the earlier version. The sound of his faxed letters from Australia – which regularly woke me at 3.00 am – was always welcome. Michael Parke-Taylor of the Art Gallery of Ontario, Toronto, gave me a uniquely helpful list of the fax numbers and e-mail addresses of those staff in Canadian galleries who would be willing and able to answer my enquiries. David Scrase at the Fitzwilliam Museum, Cambridge; Tim Craven at Southampton City Art Gallery; Alistair Smith at the Whitworth Art Gallery, Manchester; Andrew Barlow at Brighton Museum and Art Gallery; and Brendan Bell at the Tatham Art Gallery in Pietermaritzburg, all went out of their way to find information outside the scope of their own institutions.

In 1979 I wrote about the impetus my work on Camden Town painters received when the late Dr Malcolm Easton gave me his research papers. I must again acknowledge my great debt to him. Other scholars who helped me in the 1970s have continued to share their knowledge with me. In particular I am grateful to Professor Andrew Causey, to Anne Thorold and to David Buckman, authorities on Gilman, Lucien Pissarro and Manson respectively. Dr Pamela Taylor gave me the results of her investigations into the places where William Ratcliffe had lived in Barnet, and Kevin Driscoll told me of the photograph of 19 Fitzroy Street (fig.2).

The private owners of paintings illustrated in this book – some acknowledged by name in the following pages, some not – have been generous with their time and trouble. I thank them all. Collecting photographs and transparencies of far-flung paintings is always a nightmare. Writing an illustrated book demands the co-operation of many people besides the current owners of the pictures concerned. I was fortunate to obtain the unstinting help of Rachel Hidderley at Christie's, Mark Adams at Sotheby's, Jenna Burlingham at Phillips, Robin Vousden at the Anthony d'Offay Gallery and Peyton Skipwith at the Fine Art Society. I would also like to thank Richard Littlewood and Alan Stewart for their help with photography.

One of the pleasures of studying the work of painters of the near, rather than the distant, past is to meet their families. I have greatly enjoyed my continuing contact with Frederick Gore (son of Spencer Gore) and his wife Connie. I am indebted to them for so generously sharing with me their enthusiasm as well as their expertise. While preparing this book I made two new friends: Barbara Duce, niece of Gilman, and Monica Beck, niece of Ratcliffe. My deep thanks to them both for their encouragement.

Sadly many of the people who helped me in the past have since died. I remember in particular John H. Gilman (son of Harold Gilman), Miss Mary Manson and Mrs Jean Goullet (daughters of J. B. Manson) and Mrs Ruby Ginner Dyer (sister of Ginner). Many of the former copyright holders have died since the late 1970s. In most – but not all – cases I have traced the new copyright holders. Copyright is not an issue which much exercised the Camden Town Group painters and their heirs. It is, however, an issue which in an increasingly bureaucratic and litigious age must be addressed by writers and publishers. Bevan, Gilman, Gore, Innes and Lightfoot are out of copyright; Bayes, Drummond, Ginner, Grant, John, Lamb, Lewis, Manson, Pissarro, Ratcliffe, Sickert and Turner are still in copyright. I am grateful to the following for their permissions: James Drummond, Henrietta Garnett, Julius E. White, Henrietta Phipps, Omar S. Pound, Dennis Nicholson, Dr Simon Shorvon, Monica Beck, and DACS on behalf of Sickert's estate. I have been unable to trace the current copyright holders of Bayes, Ginner and Turner. If anyone knows who they are, please let me know through my publishers. I much appreciate the efforts of all those who have helped me try – unsuccessfully – to find the relevant names and addresses. I would especially like to thank Miss E. H. Crowe (friend of Mrs Ruby Ginner Dyer) and Mrs F. R. May of the solicitors Slade Son and Taylor who handled Mrs Dyer's estate.

I thank the following curators and registrars of museums and galleries worldwide: Jill Adelson; Rosamund Allwood; Maureen Attrill; Adrienne Avery-Gray; Sue Backhouse; Richard Beresford; John Bernasconi; Mark Bills; Miriam Biran; Danielle Blanchette; Jennifer Bossmann; Brigitte Bouret; Sarah Bridges; Rachel Brodie; Ron Brownson; Erik Burnett-Godfree; Richard Burns; Richard Calvocoressi; Jillian Carman; Ron Aquila Clarke; Matthew Clough; Beverley

Cole; Alison Cowling; Bridget Crump; Richard Davies; Sonia Dean; Hilary Diaper; Ann Dorsett; Leanne Engelberg; Peter Entwhistle; Kate Eustace; Dr Mark L. Evans; Brendan Flynn; Melanie Gardner; Mireille Galinou; Dionissia Giakoumi; Anne Goodchild; Janda Gooding; Richard Green; Deanna M. Griffin; Helen Hadden; Robert Hall; Rosalind Hardiman; Nigel Herring; Dr Melanie Hillebrand; Kimberly K. Hirst; Elizabeth Hopkin; Christine Hopper; Angela Horn; David Fraser Jenkins; Jill Jimenez; Isobel Johnstone; Dr Brian Kennedy; Laura Kidner; Alex Kidson; Isobel Kindley; Brian J. Lang; David Law; Adrian Le Harivel; Jillian Lloyd; Thembinkosi Mabaso; Sheila McGregor; Vera Magyar; Sandra Martin; Mary Matthews; Dallas M. Mechan; Lee Mooney; Christine Nielsen; Lisa O'Connor; Michael Pantazzi; David Patterson; Stephen B. Phillips; Alison Plumridge; Evelyne Pomey; Hayden Russell Proud; Stefan van Raay; Denis Rainforth; Jane Richards; Alex Robertson; Fiona Robertson; Laura Rosenstock; Liz Salmon; Judith Sandling; Pat Saunders; Jane Sedge; Tracy Sibson; Sue Sloman; Sheena Stoddard; Alan Suddes; Penny Thompson; Ruth Trotter; Amanda Vye; Alexandra Walker; Jean Walsh; Malcolm Warner; Angela Weight; Toby Whatley; Lucy Whetstone; Carolyn Wingfield; Maime Winters; Caroline Worthington; Joanne Wright; Stephen Yates; Clara Young; Kai Kin Yung; and Tanya Zhilinsky.

My editors Pamela Edwardes, Sue Moore and Maureen Street have each contributed to the coherence of the final text. Any infelicities and inconsistencies which remain should be credited to me.

List of abbreviations

General

AAA	Allied Artists' Association
AC	Arts Council of Great Britain
FAS	Fine Art Society, London
LG	London Group
NEAC	New English Art Club
RA	Royal Academy of Arts
RBD	Roland, Browse & Delbanco, London
rep.	reproduced

For inscriptions

bc	bottom centre
bcr	bottom centre right
bl	bottom left
br	bottom right
tl	top left
tr	top right

References to books

Baron 1973	Baron, Wendy, *Sickert*, London: Phaidon, 1973.
Baron 1977	Baron, Wendy, *Miss Ethel Sands and her Circle*, London: Peter Owen, 1977.
Baron 1979	Baron, Wendy, *The Camden Town Group*, London: Scolar Press, 1979.
Bevan 1965	Bevan, R.A., *Robert Bevan 1865–1925: A Memoir by his Son*, London: Studio Vista, 1965.
Browse 1960	Browse, Lillian, *Sickert*, London: Rupert Hart-Davis, 1960.
Connett 1992	Connett, Maureen, *Walter Sickert and the Camden Town Group*, London: David & Charles, 1992.
Easton and Holroyd 1974	Easton, Malcolm, and Holroyd, Michael, *The Art of Augustus John*, London: Secker & Warburg, 1974.
Fothergill 1946	Fothergill, John, *James Dickson Innes*, London: Faber, 1946 (reproductions collected and edited by Lillian Browse).
GLK 1924	G. L. K[ennedy], *Henry Lamb*, London: Ernest Benn, 1924.
Jenkins 1975	Jenkins, A. D. Fraser, 'J. D. Innes at the National Museum of Wales', Cardiff: National Museum of Wales, 1975.
L&F 1919	Lewis, Wyndham, and Fergusson, Louis F., *Harold Gilman: An Appreciation*, London: Chatto & Windus, 1919.
Michel 1971	Michel, Walter, *Wyndham Lewis Paintings and Drawings*, London: Thames & Hudson, 1971.
Rothenstein 1944	Rothenstein, John, *Augustus John*, London: Phaidon, 1944.
Shone 1976	Shone, Richard, *Bloomsbury Portraits*, London: Phaidon, 1976.

Shone 1988   Shone, Richard, *Walter Sickert*, Oxford: Phaidon, 1988.

Thorold 1983   Thorold, Anne, *Catalogue of Oil Paintings by Lucien Pissarro*, London: Athelney Books, 1983.

Watney 1980   Watney, Simon, *English Post-Impressionism*, London: Cassell, 1980.

References to exhibitions and their catalogues

Aberdeen 1998   Aberdeen Art Gallery, 1998–9, 'An Ordinary Life: Camden Town Painters'.

AC 1953   The Arts Council of Great Britain touring exhibition, 1953, 'The Camden Town Group'.

AC 1953–4   The Arts Council of Great Britain touring exhibition, 1953–4, 'Charles Ginner 1878–1952: Exhibition of Paintings & Drawings'. Catalogue introduction by Hubert Wellington.

AC 1954–5   The Arts Council of Great Britain touring exhibition, 1954–5, 'Harold Gilman 1876–1919'. Catalogue introduction by J. Wood Palmer.

AC 1955   The Arts Council of Great Britain touring exhibition, 1955, 'Spencer Frederick Gore 1878–1914'. Catalogue introduction by J. Wood Palmer.

AC 1956   The Arts Council of Great Britain touring exhibition, 1956, 'Robert Bevan 1865–1925'. Catalogue introduction by J. Wood Palmer.

AC 1960   The Arts Council of Great Britain at the Tate Gallery, London, Southampton Art Gallery and Bradford City Art Gallery, 1960, 'Sickert Paintings and Drawings'. Catalogue introduction by Gabriel White.

AC 1963–4   The Arts Council of Great Britain touring exhibition, 1963–4, 'Malcolm Drummond 1880–1945'. Catalogue introduction by Quentin Bell.

AC 1974   The Arts Council of Great Britain, Hayward Gallery, London, 1974, 'Vorticism and its Allies'. Catalogue by Richard Cork.

AC 1981–2   The Arts Council of Great Britain touring exhibition, 1981–2, 'Harold Gilman 1876–1919'. Catalogue by Andrew Causey and Richard Thomson.

AC Edinburgh 1953 The Scottish Committee of the Arts Council, Royal Scottish Academy, Edinburgh, 1953, 'Sickert 1860–1942'.

Adelaide 1997   Art Gallery of South Australia, Adelaide, 1997, 'Bohemian London: Camden Town and Bloomsbury Paintings in Adelaide'. Catalogue by Angus Trumble.

Applehayes 1986 Herbert Art Gallery, Coventry, and Plymouth City Museum and Art Gallery, 1986, 'Artists at Applehayes: Camden Town Painters at a West Country Farm, 1909–1924'. Catalogue by Rosalind Billingham.

Barbican 1997   Barbican Art Gallery, London, 1997, 'Modern Art in Britain 1910–1914'. Catalogue by Anna Gruetzner

	Robins, published by Merrell Holberton, London, 1997.
Bedford 1969	Cecil Higgins Art Gallery, Bedford, 1969, 'The Camden Town Group'.
Brighton 1913–14	Brighton Art Gallery, 1913–14, 'English Post-Impressionists, Cubists and Others'. Catalogue introductions by J.B. Manson and Wyndham Lewis.
Brighton 1962	Royal Pavilion, Brighton, 1962. 'Sickert Exhibition'.
Christie's 1988	Christie's, London, 1988, 'The Painters of Camden Town, 1905–1920'. Catalogue by Francis Farmar with introduction by Wendy Baron.
CMG 1915	Goupil Gallery, London, 1915, 'Cumberland Market Group'.
Colchester 1961	The Minories, Colchester, 1961, 'Camden Town Group'. Catalogue preface by R. A. Bevan.
Colchester 1969	The Minories, Colchester, Ashmolean Museum, Oxford, and Graves Art Gallery, Sheffield, 1969, 'Harold Gilman 1876–1919: An English Post-Impressionist'. Catalogue by Julian Agnew.
Colchester 1970	The Minories, Colchester, Ashmolean Museum, Oxford, and Graves Art Gallery, Sheffield, 1970, 'Spencer Gore 1878–1914'. Catalogue by John Woodeson.
CTG 1	Carfax Gallery, London, June 1911, 'Camden Town Group'.
CTG 2	Carfax Gallery, London, December 1911, 'Camden Town Group'.
CTG 3	Carfax Gallery, London, December 1912, 'Camden Town Group'.
d'Offay 1974	Anthony d'Offay Gallery, London, 1974, 'Spencer Frederick Gore 1878–1914'. Catalogue introduction 'Spencer Gore: A Memoir by his Son' by Frederick Gore.
d'Offay 1979	Anthony d'Offay, London, 1979, 'Paintings of London by Members of the Camden Town Group'.
d'Offay 1983	Anthony d'Offay, London, 1983, 'Spencer Frederick Gore 1878–1914'. Catalogue by Frederick Gore and Richard Shone.
Doré 1913	Doré Galleries, London, 1913, 'Post-Impressionist and Futurist Exhibition'. Foreword by Frank Rutter.
FAS 1973	Fine Art Society, London and Edinburgh, 1973, 'Sickert'. Catalogue by Wendy Baron.
FAS 1976	Fine Art Society, London, and Graves Art Gallery, Sheffield, 1976, 'Camden Town Recalled'. Catalogue by Wendy Baron.
FAS 1985	Fine Art Society, London, 1985, 'Charles Ginner 1878–1952'. Catalogue by Brian Sewell.
Leeds 1942	Temple Newsam, Leeds, 1942, 'Exhibition of the Life Work of Walter Richard Sickert'.
Lefevre 1950	Lefevre Gallery, London, 1950, 'Paintings by some members of the Camden Town Group'. Foreword by Maurice de Sausmarez.

Leicester 1940   Museum and Art Gallery, Leicester, 1940, 'Paintings and Drawings by Members of the Camden Town Group'. Preface by Maurice de Sausmarez.

Leicester Galleries 1930 Leicester Galleries, London, 1930, 'The Camden Town Group: A Review'.

Manchester 1984   Manchester Art Gallery, 1984, 'Henry Lamb'. Catalogue by Keith Clements and Sandra Martin.

Norwich 1976   Norwich Castle Museum, Southampton Art Gallery and Oxford Museum of Modern Art, 1976–7, 'A Terrific Thing: British Art 1910–16'. Section on the Camden Town Group.

Oxford 1991   Ashmolean Museum, Oxford, 1991, 'The Camden Town Group'. Catalogue by Bernadette Nelson.

Plymouth 1974   City Museum and Art Gallery, Plymouth, 1974, 'The Camden Town Group and Related Pictures'.

Pontoise 1998–9   Musée de Pontoise and Château Musée de Dieppe, 1998–9, 'Lucien Pissarro et le Post-Impressionisme Anglais', incorporating work by Harold Gilman, Spencer F. Gore, Lucien Pissarro and Walter R. Sickert. Catalogue contributions by Andrew Causey, Frederick Gore, Anne Thorold and Wendy Baron.

RA 1992   Royal Academy, London, and the Van Gogh Museum, Amsterdam, 1992–3, 'Sickert Paintings'. Catalogue edited by Wendy Baron and Richard Shone, published by Yale University Press, 1992.

RBD 1951   Roland, Browse & Delbanco, London, 1951, 'Sickert: Forty of his Finest Paintings'.

RBD 1960   Roland, Browse & Delbanco, London, 1960, 'Sickert 1860–1942'.

Redfern 1939   Redfern Gallery, London, 1939, 'The Camden Town Group'. Sale exhibition supported by a few loans.

Richmond 1996–7 Museum of Richmond, 1996–7, 'Spencer Gore in Richmond'. Catalogue by Frederick Gore and Robert Upstone.

Southampton 1951 Southampton Art Gallery (in association with the Arts Council of Great Britain), 1951, 'The Camden Town Group'. Catalogue introduction by Eric Westbrook.

Southampton 1977 Southampton Art Gallery and tour, 1977–8, 'James Dickson Innes'. Catalogue by John Hoole.

WAG 1972   Walker Art Gallery, Liverpool, 1972, 'Maxwell Gordon Lightfoot'. Catalogue by Gail Engert.

Ware Gallery 1967 William Ware Gallery, London, 1967, 'The Camden Town Group & English Painting 1900–1930's'.

Whitechapel 1914 Whitechapel Art Gallery, London, May 1914, 'Twentieth Century Art: A Review of Modern Movements'.

Yale 1980   Yale Center for British Art, New Haven, 1980, 'The Camden Town Group'. Catalogue by Wendy Baron with introduction by Malcolm Cormack.

List of plates

List of figures and maps

Chart of exhibition/membership participation

	CTG EXH June 1911	CTG EXH Dec 1911	2 P-I EXH Oct to Jan 1912-13	CTG EXH Dec 1912	DORÉ EXH Oct 1913	FSG 25 Oct 1913	FSG 15 Nov 1913	FSG 22 Nov 1913	FSG 29 Nov 1913	FSG ELECT LG 6 Dec 1913	BRIGHTON EXH Dec to Jan 1913-14	FSG ELECT LG 3 Jan 1914	FSG ELECT LG 7 Feb 1914	LG EXH Mar 1914	FSG ELECT LG 7 Mar 1914	FSG 14 Mar 1914
Bayes	●	●		●		○	○	○	○	○	●	○	○	●	○CH	
Bevan	●	●		●	●	○	○	○	○	○	●	○	○	●	○	○
Drummond	●	●		●	●	○	○	○		PR	●			●		
Gilman	●	●		●	●	○	○	○	○	○	●	○	○	●	○	○
Ginner	●	●		●	●	PR	○	○	○	○	●	○	○	●	○	○
Gore	●		●	●	●	○	○	○	○	○	●	○	○CH	●	○	○CH
Grant		●	●			○										
Innes		●										NM				
John	●															
Lamb	●	●	●	●			○			PR		PR				
Lewis	●	●	●	●	●	○	○	○	○	○	●	PR	○	●	○	
Lightfoot	●	dead														
Manson	●	●		●	●	○	○	○	○	○	●	○	○	●	○	○
Pissarro	●	●		●	●					PR	●	○				R
Ratcliffe	●	●		●	●		○	○	○	○	●	○	○	●	○	○
Sickert	●	●		●	●	○CH	○CH	○CH	○CH	○CH	●	○CH		R		
Turner	●	●		●												
E Sands						○	○	○	○	○	●	○		●		
A H Hudson						○		○	○	○	●	○		●		
Epstein					●	○	○	○	○	○	●	○	○	●	○	○
R Finch					●	○	○	○	○	○	●	○	○	●	○	○
Sund					●	○	○	○	○	○	●	○	○	●		
Adeney	●					○	○		○	○	●	PR	○	●	○	
Etchells	●				●	○	○		○	○	●	○	○	●		
Hamilton	●				●	○	○	○	○	PR	●	PR	○	●		
Nevinson					●	○		○	○	○	●	○	○	●		○
Squire						○	○	○	○	○	●	○		●	○	
Wadsworth	●				●	○	○	○	○	○	●	PR	○	●	○	
Bomberg			●							F	●	ED		●	○	○
J Etchells										F	●	ED	○	●		○
Fox-Pitt										F	●	ED				
Gill			●									ED	R			
S Gosse										F	●	ED		●		
S de Karlowska					●					F	●	ED	○	●	○	○
T Lessore										F	●	ED	○	●		
J Nash											●	ED		●	○	
Taylor										F	●	ED				
Gaudier-Brzeska										ED	●				○	○
S Spencer												ED				

Brackets at right: Camden Town Group; Fitzroy Street Group; Founder members of the London Group [NB Grant and John probably resigned before March 1914]; Elected Members of London Group by March 1914.

KEY

● = exhibited
○ = present
CH = chairman
PR = assigned proxy
NM = declared non-member
F = failed in election
ED = elected
R = resigned
CTG = Camden Town Group
EXH = exhibition
2 P-I = 2nd Post-Impressionist
FSG = Fitzroy Street Group
LG = London Group

NB Artists who stood as candidates but failed to secure election to the London Group between 6 December 1913 and 7 March 1914 were:

Geoffrey Allfree
Horace Brodzky
J S Currie
Miss Davison
Fanny Eveleigh (3)

E Forbes-Robertson
Mark Gertler (2)
Hilda Hassell
Hamilton Hay (3)
Darsie Japp (2)

Miss Lancaster
Mervyn Lawrence
Miss Middleton
Paul Nash (2)
C Maresco Pearce

William Roberts
A Rothenstein (2)
W Rothenstein (2)
Joseph Simpson
H S Teed (2)

Hilda Trevelyan (2)
E Verpilleux (2)
C Winzer (3)
Alfred Wolmark

The numbers in brackets are the number of times some artists submitted themselves for election. Otherwise each artist stood once only.

Fig.1   Chart explaining the formation of the London Group

Introduction

Camden Town, in north-west London, gave its name both to a style of painting and to a society of sixteen artists. The society – the Camden Town Group – was formed in 1911 to hold exhibitions in a commercial London gallery and thus reach a wider public than most of its members could manage alone. Its members were Walter Bayes, Robert Bevan, Malcolm Drummond, Harold Gilman, Charles Ginner, Spencer Gore, James Dickson Innes, Augustus John, Henry Lamb, Wyndham Lewis, Maxwell Gordon Lightfoot, James Bolivar Manson, Lucien Pissarro, William Ratcliffe, Walter Sickert and John Doman Turner. Duncan Grant was elected to replace Lightfoot after the latter's death in September 1911. The group held only three exhibitions, all at the Carfax Gallery in fashionable St James's, two in 1911 and one at the end of 1912.

The 'Camden Town' style encompassed paintings domestic in scale, unpretentious in subject-matter, informal in composition and lively in execution. Its favourite themes included humble models, nude or clothed, in shabby lodgings; domestic still lifes; London townscapes (not all of the Camden Town neighbourhood) and landscapes studied on visits to the country and abroad. The surface of 'Camden Town' paintings was typically constructed from a mosaic of crusty touches of high-keyed colours, often dominated by violets and greens. This style was common to a number of painters who, from 1907 onwards, under the aegis of Sickert, together rented a studio at 19 Fitzroy Street to store their work and hold informal exhibitions at Saturday afternoon gatherings attended by potential patrons. Those who contributed to the rent of this studio were known as the Fitzroy Street Group. Membership of this group over the years was fluid.

The most cursory consideration of the names on the list of Camden Town Group members demonstrates that some (Bayes, Innes, John, Lamb, Lewis, Lightfoot and Grant) were never, in the sense of the style described above, 'Camden Town' painters. Others were already exploring alternative means of expression by the time the Camden Town Group was born. These are the dry facts. The account that follows gives substance and context to these facts, tracking the collaborations and conflicts which gripped the art world in London before the First World War. At all points in the story Sickert is omnipresent.

Sickert: the New English Art Club and the 'London Impressionists'

To understand how and why the Camden Town Group came into being, it is essential to go back to the 1880s and follow the imperative, if seemingly erratic, course of Walter Sickert's career as artist, strategist and polemicist. The central rôle played by Sickert in both the Fitzroy Street and Camden Town Groups has to be set against the background of his earlier efforts to persuade his contemporaries to collaborate professionally.

The story begins in April 1888, when Sickert joined the New English Art Club (NEAC) and exhibited his four-foot-high portrayal (since destroyed) of the music hall artiste Katie Lawrence behind the footlights at Gatti's Hungerford Palace of Varieties. *Katie Lawrence* shared the honours with Philip Wilson Steer's even larger evocation of bathers on a beach entitled *A Summer's Evening*. In a letter to Jacques-Emile Blanche, Sickert enthusiastically predicted that the NEAC 'will be the place I think for the young school in England'.[1] However, the idealistic impetus behind the creation of the club in 1886 as an exhibiting body open to painters responsive to recent innovations in France was already fading. Its members split up into mutually antagonistic factions, the most progressive of which centred around Steer. The brilliant colours and increasingly broken touch of Steer's light-drenched visions of young girls at the English seaside were derived from French Impressionism, a source disapproved of by most critics and by many of Steer's fellow-members at the NEAC. Whereas Steer's *avant-garde* reputation was earned by his handling rather than by his subject-matter, the reverse was true of Sickert, vilified for finding the bawdy cockney music hall a proper subject for painting. Trained by his master Whistler in the arts of political manoeuvring and polemics, Sickert was a valuable addition to the Steer clique. While tactfully lying low at official club meetings and exhibiting only one picture in 1889, *Collin's Music Hall, Islington Green* (since destroyed), Sickert busied himself behind the scenes, trying to recruit sympathetic new members and conspiring to secure control of the selecting jury by his own faction. He also organized the independent exhibition of this group at the Goupil Gallery in December 1889 under the title 'London Impressionists' and as author of the catalogue preface acted as spokesman.

The ten exhibitors[2] were friends, sympathetic to each other's aims. They were not members of a common movement and none but Steer could claim any real affinity with Impressionism. D. S. MacColl pointed out that 'Impressionism' was 'the nickname for any new painting that surprised or annoyed critic or public' and suggested that its use to define the Goupil Gallery exhibition was 'a rough and ready means of attracting popular attention'.[3] Sickert, with his keen appreciation of the publicity value of catchy – if misleading – appellations, probably urged the adoption of the exhibition title. As a definition of the artists showing at the Goupil Gallery, 'London Impressionists' presages the inaccuracy of 'Camden Town' to define the group of sixteen exhibitors at the Carfax Gallery in 1911. This does not mean that the management of Goupil's (who in April 1889 had exhibited twenty 'Impressions by Claude Monet') was in any doubt about the meaning of the term 'Impressionism'. Nor was Sickert, though he tiptoed round this issue in his catalogue preface.

This preface[4] is Sickert's earliest coherent manifesto. He repudiated decorative painting and articulated his passionate belief that what mattered above all in a painting was 'quality', the fitness of its execution (even if this seemed 'ragged' or 'capricious') in expressing the artist's response to his subject. He then turned to Impressionism:

The word 'Impressionist' has certainly been for years an elastic one … Essentially and firstly it is not realism. It has no wish to record anything merely because it exists. It is not occupied in a struggle to make intensely real and solid the sordid or superficial details of the subjects it selects. It accepts, as the aim of the picture, what Edgar Allan Poe asserts to be the sole legitimate province of the poem, beauty. In its search through visible nature for the elements of this same beauty, it does not admit the narrow interpretation of the word 'Nature' which would stop short outside the four-mile radius. It is, on the contrary, strong in the belief that for those who live in the most wonderful and complex city in the world, the most fruitful course of study lies in a persistent effort to render the magic and the poetry which they daily see around them.

His lifelong creed was already formulated.

Although the 'London Impressionists' never again exhibited as a self-contained group, Sickert did not relax his attempts to publicize their activities. Two or three years later, in his Glebe Place studio in Chelsea, Sickert held the first one-man exhibition of Steer's work. He also wrote the catalogue preface to the first exhibition of another 'London Impressionist' colleague, the watercolourist Francis James, held at the Dudley Gallery in 1890. Sickert cited both these early efforts as precedents ('I have accomplished a great deal in that way') when he prophesied in a letter to Nan Hudson[5] in 1907 that the group of painters he was then organizing into concerted activity in Fitzroy Street would 'slowly do very useful things in London'.

Sickert: prelude to exile

As the 1890s progressed, Sickert and his 'London Impressionist' colleagues gradually drew apart, separated as much by their different temperaments as by their different preoccupations as painters. None possessed Sickert's restless energy, or his fierce professionalism. Their more limited ambitions were already satisfied. The Steer faction gradually gained control of the New English jury and, with the resignation or defection of other groups, came to dominate the club. Their prestige and authority were boosted when Fred Brown, Steer's original champion and one of the 'London Impressionists', was appointed professor at the Slade 1892 and when sympathetic writers – George Moore, D. S. MacColl and R. A. M. Stevenson – were appointed art critics to the *Speaker*, the *Spectator* and the *Pall Mall Gazette* respectively.

Only Steer and Sickert among the 'London Impressionists' group had ever been innovators. As the decade moved on Steer abandoned the dazzling stippled handling of his early works. He painted landscapes, portraits and (long before Sickert) informal figure studies, including nude subjects. However, from about 1894 onwards, he turned from the direct spontaneous observation which informed his intimate figure subjects and began to pillage a bewildering range of largely traditional pictorial sources. To quote Bruce Laughton, 'in his figure paintings … there is a continuous regressive change, as it were, back through evocations of Manet and Velasquez to a rather dusty version of French rococo. The landscapes … become inhibited and old-masterish.'[6] Sickert found himself isolated as the only one of the group who was still experimenting and exploring in the search for an independent artistic personality. While faithful to the tonal tradition in which he had been schooled by Whistler, Sickert recognized its dangerous tendency towards oversimplification. Many experiments during the 1890s, in both his landscapes and his portraits, were means of avoiding Whistlerian slightness of form and content. Monumental design; the use of deep, opaque colours; an extension of his tonal scale with the intermediate gradations excised (particularly in his night scenes of Venice, Dieppe and the area around Cumberland Market); the broad, untidily slashed brushwork of some of his portraits and landscapes later in the decade: these were among his methods of rejecting the subdued, refined effects favoured by Whistler and his followers. The several versions of Sickert's major music hall subject during the 1890s, *The Gallery of the Old Bedford, Camden Town*, demonstrate that he could transcend the influence of Degas as well as of Whistler. His earlier Degas-inspired representations of a floodlit stage seen behind silhouetted heads in a darkened auditorium (revived by Gore in the next century) were forgotten as Sickert concentrated on the rapt occupants of the gallery. He omitted all reference to the stage. The sophistication of his design produced compositional and psychological tensions which did not need explicit support or explanation. When Sickert returned to the music hall as a subject for painting in 1906 it was the spectators, often in the gallery, who recaptured his attention (see pl.25).

Sickert valued his independence, but did not relish isolation. Personal difficulties contributed to his depression and disillusion in the latter half of the 1890s. His marriage broke down. He was publicly slighted by his former master Whistler.[7] In the winter of 1898 he decided that he could no longer tolerate the apathetic insularity which characterized his professional colleagues in Britain. He escaped across the Channel, gave up portrait painting and settled down to paint the architecture of Dieppe.

Sickert abroad, 1898–1905

Dieppe remained Sickert's base until 1905. He punctuated his residence there with several long visits to Venice, and Venetian landscapes helped relieve the monotony of his concentration on the topography of Dieppe. Then, at the age of 43, on his visit to Venice of 1903–4, Sickert discovered a new and consuming interest in painting figures in his shabby rooms on the Calle dei

Frati. Back in Dieppe he continued to paint intimate figure subjects, posing his mistress Madame Villain, doyenne of the fishmarket, nude on the tousled sheets on an iron-framed bed.

During his absence Sickert maintained some contact with England, and even made fleeting visits to London. He occasionally sent his work over for exhibition at the NEAC, although he had resigned his membership in 1897. Ernest Brown of the Fine Art Society arranged to exhibit some of his landscape drawings in London. However, Sickert's main link with London was sustained through his friendship with William Rothenstein. Rothenstein, who had attended Sickert's evening classes in The Vale, Chelsea, in 1893 and had taken over Sickert's studio in Glebe Place in 1894, now worked in an advisory capacity for the Carfax Gallery, which began acquiring Sickert's work in 1899. The gallery had been started by a young painter and archaeologist, John Fothergill, in 1898; its staff then included Arthur Clifton (in charge of the business side) and Sickert's younger brother Robert. It was William Rothenstein's younger brother Albert (later Rutherston) who, on a painting trip in Normandy with Walter Russell and Spencer Frederick Gore, took Gore – future president of the Camden Town Group – to visit Sickert in Dieppe in 1904. Sickert's reputation as the *enfant terrible* of British art during the later 1880s and the 1890s had survived his absence. Gore had probably seen his pictures at the NEAC. Sickert was hungry for news of art in London.

Gore had studied at the Slade from 1896 to 1899, coinciding or overlapping not only with Albert Rothenstein but also with Harold Gilman, Wyndham Lewis and Augustus John. His account of these young painters' gifts encouraged Sickert to consider returning to London. He had exhausted his interest in painting the architecture of Dieppe. London, with its drab and sleazy suburbs, its forbidding tenement houses full of dusty high-ceilinged rooms barely letting the cold grey light filter through begrimed windows, was the ideal setting for the kind of figure pictures he now longed to paint. He was later to advise Nina Hamnett to exploit the unique flavour of English subjects in her painting: 'aren't we canaille enough for you?', he asked. 'Didn't Doré and Géricault find English life sordid enough?'[8] In London, Sickert could once again orchestrate the careers of his colleagues. Gore and his generation evidently needed the support of a mature, established, but nonetheless independent and original, artist. Steer, who now taught at the Slade, was not prepared to enter the fray on behalf of his young pupils. By 1905, as J. B. Manson (future secretary of the Camden Town Group) was later to recall, the NEAC 'had already found its respectable level; it had reached a point of safety. It was too tired or too wise to venture further.'[9] An active role awaited Sickert in London.

Sickert in Camden Town

On returning to London Sickert rented two studios in the neighbourhood around Fitzroy Street, an area long favoured by artists. The painter Clive

Newcome, fictional hero of Thackeray's *The Newcomes*, was housed in Fitzroy Square. In real life one of Sickert's studios (at 76 Charlotte Street) had formerly been used by Constable; the other (at 8 Fitzroy Street) was in the house where Whistler had once rented a studio. The northern boundary of the district was defined by a broad avenue constructed in the mid-eighteenth century to serve as a London bypass. A hundred years later this 'New Road', renamed along its course as the Marylebone, Euston and Pentonville Road, no longer circumvented London but divided the Fitzroy Street area in the borough of St Marylebone from densely populated Camden Town in the borough of St Pancras.

Camden Town was named after Lord Camden who in 1791, as ground landlord, had leased the pleasant fields north of the New Road for the building of 1,400 houses. John Nash was among several architects and builders who planned the layout of streets and buildings. The fine curve of Mornington Crescent, which faced leafy gardens until the Carreras cigarette factory was built on the site in 1926, marked the northern edge of the area conceived in outline by Nash and rapidly developed during the early years of the nineteenth century. Nash envisaged this area as a service background for his elegant terraced residences facing Regent's Park. Between Albany Street (running alongside the park) and Hampstead Road, Nash planned shops, three markets (Clarence, York and Cumberland) served by the Canal basin, and a criss-cross network of little streets lined with well-proportioned but relatively modest houses. The area on the opposite (eastern) side of Hampstead Road was developed soon afterwards. Almost as soon as the handsome houses were completed the district was blighted by the arrival of the railways. The construction of three great termini nearby – Euston completed in 1838, King's Cross in 1852 and St Pancras in 1870 – brought dirt, noise and a shifting population of navvies into the area. Houses built as substantial middle-class homes were divided into temporary lodgings for a working-class population. The railway lines, particularly those serving Euston, swallowed up large tracts of residential land. Property in neighbouring streets fast declined in status.

Sickert had discovered north-west London early in his career. After his marriage to Ellen Cobden in 1885, he had moved from Chelsea to West Hampstead and used the top floor of their house in Broadhurst Gardens as his studio.[10] His favourite music hall, studied in countless paintings and drawings between 1888 and 1898, had been the Bedford off Camden High Street. A statue of his wife's father, the prominent advocate of Free Trade Richard Cobden, dominated – and still dominates – the busy intersection of roads outside Mornington Crescent station. In 1894 he had taken a studio in Robert Street which, linking Hampstead Road and Albany Street, passed between Clarence Gardens (see pl.53, the residential square intended by Nash as a vegetable market) and Cumberland Market (see pl.18, the hay market).[11] William Rothenstein, who had inherited Sickert's studio in Glebe Place, Chelsea, was ever amazed by his friend's 'taste for the dingy lodging-house atmosphere' and his 'genius for discovering the dreariest house and most forbidding rooms in which to work'.[12] After separating from Ellen in 1896,

Sickert went to live as well as work in Robert Street. During the later 1890s he painted both Cumberland Market and Munster Square (where Nash had planned a meat market). He even retained his Robert Street studio for several months after his move to Dieppe in the winter of 1898, giving it up only after his divorce in the summer of 1899.

When Sickert resettled in London, towards the end of 1905, he took lodgings and a studio at 6 Mornington Crescent. The railway track passed the end of the garden. During the next six years he rented many more premises in Camden Town to use for studios, private art schools and living purposes. He had a studio in 247 Hampstead Road, set astride the rail tracks on the corner of Granby Street, a building better known as the Wellington House Academy, where Charles Dickens had been educated from 1824 to 1826. He ran schools for etching at 31 Augustus Street (called by Sickert 'Cruikshank's House' because the illustrator George Cruikshank had maintained his mistress and their large family there) and at 209 Hampstead Road. He lived for a time in Harrington Street, and on his second marriage, in 1911, set up home with his wife in Harrington Square. In 1910 he took over the whole of an end-of-terrace house at 140 Hampstead Road to establish 'Rowlandson House', his most ambitious private school; once again the trains to and from Euston passed just outside his garden walls (see pl.55).

Sickert: return to London and relationship with Gore

Sickert's return to London in 1905 was provisional. He spent the year partly in England and partly in France. He kept his house in Neuville, on the outskirts of Dieppe. He exhibited at the *Salon d'automne* in Paris but not at the NEAC in London. However, by 1906 he had fully committed himself to London. He had rooms at 6 Mornington Crescent, kept on his studio at 8 Fitzroy Street (but gave up Constable's studio in Charlotte Street) and rejoined the NEAC. Just as his introduction to the club's exhibitions in April 1888 had been effected with a major music hall picture, so he chose to re-introduce himself in June 1906 with *Noctes Ambrosianae* (pl.25), an expressive evocation of the dark gallery at the Middlesex Music Hall, with faces glimmering weird and lop-sided between the rails. In the winter he exhibited some of his Venetian figure studies of 1903–4. His pictures were greeted with relief by the *Athenaeum*'s reviewer: 'May we look to Mr Sickert for a revival of that diablerie which we associate with his name, and which is a little wanting in the heavier-handed New English artists of this generation?'[13]

The author of this remark was probably Walter Bayes, a painter in oils and watercolour who since 1890, when he was still a student, had exhibited with the Royal Academy. Bayes had to wait two years for Sickert to reciprocate this recognition. In 1906 Sickert's closest associates were the Rothenstein brothers and, above all, Gore.

The earliest landscapes by Gore to survive are a few tentative paintings done in Normandy in 1904 which reveal the influence of Corot. In 1905 he went to central France where the constructive perspective of his wide-ranging views around the village of Billy on the River Allier suggests that he was grafting knowledge of seventeenth-century Dutch landscape onto his training by Steer at the Slade. A more adventurous streak can be detected in Gore's early music hall subjects.

Frederick Gore has told[14] how early drawings show his father's fascination with Goya's carnival scenes. Gore's emotional response to the romantic expressionism of early nineteenth-century Spanish art was reinforced when, in the company of Wyndham Lewis, he visited Madrid in the winter of 1902–3. The chief legacy of this visit was Gore's readiness to turn to popular theatre as a fertile source of subjects. His taste was for stage subjects of especial lunacy. These he found from 1903 in the spectacular ballets staged at the Empire Music Hall, for example *The Masked Ball* of 1903 (a scene from 'The Duel in the Snow', rep. d'Offay 1983, no.1) and *'The Dancing Doll'* of 1905 (rep. d'Offay 1974, no.1, and in Baron 1979, pl.2, wrongly identified in both as *'The Mad Pierrot' Ballet*; see the note to pl.20). In both paintings, Gore adopted a straightforward compositional arrangement of horizontal planes to represent stage and orchestra pit (recalling Sickert's music halls of the 1880s); in both, the scene on stage is freakish, with wildly disproportionate figures and a tower of acrobats in *The Masked Ball*, an elephant alongside absurdly dressed cavorting dancers in *The Dancing Doll*. In these, as in many of his later music halls, Gore betrayed a streak of fantasy rarely found in Sickert's work. It may be concluded that while Sickert's example encouraged Gore to persevere with music hall pictures, his influence on their style and conception was minimal. *The Dancing Doll*, with its romantic sense of colour, its impasto and its eccentric subject, points to an alternative source of inspiration in Adolphe Monticelli's paintings of itinerant troupes of players. Monticelli, a French painter of Piedmontese origin, had died in 1886 but his work enjoyed something of a vogue, especially among painters, in both France and England during the late nineteenth and early twentieth centuries.

From 1906 Gore's favourite music hall was the Alhambra in Leicester Square, which specialized in sumptuous ballet displays with luscious backdrops and ornate costumes. Sickert never painted there. Occasionally Gore accompanied Sickert to the Bedford in Camden Town and once sketched the precise view Sickert was studying intensively as preparation for a painting (see Baron 1979, pl.3). In a few music hall paintings, such as *Rinaldo the Mad Violinist* of c.1911 (rep. Baron 1979, pl.5) he forsook his own preference for pure colours in favour of Sickert's more muted and muddy range of browns and ochres. The heads of the audience, silhouetted large on the surface, and the free, slashed application of thin paint also refer to Sickert. However, soon after Gore painted *Rinaldo* he produced *The Balcony at the Alhambra* (City Art Gallery, York) which in style and treatment introduces the brilliant phase in Gore's career, cut short by his premature death, during which he explored a novel combination of Post-Impressionist sources to produce pictures of everyday life ruthlessly reduced to their essential formal components of constructive design and colour.

Pictures of music halls did not become a part of the vocabulary of Sickert's Camden Town associates other than Gore and, as we have seen, Gore might well have come to this subject without Sickert's help. Remembering the disparity in their ages, Sickert 46 in 1906 and Gore 28, it is arguable that Gore might independently have developed his interest in all sorts of Sickertian subject-matter. As it happened, Sickert was directly responsible for taking Gore straight from his relatively conventional landscape painting into the Camden Town bedrooms he used as studios, and there introduced him to the themes which established the identity of Camden Town painting.

Sickert had himself been painting intimate interiors only since 1903. In London from 1905 to 1906, besides continuing with his series of nudes on metal-framed beds begun in Dieppe in 1904, he had been developing his ability to integrate figures (clothed and unclothed) and their settings into pictures which appeared convincing as aspects of ordinary life. In 1906 he worked at this problem in his Mornington Crescent studio with Gore at his side. Sickert's *Mornington Crescent Nude: Contre-Jour* (rep. Baron 1979, pl.8) and Gore's *Behind the Blind* (pl.27) demonstrate their close collaboration.

In the summer of 1906 Sickert lent his house at Neuville to Gore and joined him there for a few weeks. Writing in 1910, four years later, Sickert credited Gore with helping him to recast his painting entirely 'and to observe colour in the shadows'.[15] With a fine disdain for chronology, Sickert stated that this process of revision had begun 'about six or seven years ago', that is in 1903–4. Obviously Gore's influence on Sickert's development could not have begun until they were working in close association from 1906 onwards. *Behind the Blind* is lighter in tonality and more varied in colour than Sickert's contemporary interiors. Similarly, Gore's Dieppe landscapes of 1906, painted while he stayed in Sickert's house, tended to be brighter in colour and more broken in execution than Sickert's landscapes. Nevertheless, Gore's observation of colour in the shadows was still haphazard at this date, and he was not yet using the pure colours on a white ground, the constructive *pointilliste* brushwork and the divided tones which became general in his work from 1907 onwards. He was indeed swaying in a variety of directions in 1906. Sometimes he adopted the attractive *plein-air* style favoured by the NEAC (for example *The Cross Roads, Neuville*, rep. Baron 1979, pl.10) and sometimes (in his small-scale panoramic studies of Dieppe with their sharply drawn accents and reddish-brown tonality, for example Baron 1979, pl.11) he embraced the objective Sickertian approach to the sketching of landscape.

Sickert went on to Paris from Neuville in 1906. He spent the autumn and part of the winter painting nudes in his hotel room and, for the first time, studying the music halls of Paris. Because he lingered in Paris Sickert could not serve, as he had promised, on the NEAC jury that winter, although he did send over for exhibition the Venetian pictures welcomed by Bayes in the *Athenaeum*. Gore, who had shown two French Billy landscapes with the club in the summer, had one of his Neuville landscapes accepted for the winter exhibition. Meanwhile, in Paris, Sickert prepared for a big one-man show of his work at Bernheim Jeune to open in January 1907 and he exhibited ten pictures at the *Salon d'automne*. When viewing this *Salon* Sickert was much impressed by a view of Venice, *Le Canal de la Giudecca*, by a painter listed as Mme Hudson with an address in Paris. He contemplated writing to request an exchange of pictures. In the spring of 1907 he discovered that Mme Hudson was the American Miss Anna Hope (Nan) Hudson whom he had already met in Paris and in London where she lived with the American-born Miss Ethel Sands.

Birth of the Fitzroy Street Group

On his return from Paris, in the spring of 1907, Sickert decided to implement a scheme he had been considering for some time. He had formed the habit of keeping open house in his studio at 8 Fitzroy Street on Saturday afternoons. His circle had not much altered since he had resettled in London in 1905 and his most regular Saturday visitors were William and Albert Rothenstein, Walter Russell and Gore. In February 1907 Sickert met Harold Gilman, who had been a friend of Gore during their student days at the Slade.[16] Gore and Gilman had then gone their separate ways, although they perhaps met when Gore and Wyndham Lewis visited Spain in 1902. Gilman spent well over a year in Spain, largely occupied with studying and copying the paintings of Velazquez and with wooing an American girl whom he married in Madrid in February 1902. In 1903 he was back in England, and in the spring of 1904 exhibited a *Still Life* at the NEAC.[17] Living in the country with family responsibilities, Gilman developed his art during these early years free from the influence of his Slade contemporaries. He painted portraits of his wife and children and charming Edwardian interiors in a smoothly blended range of cool tones and colours. In 1907, although he still lived outside London, he evidently began visiting the capital more frequently. He was certainly one of the painters (the others being Russell, Gore and the Rothenstein brothers) who, under Sickert's direction, rented a first floor and a store room at 19 Fitzroy Street (fig.2). There they hoped to show pictures to anyone who cared to come, every Saturday, year in, year out, under the formula 'Mr Sickert at Home'. When Sickert discovered that Miss Sands and Miss Hudson were not amateur lady-painters, but had their work on sale, he asked if they would join his group. He explained the practical arrangements – the equal division of the rent at £50 a year – and his motives:

I do it for 2 reasons. Because it is more interesting to people to see the work of 7 or 9 people than one and because I want to keep up an incessant proselytizing agency to accustom people to mine and other painters' work of a modern character. Every week we would put something different on the easels. It is agreeable sometimes to show something 'lucky' you have done at once to anyone it may interest. All the painters interested could keep work there and would have keys and could show anything by appointment to any one at any time ... I want to create a Salon d'automne milieu in London and you could both help me very much.[18]

Ethel Sands and Nan Hudson accepted the invitation, although their busy

Fig.2 Exterior, 19 Fitzroy
Street in 1966

25

social lives did not permit attendance each Saturday. The rooms at 19 Fitzroy Street were not immediately ready for use and the first selected gatherings of the Fitzroy Street Group were still held at Sickert's studio at 8 Fitzroy Street. Urging Ethel Sands and Nan Hudson to send two pictures each for the last of the 'At Homes' at No. 8, Sickert expanded on his aims for the future:

Accustom people weekly to *see* work in a different notation from the current English one. Make it clear that we all have work for sale at prices that people of moderate means could afford. (That a picture costs less than a supper at the Savoy.) Make known the work of painters who already are producing *ripe* work, but who are still elbowed or kept out by timidity etc. …

And of course no one will feel we are jumping at the throats to buy. That comes of its own accord. People pay attention to things seen constantly and judiciously explained a little.

Further I particularly believe that I am sent from heaven to finish *all* your educations!! And, by ricochet, to receive a certain amount of instruction from the younger generation.

It is surprising that Sickert felt that his group represented the younger generation; that he felt their work, within an English context, was modern; and that he believed them to be struggling against the establishment. At 47 Sickert was the oldest of the group, but Russell was only seven years his junior. All except Gore and Albert Rothenstein were over 30. Furthermore, of the eight original members three belonged to the NEAC establishment (Sickert, Russell and William Rothenstein), serving on its juries and committees. Albert Rothenstein was a member of the NEAC and Gore usually had his work accepted for exhibition. Russell, a close friend of Gore, had exhibited at the Royal Academy since 1898, and had been assistant professor at the Slade School since 1895. Nothing in his fresh and charming portraits or landscapes could possibly have offended public and critics in 1907. Sickert seems to have been tilting at windmills.

Sickert soon began to think of expanding the membership of Fitzroy Street. He approached George Thomson, one of the 'London Impressionists' of 1889 and now a teacher of perspective at the Slade and head of the Department of Art at Bedford College, but Thomson resisted recruitment. Lucien Pissarro, another respected member of the NEAC, was invited to join the group and accepted in the autumn of 1907. Sickert was delighted when, as he told Nan Hudson, the £2 collected from each member enabled him to buy not only gas-fittings but also chairs 'like at the New English 21 shillings a dozen'. He busied himself with the practical arrangements, such as the layout of furnishings (fig.3). Nan Hudson was again the recipient of Sickert's views on how the group should conduct itself:

I want (and this we can all *understand* and never *say*) to get together a milieu rich or poor, refined or even to some extent vulgar, which is interested in painting and in the things of the intelligence, and which has not … an *aggressively* anti-moral attitude. To put it on the lowest grounds, it interferes with business.

At this early stage Sickert clearly envisaged the Fitzroy Street Group as a co-

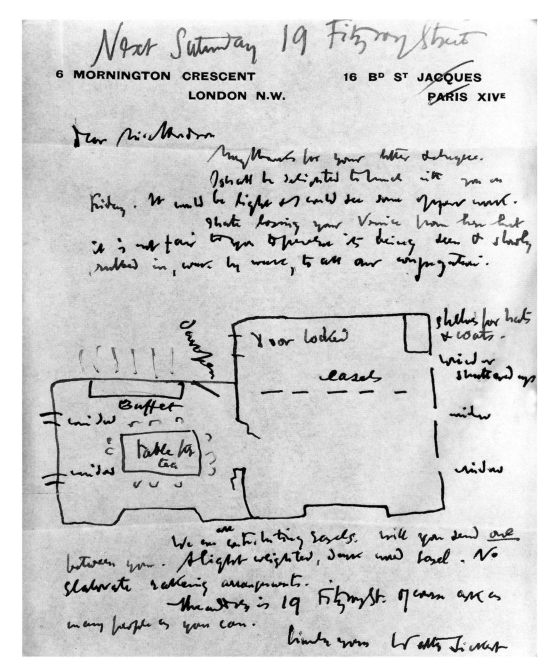

operative commercial enterprise, run by a partnership of socially acceptable friends who broadly represented an offshoot of the NEAC. It soon attracted a small but faithful clientele. The virtuoso collector Sir Hugh Lane, Steer's patron Cyril Butler, Hugh Hammersley, Judge William Evans, Sir Louis Fergusson, Walter Taylor (a watercolourist as well as an avid collector of contemporary British art) and several discerning ladies, including Mrs Charles Hunter, Mrs Donaldson Hudson and Mrs Salaman, talked, drank tea, sometimes listened to an informal concert and, bypassing the dealers, bought pictures at these Saturday meetings in 1907. Together with their male colleagues, Ethel Sands and Nan Hudson contributed easels (light-weight, of dark wood) which were arranged to form a screen with a picture by each artist displayed on his or her own easel. In 1908 this method was altered; the easels stood empty with pictures in the stacks behind and visitors were taken through each artist's stock. Nan Hudson's Venetian picture from the 1906 *Salon d'automne*, which had been acquired by Sickert, was removed from his rooms in Mornington Crescent in 1907 to hang at Fitzroy Street where it could be 'seen and slowly rubbed in, week by week, to all our congregation'. Occasionally one of their pictures sold. A report made by Sickert to Miss Sands and Miss Hudson of sales made in their absence on a Saturday in May gives a flavour of the commercial activity at Fitzroy Street gatherings:

one Gore	£10 to Mrs Donaldson Hudson
one watercolour Russell	£10 to Walter Taylor
one panel by me	£5 to Mrs Donaldson Hudson
one sketch by me	£5 a present from Mr Taylor to Miss Russell.

Camden Town painting

Although the Fitzroy Street Group was never intended to represent a movement or school, it did come to nurture a distinct and important episode in the history of British art which is most suggestively described as Camden Town painting. What is thought of as Camden Town painting is a blend of several characteristics. The pictures tended to be small: 'little pictures for little patrons', to quote one of the latter.[19] Its favourite themes established an unmistakable vocabulary: nudes on a bed, washing or just naturally inhabiting their shabby lodgings in Camden Town; informal portraits of friends and coster-girl models in humble interiors; domestic still lifes rather than tasteful arrangements of *objets d'art*; and townscapes of commonplace London streets, squares and gardens. It shunned the pretentious. Pompous exhibition pictures on an inflated scale, paintings of august sites, of drawing-room beauties and idealized nudes were abjured.

Sickert, but not the others of his group, developed a peculiar brand of conversation piece. He embellished his two-figure subjects with anecdotal interest by adding piquant titles. The pictures seem to read like pages from a novel – by de Maupassant, Zola or George Gissing. Virginia Woolf wrote in 1919 how she would like to possess Sickert's works in order to describe them.[20] In 1933, in the context of a discussion of an exhibition of Sickert's work at Agnew's, she wove a short story out of *Ennui* (see the note to pl.6). Her description has literary, but not literal, truth. When we seek to verify her interpretation of *Ennui*, the structure falls apart. Sickert's figure subjects are like dreams; their convincing emotional and material realism dissolves when tested by an alert intelligence. They are more poetry than prose, looking forward to the ambiguous images of T. S. Eliot rather than backwards to the gritty realism of Emile Zola. Sickert's habit of selecting titles for his paintings as afterthoughts – often interchangeable – proves that their ambiguity was deliberate. For example, paintings of a reclining nude woman, her form dissolved into myriad particles by the filtered light which throws the figure of a clothed man seated at her side into *contre-jour* silhouette, have been variously known as *The Camden Town Murder*, *'What shall we do for the rent?'* and *Summer Afternoon* (see, for example, pl.32).

Another characteristic of Camden Town painting is closely related to its vocabulary. Every theme was treated with objective perceptual honesty. The method taught by Sickert, and adopted by many of his close colleagues, was to work from drawings in which the relationships of figures and objects to their settings and to each other were recorded with dispassionate accuracy. The objective approach did not imply indiscriminate transcription of everything before the painter's eye. 'Realism' as defined by Sickert in his 'London Impressionists' catalogue preface (the 'struggle to make intensely real and solid the sordid or superficial details' of its subjects) was not its aim. On the contrary, selection was essential so long as it was dictated by the individual temperament of the painter and reflected his honest visual and emotional response to the subject rather than his preconceptions of picture-making.

Sickert, virtually single-handed, inspired both the vocabulary and the objective perceptual approach of Camden Town painting. In his 'London Impressionists' catalogue he had asserted that magic and poetry were to be found in the everyday urban surroundings of the artist. While he himself found beauty in the cockney music halls and the bustling port and narrow streets of Dieppe, as a disciple of Whistler in the 1880s he had accepted limpid views of the Thames and Chelsea as equally valid pictures of everyday subjects. However, over the next twenty years his admiration for Whistler became qualified and by 1908 he had concluded that the infiltration of Whistler's ultra-refined taste and dandified personality had vitiated his achievement: 'Taste is the death of a painter. He has all his work cut out for him, observing and recording. His poetry is the interpretation of ready-made life. He has no business to have time for preferences.'[21]

In a series of articles Sickert inveighed against the tastefulness and the 'puritan standards of propriety' to which he attributed the 'insular decadence'[22] of British painting. In 1910 he wrote perhaps his most quoted dictum:

The more our art is serious, the more will it tend to avoid the drawing-room and stick to the kitchen. The plastic arts are gross arts, dealing joyously with gross material facts … and while they will flourish in the scullery, or on the dunghill, they fade at a breath from the drawing-room.[23]

In the same year he advised the artist to follow a typical little drab, quaintly christened 'Tilly Pullen', into the first shabby little house, into the kitchen or better still into the bedroom.[24]

The fact that pictures of less than beautiful nudes on iron-framed beds have come to personify Camden Town painting is an historical distortion directly attributable to the dominant position Sickert held within the Fitzroy Street Group. Besides Sickert only Gore (see pl.29), Gilman from about 1910 (see pl.19) and, very occasionally, Malcolm Drummond painted intimate, as opposed to idealized, nude subjects. However, Sickert's treatment of the subject was so powerful that even his contemporaries tended to overlook the rest of his production. With his flair for publicity Sickert borrowed the title 'The Camden Town Murder' (as the press christened the murder of Emily Dimmock in September 1907) for many of his pictures representing a nude woman and a clothed man (see pls 32, 33). None of these pictures, even the most dramatically composed and brutally treated variant (pl.33), was a recreation of the event as it actually happened. Sickert's juxtapositions of naked and clothed figures were primarily dictated by aesthetic principles. He declared that *Le Bain Turc* by Ingres, a composition consisting entirely of nude figures, suggested 'an effect like a dish of spaghetti or maccheroni'.[25] He expressed his own preferences in 1910:

The nude occurs in life often as only partial, and generally in arrangements with the draped ... Perhaps the chief source of pleasure in the aspect of a nude is that it is in the nature of a gleam – a gleam of light and warmth and life. And that it should appear thus, it should be set in surroundings of drapery or other contrasting surfaces.[26]

Sickert's love of the contrast of living flesh and inanimate drapery explains why so many of his single-figure nude paintings show the model in bed, gleaming amid the crumpled bedclothes. The locations, poses and relationships of his figures were chosen primarily for their pictorial possibilities. Yet Fred Brown, professor at the Slade and formerly one of the 'London Impressionists', felt impelled during the First World War to write and tell the artist that the sordid nature of his pictures since the Camden Town Murder series made it impossible to continue their friendship.[27] The powerful image of Sickert's pictures even coloured the retrospective memory of Fitzroy Street participants. Miss Ethel Sands remembered how news that Gore's uncle, the Bishop of Oxford, was expected one Saturday caused a scramble to find pictures more suited to the episcopal eye than the naked women in bed everyone had painted.[28] It is inconceivable that all the members of Fitzroy Street had painted nudes. The only explanation is that Sickert's pictures, perhaps supported by Gore's and Gilman's, wiped all sorts of acceptable subjects from her memory.

The last major characteristic of Camden Town painting was the handling of paint, often seen as a late flowering of English Impressionism, developed by a nucleus of Fitzroy Street artists. This characteristic is both the simplest to define – as an interest in colour analysis and the development of a broken touch – and the hardest to confine to Camden Town. Several future Camden Town Group members, such as Drummond and Sickert, flirted only temporarily with this handling. For others, such as Bevan, Gore and to a lesser extent Gilman, it was an important stage in their development. Pissarro and Manson used it consistently but their almost exclusive concentration on rural landscape rather than on figure or townscape subjects sets them apart from the central core of Camden Town painters. Despite these qualifications, a broken touch and broken colour were common to many painters belonging to the Fitzroy Street Group between 1907 and 1911.

Lucien Pissarro, eldest son of the classic French Impressionist Camille Pissarro, was the chief inspiration behind this development. The debt to

Pissarro was recognized and acknowledged at the time. As Sickert wrote in 1914:

Pissarro, holding the exceptional position at once of an original talent, and of the pupil of his father, the authoritative depository of a mass of inherited knowledge and experience, has certainly served us as a guide, or, let us say, a dictionary of theory and practice on the road we have elected to travel.[29]

Lucien had settled in England in 1890 but for many years devoted his main energies to the design, illustration and printing of books for the Eragny Press, which he created in 1894. His paintings were seldom seen in England until he began exhibiting at the NEAC in 1904. He became a member in 1906. His suburban and rural landscapes were deeply influenced by his father. While his pictures of railway cuttings at Acton (pl.34) hark back to Camille Pissarro's *Lordship Lane, Upper Norwood* of 1871 (Courtauld Institute of Art, London), most of his sensitive, scrupulously realized landscapes were executed in solid pigment, applied in separately coloured touches of light-toned pure colour, a handling closely based upon his father's later, more Neo-Impressionist, treatment. Like his father, Lucien Pissarro ignored the rigid scientific basis of Neo-Impressionism which predetermined the colour of each touch of paint, yet he adopted the characteristic disciplined *pointilliste* execution developed to express this theory. By temperament he preferred the constructed design of Neo-Impressionism to the more haphazard and spontaneous compositions of the original Impressionists.

Lucien Pissarro's painting deeply impressed Gore just when he needed guidance to help him emerge from the influence of Steer, Corot and the Dutch landscape tradition. He was already naturally inclined to the use of brighter, purer colour than many of his contemporaries. Lucien Pissarro's example showed him how to manipulate his colours and control his touch. Although Pissarro did not join the Fitzroy Street Group until the autumn of 1907, Gore's ready assimilation of the elder artist's method was already demonstrated in the landscapes he painted during the summer of 1907 on a trip to Yorkshire with Albert Rothenstein and Mr and Mrs Walter Russell. Gore's response was also sufficiently sensitive to allow him to adapt his new execution to the painting of music halls, portraits and figure studies.

Sickert's relationship with Lucien Pissarro was curious. Sickert had attended a lecture on 'Impressionism in Art' given by Pissarro in 1891 to the Art Workers' Guild, and sought the lecturer out. Lucien wrote to his father: 'Sickert – a young man who knows Degas – asked me to lunch. I went to his place … then I went to his studio. Deplorable!!'[30] This antipathy was not reciprocated by Sickert, but there was little rapport between the two. Lucien Pissarro disparaged any painter who had not banished black from his palette and who did not divide tones by applying paint in separately coloured crusty touches. Sickert was his own man and had little respect for authority and precedent unless they supported his current intentions and preoccupations. From time to time since the 1890s, Sickert had experimented with broken brushwork, and in his landscapes and figure pictures of 1906 he had begun to use small dabbed touches of thicker paint. His colours, however, were still based on blacks, browns and greens.

Nonetheless it would seem that at the period when Sickert was orchestrating the Fitzroy Street Group as a collaborative venture he chose, perhaps for polemical reasons, to stress the interdependence of its members. In 1910 his appointment as art critic on the weekly journals the *Art News* and the *New Age* gave him a ready platform. In 'The New English – and After'[31] he attributed the evolution of the method of painting 'with a clean and solid mosaic of thick paint in a light key' to the combined efforts of a group of artists ('for these things are done in gangs, not by individuals') belonging to the New English Art Club (he was probably thinking of the Fitzroy Street offshoot of the NEAC rather than the club proper). In the article, aptly named 'The Spirit of the Hive', quoted above (p.23) in relation to his debt to Gore, he acknowledged that the Pissarros, father and son, had also helped him learn to recast his painting 'to observe colour in the shadows'. Certainly, his decision to invite Lucien to join the Fitzroy Street Group occurred just at the time when, early in 1907, Sickert became increasingly preoccupied with the problem of expressing reflected light on figures and objects. Sickert's interest in reflected light coincided with a period of critical self-examination which led him to the conclusion that he had done too much sketching and too little 'considered, elaborated work'. As a 'punching-ball' he settled down to paint 'a life-sized head of myself in a cross-light which will I think become something in time'.[32] This head is *The Juvenile Lead* (pl.1), a title given to the picture by Sickert at a later date when he perhaps looked back with irony at his rôle in 1907 as the middle-aged actor-manager of Fitzroy Street. Although *The Juvenile Lead* is still deeply sombre in tone and colour, the modelling, especially where the obliquely falling light is reflected in the face, is more consistently and constructively built up in small overlapping dabs and smears of rough, crusty paint. Soon afterwards he painted another self-portrait in the studio which, when exhibited at the NEAC in the summer, caused Walter Bayes as critic of the *Athenaeum* to remark that its consistently crumbling *facture* made 'this kind of handling a formal decoration'.[33] By the summer Sickert was so engrossed in a series of Mornington Crescent *contre-jour* interiors, which he described to Nan Hudson as 'Studies of illumination', that he put off going to France. He lent his Neuville house to the Gilmans and settled down to paint from a nude model (see pl.26) and from a 'little Jewish girl of 13 or so with red hair' (see pl.3), on alternate days. It was in these Mornington Crescent interiors that Sickert introduced a brighter and more varied range of colours into his palette, including the violets and greens typical of Impressionism. The tones, though subtly muted, are less sombre than previously. The quality of the paint, applied in disciplined but delicate stippled touches, is rich and sensuous. The affinity between Gore's *Some-one waits* (pl.28), Pissarro's *The Turban* (pl.42) and Sickert's *Little Rachel* (pl.3), all paintings of 1907, confirms Sickert's admission that these two were the primary influences behind this development in his handling. However, such was the reciprocal nature of relationships within Fitzroy Street that Sickert's sensitive adaptation of the method to suggest *contre-jour* effects of light on a figure in turn inspired Gore to paint similar pictures, for example *Morning: The Green Dress* (pl.30).

This type of handling never became a formula for Sickert. He merely assimilated the use of thicker paint, applied in broken touches of lighter and brighter colour, into his technical repertoire. In his pictures of 1907–10 he made free use of the variety of texture, brushwork and colour it afforded to paint such pictures as *Sally – the Hat* (pl.31), a scintillating study of a nude bathed in shimmering light, and *The New Home* (pl.4), the quintessence of Camden Town portraiture and the direct prototype of pictures like Gore's *North London Girl* (Tate Gallery, London) and Gilman's *Contemplation* (City Art Gallery, Glasgow).

Meanwhile J. B. Manson, Paris-trained but as yet unknown to the Fitzroy Street Group, had in his Brittany landscapes of 1907 developed an Impressionist style of execution independently. Gilman, on the other hand, remained unaffected by his colleagues and continued to paint gentle domestic interiors and occasional landscapes in a smoothly blended range of cool tones. The wider spread of the use of 'a clean and solid mosaic of thick paint in a light key' awaited the capture of new recruits by the Fitzroy Street Group.

The Allied Artists' Association and the expansion of the Fitzroy Street Group

The character and composition of the Fitzroy Street Group altered fundamentally in 1908. Without official records it is impossible to distinguish definitively its members (that is those who contributed to the rent of rooms at 19 Fitzroy Street and were thus entitled to store and show their pictures there) from the many painters who attended the Saturday gatherings to discuss art and its politics. Moreover, membership of the group was fluid. While we may assume that the artists who were to make up the Camden Town Group in 1911 were primarily selected from active and current members of the Fitzroy Street Group at that date, it is harder to say who were the paying members three years earlier. An interim clue is found in the *New Age* of 27 January 1910 when the formation of 'a London Group', composed of Bevan, Gilman, Gore, Lucien Pissarro, Augustus John, Albert Rothenstein, Walter Sickert, Miss Hudson and Miss Sands, was announced. The prophetic title of this group was, in fact, a synonym for the Fitzroy Street Group and described no more than the old activities: 'It exhibits every Saturday afternoon in Sickert's studio at 19 Fitzroy Street and will be glad if anyone will call in an informal way and become acquainted with its pictures and with the members.' Two founder-members, William Rothenstein and Walter Russell, are lacking from this 1910 list, and it is probable that they had ceased to be active members long before this date. Albert Rothenstein's inclusion is surprising and perhaps represents a temporary resurrection, for he too seldom participated in group activities after 1908. Augustus John is listed. His name, like that of Sickert, lent prestige to the group, but his involvement in its activities was limited. From time to time, in the intervals between his travels, he attended meetings; presumably he contributed to the rent.

A cryptic note sent by Sickert to Pissarro asking for the rent due for two quarters[34] provides another, less definitive, clue. The note is undated, but spring 1908 is the most likely time of its expedition. The rent still stood at £50 a year, as it had been when the group was formed, but this sum was now divided among eleven members. Who the eleven were, at the uncertain date of the note, is not known. Even if we accept that all the original members (that is including William Rothenstein and Walter Russell) were still paying partners in the enterprise, and add Pissarro to their number, only nine are accounted for. The explanation could be that John had already joined the group, and that James Dickson Innes was the eleventh member. Innes was not included in the 1910 announcement, but at that time he was living away from London. His close friendship and artistic collaboration with John dates from 1910; in 1907 they were no more than acquaintances. However, Innes could have become known to members of the Fitzroy Street Group independently because in the winter of 1907, while still studying at the Slade, he moved to Fitzroy Street. In spite of frequent absences in 1908 he retained an address in Fitzroy Street, and some of his paintings of about this date – uncharacteristic interiors such as *Resting* (rep. Baron 1979, pl.48) – support the suggestion that he was in contact with the group.

Any defections, whether temporary or permanent, that occurred within the Fitzroy Street Group during 1908 were offset by the new recruits discovered at the first exhibition of the Allied Artists' Association (AAA). Frank Rutter, then art critic of the *Sunday Times* and the force behind the creation of the AAA, has detailed its history.[35] London lacked a non-jury exhibiting platform of the kind provided in Paris by the *Salon des Indépendants*. Foreign artists were weary of paying for the transport of their pictures to London only to have them rejected by the various exhibiting societies. They pressed for a subscription organization which would entitle them to exhibit. Native artists also suffered from restrictive selection procedures. Rutter canvassed opinion in London. By Christmas 1907 he had been promised active support from a reasonably wide circle, including Sickert, Gore and Lucien Pissarro from the Fitzroy Street Group.[36] Walter Bayes – as yet unknown to the Fitzroy Street circle – was won over when Rutter disarmingly admitted that the exhibitions would be 'bigger and worse' than the Royal Academy: 'Why pay a shilling to see two thousand works at the Academy when for the same money you can see four thousand at our exhibition?' During the winter of 1907–8 Rutter met Jan de Holewinski who had come to London to organize an exhibition of Russian arts and crafts. Rutter decided that, like the Paris *Salon des Indépendants*, a foreign section should be a feature of his creation. They joined forces to look for a location, found and booked the Albert Hall for July 1908 and formally registered the society in February. The name Allied Artists' Association was chosen for a variety of reasons, including its alphabetical advantages. Sickert took a leading part at the meeting to decide its rules. He pressed for total impartiality, even insisting that the catalogue order should be decided by ballot rather than printed in the alphabetical order used by their Parisian prototype. He made the famous retort to one founder-member who thought that the best pictures by the best artists should be hung in the best places: 'In this society there are no good works or bad works: there are only works by shareholders.' Every subscriber was entitled to show five works, reduced to three the following year because of the overwhelming response. The 1908 catalogue lists 3,061 works, not counting the Russian section; more works were submitted too late for publication. Forty founder-members, among them Sickert, were allotted sections to hang. Exhaustion overcame all the supervisors except Sickert who had the sense to superintend from a chair placed in the middle of his section. Rutter, with overall responsibility, covered an enormous mileage round and round the vast hall; the following year he had the happy idea of conducting his operations on a bicycle.

When the exhibition opened members of the Fitzroy Street Group admired pictures by two artists in particular: Walter Bayes and Robert Bevan. Sickert noticed the work of Bayes who had submitted some decorative panels large enough (and at £157.10s expensive enough) to attract notice whatever the competition. The whereabouts of very few pictures exhibited and/or painted by Bayes between 1908 and 1911 are known, but we may infer from his earlier and later work, as well as from his idiosyncratic critical writings, that they possessed a strong sense of design and possibly an element of humour. It is strange that Sickert and Bayes, both active supporters of the creation of the AAA, did not meet before the exhibition. Moreover, in his art reviews, admittedly published anonymously, Bayes had been singling out Sickert's work for especial praise since 1906. Rutter reports Sickert's reaction on first sighting Bayes's work at the Albert Hall: 'Who is this man Bayes? His paintings are very good.' In 1951 Bayes recalled their first meeting: 'I found him eloquently holding forth to a group of bemused spectators before one of my pictures.'[37] Sickert certainly adopted him as a protégé (a relationship acknowledged by Bayes in 1951) and undoubtedly brought him to Saturday meetings. It is possible that Bayes became a formal paying member of the group in 1908; if he did, his membership must have lapsed by 1910 because his name is not included in the list of members of the synonymous 'London Group' published in the New Age in January.

Rutter credits Bayes with the introduction of Robert Bevan to the Fitzroy Street Group in 1909. In that year it was decided that all members should be eligible to serve on the Hanging Committee of the AAA, and that invitations should be issued on an alphabetical basis. Bayes chaired the committee on which Robert Bevan served and, according to Rutter, this fortuitous circumstance led to Bevan's recruitment. However, all other writers, including R. A. Bevan in his Memoir of his father[38] state that Gore and Gilman spotted Bevan's pictures at the 1908 AAA show and invited him to join their group in that year.

Bevan was only five years younger than Sickert. He too had lived and worked abroad. Having trained in Paris, he had visited Pont Aven in Brittany from 1893 to 1894 and there met, and been influenced by, Gauguin. He also had first-hand knowledge of the work of the earlier generation of Impressionists. In 1900 he had settled in London with his wife, the Polish painter Stanislawa de Karlowska. His work remained almost unknown for another eight years, having been displayed only in one virtually unnoticed show in 1905 in the Baillie Gallery, then off the beaten track in Bayswater. In 1908 a second exhibition at the Baillie Gallery, now more centrally placed in Baker Street, attracted little more attention than the first although it included one of his finest paintings of this period, *Ploughing on the Downs* (Art Gallery, Aberdeen).

None of the pictures exhibited by Bevan at the 1908 AAA can be identified with certainty. It is safe to assume that they were strongly coloured poetic landscapes, executed in a broken technique, possibly in the considered divisionist touch which Bevan had recently been developing. With his firm drawing, his confident and educated handling and his uninhibited approach to colour, Bevan was a valuable addition to the Fitzroy Street Group.

Gore is thought to have noticed Charles Ginner's pictures at the 1908 Allied Artists' exhibition (three illustrations to the work of Edgar Allen Poe, a study of a head and a river landscape) but was unable to seek him out because Ginner lived in Paris. Ginner did not exhibit at the AAA in 1909. In 1910, having settled in London late in 1909, he not only submitted his work but his surname brought him to serve alongside Gore and Gilman on the Hanging Committee. The three 'Gs' established an immediate and lasting rapport.

Ginner, the French-born son of British parents who lived in Cannes, had trained in Paris and knew the work of the Post-Impressionists. His admission to the Fitzroy Street Group in 1910 further strengthened its cross-Channel relationships. *The Sunlit Wall* of 1908 (rep. Baron 1979, pl.84a) is one of the few paintings to survive from his early years in France. Its thick paint and vivid colour proclaim an immature admiration for Van Gogh. When Ginner decided to include this early painting as one of his four contributions to the first Camden Town Group exhibition in 1911, it eclipsed, in the eyes of some reviewers, nearly all the other pictures in the show. The critics were dazzled by its sense of colour. To quote just one example of the kind of comment it elicited: 'One hesitates to use the phrase "crushed jewels", which has been so often applied to Monticelli, but "The Sunlit Wall" really glows like jewels themselves. It is quite Bacchic in its voluptuous beauty.'[39] Another work of 1908, a rare survivor of a series of still-life paintings entitled by the artist 'tâches décoratives' (rep. Baron 1979, pl.50), although smaller in scale, illustrates the extraordinary violence of Ginner's execution. Rutter remembered that he answered Gore's questions about Ginner by saying that 'his pictures were a nuisance to handle because the paint stood out in lumps and was still wet'. The example of Ginner's prodigal use of paint was new to London. By the time he arrived in the winter of 1909 the basis of his life-long style was already established, although the small, tight touch and the strong feeling for pattern which discipline his meticulously observed transcriptions of nature were not fully developed for another year or so. Worms of paint still trail in haphazard fashion across his famous interior *The Café Royal* (pl.43), first exhibited at the AAA during the summer of 1911.

At the 1910 AAA Ginner exhibited two portraits, one of his mother and one, *A Classical Dancer*, probably of his sister. Neither is extant.[40] His third exhibit, *A Corner in Chelsea* (pl.38) painted in 1910, was a work of startling ambition. When Ginner first settled in London he lived in Chelsea, but far from seeing the picturesque neighbourhood in the spirit of Whistler and his followers, Ginner approached the much-painted townscape with the innocence of a primitive to depict a totally new aspect of the scene around him. He painted a big atmospheric roofscape. Presumably his painting grew out of the little sketches on panel, such as *Battersea Roofs* and *Chelsea Chimneys* (both now in private collections), made by Ginner in 1909. *A Corner in Chelsea* introduced a distinctive theme into Ginner's vocabulary (he was later to paint the roofs of Leeds, of Hampstead and of Belfast, among other cities). It perhaps also encouraged members of the Fitzroy Street Group to study the urban scene more intently and thus to find subjects in unusual aspects of their immediate environment.

London scenes in Camden Town painting

Until 1910 the nucleus of Camden Town painters within the Fitzroy Street Group had tended to concentrate on figure subjects when working at home and on landscapes when in the country or abroad. Ginner's arrival in their midst may have helped to break this routine. From 1910 onwards townscapes of London occupied an increasingly prominent place in the activities of Camden Town painters. In that year Bevan began to paint his own Swiss Cottage neighbourhood and tackled a series of cab-yard subjects which, together with his pictures of horse sales, became so distinctive a feature of his *œuvre*. Bevan, a keen horseman, had often included horses in his landscapes, but it is possible that the belief, fundamental to Sickert and his circle, that the painter could find beauty in every aspect of his environment encouraged him to paint his equine London subjects.

Gore had occasionally painted Mornington Crescent Gardens before 1910, but his pictures of young people playing tennis on the grass seem unrelated to urban life outside the garden railings. They could just as well have been painted at his mother's home in Hertingfordbury. Gore began to paint more extensive views of the architecture of Camden Town in 1910, in particular the view towards the underground station seen from his studio window at 31 Mornington Crescent (see pl.16). In 1911 he spent the entire summer in London. Sickert gave him the use of Rowlandson House at 140 Hampstead Road during the school's vacation. He painted the railway tracks to Euston from its upper-floor windows (see pl.55) and glowering rows of terrace houses glimpsed over its garden walls. In the winter of 1912–13, Gore found inspiration in the rear elevations and dreary rectangular back gardens seen from an upper window of the house at 2 Houghton Place (an example is in the Whitworth Art Gallery, Manchester) where he moved after his marriage. Although his method and his style were totally different from Ginner's, he too

Fig.4 Sickert and Gore (seated) in the garden of Rowlandson House reading press cuttings of the first Camden Town Group exhibition, June 1911

was excited by the patterns which could be extracted from the most unpromising architectural subjects.

Sickert and Gilman also painted views of Camden Town at this period. Sickert was a master of townscape. In his paintings of Dieppe between 1898 and 1905 he had produced one of the most complete records of an urban environment ever created by an artist. Yet, apart from a few paintings of the area around Cumberland Market studied when he had a studio in nearby Robert Street during the 1890s, he had seldom painted London before 1910–11. Even then he did not range outdoors far beyond the studio. Almost all Sickert's paintings and drawings of London were confined to the view from and of his own back garden at 140 Hampstead Road. Gilman had not tackled London subjects since painting Whistlerian views of the Thames in 1907–8. Although he often lived in London, he had no permanent address there until 1914 when he took a studio in Maple Street near Fitzroy Street. Like Sickert, in 1911–12 he too painted several Camden Town landscapes in which the freedom of his execution matched the informality of his subject-matter. These pictures include two views of Clarence Gardens (Ferens Art Gallery, Hull, and Odin's Restaurant, London) where he may have gone to paint with his friend and protégé, William Ratcliffe, who also produced two paintings of this square in 1912 (see pl.53). Another Gilman townscape of this period known (perhaps incorrectly) as *Mornington Crescent* (National Museum of Wales, Cardiff) shows Gilman, like Gore in his Houghton Place pictures, studying the bleak prospect of a row of terrace houses seen from the back. Malcolm Drummond, who entered the Fitzroy Street circle in 1910–11, was also to make house backs a subject for painting when, around 1914, he executed *Backs of Houses, Chelsea* (Southampton City Art Gallery). The inclusion of *Paddington Station* (present whereabouts unknown) among the four pictures Drummond showed with the Camden Town Group in June 1911 suggests that Drummond's enthusiastic adoption of urban architectural themes developed as soon as he entered the Fitzroy Street Group.

The Fitzroy Street Group in 1910

By the end of 1910 the Fitzroy Street Group meetings were patronized by a huge circle of painters. Every progressive artist in London came, at least sometimes, to its Saturday afternoons. The gatherings were composed of a cat's cradle of strands based on friendship and professional relationships.

When the Camden Town Group was created in the following year its members became, *ipso facto*, members of the parent society. It is, however, impossible to list with any accuracy which members of the new society were recent recruits to the old. Many of the old-established members of the Fitzroy Street Group introduced their colleagues, friends, protégés and pupils to the Fitzroy Street circle in 1910–11, but whether as welcome visitors or paying members is not known.

Manson, hoping to write an article on Pissarro, was brought to view paintings at Fitzroy Street in November 1910.[41] As their friendship ripened, Pissarro brought Manson on further occasions, although it is probable that the future secretary of the Camden Town Group had to wait some six months before he was accepted as a full member of Fitzroy Street. Henry Lamb, perhaps persuaded by Augustus John, visited Fitzroy Street and may or may not have become a formal member at this period.

Sickert, who had been teaching night classes at the Westminster School of Art since 1908, introduced his more promising pupils to the Saturday meetings. Chief among these was Malcolm Drummond, who had exhibited his work for the first time with the AAA in 1910. Frank Rutter wrote that his *Sculptor's Studio* (rep. Baron 1979, pl.63; coll. Waterman Fine Art, London, 1998) would 'be raved about a few years hence if his name becomes widely known'.[42] The point of departure for Drummond's novel approach to the painting of church and congregation in *Brompton Oratory* (pl.37) was Sickert's striking vertical interior *The New Bedford*, exhibited at the AAA and the NEAC in 1909 (rep. Baron 1979, pl.4). Music hall and church are seen from an equivalent viewpoint, so that the grouping of the figures and their relationship to the architectural setting are similar in both. However, Drummond replaced Sickert's crusty polychrome with a flatter application of simplified areas of strong colour. He limited his palette to a few basic colours using, for example, the red of his architecture for the flesh tones and chair backs. Whereas Sickert's forms are open, Drummond's are self-contained. This painting reveals that Drummond's feeling for emphatic patterns antedated his association with Ginner, who entered the Fitzroy Street circle after the AAA exhibition. It also proves that, unlike most of Sickert's pupils, Drummond's artistic personality was sufficiently mature and well-defined to assimilate his master's methods (that is to work from drawings, to relate figures and setting, to observe tonal values and relationships) without imitating his mannerisms. Once admitted to the Fitzroy Street circle Drummond, with his innate attraction towards strong, tidy patterns running counter to his training by Sickert at the Westminster, must have found Ginner's example particularly encouraging. They became close friends and developed independently, but in parallel, ways of expressing the bustle of London streets and the shapes of urban architecture so as to emphasize both the decorative and the atmospheric qualities of their subjects. The depth of their understanding is revealed in Drummond's remarkable *Portrait of Charles Ginner* of 1911 (pl.39).

Gore acquired a pupil in 1908, a deaf stockbroker's clerk in his middle thirties, J. Doman Turner, to whom he gave instruction by correspondence in the art of drawing. While it may be assumed that Doman Turner – who was sensitive and talented, as his extant watercolours prove – was too shy and retiring often to intrude on the lively gatherings at Fitzroy Street, he had probably become a member in time to join the Camden Town Group in 1911.

Gilman, who had no family commitments since his wife had returned with their children to her family in Chicago in 1909, became an ever-stronger voice in the discussions at Fitzroy Street. He too introduced a newcomer to his London circle: William Ratcliffe. Ratcliffe, who had studied at Manchester School of Art, had been working as a wallpaper designer for about twelve years when, probably in Letchworth, he met Gilman in 1908. It tells much about the power of Gilman's personality that he persuaded Ratcliffe, a diminutive and shy man aged 40, to take up painting again by studying part-time at the Slade in 1910 and by spending his Saturday afternoons in the Fitzroy Street Group studio.

Meanwhile Gilman himself, under the influence of his colleagues, abandoned his liquid, tonal handling and quickly developed confidence in the use of richly impasted paint and full colour, qualities already fully demonstrated in *The Blue Blouse* (pl.36), exhibited at the NEAC in the summer of 1910.

As the Fitzroy Street Group increased in size, influence and prestige, its members gained entry to the NEAC exhibitions. Sickert, Pissarro and John were members of the NEAC, where their pictures were always hung. Gore's work had been regularly accepted for exhibition since 1906. Pictures by Innes and Lamb were sometimes included and once, in the spring of 1904, a *Still Life* by Gilman had been exhibited. However, it was not until 1909 that a real change in the attitude of the NEAC establishment towards the Fitzroy Street painters became apparent. In that year Gore was elected a member of the club. Gilman's work was re-admitted after an interval of five years, and pictures by Walter Bayes, Nan Hudson and Manson (not yet a member of Fitzroy Street) were accepted for the first time. This lenience continued in 1910, in spite of Sickert having resigned his membership of the NEAC meanwhile. Pictures by the same non-members were again accepted for both the summer and winter shows and Robert Bevan's paintings were included for the first time.

At the NEAC exhibition in the winter of 1910 the Fitzroy Street artists may have noticed three works by Maxwell Gordon Lightfoot, who had finished his training at the Slade a year before. His NEAC pictures cannot be certainly identified but they probably included a painting of Conway executed in a delicate stippled touch, and examples of his strongly expressive and individual drawings of trees from nature. However, although within a few months Lightfoot was to join the newly formed Camden Town Group, he did not become a member of the Fitzroy Street Group. He joined the Friday Club, founded in 1905 by Vanessa Bell to hold meetings, lectures and annual exhibitions. Its membership sometimes overlapped that of the Fitzroy Street Group (Henry Lamb and James Dickson Innes) but on the whole it incorporated artists of different temperament and aesthetic ideals. These included Roger Fry, Duncan Grant, Derwent Lees and, from 1910, Mark Gertler who, together with Stanley Spencer, Eric Wadsworth and C. R. W. Nevinson, had been among Lightfoot's closest friends at the Slade.

'Manet and the Post-Impressionists' at the Grafton Gallery

In the winter of 1910–11 Roger Fry, hitherto known as a mediocre painter, a respected connoisseur of Old Masters and a brilliant lecturer and critic, staged the exhibition 'Manet and the Post-Impressionists' at the Grafton Gallery. The exhibition and its effects are discussed in almost every survey of British art during this period. All that need be said here of its contents is that Manet served as an introduction to the main body of the show – a large selection of pictures by the most noted French Post-Impressionists. There were paintings by living artists, including Matisse, Picasso, Derain and Vlaminck, but the main emphasis was on the great trio, Van Gogh, Cézanne and Gauguin.

The visual impact of this exhibition on English artists has perhaps been overstressed at the expense of proper emphasis on its political consequences.

By 1910 there were few progressive painters working in England who were completely unaware of the French achievements illustrated by Fry's exhibition. As an assembly of stunning pictures the exhibition undoubtedly confirmed and accelerated the direction in which many of these painters were developing. A few painters, like Gore and Gilman, had never before had an opportunity to study so comprehensive a review of French Post-Impressionist art. The exhibition was well timed to provide the necessary stimulus to the natural evolution of their style and handling.

Ginner, with his feeling for strong pure colour and the unified decorative quality evident in the construction of his pictures, was already taking over from Sickert as Gilman's mentor. The sight of a fine group of Post-Impressionist paintings must have encouraged Gilman towards this change of allegiance.[43] A visit to France in 1911 with Ginner, who acted as his guide around the galleries of Paris, confirmed the new direction in which Gilman's art was beginning to develop. In *Le Pont Tournant* (pl.11), painted while they were both in Dieppe in 1911, Gilman was already reaching out towards his vision of nature seen in terms of the relationships of pure and brilliant colours. Wyndham Lewis's report of Gilman's later rejection of Sickert is no doubt exaggerated, but nonetheless illuminating:

He would look over in the direction of Sickert's studio, and a slight shudder would convulse him as he thought of the little brown worm of paint that was possibly, even at that moment, wriggling out onto the palette that held no golden chromes, emerald green, vermilions, only, as it, of course, should do.[44]

Gore's reaction to the Post-Impressionist exhibition was less delayed than Gilman's. In 1910 his vibrant *pointilliste* application had already begun to give place to a smoother handling. In some of his paintings of 1911 (for example, *Rinaldo, the Mad Violinist*) the broad, summary execution is similar to Sickert's work of about the same date, but in others he began to group the colours into self-contained areas. When he was staying in Sickert's house at Neuville in 1906 it is possible that Gore visited Paris to see the large Gauguin retrospective on show at the *Salon d'automne*. If so, an understanding of Gauguin's art may have been simmering in Gore's mind, awaiting only fresh contact to trigger off an immediate reaction. Gauguin's effect on Gore's vision is clearly demonstrated in *The Balcony at the Alhambra* (Art Gallery, York) with its strong pattern of flat areas of colour, its slight sense of distortion in the drawing and its high-angled viewpoint. In another *tour de force*, *Gauguins and Connoisseurs at the Stafford Gallery* (pl.21) of 1911–12, showing the gallery during an exhibition of paintings by Gauguin and Cézanne held in November 1911, subject and treatment were united by Gore in an explicit gesture of homage.

If Fry's exhibition inspired the younger and less travelled British artists, it held no surprises for such Fitzroy Street members as Bevan, Ginner, Pissarro and Sickert. Sickert lectured on the exhibition at the Grafton Gallery, and wrote the substance of his exuberant criticism in an article for the *Fortnightly Review*.[45] He could not see what all the fuss was about. He had known the work of the artists shown for many years. He then proceeded to treat them neither as gods nor as devils, but as ordinary painters subject to successes, failures and external influences just like anyone else. He allowed himself to wonder, 'since "post" is Latin for "after", where are Bonnard and Vuillard?' However, Sickert's attempt to restore a sense of perspective failed. The public, most of the critics and the figureheads of the art world united to condemn the exhibition as an outrage. The old guard of the NEAC, led by Tonks, Steer and D. S. MacColl, were among the most hostile. In the backlash following the exhibition, it was obvious that the grudging tolerance recently displayed by the NEAC towards Fitzroy Street and its allies would be abruptly withdrawn. Any younger painter not yet firmly established, whose work betrayed non-traditional foreign allegiances, would almost certainly be rejected by the club. As the critic of *The Times* was to write in 1913, the NEAC had become 'one of the strongest conservative forces in the country. What was an adventure has become an institution.'[46] This political fact of life was the main impetus behind the creation of the Camden Town Group.

Formation of the Camden Town Group

Disaffection with the New English Art Club was the chief topic of discussion among the members and satellites of the Fitzroy Street Group early in 1911. The relative merits of capturing control of its jury or of setting up a rival exhibiting society were hotly debated both at general meetings and in private conversation. Manson was kept informed of developments by Pissarro and took a keen interest.[47] On 22 March 1911 he wrote to Pissarro:

I am preparing a list of people I might approach with regard to the formation of a Society such as we spoke of.

You will, of course have a number of names. I shall, I expect, see you on Saturday when we might discuss how many people it would be possible to start with, etc.

Perhaps abashed at his temerity, Manson was less pushing in his next letter to Pissarro, written on the following day:

I should like to join the NEAC but can't afford it at the moment.

If you do manage to form a new society I should like to be in it and anyhow I would support it.

Pissarro's reply reflects the vacillating opinions and decisions current in Fitzroy Street:[48]

I feel I owe you an explanation. For the present our new society is given up for want of gallery and funds. At the same time the NEAC like a better known Club in the house of Lords is very anxious to reform itself. We, unlike the house of Commons have kindly consented to allow them to do so by admitting a certain number of members with advanced tendencies. I am not very pleased with the turn things have taken, but I don't see what else to do. I hope that at some future time we may manage to form the new Society.

Manson's answer was written immediately (24 March):

Under the circumstances, I will avail myself of yr. kind offer to propose me for the NEAC.

I couldn't afford to subscribe to that and to the New Society which I hoped you would be able to form. So if the NEAC is trying to reform itself I should like to be in it (if they'll have me!)

Of course, the advanced society *must* someday come into existence. We must work for it. It ought to be and it must be.

Events did not rest. Pissarro's reservations were felt more strongly by other members of the Fitzroy Street Group. Sickert and Gore temporized, but on the whole they had little faith in the ability of the NEAC to reform itself, and less in the practicability of their capturing control of its jury. Gilman argued fiercely and powerfully for a total break with the club.

The precise circumstances which resulted in the formal foundation of the Camden Town Group have been related by Ginner.[49] A nucleus of Fitzroy Street members used to eat together after their Saturday meetings. Dining at Gatti's, probably in April, Sickert, Ginner, Bevan, Gore and Gilman made their decision. They would indeed create a new society. Sickert, playing the *grand maître*, exclaimed, 'We have just made history.' Discussion continued at 19 Fitzroy Street and then at a larger dinner at the Criterion when practical issues were decided such as who to invite as members. A full meeting took place in a restaurant in Golden Square. Walter Bayes, in his account of the group,[50] told how Sickert 'invented the name Camden Town Group, averring that that district had been so watered with his tears that something important must sooner or later spring from its soil'. Gore, rather than the more truculent Gilman, was elected president. Manson, by now a member of Fitzroy Street, was made secretary.

Although the reactionary attitude displayed by the controlling faction of the NEAC was the main impetus behind the creation of the Camden Town Group, Ginner recorded another ideal. The Fitzroy Street friends wanted to collect 'a group which was to hold within a fixed and limited circle those painters whom they considered to be the best and most promising of the day'. Naturally there were arguments as to who these painters were. Pupils and disciples gained relatively easy entry. Just as Pissarro had secured Manson's membership of the Fitzroy Street and thus of the Camden Town Group, Gore may have proposed Doman Turner, Gilman proposed Ratcliffe and Sickert and Ginner proposed Drummond for membership of one or both groups. The suggestion that Wyndham Lewis be invited to join the Camden Town Group caused most dissension, for he was already leaning towards the angular distortions of Cubism and his temperament was uncomfortably fiery. Gilman, probably supported by Gore, pressed in his favour and won the day.

Sickert and Gilman agreed on one key rule: that there should be no women members. Dr Malcolm Easton has quoted a letter written by Manson to Lucien Pissarro's wife in answer to pressing demands that her friend Diana White[51] should be elected to the Camden Town Group.[52] In his letter Manson explained that the bar against women arose 'from the disinclination of the Group to include Miss S. and Miss H. of Fitzroy Street in the list of members'. This explanation helped Manson out of a delicate situation *vis-à-vis* Mrs Pissarro; it probably also reflected his own and Pissarro's views. Pissarro was later to accuse Sickert of destroying the art value of Fitzroy Street by diluting the group 'in a sea of amateurs and pupils of his'.[53] However, Ginner's accurate factual account gives a different, and psychologically more convincing, reason for the ban on women:

Gilman, strongly supported by Sickert … contended that some members might desire, perhaps even under pressure, to bring in their wives or lady friends and this might make things rather uncomfortable between certain of the elect, for these wives or lady friends might not quite come up to the standard aimed at by the group.

Miss Sands and Miss Hudson qualified as neither wife nor mistress, but the convenient blanket ban excluded them. Sickert bluntly explained the situation: 'As a matter of fact, as you probably know, the Camden Town Group is a male club, and women are not eligible. There are lots of 2 sex clubs, and several one sex clubs, and this is one of them.'

It was left to find a gallery in which to exhibit. Sickert, who had recently held an exhibition at the Carfax Gallery, persuaded Arthur Clifton (who had taken charge of the gallery) to lend them his premises in June. Over the next two years the Carfax Gallery under Clifton's management not only hosted the three Camden Town Group exhibitions but also sponsored many of the members with individual shows. Without Clifton's support, the Camden Town Group would have foundered.

Consideration of the list of sixteen members of the Camden Town Group – Bayes, Bevan, Drummond, Gilman, Ginner, Gore, Innes, John, Lamb, Lewis, Lightfoot, Manson, Pissarro, Ratcliffe, Sickert and Doman Turner – suggests that the founders of the group felt that the best and most promising painters of the day were, on the whole, members or satellites of their own Fitzroy Street Group. Lewis and Lightfoot were the only recruits from outside their immediate circle. Following Lightfoot's resignation, the policy of recruiting from the Friday Club was repeated and Duncan Grant became a member. While developing as an artist Grant had, on occasion, yielded to the influence of Sickert and Fitzroy Street. However, by 1911 Grant's art was evolving in a totally different direction and his energies, both artistic and political, were bound up with Roger Fry and Clive Bell. He took little part in the group, sending only one picture to the second exhibition in December 1911 and nothing at all to the third and last exhibition a year later in December 1912.

Ginner's explanation of the ban on women stressed the qualitative standard the Camden Town Group wished to sustain. Manson, on the other hand, suggested that the group in 1911 'represented a coherent homogeneous school of expression; differing in degree as to the work of individual members, but with the unity of a common aim'.[54] It is difficult to pinpoint the nature of this common aim in artistic terms. Manson probably had in mind what he had characterized in 1911 as 'that quiet but persistent and virile movement of English impressionism of which Messrs. Lucien Pissarro, Walter Sickert, Spencer Gore, Harold Gilman, and some others are the bright and shining lights'.[55] A review by Manson of the second Camden Town Group exhibition[56] reveals that he saw the Camden Town Group primarily as a challenge to Burlington House: unlike that 'concentrated block of bourgeois sentimentality known as the Royal Academy', the group found its subjects in everyday life; its members were blessed with gifts of perception in front of nature which each expressed in his different way, through colour, tone, design and so on.

The Camden Town Group was, in fact, even less representative of a particular movement in painting than the Fitzroy Street Group. Drummond and Ratcliffe were broadly aligned with the nucleus of Camden Town painters: Bevan, Gilman, Ginner, Gore and Sickert. However, by 1911 this nucleus was rapidly losing its self-contained identity as each of its members began to outgrow the teaching of Sickert and Pissarro and to explore new stylistic avenues. If we define Camden Town painting as the objective record of aspects of urban life in a basically Impressionist-derived handling, and recognize it as a distinct movement in British art, then we must accept that the heyday of Camden Town painting was over by the time the Camden Town Group was born.

The core of the group retained the subject-matter, if not the handling, evolved within Fitzroy Street. Manson and Pissarro remained painters of Neo-Impressionist landscape. The imagery of John, Innes and Lamb was more romantic, and their style, with its fluent draughtsmanship and lyrical sense of colour, totally at variance with those painters who had evolved their handling through Impressionism. The painting of Walter Bayes was closer in style and subject-matter to this last group. He too painted figures in a landscape, but his approach was cooler, conditioned more by his sense of design than by a subjective emotional response to his subject. Doman Turner as a non-painter in oils, Lewis as an embryonic Vorticist and Lightfoot, whose uniquely sensitive revival of the best academic traditions of draughtsmanship and tonal painting defy classification within a twentieth-century context, each stood on his own. Contemporary critics soon recognized that the group was 'not a school, but only a convenient name for a number of artists who exhibit together',[57] and that basically what they had in common was 'the Carfax Gallery in which they exhibit'.[58]

1911: the first two exhibitions of the Camden Town Group

The basement in Bury Street, St James's, which housed the Carfax Gallery imposed its own limitations on the Camden Town Group exhibitions. Each of the sixteen members was entitled to show four reasonably sized works, which were hung together, rather than mixed at random, on the walls. In fact only fifty-five, instead of the maximum of sixty-four, pictures were shown in June 1911; Innes did not exhibit, while Lamb with three, and Lewis and John with two pictures each, did not take up their full quota. The second exhibition in December 1911 included fifty-three pictures, and the third in December 1912 only forty-five pictures.

The support given to the group by such established artists as John and Sickert was largely motivated by their desire to help less renowned colleagues. Gore's counsel had prevailed against Gilman's demand that membership of the new society should entail breaking totally with the NEAC. Nevertheless, John refrained from exhibiting with the NEAC in the summer of 1911, but sent two Welsh landscapes to the Camden Town Group. His choice of small, informal pictures may perhaps be interpreted as an effort to indicate his support without outshining less recognized and less popular talents. Having made this gesture he neither exhibited again with the group, nor attended their committee meetings.

Sickert did exhibit with the NEAC in the summer of 1911, as did Bevan, Gore, Lamb and Pissarro. In the first Camden Town Group exhibition he included two related two-figure subjects given the 'Camden Town Murder' title, undoubtedly as a bait to bring the public into the Carfax Gallery.

On the whole the press reacted favourably from the beginning (see fig.4); as one critic remarked, their nerves had been steeled by 'recent experiences'.[59] Compared with the more radical distortions of form and colour demonstrated by the French Post-Impressionists at the Grafton Gallery, the pictures decorating the Carfax Gallery in June 1911 presented little to disturb even an insular critic. There were fresh landscapes of both rural and urban scenes, Camden Town figures in interiors, two music hall subjects by Gore and two cab-yards by Bevan. However idiosyncratic were Sickert's contributions to an exhibition, and however unappealing his subject-matter, critics had learned that he was a master to be respected and praised for his craft. John's presence was reassuring. Every reviewer could recognize and admire the qualities of design and draughtsmanship, as well as the technical fluency, of Lightfoot and Lamb.

Lightfoot himself regretted his inclusion and alleged in an interesting letter to his Slade contemporary Rudolph Ihlee that he had never consented to becoming a member of the Camden Town Group.[60] He harshly condemned the exhibition: Lamb's work was 'paltry'; John's sketches were 'wild' and he judged that Adrian Allinson would soon match John's achievement ('For he is equal to him now in lack of humbleness – he has only got to practice drawing wild lines'); Gore's theatre pieces were 'as pretty as any young lady would wish to see – drawing, none – colour pretty – but not by any means good. He approaches as many schemes of colour in one picture as Whistler did in the whole of his lifework.' Lightfoot evidently resigned from the Camden Town Group forthwith, telling Ihlee in the same letter: 'I swear on my oath I will never show with the crowd again. It is 19 Fitzroy Street to the core. My stuff looks as much out of place and absurd as I do when I go to the Saturday afternoon lying competition at Sickert's.' He did, however, welcome the good relationship he had established with Clifton and hoped to exhibit at the Carfax Gallery, alone, in the future.

Only Wyndham Lewis excited almost unanimous critical derision. He had contributed two angular pen and ink drawings of a man's head, both entitled *The Architect* (see pl.50). They were the first works Lewis had exhibited in London since the NEAC in 1904. The critic of the *Morning Post*[61] conveys the pain, which had replaced fury, of popular reaction to such advanced art:

As an imaginary portrait of the man who designed most of the modern buildings in London, it may be welcomed as a caricature nearer the truth than perhaps the artist intended. But what was the aim of the draughtsman? … Mr Lewis, who enjoys a high reputation among his friends as poet and draughtsman, introduces a note of insincerity that is well enough in criticism but regrettable in serious art, and entirely foreign to the present exhibition.

Lewis remained the chief thorn for reviewers of the next two exhibitions. He also caused dissension within the Camden Town Group. The Pissarro archives in the Ashmolean Museum contain the undated draft of a letter from Pissarro to Gore, as president of the group. The reference within it to 'pictures' and 'canvases' in the plural suggest it was penned in December 1911, on the occasion of the second exhibition:

I am quite upset by what I saw this afternoon at the Camden Town Group exhibition. The pictures of Lewis are quite impossible! Either ours is a serious movement or else a farce! I dont feel inclined [to] let my pictures remain if he persists in showing these particular canvases. I was not consulted when he was asked to join our society – we all took him from Gilman's recommendation without knowing his work. If the principle of the group were like the AAA, I would say nothing, but as we are quite a closed society I dont see why we should put up with such rubbish.

Pissarro asked Gore to meet him at the Carfax Gallery the following day. If this draft was sent we can only assume that Gore managed to unruffle Pissarro. Certainly, apart from Lewis, the Camden Town Group was accepted by the press as a band of 'intensely serious artists who … show neither eccentricity nor a desire to épater le bourgeois but are clearly inspired by the longing for self-expression in what each considers the most suitable language'.[62]

Expansion of the Camden Town Group: first ideas

The question of new membership of the Camden Town Group was raised before the second exhibition opened in December 1911. The election of Duncan Grant to fill the vacancy created by Lightfoot's suicide in September 1911 may have triggered consideration of this matter. The idea of increasing the size of the group was formally tackled at a meeting on 2 December 1911, attended by all the members except Grant, John and Innes. Sickert opened the discussion. He, Manson and Doman Turner preferred a small, exclusive society, but most members were in favour of expansion. Their opinions ranged from Gilman's belief that anyone whose work was interesting to the group should be elected, to the cautious view expressed by Bayes that there were disadvantages in keeping the size of the group permanently the same, although under present conditions at the Carfax Gallery he saw no alternative to the status quo. Procedures to elect new members were then discussed. Pissarro had taken the precaution of preparing a draft of his proposals and rules in advance.[63] His suggestion that candidates should show their work on probation at 19 Fitzroy Street prior to election was vetoed by Sickert who felt this use of the parent society's premises was improper. Pissarro also proposed that women be eligible for election, and that at each exhibition four members in turn should have the right to invite a guest, man or woman, to contribute two pictures. Pissarro may have taken this opportunity to promote his wife's ambition that Diana White should show with the group. Finally, he suggested an escape clause whereby if two-thirds of members felt the work of another member was out of harmony with the aims of the society, that member should be asked to retire. Like Manson, Pissarro seems to have had a clear, if personal, concept of the nature of such aims. However, while discussion of these matters was under way, Gilman intervened to propose that there should be no increase in membership under the present conditions of exhibition at the Carfax Gallery. He had perhaps been pondering the point made earlier by Bayes that an increase in the number of members would involve a decrease in the number of works each could show. He may also have been alarmed at Pissarro's attempt to re-open the question of women members. Gilman's motion, oddly enough seconded by Pissarro, was carried by eight votes to three. Gilman then proposed that a new and larger gallery should be found as soon as possible. This motion was carried unanimously. As it happened it took two years to find satisfactory alternative accommodation, so the membership problems were shelved.

1912: members' activities

The Camden Town Group's decision to seek new premises delayed active consideration of their next exhibition. Twelve months elapsed between the second and third showings of the group's work at the Carfax Gallery. Nevertheless, however dormant the society was as a whole, several of its individual members enjoyed an exceptionally stimulating year.

Gilman boldly experimented with his handling and subject-matter. Emulating Ginner's theme, he painted the interior of the Café Royal (rep. Baron 1979, pl.109), laying out the design of the complex setting with free, confidently drawn strokes of the brush and modelling his forms in closely integrated flat planes of rich colour, pinks and blues and greens. During the summer he broke new ground by painting landscapes and interiors in Sweden. There he drew liberally on a wide range of styles and treatments, extending from the flat colours and almost childishly simple drawing of *A Swedish Village* (National Gallery of Canada, Ottawa) to the striated paint of his Van Gogh-inspired *The Reapers* (Art Gallery, Johannesburg).

While Gilman was away he lent his house in Letchworth to Gore, who responded vigorously to the novel environment of garden city, burgeoning industry and domesticated landscape in a series of brilliant experimental canvases (see pls 22, 23).

Existing friendships were consolidated in the course of this year. Innes and John again spent some time together in North Wales. The sympathy between Manson and Pissarro grew stronger. And new allegiances were formed. During the late summer and autumn Bevan and Ginner, both for the first time, stayed at Applehayes, Clayhidon, home of the hospitable H. B. Harrison, retired rancher and amateur artist. Each produced his own version of their host's Somerset landscape. Temporarily, Bevan seems to have reacted to Ginner's influence. His *Evening in the Culme Valley* (rep. Bevan 1965, pl.41) is not only close compositionally to Ginner's *West Country Landscape* (rep. Baron 1979, pl.116), it has the same feeling of swirling movement (in spite of Bevan's larger, looser stroke) and it is similar in colour. This kind of treatment represents an unexpected interlude in the natural evolution of Bevan's style. His affinities as a painter were much closer to Gore than to Ginner. For example, the firm structured pattern, the schematic drawing and the angular modelling of such Bevan landscapes as *The Town Field, Horsgate* (pl.58) of 1914 echo qualities found in Gore's *Croft's Lane, Letchworth* of 1912 (rep. Baron 1979, pl.111), a painting which belonged to Bevan. A comparison of their self-portraits of *c.*1914 (both in the National Portrait Gallery, London) underlines the depth of their innate stylistic affinity.

The interlude in Somerset occurred several months after the close association of Gore and Ginner in what was probably the most exciting, and certainly the most exacting, collaborative venture of 1912. Madame Frida Strindberg, briefly the second wife and by 1912 the widow of the Swedish dramatist August Strindberg, indulged her passion for the bohemian life of advanced art and letters by launching the Cabaret Theatre Club in Heddon Street, Soho. This establishment, better known by the more evocative name of its inner sanctum, 'The Cave of the Golden Calf', opened on 26 June 1912. Its decorations were designed and executed by Wyndham Lewis, Gore, Ginner and Jacob Epstein. Additional decorations by other artists, including a calf by Eric Gill, were envisaged but never carried out. In 1914 the night club went into liquidation. During the war Madame Strindberg and all the transportable decorations disappeared, reputedly together, to America. The paintings by Lewis, Gore and Ginner have yet to re-emerge.

The general character, if not the detail, of the decorative scheme can be deduced from personal reminiscences, documents and above all from surviving studies by Gore and Ginner for their contributions.[64] Lewis painted 'a huge and hideous raw meat drop curtain',[65] some screens and wall paintings. As a friend of Madame Strindberg, Lewis had probably suggested that Gore and Ginner be commissioned to provide more wall decorations and that Epstein should provide the reliefs which decorated the columns supporting the interior. Gore, perhaps because his artistic gifts were matched by his extraordinary ability to remain on good terms with everybody and thus mediate between the most conflicting temperaments, was appointed to guide and supervise the whole scheme.

The existing evidence suggests that this scheme had little iconographic structure. Gaiety was the chief requirement and each artist was left to react individually to the hedonistic concept of the total environment. Lewis referred to his murals as 'somewhat abstract hieroglyphics'.[66] His extant designs for the prospectus, programme and menu (reproduced Michel 1971, pls 14–16) are nonetheless figurative, although the drawing is distorted to convey kinetic frenzy. Both Gore and Ginner, probably working in close co-operation, chose exotic jungle and hunting scenes to convey the necessary atmosphere. Ginner made three highly stylized, decorative panels: *Chasing Monkeys* (over eight feet by six); *Birds and Indians* (an irregular picture, with a segment cut out in the centre of the lower half, measuring nine feet by six overall); and *Tiger Hunting* (some six feet square flanked by two narrow side panels). Ginner's notebooks record what he was paid for such yardage: £12 for the three, intended as an advance but not settled until 1913, plus another £6.10s.3d obtained as a percentage of money due to him after the liquidation. He also sold two posters in distemper to the club. Their themes suggest that they were executed independently (and then bought as decorations for £2.10s each) rather than commissioned as advertisements by Madame Strindberg. Both are lost but one, entitled *Piccadilly Circus*, perhaps anticipated the composition of the painting (pl.54) exhibited by Ginner later in the year with the Camden Town Group.

Whereas Ginner's animals were presented as two-dimensional patterns, Gore's surviving sketches suggest that his huntsmen on horseback and his racing animals peopled imaginary landscapes. His confident integration of landscape and figures into a synthetic pattern in which the basic forms are translated into simplified, brightly coloured, flat shapes, each strongly demarcated with dark outlines, reveals that he had assimilated, and could exploit at will, a variety of Post-Impressionist sources. Gauguin, Matisse and possibly the German *Blaue Reiter* group, in particular the Russian-born Wassily Kandinsky who had been known in England since the first exhibition of some of his paintings in 1909 with the AAA, may all have contributed to Gore's inspiration.

Ginner's experience with these night-club decorations seems to have had little effect on his future work. Jungle scenes emanating from the imagination had no place in the development of an artist increasingly devoted to the most scrupulous study of the external detail of nature. Wyndham Lewis's designs for the club probably contributed towards the evolution of *Danse*, painted during 1912, but unfortunately this large picture is another of Lewis's lost early works. In Gore's case, however, the decorations can be positively assessed as relevant to his future development. The strong patterning, the synthetic organization and the brilliant colours of the paintings he did in Letchworth in the summer must have drawn part of their impetus from the night-club decorations so recently completed.

The third Camden Town Group exhibition and the 'Second Post-Impressionist Exhibition'

At the third and last Camden Town Group exhibition at the Carfax Gallery in December 1912, thirteen members showed a total of forty-five pictures. Grant, John and Innes abstained. Each had exhibited only once with the group, to which they had never felt deeply committed. Grant was involved politically and artistically with Roger Fry, Vanessa Bell and the Friday Club; John and Innes were members of the NEAC and allied commercially to Jack Knewstub of the Chelsea Chenil Gallery, rather than to Arthur Clifton of the Carfax.

The absence of these three artists meant that the overall character of the paintings on view at the Carfax Gallery was more uniform than in 1911. Only Bayes, Lamb and Lewis remained to represent artistic styles developed outside the influence of the original nucleus of Fitzroy Street Group painters. Yet, paradoxically, this 1912 exhibition appeared to be less 'Camden Town'-orientated than those of 1911. There were no music hall pictures. Only Drummond and Sickert contributed interiors with figures. Of these only Sickert's three paintings represented humble models in humble surroundings; one of these, *Summer in Naples*, was also the sole nude in the entire show. The bulk of the exhibition was made up of colourful rural landscapes characterized by 'a common liking for undertones of a purplish tinge'.[67] In the face of this display, Manson's outrageously partisan review of the exhibition, under the title 'London Impressionists',[68] can almost be excused. Manson composed a panegyric on Lucien Pissarro, 'the leader of the movement in England … honoured … by the small band of modern artists who are producing the work of which posterity will take account'. He described Sickert as 'the pill in the jam of modern art' and consigned him to the tailpiece of his review.

There were only two distinctly provocative paintings in the exhibition. One was Sickert's *Summer in Naples*, representing a fat and ugly nude woman seated on a metal-framed bed back to back with a shabbily dressed man. This painting now bears the more appropriate title *Dawn, Camden Town* (rep. RA 1992, pl.71). It is probable that Sickert chose both to exhibit this unusually brutal painting and to designate it with an exceptionally perverse title, in order to remind critics and his fellow-exhibitors that this was the kind of subject which, under his guidance, the Fitzroy Street Group had introduced into English art.

The other provocative, and much more obviously nonconformist, work was Wyndham Lewis's (now lost) painting *Danse*. However, although critics of the popular press continued to huff and puff when confronted with the angular distortions of Lewis's design, others were gradually becoming reconciled to this new mode of vision. For example, while the *Star*[69] dismissed *Danse* as 'a piece of "cubism"' which might more properly be exhibited in the Zoo or Madame Tussaud's, *The Times*[70] commented that 'though we see no dance in it, we do see a kind of geometrical logic in the design, which gives us more pleasure than we get from a quite commonplace and intelligible picture'.

Several critics again found Walter Bayes's paintings equally out of character with the main body of work on exhibition, but at the opposite extreme to Lewis. He was admired for combining the modern (his gifts for synthesis and simplification) and the classical (his concern with design and rhythm). Reassuring echoes of Poussin were recognized in his large-scale designs. When he looked back on this period to write his article on the Camden Town Group for the *Saturday Review* in 1930,[71] Bayes was to disparage the practice current within the group of working from nature, 'returning again and again to the same study' as if this in itself 'was in some sort an evidence of seriousness, as the working from cumulative knowledge was not … For perennial repainting from Nature their execution had the great advantage that you could always poise another lump of stiff paint on a surface already so rough and corrugated that it would not show as a scar.'

In spite of the preponderance of rural landscapes – English, French and, from Gilman, Swedish – there were more exciting pictures to reflect the new departures in subject-matter made by their painters during 1912. Bevan showed paintings of the London horse sales instead of his former cab-yards. His son has recorded[72] how he gave up cab-yard subjects because he did not wish 'to be accused of sentimentalizing about an almost vanished feature of London life', and indeed the critic of the *Globe*[73] in praising *The Cabyard, Night* (pl.14), in the second Camden Town Group show, had remarked that nevertheless his technique seemed 'antiquated, as will his subject in a year or two, when the last hansom has disappeared'. The horse-sale subjects, filled with hard-faced traders, studied instead one of the toughest aspects of a great commercial city. Moreover, as his art matured, Bevan turned away from the broken divisionist handling which had enlivened his paintings since around 1907, his drawing became more angular and schematic and his choice of local colour more arbitrary.

Aspects of contemporary life in central London were also presented by Ginner, Drummond and Ratcliffe. Ginner showed *Piccadilly Circus* (pl.54), one of his earliest brilliantly coloured, tautly constructed London street scenes filled with a bustling throng of traffic and figures. The year between shows had allowed time for the talents of less-experienced exhibitors to mature. For example, among the paintings which survive and can be identified from this third exhibition are Drummond's *St James's Park* (pl.17) and Ratcliffe's *Clarence Gardens* (pl.53). These two London prospects represent high points within the context of each artist's development. The tidy geometry and the tightly stippled application of high-toned colours used by Ratcliffe in *Clarence Gardens* reveal that he had already developed the disciplined approach which supported him throughout 1913, his most productive and successful year as a painter. In *St James's Park* Drummond achieved a consummate balance between prose and poetry. The skilful, almost pedantic, perspective construction provided a prosaic framework within which Drummond set free his poetic imagination to express his subject in an range of rich, unrealistic, confectionery tints. The product is an idyllic vision of Londoners at leisure which recalls, albeit on a smaller and less ambitious scale, Seurat's description of Parisians enjoying Sunday afternoon on *la Grande Jatte*.

Drummond and Ratcliffe undoubtedly sent their most important pictures of the year to the Camden Town Group in December 1912. Other members, whose work was seldom accepted for exhibition elsewhere in London except in the annual AAA jamboree, probably did likewise. Among these members were Gilman and Ginner, although the latter also exhibited each year with the *Salon des Indépendants* in Paris and had been, in May 1912, among the small group of artists selected by Roger Fry to represent contemporary (thus by Fry's lights Post-Impressionist) British art at the Galerie Barbazanges in Paris. A few members of the Camden Town Group in 1912 clearly reserved their more radical work for an alternative showplace.

Roger Fry's 'Second Post-Impressionist Exhibition' opened at the Grafton Gallery in October 1912. Unlike the first exhibition, this one incorporated an 'English Group' selected by Clive Bell. Four members of the Camden Town Group – Gore, the Australian-born Lamb, the half-American Lewis and the Scot Duncan Grant – were among the painters invited to exhibit under this 'English' heading. Lewis and Grant had both been included in Roger Fry's show at the Galerie Barbazanges, but Bell dropped Ginner as a Post-Impressionist in favour of Gore and Lamb. The Grafton Gallery exhibition ran on into the new year, thus totally overlapping the Camden Town Group show which opened in December.

Duncan Grant's commitment to the Camden Town Group had ceased after December 1911. He sent nothing to the December 1912 exhibition at the Carfax Gallery. However, the three painters who contributed to both exhibitions had to choose which context was more appropriate to particular paintings. Neither Lewis nor Lamb belonged to the nucleus of artists responsible for creating the Camden Town Group. Gore, on the other hand, was its president. His choice of which pictures to exhibit where thus indicates the shifting balance in the structure of non-conformist politics in the London art world.

Lamb's priorities were slightly weighted towards the Grafton Gallery. Whereas he sent two studies of heads (probably representing Irish girls he had just painted in Donegal) to the Carfax Gallery, he chose to exhibit a recent *Portrait of Lytton Strachey* and a picture from Lady Ottoline Morrell's collection with the Post-Impressionists. He cared enough about the Grafton Gallery show to complain bitterly that the wrong picture was collected, in his absence, from Lady Ottoline's house.[74]

Wyndham Lewis, who showed only *Danse* at the Carfax Gallery, had eight important drawings and two major paintings on view at the Grafton Gallery. One of his paintings, *Creation* (another lost work), was illustrated in the catalogue.

Gore showed his full complement of four paintings at the Carfax Gallery. One was a Camden Town landscape of 1911, shown as *Euston from the Nursery* (pl.55), remarkable not so much for its style and handling as for the effective use of a grid of vertical bars through which the railway tracks and station are seen. *The Pond*, described in the press as 'gold and green ... rhythmical in design',[75] may be the painting of that title and colouring now in the Worthing Art Gallery, a somewhat dour work in which the angular handling of the landscape and cloud forms, as well as the Derain-derived colour harmony, recall Roger Fry's landscapes; alternatively it might be *The Pond, Richmond Park* in the National Gallery of Canada. Press descriptions of *Letchworth Common* and *The Broken Fence* imply that they were pleasant, unexceptional studies from nature. The former may be the painting now in the Tate Gallery, London, one of Gore's least radical Letchworth subjects of 1912. The latter may be an Impressionist Panshanger landscape of 1908–9. Evidently

Gore did not exhibit his more daring, experimental paintings of 1912 at the Carfax Gallery.

Gore exhibited *The Tree* and *Letchworth Station* (National Railway Museum, York) at the Grafton Gallery. When the exhibition was unexpectedly extended from December 1912 to January 1913 he added *The Cinder Path* (Tate Gallery, London) to help fill gaps on the walls caused by some artists having to withdraw their exhibits. *The Tree* may be one of two pictures of a fig tree (one in a private collection as *The Tree*; the other in the Tate Gallery as *The Fig Tree*) painted from a back window of 2 Houghton Place where the Gores lived in 1912. *The Cinder Path*, showing the track crossing the fields outside Letchworth towards Baldock, clearly illustrates Gore's increasing preoccupation with the underlying three-dimensional structural relationships of his subject and the two-dimensional pattern of his picture surface. He expressed the component volumes of his scene – trees, fields, sky and clouds – as separate rhomboidal blocks of distinct colours. The path itself, plunging down at right angles to the picture plane and coloured a deep violet, both defines the spatial recession and articulates the flat pattern on the surface. Gore processed his perception of nature even more radically in other contemporary Letchworth subjects, such as *The Beanfield* (pl.22) in which the rows of beans are condensed into zigzag coloured stripes, *The Icknield Way* (pl.23), and *Letchworth Station*. *Letchworth Station* was illustrated in the Grafton Gallery catalogue: it could be a scene from Noddy's *Toytown*. The bright and varied colours emphasize the unreal aspect of the picture. Gore had long understood the emotive force of colour as used by French Post-Impressionist painters like Gauguin and Matisse. However, his use of colour was not arbitrary. It sprang rather from his training as an objective student of nature. He took the colours he perceived, organized them into family groups and heightened them in tone. Thus in *The Beanfield* the zigzag stripes of greens and reds are inspired by the actual colours of a plot of beans in flower. The colours of *Letchworth Station* are also based on nature, except that the inclusion of clothed figures gave Gore more leeway in his choice of harmonic accents.

The way in which Gore orchestrated his response to nature – grouping, patterning and organizing what he saw into a structure of shapes and colours – accorded with Clive Bell's statement in his preface on 'The English Group' for the Grafton Gallery catalogue: 'We expect a work of plastic art to have more in common with a piece of music than with a coloured photograph.' Nevertheless, Gore was not one of the painters singled out by Bell for special mention in this preface. Perhaps Gore's rejection of the 'descriptive' art so much abominated by Bell was not sufficiently explicit to ratify his total commitment to the kind of modernism advocated by the Grafton Gallery clique. Gore was, after all, still politically and artistically very much a member of the Camden Town Group which constituted, to quote from Sir Claude Phillip's review of their third exhibition,[76] 'a sort of link between the extremism of the Grafton Galleries and the more sober modernity of Suffolk Street' (the latter address being the headquarters of the New English Art Club). However, while the coincidence of these two exhibitions served to polarize their respective characters in the eyes of critics and public, the overlap of exhibitors tended to blur such distinctions in the eyes of the participants and their sympathetic colleagues. The Camden Town Group had not been created to act as a neutral buffer between conservatives and radicals: invidious comparisons threatened its continued viability.

1913: one-man exhibitions by members of the Camden Town Group

The three Camden Town Group exhibitions had not been successful financially and it is doubtful whether Arthur Clifton could have afforded to play host to a fourth group exhibition. However, he continued to sponsor the work of its members in a series of exhibitions at the Carfax Gallery in 1913. He launched his programme with a joint show by Gore and Gilman in January (see fig.4). Gore had already held a one-man exhibition of twenty-nine paintings at the Chenil Gallery in March 1911. He showed twenty-six pictures at the Carfax Gallery where *The Beanfield* (modestly priced at twelve guineas) and another smaller version of *The Cinder Path* (Ashmolean Museum, Oxford) were among several Letchworth landscapes. This joint exhibition was Gilman's first opportunity to show a substantial body of his work. He was not tempted to seize the opportunity to demonstrate his past achievement. Instead, with one exception (*The Cave Dwellers, Dieppe* of 1907; Ashmolean Museum, Oxford) his twenty-four paintings were recent works. These included four nudes, seven Swedish subjects (three previously exhibited with the Camden Town Group a month before) and two paintings of the interior of the Café Royal.

In March the Carfax Gallery mounted an exhibition of studies and etchings by Sickert, one of many Sickert shows held at the gallery between 1911 and 1916. Forty-eight paintings and drawings by Bevan occupied the Carfax Gallery in April in an exhibition which amounted to a retrospective survey covering all aspects of Bevan's style and subject-matter. Lucien Pissarro's first one-man exhibition, incorporating thirty-six paintings executed from the 1880s onwards, followed in May. The last of these 1913 exhibitions at the Carfax Gallery by Camden Town Group members was held in October, when Walter Bayes showed forty-five recent paintings.

Art politics and the Fitzroy Street Group in 1913

As in previous years, 19 Fitzroy Street remained a central meeting-point where members of the Camden Town Group were joined by a wide spectrum of visitors to the weekly gatherings of the parent society. Whereas membership of the Camden Town Group remained static and closed, that of the Fitzroy Street Group was open to expansion. In April 1913 Sickert, with some misgivings, decided not to veto Epstein's admission to the group: 'We shall see what we shall see', Sickert commented darkly to Ethel Sands. For the time

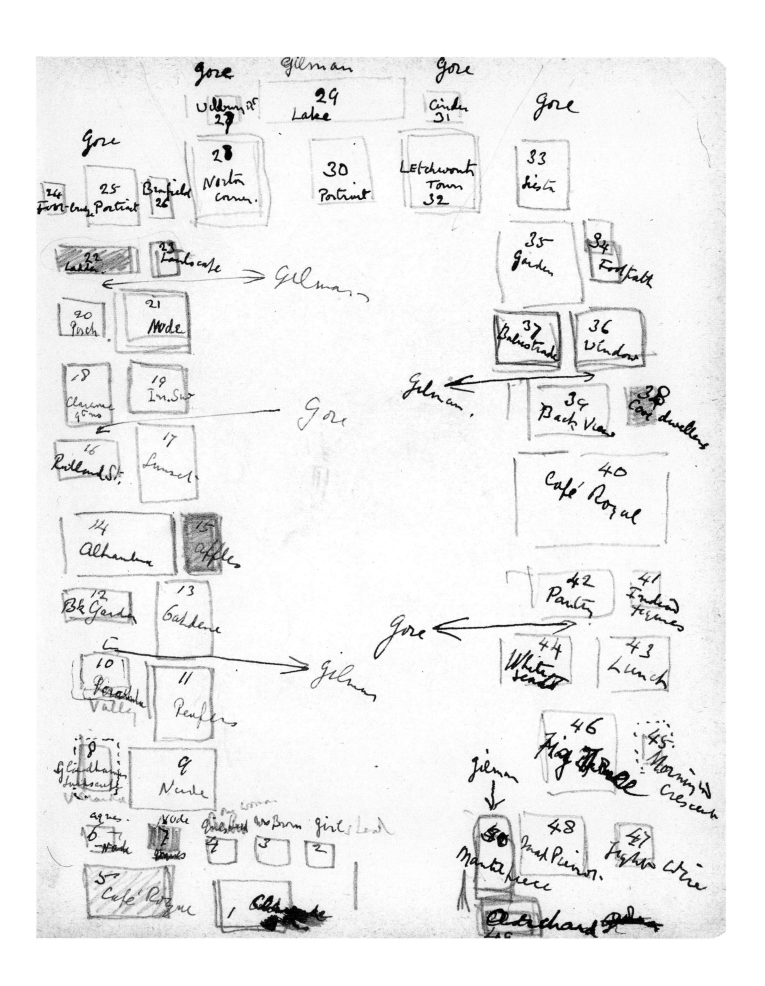

being he allowed himself to be swayed by Gore's opinion of his erstwhile colleague at the Cabaret Theatre Club, that the 'danger' was exaggerated and that the other members would be able 'to insist on not having anything too too'. As a counterbalance to potential subversion Sickert immediately lobbied on behalf of two of his former pupils, Madame Renée Finch and Sylvia Gosse. Miss Gosse's bid for membership failed, but Renée Finch and her husband Harald Sund both became members at some time between the spring and the autumn. It is possible that Madame Finch's election was materially aided by the furore caused by her submission of a male nude, with blue pubic hair, to the 1913 Allied Artists' Association exhibition. Accused of immorality, and threatened with police action, the artist had to withdraw the offending picture although, under the title *Reginald*, it was duly displayed in the 1914 AAA exhibition.

Roger Fry and his friends occasionally came to Fitzroy Street gatherings. It seems that when the 'Second Post-Impressionist Exhibition' was extended in December 1912 there was even talk current in Fitzroy Street of transferring the Camden Town Group show at the end of its run to the Grafton Gallery. This is the only possible explanation of an exchange of letters between Manson and Pissarro on 19 December 1912.[77] Manson tried to persuade Pissarro to overlook his distaste if such a course were ratified: 'You are very loyal to the C.T.G. but I think that you ought to benefit by any opportunity which might be useful to you. Of course, one does not care to accept anything from Roger Fry.' In a postscript Manson added: 'You see the rest of the C.T.G. are young and probably would not consider you in the same way. I fancy Sickert can look after himself!' The wind must have been taken out of Manson's sails by Pissarro's reply:

I am afraid you give me credit for more loyalty than I have. I don't feel it would be an advantage to be among the 'Post', but if the C.T. were to exhibit at the Grafton en bloc, I should of course be glad to join as one of them tho' I think we are all better out of it.

These loyalties were not put to the test in an exhibition, but relations grew more cordial between the two cliques. On one Saturday afternoon 'At Home' in the spring of 1913 Sickert brought Théodore Duret, the distinguished art historian and friend of the French Impressionists, to 19 Fitzroy Street where he introduced him to Fry and to Vanessa and Clive Bell. Fry, who had been up at Cambridge with Sickert's brother Oswald during the early 1890s, was a long-standing friend of the whole Sickert family and a one-time pupil of Walter Sickert. Mutual respect and much affection also existed between Sickert and Vanessa Bell. Nevertheless, the cluster of artists most intimately associated with Fry tended to keep themselves aloof from the Fitzroy Street Group. Besides divergences in their artistic tastes, their own activities left little spare time to attend alternative assemblies. The Friday Club survived to hold annual exhibitions. While it had attracted several of the most adventurous young artists trained at the Slade in these years, including Mark Gertler, Edward Wadsworth, Christopher Nevinson and David Bomberg, it had by 1913 also gathered together a large and amorphous crowd of lesser talents. The old guard of the club – Fry, Grant, Frederick Etchells and Vanessa Bell – therefore established a splinter society, the Grafton Group, and abstained from exhibiting with the Friday Club from 1913 onwards.

The first exhibition of the Grafton Group, at the Alpine Club Gallery, was held in March 1913. In anticipation of the imminent creation by Fry of the Omega Workshops, the exhibits were displayed anonymously and several items of applied art were included. The Camden Town Group was represented at the Grafton Group show not only by Grant, but by Lewis and Gore, who chose this forum to air his most striking Letchworth painting, *The Icknield Way* (pl.23). In April, Fry leased 33 Fitzroy Square to house the Omega Workshops, a fascinating co-operative venture in which artists could be employed on a regular, though part-time, basis to design, execute and decorate objects of applied art. Fry, Grant and Vanessa Bell were co-directors, and among the artists working for Omega by the time of its formal opening in July were Lewis, Etchells, Cuthbert Hamilton and Wadsworth.

Radical art politics were in a state of constant flux by 1913. Factionalism and cross-fertilization were rife as groups formed, overlapped and re-formed. Work by Gore, Lewis and Grant could be seen in nearly every context. Both the Friday Club and the Fitzroy Street Group had been created at a time when young, unrecognized artists had almost no opportunity either to exhibit and sell their work or to congregate in congenial company to discuss common concerns. This situation had since changed, largely through the efforts of the activists in both societies. Although their work was still unacceptable to the art establishment, young artists could now exhibit in shows which were widely, if not always flatteringly, reviewed in the press. A small, but faithful and ever-growing, band of clients collected contemporary art. If we except Frank Rutter's efforts on behalf of the broad majority, Roger Fry and Sickert were the two individuals most responsible for creating these conditions more favourable to progressive art, and there were similarities in their pragmatic approach to the task. They both realized that the priority was to educate the public towards appreciation of different methods of artistic expression; each tackled this problem head-on: Fry in his writings, lectures and exhibitions, Sickert primarily in his writings and teaching but also through the gatherings at Fitzroy Street. Both keenly appreciated that artists must earn a living, and the various groups and enterprises each created existed chiefly to promote the work of artists in whom they believed. Ironically, both Fry and Sickert were later to be accused of destroying the value of their creations. In his autobiography, Nevinson charged Fry with ruining the Friday Club, 'a remarkable little clique', by his 'amateurish dilettantism'.[78] On 22 December 1913, Pissarro was to write, with something of the same emphasis, to Manson:

As you know Sickert tries to dilute the little art elements of Fitzroy Street in a sea of amateurs and pupils of his – with probably the intention of destroying the art value of Fitzroy Street as he has destroyed the art value of the Camden Town Group.[79]

Neither attack should be taken as representing a general view. Nevinson wrote retrospectively when his account was coloured by recent animosities. Pissarro, on the other hand, satisfied with things as they had been during the early days of Fitzroy Street and Camden Town, found the turmoil of artistic developments and temperaments around him infinitely disturbing. He had never liked Sickert, and was perhaps a trifle jealous of Sickert's position of authority within Fitzroy Street. He was, therefore, more ready to blame Sickert who, as chairman at meetings, seemed to be the man in charge.

As usual, the Fitzroy Street Group went into recess during the summer of 1913. Most members left London. Sickert was in Envermeu near Dieppe where he briefly ran across Wyndham Lewis. Ginner painted in Dieppe and also joined Bevan and Gore at Applehayes, Clayhidon. Pissarro and Manson painted together at Rye. Bayes went to Brittany. Gilman visited Norway and Ratcliffe went to Sundsholm in Sweden. John passed the summer between Paris and Wales. Their summer break over, members returned to face decisions which could no longer be deferred.

The Camden Town Group was still seeking larger exhibition premises so that it could increase the number of members. The concurrence of its third exhibition in December 1912 and Fry's 'Second Post-Impressionist Exhibition' suggested that, as it stood, the Camden Town Group was no longer politically viable. As we have seen, the group had even toyed with the idea of joining Fry's show. Early in the autumn of 1913 Sickert considered recognizing a *fait accompli* by amalgamating the Fitzroy Street and Camden Town Groups with the Grafton Group. He wondered if a floor at 33 Fitzroy Square might be set aside to house this combination. And, as he told Nan Hudson, 'Any rules about the sexes ipso facto lapse distinctions having become, not only invidious, but impossible!' He was in two minds about the idea. On the one hand he maintained that 'Fry–Bell, in their critical capacity, have tried to edit film, pick and choose pictures (a disintegrating and impossible attitude), have created Ginner Post-Imp in Paris but not in London ...'.[80] On the other hand, he accepted that Gore and Lewis already fraternized (Sickert used the more picturesque verb *découcher*) with Fry's group. In conclusion he decided that 'It would make *the* only interesting crowd in London.'

Events fast overtook the birth of this plan. In October a bitter and irreconcilable quarrel occurred between Lewis and Fry. To summarize the well-known story,[81] Lewis believed that Roger Fry had wilfully appropriated an exciting commission, to decorate a complete 'Post-Impressionist Room' for the Ideal Home Exhibition in October 1913, which had originally been intended for himself and Gore – presumably as a result of their successful collaboration at the Cabaret Theatre Club. Gore had apparently been approached personally by the *Daily Mail* organizers who had also suggested that the room might contain Omega furniture. Gore, not himself an Omega artist, had left a message to this effect at Fitzroy Square for Lewis and Fry. Without telling Lewis, Fry received the message, approached the organizers and accepted the entire commission for Omega. Fry later asked Lewis to carve a mantelpiece for the room. Shortly afterwards Lewis learned, through Gore, that the *Daily Mail* commission had been intended primarily for himself and Gore, not for Omega.

In retaliation Lewis circularized a virulent letter among his friends and among the customers and shareholders of Omega, denouncing Fry as dishonest in his management. He also accused Fry of having withheld letters of invitation to himself and Etchells to show work in the 'Post-Impressionist and Futurist' exhibition being organized at the Doré Galleries by Frank Rutter. This abusive letter was signed not only by Lewis, but also by Etchells, Hamilton and Wadsworth. All four walked out on Omega. Gore supported Lewis's case. Even Sickert favoured Lewis rather than Fry in this matter. He wrote to Nan Hudson, 'I do not wish to send you the Lewis circular because I do not wish mine to be the hand to give it to you. I don't approve of its wording, though I think they were quite justified in leaving.' Obviously amalgamation with the Grafton Group was now impossible.

'Post-Impressionists and Futurists' at the Doré Galleries

The rift between the Grafton Group–Omega artists and Fitzroy Street was emphasized, perhaps unintentionally, by the Doré Galleries exhibition in October 1913. No works by Fry, Grant or Vanessa Bell were included in an otherwise remarkably comprehensive survey of 'Post-Impressionist and Futurist' art in Britain and abroad. The show was frankly didactic. Its organizer, Frank Rutter, wrote a preface in the catalogue outlining the developments in art which sprang from, or occurred after, Impressionism. He was anxious to explain that the umbrella definition 'Post-Impressionism' embraced a variety of movements, and he selected his exhibition accordingly. Paintings by Camille Pissarro represented classic Impressionism, and works by Cézanne, Van Gogh and Gauguin classic Post-Impressionism. Neo-Impressionism (Signac, Henri Edmond Cross and Theo van Rysselberghe), Intimism (Bonnard and Vuillard) and Fauvism (Matisse) were likewise demonstrated in what amounted to an illustrated lecture on modern art. Three photographs of works by Picasso stood in for Cubism. There were no paintings by the Italian Futurists but a work by Robert Delaunay, illustrating the parallel French development christened Orphism, was included. Twentieth-century German art was represented by loans from Professor Sadler's outstanding collection. Rutter then illustrated the developments, at home and abroad, inspired by these principal movements. His selection of contemporary British art ranged much wider than Fry's and Bell's partisan choices for the Barbazanges and Grafton Gallery exhibitions in 1912. There were, for example, pictures by Alfred Wolmark; the Scot J. D. Fergusson was chosen together with the American Anne Estelle Rice to represent an individual offshoot of Fauvism; pictures by Renée Finch and Harald Sund were included; and Epstein exhibited two works in a small sculpture section containing three pieces by Zadkine and one by Brancusi. Ten members of the Camden Town Group exhibited (the absent six being Bayes, Grant, Lamb, Innes, John and Doman Turner), nine as the 'Intimists' of England and the tenth, Lewis, as the spearhead of the Futurist–Cubist-orientated movement in London. Important pictures by Nevinson (among them *The Departure of the Train de Luxe*, inspired by Severini), Wadsworth, Etchells and Hamilton vigorously supported the impact of this section and justified the distinction conferred by the separate mention of Futurism in the exhibition title.

The only precedents for so comprehensive and diverse a display of contemporary talent were the non-selected AAA exhibitions, also organized by Rutter. However, the AAA shows suffered from their size and lack of quality-control. The catholic taste demonstrated by Rutter in his selection for the Doré Galleries must have impressed members of the Fitzroy Street and Camden Town Groups. Moreover, this proof that non-partisan groupings were possible occurred just at the moment when William Marchant's offer of his commodious Goupil Gallery for their exhibitions made the immediate expansion of the Camden Town Group imperative.

Formation of the London Group

See fig.1, page 14, for an outline of these developments.

As we know, expansion of the Camden Town Group had been considered in 1911. When the group was first formed a newspaper report had announced that one of its rules was 'the unusual one that the Society shall be dissolved and reformed every five years in order to prevent the growth of undesirable "traditions"'.[82] However, the first formal consideration of what, for the time being, was called 'the New society' is recorded in the minutes of a Fitzroy Street meeting on 25 October 1913.[83] The substance of this meeting was known in advance, at least to some members. Ginner, unable to attend, wrote a note to Manson (secretary of the group) on 23 October expressing his regret at missing a meeting on the important subject of a new society; he appointed Gilman his proxy.[84] Nan Hudson feared that the business might be conducted as an attack on Roger Fry, and Sickert wrote to reassure her on 21 October:

No demonstration against Roger will be permitted by me either. That is understood. Unless forming a society of which he is not a founder-member is a demonstration. As he has not included you in his group and I have, I think your bread is buttered on my side. Personally I should later wish Roger and anyone interesting to be elected. But we needn't put that forward while the Roger–Lewis quarrel is acute.

Duncan Grant, perhaps to forestall such an offensive, braved Lewis and Gore to make one of his rare appearances at Fitzroy Street for this meeting. He took no active part in the proceedings and never attended again. It is possible that he resigned from the group, although this is not recorded in the minutes. He was certainly not a member of the new society launched at this meeting. Nor were Innes and John. Advanced consumption was about to drive Innes abroad to the sun, but lack of interest as well as ill-health had long caused his participation in the Camden Town and Fitzroy Street Groups to cease. On 3 January 1914 Innes's membership was formally rescinded, and in August he died. John's membership of both groups had also lapsed but whether he took the trouble to resign is uncertain. The other Camden Town absentees on 25 October were Lamb, Pissarro, Ratcliffe and the deaf, diffident Doman Turner, who found meetings such a strain that he attended none over the winter of 1913–14. Ethel Sands, Nan Hudson and Epstein, as members of the Fitzroy Street Group but not of Camden Town, were present. The main outcome of this meeting was that henceforth these two groups were amalgamated to form the new society. There was, besides, much discussion of how new members should be elected, and it was decided to limit membership to residents of the United Kingdom.

The next meeting at 19 Fitzroy Street of which minutes survive was on 15 November. Interesting things had happened during the intervening three weeks. Because members of the amalgamated Fitzroy Street and Camden Town Groups were to be, *ipso facto*, founder-members of the new society, several artists realized that if they stormed the more flexible defences of Fitzroy Street in advance they could bypass the potentially stringent, although as yet undecided, election procedures to the new society. In any event six, possibly eight, new members of the Fitzroy Street Group were present. Renée Finch and Harald Sund explain this numerical discrepancy. They were absent from the meeting on 25 October. While it is probable that they were already members by this date, no proof of the time of their election exists and their first documented appearance at Fitzroy Street was on 15 November. The other six new members were Bernard Adeney and Harold Squire, who both exhibited with the Friday Club, and Nevinson, Hamilton, Wadsworth and Etchells. This invasion from Lewis's Futurist–Cubist camp significantly altered the political and artistic balance of the society. It marks the moment when the two erstwhile mentors of the Fitzroy Street Group, Pissarro and Sickert, lost control of the enterprise.

Pissarro had missed the meeting when the new members were elected. Manson wrote to him on 5 November to tell him the results were not 'entirely satisfactory'.[85] A week later he tried to reconcile Pissarro to the *fait accompli*: 'Judging from the exhibition at the Doré I think we gain rather than lose by the presence of these outrageous cubists.'

Pissarro stayed away from the meeting on 15 November. Indeed he and Nan Hudson were the only active founder-members of the Fitzroy Street Group absent when, with Sickert as usual in the chair, the new society settled on a title. According to Ginner it was Epstein who suggested that 'The London Group' was a fitting banner to embrace the more broadly based membership.[86] Gilman replaced Gore as president, Bevan was appointed treasurer and Manson continued as secretary. Following the precedent set by the Camden Town Group it was resolved that the pictures exhibited by each artist should hang in separate groups. Arrangements for a first exhibition in the spring of 1914 were initiated. The difficult problem of how new members should be elected was not considered, except to decide that a special meeting was necessary for voting.

Three days later Manson again summoned up the courage to try to win Pissarro over to acceptance of the way the new society was evolving:

I feel that by denying these new movements a right to express themselves, we should be acting exactly as the Academicians did with regard to the Impressionists and precisely as the N.E.A.C does when it says with regard to Fitzroy St: 'You may be alright from your own point of view but we shan't show yr. work.'

I have no sympathy with that attitude and I do not want to support it, so I think that I shall stay with the 'London Group'.

I feel the other attitude of intoleration is rather narrow.

I don't think we have any reason to be afraid of a few extreme young men; nor ought we to run away from them.

Perhaps to soften his intransigence, Manson suggested that Pissarro propose Diana White as a candidate for the next election. Pissarro composed a long and detailed reply on 20 November:

You are right in a way, but I must say that your attitude is much more concerned with philanthropy than with Art.

Of course the N.E.A.C. is conducted by a clique, so are the Academy and the Camden Town Group! There is only one society which is not supposed (?) to be cliquy [sic] and that is the A.A.A. Whatever one does, things *always* turn to be governed by a clique. I think the N.E.A.C. constitution is the most perfect I ever heard of, and really done honestly with the intention to admit all possible developments, and you see the result! I do not believe for a moment that the London Group will be more liberal and fair than any of the other societies – What I object to is that it is the wrong clique that has gained influence.

Things being so, I maintain that the real force of a group is to be cliquy, without shame, to claim highly and openly to be cliquy, and to make a glory of it! and so form a small society of tendance rather than of numbers.

Fancy people joining with the idea of forming a teetotaller society and coming to the conclusion that in order not to be narrow minded, they should admit some drunkards!

My dear Manson, there is only one thing to consider, that is our ideal in Art. Others with different ideas may fight their battle, that is not our business, we must fight ours. I firmly believe that our friends have some broad aim in common with us which is quite wide enough to permit all individual developments and at the same time to allow us to join together – that broad principle is that they do not turn their backs to Nature. The new members are looking for something different (I dont say that they wont arrive at some fine things in time) but what I say is that we, worshippers of nature, are not concerned with their aim. It may be that our friends want to follow that lead, because it is the fashion – or perhaps are they more in sympathy with them than with us – but then, I fail to understand why some of them have taken the title of Neo-Realist – I fear they dont quite know where they are going and as true opportunists want to be ready to turn with the wind.

Well, as I can not form a group all alone I will stay until I see more clearly in what direction things will go, and then I will act according to my *interest*, for I see now that interest is the only thing to be considered, conviction seems to enter so little in all these considerations.

P.S. Dont trouble about proposing Miss White, she would not now care to belong.

Pissarro's letter demanded a reply. On 22 November Manson wrote back to justify his own position as an active supporter of the London Group and to persuade Pissarro, whose rejection of the London Group was still in the balance, back into the fold:

My attitude may be more concerned with philanthropy than with art, but I must say exhibitions and societies are more concerned with business than with art: more concerned with selling pictures, with advertising painters etc. I detest exhibiting and exhibitions except one-man shows. When I see beautiful, refined, delicate, subtle pieces of painting looking their worst in exhibitions I feel extremely sorry that they have to be shown in that way and in an environment which demands an unusual degree of discrimination on the part of the onlooker before he can really *see* the good picture so I do not think we can adopt any very idealistic attitude or imagine that any art society exists primarily for the benefit of art. Therefore, speaking very broadly, it does not matter much where one exhibits …

The new members – the young mathematical painters – are still young and foolish. They have not gained influence. They are in a minority of 7 to 19![87] You are quite content to be a member of the N.E.A.C. where you are practically all alone among a whole crowd of reactionaries: while as a member of the London Group you would have at least 11 followers, you would be among friends, people who honour and admire, a few who love you. I know, because I have talked to them intimately about it.

If we take that standpoint, what possible good service does one do to Art by exhibiting at the New English? Its very name is a mockery. I cannot feel that I should be considering my ideal in art by exhibiting with them. I have nothing in common with any other member but yourself. On the other hand I am in sympathy (more or less) with nearly ¾ of the London Group.

Of course my ideal would be a group like the original splendid French Impressionist group; but that appears to me to be impossible here. How could we form a society that would be important enough to justify its existence? If you see a way or see a way later I should like to be in it … the London Group seems to be the best thing going at the moment … don't do anything hastily. The AAA is no good because it opens its doors to reactionary bad old stuff. 98% of it is very bad. And after its treatment of Mrs Finch I shall leave it.

I think a society might open its doors to admit a certain amount of work representing new movements for I think that new thought and new ideas should be allowed to say what they have to say, that is all.

The mathematical-cubists are in a proportion of about 1 to 3 and quite harmless. Believe me, they have very few admirers besides themselves among the members of the London Group. I think it a *positively* good thing to give these new movements a chance of displaying themselves. They will soon cease to beg them.

Manson wrote this letter on the day of a meeting from which Pissarro was obviously again absent, as were Lamb, Nevinson and Etchells. Several practical resolutions were passed (about proxy votes, the annual subscription and such like). It was also decided that candidates for membership should now be invited to submit work for inspection, and that the possibility of two exhibitions a year should be explored. The only political decision taken was that members of the London Group should become, *ipso facto*, members of the Fitzroy Street Group. This resolution recognized the fact that the London Group took over the functions of the Camden Town Group as an exhibiting society, but left unsatisfied the needs of artists to store their work, show it to clients and meet together for informal discussion; all these privileges were conferred by membership of the Fitzroy Street Group.

The meeting on 29 November was mainly concerned with voting procedures. One adverse vote should cancel one favourable vote, and to secure election a candidate must secure the votes of at least half the total number of members. Manson's draft of the Rules and Constitution of the London Group must have been made after 29 November because it incorporates rules passed at this and all the preceding meetings. However, he inscribed the date '25/10/1913' at the top.

Every active member of the London Group turned up, or assigned a proxy, for the all-important meeting on 6 December when, for the first time, an election for new members was held. Manson had taken the precaution of asking if he could stand proxy for Pissarro on 28 November, when he already knew that 'one or two objectionable people' were to be put up for election. All fourteen candidates failed to pass the test. Just as the founder-members of the London Group represented a wide range of artistic styles and allegiances, so the candidates included artists as various as William Rothenstein, the watercolourists Walter Taylor and Douglas Fox-Pitt, Stanislawa de Karlowska (Mrs Bevan) and Sickert's disciple Sylvia Gosse, as well as Jessie Etchells (sister of Frederick), Gertler and Bomberg. It became obvious that the political complexions represented by both voters and candidates made a majority consensus impossible. Therefore Epstein proposed that the votes of one-third rather than one-half of the total number of members be sufficient to secure election.

On 3 January, the next election date, every active participant except Drummond either attended or assigned a proxy. Twenty-six candidates put themselves forward and nine secured election. The unsuccessful candidates included Gertler and the Rothenstein brothers, Albert and William. William Rothenstein secured the impressive total of minus ten votes, only surpassed by two complete outsiders. On the whole friends and relations of the old guard of Camden Towners did best. Stanislawa de Karlowska became a member, as did three of Sickert's disciples and friends, Sylvia Gosse, Fox-Pitt and Taylor; Thérèse Lessore, who was to become the third Mrs Sickert in 1926 but who was currently the wife of Bernard Adeney, was also elected. The other successful candidates were Jessie Etchells, John Nash (his brother Paul failed), Bomberg and the sculptor Eric Gill.

Pissarro had actually attended the 3 January meeting in person, the only time he did so. In December he had evidently decided to revise his policy of aloofness and began to busy himself behind the scenes. He concentrated his efforts upon Fitzroy Street rather than the London Group. On 16 December he wrote to Manson:

I shall be glad to talk to you about Fitzroy St. I think we must make an effort to keep it alive, for if the London Group comes to grief, as I expect it will, our own little center will again be able to spring in another direction. We ought to take this excellent opportunity, now that we have a pretext, to get rid of W. Bayes. If we want some new members to help the financial part Miss White, Conway[88] and perhaps Mrs Finch, will be willing to join.

The background to this letter, in particular the 'pretext' for reorganizing Fitzroy Street by purging it of unwanted members, is undocumented. It sounds as if a suggestion to disband Fitzroy Street altogether, and then to reconstitute it, was afoot. Why else should Pissarro suggest that Mrs Finch (already a member) might join? It is within this context that Pissarro's letter to

Manson of 22 December (quoted p.59), complaining of Sickert's destruction of the 'art value' of Fitzroy Street, must be understood. The letter did not refer to developments within the London Group, where Pissarro objected primarily to Wyndham Lewis and his followers; nor did it refer to the admission of several of Sickert's friends and disciples to this group, because it was written nearly two weeks before their election. It reflects Pissarro's fundamental antagonism to Sickert as a man and an artist, and his consequent inability to reconcile himself to the fact that Sickert commanded respect and loyalty within Fitzroy Street from such odd quarters as Walter Bayes.

Pissarro found allies in his endeavours to oust Sickert and his friends from their hold upon Fitzroy Street. Gilman arranged an unofficial meeting to discuss the situation, attended by Pissarro, Ginner and Bevan. The outcome of their talk, and whether they even agreed, is unknown. If, as is probable, the pretext they were to use to secure the disbandment of the Fitzroy Street Group was that this group would lose its identity and purpose when the entire London Group was admitted to its bosom, then they were outmanoeuvred. At the meeting on 3 January Bayes anticipated objections by proposing that the rule relating to amalgamation of the London and Fitzroy Street Groups be rescinded. Etchells seconded the motion, which was carried unanimously. Thus the privileges of Fitzroy Street were preserved for a slightly less motley crew of members, although from Pissarro's point of view undesirables remained. A week or so later Pissarro went to Eragny and did not return to London until April 1914. In March he resigned, by letter, from the London Group and the Fitzroy Street Group.

At the next election on 3 February 1914, ten candidates were proposed for election, of whom only Henri Gaudier-Brzeska was successful (at his first attempt). A few days earlier Eric Gill had declined to take up his membership, explaining in a letter to Manson that he disliked exhibitions and exhibition societies.[89] A more significant absentee from this meeting was Sickert, who until then had always taken the chair. For reasons shortly to be explained he stayed away from subsequent meetings and resigned his membership of both Fitzroy Street and the London Group before the exhibition opened in March. Henry Lamb's participation in the group also ceased after January. Manson himself withdrew from the London Group towards the end of March, disheartened by Pissarro's resignation and perhaps by the animosities within the group. Unlike Pissarro, he contributed to the first exhibition but, as secretary, he kept minutes of only two more meetings.

From these minutes we learn that Stanley Spencer was the only successful candidate out of six at the election of 7 March, with Horace Brodzky (a friend of Gaudier-Brzeska) and Wolmark among the failures. The first London Group exhibition had by then already opened in the upstairs room at the Goupil Gallery, so that no work by Spencer could be included.

The most significant absentees among the exhibitors were Sickert and Pissarro. Their withdrawal evidently worried William Marchant. He had originally agreed to sponsor the exhibitions of a new society formed from, and by, the Camden Town Group. He was now supporting a group from which the two leading figures were missing, besides other notable artists such as Henry Lamb. The meeting on 7 March was, therefore, faced with a letter from Marchant asking for some guarantee of the 'constitution' of the London Group for the spring 1915 exhibition. Puzzled by the ambiguous import of this document, the members resolved to find out just what Marchant meant. Their answer came a week later, at the meeting on 14 March, when a letter from Marchant suggested that a total of five resignations should liberate him from his agreement. In fact another matter altogether finally led Marchant to terminate his agreement with the London Group during the war. In October 1916 he announced that he would not house exhibitions which included work by conscientious objectors. The London Group by then included two objectors, one being Adrian Allinson. They stood down for the winter 1916 exhibition while the London Group sought alternative premises. The 1917 exhibition was removed to Heal's Mansard Gallery.

1913–1914: the Brighton exhibition

The history of resolutions, elections and resignations recorded in the minutes of London Group meetings between October 1913 and March 1914 reflects private reactions to more public events. Chief among these events was a large exhibition entitled 'English Post-Impressionists, Cubists and Others' held at the Brighton Art Gallery from 16 December 1913 to 14 January 1914. The Camden Town Group, under the presidency of Gore, was invited to select this exhibition and thus, on paper at least, enjoyed a brief reprieve from extinction. In fact suggestions for selection were probably made by the entire Fitzroy Street Group, in other words by the founder-members of the London Group. Because exhibitors did not have to pass the stringent election processes used by the London Group, the Brighton exhibition included many artists who had failed on one, more or all their attempts to be admitted to the new society. It was obviously difficult to find a title appropriate to such a mixed exhibition of contemporary art. As the director of the Art Gallery wrote in an introductory catalogue note, the chosen title, 'English Post-Impressionists and Cubists', was 'hardly sufficiently explanatory, as there are many works exhibited which do not come under either of these titles. It is, however, sufficiently indicative of the general tendency of the exhibition.'

All eleven active members of the Camden Town Group exhibited at Brighton (those absent being Doman Turner, Grant, Innes, John and Lamb). All eleven non-Camden Town members of the Fitzroy Street Group exhibited, as did eight of the nine artists elected to the London Group on 3 January (the abstainer being Eric Gill). These thirty exhibitors were joined by six more artists of whom four (Mervyn Lawrence, Paul Nash, Hamilton Hay and Fanny Eveleigh) were unsuccessful candidates for election to the London Group on one or more occasions before March 1914. The remaining two were Martin Ogilvie and Ruth Doggett (whose name was misprinted as Duckett in the catalogue), a talented pupil of Sickert and later of Gilman.

A rift divided these exhibitors from the start. Not only were the exhibits physically separated, but two separate catalogue introductions were found to be necessary. Manson wrote the introduction to Rooms I and II; Wyndham Lewis introduced Room III, subtitled 'The Cubist Room'. Manson's introduction gently traced the history of the Fitzroy Street and Camden Town Groups – incidentally antedating the institution of the former by some two years. He acknowledged Sickert's original realization that scope must be given to the 'free expression of newer artistic thought', that Gore and Gilman led the movement forward and that Lucien Pissarro provided the crucial link with traditional art. Stressing the right of free speech in art, he referred to the current formation of the London Group which would extend 'the means of free expression ... to other artists who were experimenting with new methods'. In a glowing appreciation of what the London Group could achieve Manson wrote:

More eclectic in its constitution, it will no longer limit itself to the cultivation of one single school of thought, but will offer hospitality to all manner of artistic expression provided it has the quality of sincere personal conviction. The Group promises to become one of the most influential and most significant art movements in England.

To conceive a limit to artistic development is an admission of one's own limitations. Nothing is finally right in art; the rightness is purely personal, and for the artist himself. So, in the London Group, which is to be the latest development of the original Fitzroy Street Group, all modern methods may find a home. Cubism meets Impressionism, Futurism and Sickertism join hands and are not ashamed, the motto of the Group being that sincerity of conviction has a right of expression.

This Messianic vision was immediately put to the test in the exhibition, although not specifically in Wyndham Lewis's introductory text. The only mildly combative statements in Lewis's highly charged account of his own relationship with Futurism and Cubism was his description of himself, Nevinson, Etchells, Hamilton and Wadsworth as 'a vertiginous, but not exotic, island in the placid and respectable archipelago of English art' and that Epstein was 'the only great sculptor at present working in England'.[90] Nevertheless, his essay amounted to a credo announcing the imminent birth of Vorticism, and its tone was fundamentally rejectionist.

One artist, Adeney, exhibited in both the Camden Town–Fitzroy Street rooms and the Cubist Room. Otherwise segregation was total. Both the artistic content of and critical reaction to this Cubist Room – containing major works by Epstein, Hamilton, Wadsworth, Etchells, Bomberg, Nevinson and Lewis, supported by contributions from Jessie Etchells, Fanny Eveleigh and Adeney – have been fully discussed by Richard Cork[91] and are outside the scope of this text. The response to the Brighton exhibition by the old Camden Town Group members is relevant here. Pissarro's disgust with the Cubist Room must have encouraged his decision to resign from the London Group, although he was perhaps equally disillusioned with the hotchpotch miscellany hung elsewhere. Sickert's reaction was more forthright, but delayed. He had opened the exhibition with a speech. However, as he told Nan Hudson two months later, 'At Brighton the Epstein-Lewis-Etchells room made me sick and I publicly disengaged my responsibility.' This disengagement must have been declared within his opening speech, because Sickert did not publish his attack on the Cubist Room exhibits until March 1914.

The London Group: factions and Sickert's resignation

For once Gore's attempts to heal the breaches between his colleagues failed. Gilman also made efforts to reconcile opposing factions when, in an interview published in the *Evening Standard* on 3 February 1914, he was at pains to define the common aims possessed by 'realists' and 'formulists' in the London Group: 'They both arise from the revolt against naturalism, and they support one another in the sense that one can learn from the other.'[92] Demonstrating with a small potted cactus, he explained that if he were a formulist

he would simply paint a very obviously heartshaped object with a sort of elliptic circle underneath it to represent the pot and it wouldn't matter what colour it was. 'That is to say, I am rendering so much of it as consists of planes and curves … On the other hand, if I am a realist I want the object to remain a cactus after I have painted it.'

Gilman ranked himself with the realists. Indeed, when they exhibited in the Goupil Gallery Salon in the autumn of 1913 he and Ginner had already inserted the subtitle 'Neo-Realist' after their names in the catalogue.

What Ginner and Gilman meant by this epithet was explained on 1 January 1914 when Ginner published 'Neo-Realism' in the *New Age*; the essay reappeared as the catalogue preface to their joint exhibition at the Goupil Gallery in April to May 1914. It is a very personal document. Like Gilman in his *Standard* interview, Ginner rejected 'Naturalism' as 'the production of a Realist with a poor mind'. The Naturalist merely copies nature, 'with a dull and common eye', but possesses 'no personal vision, no individual temperament … no power of research'. However, the main object of his article was to attack those English Post-Impressionists (in particular the Fry–Bell clique) who had adapted a formula, or a series of formulae, from methods personal to Van Gogh, Gauguin and Cézanne. These formulists, whom Gilman in his interview was more ready to accept, were rejected by Ginner as the new Academics:

The Academic painters merely adopt the visions which the creative artists drew from the source of nature itself. They adopt these mannerisms, which is all they are capable of seeing in the work of the creative artist, and make formulas out of them.

They are copyists. They are the poor of mind.

Thus Ginner articulated his opposition both to English Post-Impressionsim as practised by most of his colleagues and to Naturalism which, he maintained, dominated such establishment institutions as the Royal Academy and the Paris Salon. His own doctrine of Neo-Realism was basically a dogmatic assertion that original and great works can only be produced by an artist who intimately and searchingly studies an aspect of nature which especially appeals to him, and then deliberately and objectively transposes what he sees onto canvas. Regarding subject-matter he wrote:

Each age has its landscape, its atmosphere, its cities, its people. Realism, loving Life, loving its Age, interprets its Epoch by extracting from it the very essence of all it contains of great or weak, of beautiful or of sordid, according to the individual temperament.

Ginner also had something to say on the handling of paint. He disliked 'slap-dash, careless, and slick painting', and despised the sketch as a finished product. 'Good and sound craftsmanship', he maintained, necessarily resulted from a Neo-Realist approach to nature. He added, 'Furthermore, in this matter of medium, it is only out of a sound and solid pigment that good surface and variety can be got, and durability in ages to come.'

Gilman, in his February interview, had assumed that the main breach within the London Group lay between the Realists (the old guard of Camden Town) and the Formulists (the Wyndham Lewis gang). Ginner's article threw into relief less clear-cut, but no less divisive, factions within the old guard. Sickert and Pissarro, for different reasons, rejected Neo-Realism.

In his letter to Manson of 20 November Pissarro had disparaged the term 'Neo-Realist' adopted by some of 'our friends' (that is Ginner and Gilman at the Goupil Gallery Salon) within Fitzroy Street. As far as doctrine is concerned, Ginner's emphasis on the intimate study of nature must have been approved by Pissarro. However, it is probable that he objected to Ginner's slighting references to Naturalism, even though Ginner was at pains to stress that the Impressionists were great Realists, not Naturalists. Moreover, Ginner had gone on to say that Neo-Impressionism had sunk 'into the Formula Pit'; Camille Pissarro in his later years and Lucien Pissarro had both derived their handling from this development of Impressionism.

When Ginner's article was republished for the Goupil Gallery catalogue Sickert answered in an essay in the *New Age* entitled 'Mr Ginner's Preface'.[93] He agreed with the main drift of Ginner's argument that (to quote Sickert's paraphrase) 'Art that is based on other art tends to become atrophied, while art that springs from direct contact of the artist with nature at least tends to be alive.' His few criticisms were trivial and pedantic. He disparaged Ginner's adoption of a label:

I dislike the prefix 'Neo'. It is better for a painter not to call himself 'new'. Time alone will show how his work will wear. He had also better not call himself a realist. Let us leave the labels to those who have little else wherewith to cover their nakedness. Charles Ginner is a very good name, and has gathered already around it associations of achievement and respect. 'Harold Gilman' calls up to the mind a definite tendency in painting, and both names are only obscured when they are covered by a uniform domino which would tend to merge their identities.

Sickert also quarrelled with Ginner's inclusion of Poussin in a list of the 'quagmire' of derivative painters, and with Ginner's apparent confusion of the word 'academic' with the word 'academy'. But in the main he heartily endorsed Ginner's 'sound and coherent manifesto'.

It was, in fact, the products rather than the doctrine of Neo-Realism to which Sickert took exception. In his review of the NEAC exhibition, published in the *New Age* in June 1914,[94] Sickert praised Henry Lamb for understanding the 'strict limit to the advantages of impasto'. Lamb, according to Sickert, knew that impasto was 'not in itself a sign of virility'. As he explained:

Intentional and rugged impasto, from the fact that each touch receives a light and throws a shadow, so far from producing brilliancy, covers a picture with a grey reticulation and so throws dust in the eyes of the spectator, and serves, to some extent, to veil exaggerations of colour or coarseness of drawing. It is a manner of shouting and gesticulating and does not make for expressiveness or lucidity.

Although no reference was made here to Ginner or Gilman, these two had been expressing Ginner's advocacy of 'sound and solid pigment' by using ever thicker small touches and blobs of lumpy paint. There was also, perhaps, deliberate provocation intended by Sickert when he chose to praise Lamb who, like himself, had resigned from the London Group before the first exhibition. Gilman and Ginner, in any event, read the terms in which Sickert praised Lamb as a disguised attack, and said as much in two separate letters to the *New Age*.[95] Gilman headed his letter 'The Worst Critic in London'. Sickert replied in yet another article, reserving his unkindest cut for the title 'The Thickest Painters in London',[96] which in turn sparked off an acrimonious correspondence in subsequent issues of the *New Age*.[97] This debate, conducted in the main from April to June 1914, that is after Sickert had resigned from the London Group of which Gilman was president, reflects the animosities and personal irritations current earlier in the year. However, compared with Sickert's chief quarrel within the Fitzroy Street Group, it was a mere diversionary skirmish.

Sickert's disillusion and disgust with both the London and the Fitzroy Street Groups were much more directly occasioned by the persistent and growing influence of Lewis and his colleagues on the activities of both groups. At a Fitzroy Street 'At Home', probably in February 1914, he received the *coup de grâce*. He wrote to tell Nan Hudson:

I am afraid you will think me more 'swing of the pendulum' then ever. But like the lady in bridal attire who bolts at the church door the Epstein-Lewis marriage is too much for me and I have bolted. I have resigned both Fitzroy Street and the London Group. You who have watched the stages will not think me merely frivolous. I now see the stages which led to this. First Gilman forced Epstein on me, as you know against my will. But I was in a minority. At Brighton the Epstein-Lewis-Etchells room made me sick and I publicly disengaged my responsibility. On Saturday Epstein's so-called drawings were put up on easels and Lewis's big Brighton picture. The Epsteins are pure pornography – of the most joyless kind soit-dit and the Lewis is pure impudence. Then I left, once for all, but *never again for an hour* could I be responsible or associated in any way with showing such things. I don't believe in them, and, further, I think they render any consideration of serious painting impossible.

I hope you don't think my conduct, to Gore and Gilman chiefly, cowardly or treacherous. You know that they have dragged me step by step in a direction I don't like, and it was only a question of the exact date of my revolt. It is, after all, they who believed in this thing and I who suffered it to please them, weakly I admit. But I was in a minority. It is only just that I should say to them '*You* believe in this. *You* must digest and defend it. I can't and won't'.

    ... I shall not set foot in Fitzroy Street again after my sensations when the Epsteins were on the easels and various charming and delightful people open-mouthed looking to me for explanations or defence.

Like Pissarro, Sickert felt driven out of Fitzroy Street, his own creation, by an alien invasion. Unlike Pissarro, he decided to conduct an active campaign of extermination from the outside. He felt admirably placed to do this because the *New Age*, a periodical which thrived on controversy, gave him a free hand to publish articles on whatever subjects he chose. With great optimism he told Nan Hudson, 'being a weekly I influence all the other critics. I really become the conductor of the critical orchestra in London.'

    Sickert's articles were a regular feature in the *New Age* from March to June 1914. He blasted off this series with 'Mesopotamia-Cézanne',[98] an appreciative review of Clive Bell's book *Art*, with a sting in its lengthy tail. Commending Bell's exposition of the doctrine of significant form, Sickert attacked Bell for having 'got hold of the wrong end of the wrong Messiah'. Cézanne, Sickert maintained, 'when Cubism has gone as lightly as it has come', would only be remembered 'as a curious and pathetic by-product of the Impressionist group'; the drawings of Sir Edward Poynter were more likely to guide painters of the future. In fact Sickert felt a healthy respect for some of Cézanne's qualities and adopted this extreme position, as he told Ethel Sands, 'to counter the folly of the *soi-disant* followers of Cézanne'.

    It has often been maintained that, from the time of Fry's first Post-Impressionist exhibition at the Grafton Gallery in the winter of 1910, Sickert watched the desertion of his own former disciples with ever-increasing dismay as they found new guides among the artists, dead and alive, promoted by Roger Fry and Clive Bell. However, jealousy formed no part of Sickert's make-up. He may sometimes have thought his younger friends' experiments misguided, but he never grudged them the chance of self-expression in whatever language they chose to adopt. Never, that is, until he was faced with Wyndham Lewis's maturing style, and Sickert had not counted Lewis as an artist from his own stable. Sickert's admission to Ethel Sands of his motive for adopting an extreme position when discussing Cézanne hints at the reasons behind the ultra-conservative attitudes he assumed in general at this period. Temperamentally and intellectually he was an independent. In less tolerant times he had led the campaign for progressive art; now that modern art at home and abroad had a large and articulate following he felt impelled to find another unfashionable cause, the forceful defence of the academic tradition. Moreover, he felt no compunction about overstating his case.

    Readers of the *New Age* were thus prepared for the flamboyant wit of 'On Swiftness', an article published on 26 March dealing, as he told Nan Hudson, 'delicately but firmly, with the pornometric aspect of Cubism':

We hear a great deal about non-representative art. But while the faces of the persons represented are frequently nil, non-representation is forgotten when it comes to the sexual organs. Witness Mr. Wyndham Lewis's 'Creation' exhibited at Brighton, Mr. Gaudier Brzeska's drawing in last week's New Age, and several of Mr. Epstein's later drawings. That such intention is not read into the works by me, but is deliberate, we may gather from the Cubists' own defence of themselves. Mr. Lewis writes in the preface of the Brighton catalogue of December 16 1913, 'Hung in this room as well are three drawings by Jacob Epstein, the only great sculptor at present working in England. He finds in the machinery of procreation a dynamo to work the deep atavism of his spirit.' So that the Pornometric Gospel amounts to this. All visible nature with two exceptions is unworthy of study, and to be considered pudendum. The only things worthy of an artist's attention are what we have hitherto called the *pudenda*!

Sickert was fighting a losing battle. T. E. Hulme was also employed by the *New Age* and produced *avant-garde* counterblasts to all Sickert's attacks. For instance, in December 1913 Sickert had been commissioned by the *New Age* to edit a series of illustrations called 'Modern Drawings'. His weekly selection began on 1 January 1914 and included several of his own drawings, one by Ginner (*Leicester Square*), one by Bayes and many by his little-known Rowlandson House pupils. On 19 March, instead of Sickert's choice, Gaudier-Brzcska's geometrical *Dancer* appeared, as the first in a series edited by Hulme and nicely distinguished from Sickert's selection by the title 'Contemporary Drawings'. Hulme's series, including drawings by Bomberg, Roberts, Wadsworth and Nevinson, gradually ousted Sickert's. Similarly, the issue of the *New Age* containing Sickert's 'On Swiftness' also contained Hulme's brilliantly reasoned explanation and appreciation of the works of Lewis, Bomberg, Wadsworth, Hamilton and Epstein on view at the London Group exhibition.

Sickert did not turn his personal objection to associating himself with the art of Lewis, Etchells and Epstein into an issue of loyalty, and thus he did not expect less-established colleagues to follow him into the wilderness. Ethel Sands and Nan Hudson, among others, exhibited with his explicit approval. Visiting the Goupil Gallery when the show opened in March, Sickert decided that they stood to gain by the 'universal reaction' to the exhibition. Artists like Drummond and Ratcliffe remained aloof from all dissension and treated the London Group as what it was, a convenient exhibition society where they could show their recent work. Gilman and Ginner gave a preview of their forthcoming exhibition in the same gallery by presenting a varied selection of their best paintings.

The year 1914 was crowded with exhibition opportunities for the president of the London Group and his Neo-Realist colleague. Apart from their two-man show, the first London Group and, as usual, the Allied Artists' Association display, their work was also on view at the New English Art Club exhibitions. Having presided over the warring factions within the London Group, Gilman had perhaps decided that conciliation was more practical than schism. Although he had been the most urgent advocate of a total break with the NEAC in 1911, he evidently revised this policy in 1914 when in a position of greater public responsibility. In the summer he showed *Girl with a Coral Necklace* (Brighton Art Gallery) and in the winter a portrait and a Norwegian landscape.

Progressive artists from every faction were drawn together in a vast display of 'Twentieth Century Art' at the Whitechapel Art Gallery from May to June

1914. This exhibition purported to review all the modern movements and as a rough guide the work on view was divided into four groups. The first group, according to the catalogue introduction, 'has been influenced by Mr. Walter Sickert and Mr. Lucien Pissarro. It treats common or sordid scenes in a sprightly manner and excels in a luminous treatment of landscape.' The generous representation of this group amounted to a retrospective survey of the achievements of the Fitzroy Street and Camden Town Groups. Paintings by artists (such as Lamb, Pissarro and Sickert) who had not made the full transition from the Camden Town to the London Group were again hung among the work of their former colleagues. Lightfoot's paintings and drawings reappeared in a Camden Town context, as did the work of Duncan Grant and Innes. This exhibition also provided the last opportunity for the contemporary public to appreciate paintings by Gore, the president of the Camden Town Group, side by side with those of his friends.

Four paintings by Gore had been exhibited at the London Group in March, but on the 27th of that month he died of pneumonia. Sickert had visited him in Richmond a few days before: 'We saw him lying on his bed very emaciated. One of the last things he said was "Ask the doctors to have some tea". In his delirium it was paintings and effects. The bottles were still lifes and then crowds.'[99] Everyone who had known Gore as a man and an artist grieved. Sickert took time off from polemics to publish an appreciation in the *New Age* under the title 'A Perfect Modern',[100] the term I have borrowed for the title of this book to describe Gore and his colleagues. In a private letter to Nan Hudson and Ethel Sands he confessed that Gore's example 'always gave me a kind of renewal of youthful courage'. 'It is like losing a son to me which is less natural than losing a father', he wrote in another letter. Influenced perhaps by current prejudices, he blamed overwork, particularly the stress of his involvement in the Cabaret Theatre Club decorations, for Gore's lack of resistance to infection. But he reflected:

Death in a case like Gore's is devoid of the worst sting. He has never been unhappy, or old or ill and has escaped the only intolerable things deterioration of intellect or the sufferings of self-contempt or the state when nothing has a savour. He seems to have set up with every person he met of all degrees of intelligence a personal relation of the most definite and binding kind. A wonderful gift. He was everybody's man while being the most discriminating.

The last vestige of the co-operative family spirit which had bound the principal members of the Camden Town Group together died with Gore.

Epilogue

The London Group has survived as an exhibition society to this day. When the early passions surrounding its formation cooled, artists who had been blackballed were admitted. Thus Roger Fry became a member in 1917, active as ever and the spearhead of Bloomsbury penetration. Duncan Grant and Vanessa Bell joined in 1920. Sickert acquired a more philosophical perspective and rejoined the group in 1916, explaining to Nan Hudson: 'I daresay it was a mistake to refrain from exhibiting because dear Epstein's drawings made me sick. One is only responsible for what is in one's own frames.' Even Doman Turner briefly overcame his diffidence to exhibit with the London Group in 1918. While the glorious potential of Manson's Messianic vision was never fulfilled, the London Group did eventually manage to unite disparate artistic elements and provide a useful alternative to the Royal Academy and the New English Art Club.

Nonetheless, the London Group did not repress factionalism. From the beginning its eclectic membership left various members unsatisfied. The need to establish more selected and mutually congenial groupings led to the manifold creation of splinter societies. Wyndham Lewis and his colleagues banded together to found the Rebel Art Centre in March 1914. Pissarro and Manson founded the Monarro Group in 1919, having celebrated their secession from the London Group by holding an exhibition at the Carfax Gallery in June 1914. Also included in this exhibition were Harold Squire, Malcolm Milne and Diana White, whom Pissarro continued to champion. According to Sickert,[101] Pissarro's insistence on Miss White's inclusion caused Arthur Clifton, the only dealer in London who had so far given him a one-man show, to terminate his professional relationship with the artist. Bevan, Gilman and Ginner founded the Cumberland Market Group in 1914; joined by John Nash they held an exhibition under this title at the Goupil Gallery in the spring of 1915.

Their meetings were attended by McKnight Kauffer and by Nevinson, whose relationship with the Rebel Art Centre had been strained by their repudiation of the 'Futurist Manifesto: Vital English Art' which he and the Italian Futurist Marinetti had published in June 1914. Until William Marchant lent them his Grey Room, up a steep flight of dark stairs over the Goupil Gallery, the Cumberland Market Group held Saturday 'At Homes' in Bevan's Cumberland Market studio – hence their chosen title. Besides this Camden Town base, the close-knit character of the group, their habit of drinking strong tea and their methods of showing pictures to visitors were firmly based on the early Fitzroy Street model. Following their joint exhibition as Neo-Realists, Gilman and Ginner remained particularly sympathetic to each other's aims, although Gilman developed a means of expression closer to Gore's radical paintings of 1912 than to Ginner's increasingly meticulous transcriptions of the detail of nature. However, in February 1919 Gilman died in mid-career, a victim of influenza which he had caught while nursing Ginner during the devastating post-war epidemic.

Duncan Grant lived until 1978, his longevity contrasting with the premature deaths of Lightfoot and Innes (in their twenties), of Gore (in his thirties) and of Gilman (in his early forties). Bevan died a month before his sixtieth birthday in 1925.

The historical significance of the Fitzroy Street and Camden Town Groups must be assessed both in general and in particular. Membership of these groups greatly affected the careers of some painters, but meant nothing or little to others. The Camden Town Group was of no consequence to the subsequent careers of Grant and John, nor did it influence the truncated careers of Lightfoot and Innes. For Lamb, Bayes and Lewis it presented well-timed opportunities to publicize their work, but the evolution of their styles and handling was in no way conditioned by corporate ideals.

On the other hand, the careers of the remaining members were profoundly affected professionally, artistically or both, by the existence of these two groups. Doman Turner's only claim to fame is his membership of the Camden Town Group. Ginner might never have stayed in England had he not found sympathetic friends and an exciting atmosphere of expansionist activity in Fitzroy Street. It is doubtful whether the art of Manson and Ratcliffe would have matured without the example of more self-assured colleagues. In fact, removed from their influence when the Camden Town Group dissolved and the war encouraged geographical separations, Ratcliffe's painting lost its impetus, never fully to recover. Drummond's original talent undoubtedly developed more swiftly and surely because of his friendship with Ginner. Participation in the Fitzroy Street and Camden Town Groups was of crucial importance to the careers of Gore, Gilman and to a lesser extent Bevan. Although Bevan might have developed his style, handling and subject-matter independently, the vocabulary of much of Gore's and Gilman's painting was evolved within Fitzroy Street. Similarly their handling during important episodes of their brief careers was developed in the collaborative and mutually sustaining atmosphere of the group studio. Professionally, the Camden Town Group exhibitions did much to establish the reputations of all these artists.

Neither Pissarro nor Sickert, the acknowledged leaders of the Fitzroy Street Group, had a professional need of fringe societies. Nevertheless, Fitzroy Street drew Pissarro, who had tended to work isolated from his fellow-painters in England, into the mainstream of British art. His self-confidence and sense of purpose were greatly boosted by realizing that he could teach young artists some of the lessons of French Impressionism. Even Sickert's handling at this period owed something to Pissarro and something to Gore, although within the wider context of Sickert's lifelong struggle to solve his technical problems and master his medium this episode was of but passing interest. The main significance of the Fitzroy Street and Camden Town Groups for Sickert was that they served to channel his enormous energies towards a worthwhile cause and satisfied his real psychological need to teach and direct his juniors. When Sickert retired, disenchanted, from the London Group in 1914 he could afford to abandon ship. The existence of the new society as an entity, and the factions it stimulated, represented the successful culmination of his ambition, first expressed in Fitzroy Street in 1907, to create an ambience in London wherein young painters could encourage each other towards independence and professional self-confidence.

A peculiar fascination lies in the emergence at just this time of just this group of painters, each in his own way gifted with a desire to explore and to innovate within the boundaries of figurative art. The decade before the Great War of 1914–18 was a time of unprecedented ferment in the arts, when all the traditional canons were being cast aside. In music Schœnberg, in ballet Diaghilev, in poetry Pound, in painting Braque and Picasso, all were subjecting their respective arts to processes of fragmentation, reconstruction and abstraction. Sickert and his colleagues were in, but not of, that ferment. They sought, and may be judged to have found, a *via media* between a backward-looking and ultimately sterile working of tired styles from the past and the wilder shores of experimentation to which technically and intellectually they were neither willing nor able to respond. The significance of the Fitzroy Street Group and its Camden Town satellite was not that they sheltered a belated flowering of English Impressionism but that they offered a tolerant milieu where it was possible to be modern without iconoclasm, where the patient effort to present objective records of urban life was not anachronistic and where the craft of painting was respected. Over twenty years later, when the jazz age and the machine age had passed, the Euston Road School drew inspiration from its north-west London forebears. The legacy persists.

Notes

1   Jacques-Emile Blanche, *Portraits of a Lifetime* (London: Dent, 1937), p.301.

2   The ten exhibitors were Francis Bate, Fred Brown, Francis James, Paul Maitland, Theodore Roussel, Walter Sickert, Bernhard Sickert (a brother of Walter), Sidney Starr, Philip Wilson Steer and George Thomson.

3   *Life Work and Setting of Philip Wilson Steer* (London: Faber, 1945), p.31.

4   Reprinted in *Sickert Paintings*, ed. W. Baron and R. Shone (New Haven and London: Yale University Press, 1992), pp.58–9.

5   All the letters quoted here from Sickert to Nan Hudson and to Ethel Sands, once in a single private archive, are now deposited in the Archives Department of the Tate Gallery, London. Very few are inscribed with a date, though most can be dated approximately from internal evidence (see Baron 1973 and Baron 1977).

6   *Philip Wilson Steer* (Oxford: Clarendon Press, 1971), p.57.

7   In April 1897 Whistler appeared as a witness for Joseph Pennell in the latter's libel suit against Sickert and Frank Harris. Sickert, in an article on 'Transfer Lithography' published in December 1896 in the *Saturday Review*, edited by Harris, had written that the prints made by Pennell, using transfer paper applied to stone, were not true lithographs. Pennell won the case.

8   Letter of 1918, quoted more fully in Wendy Baron, *Sickert* (London: Phaidon, 1973), p.184.

9   Introduction to the catalogue of the exhibition 'English Post-Impressionists, Cubists and Others', Brighton Art Gallery, 1913–14.

10 Before his marriage Sickert lived and worked in Claremont Square, off the Pentonville Road, and in 1884 he had rooms at 13 Edwardes Square, Kensington. There is no evidence that Sickert ever had a studio in Cleveland Street (as was claimed by Stephen Knight in his *Jack the Ripper: The Final Solution* (London: Harrap, 1976)).

11 Most of this area, having been destroyed by bombs during the Second World War, has since been rebuilt as housing estates. The layout of some of the original roads has been lost.

12 *Men and Memories: Recollections of William Rothenstein 1872–1900* (London: Faber, 1931), p.167.

13 15 December 1906.

14 'Spencer Gore: A Memoir by his Son', preface to the catalogue of the Gore exhibition at the Anthony d'Offay Gallery, London, 1974.

15 *New Age*, 26 May 1910, 'The Spirit of the Hive'.

16 This first meeting is documented in an unpublished letter from Gilman's wife to her mother in America (John Woodeson, 'Spencer F. Gore', unpublished MA report, University of London, 1968).

17 Gilman's address in 1904 was The Rest, The Moors, Pangbourne, Berks. The Gilmans then seem to have stayed for some time in his father's rectory at Snargate, Kent, before moving late in the summer of 1908 to 15 Westholme Green, Letchworth, Hertfordshire.

18 Wendy Baron, in *Miss Ethel Sands and her Circle* (London: Peter Owen, 1977), incorporates these and other extracts from Sickert's letters to Nan Hudson and to Ethel Sands.

19 Sir Louis Fergusson, in *Harold Gilman: An Appreciation* (by Wyndham Lewis and Louis Fergusson) (London: Chatto & Windus, 1919), p.19.

20 Letter to Vanessa Bell, 16 February 1919, in Virginia Woolf's *Collected Letters*, vol.II: *1912–22, The Question of Things Happening* (paperback edn, London: Hogarth Press, 1994), p.331.

21 *Fortnightly Review*, 84, December 1908, 'The New Life of Whistler'.

22 Phrases taken from 'A Critical Calendar', *English Review*, March 1912.

23 *Art News*, 12 May 1910, 'Idealism'.

24 *New Age*, 16 June 1910, 'The Study of Drawing'.

25 *English Review*, April 1912, 'The Futurist Devil among the Tailors'.

26 *New Age*, 21 July 1910, 'The Naked and the Nude'.

27 Sickert quoted this incident in a letter to Miss Ethel Sands (see n.5, above). It is, however, possible that Brown used the unpleasantness of Sickert's subjects as an excuse to terminate their friendship. In the autumn of 1915 Sickert, after a three-year break, resumed his teaching post at the Westminster Technical Institute and thus displaced Gilman who had held the post in Sickert's absence. Not only was Gilman much embittered by Sickert's action, but many of his fellow-painters and teachers, including Brown and the staff at the Slade, felt that Sickert had dealt treacherously in the matter.

28 Letter written in 1954 by Ethel Sands to Quentin Bell. I am indebted to Professor Bell for giving me a copy of Miss Sands's letter.

29 *New Age*, 28 May 1914, 'Whitechapel'.

30 Quoted in W. S. Meadmore, *Lucien Pissarro – Un Coeur Simple* (London: Constable, 1962), p.60.

31 *New Age*, 2 June 1910.

32 These quotations are taken from a letter written in 1907 by Sickert to Nan Hudson (see n.5, above).

33 1 June 1907.

34 In the Pissarro papers in the archives of the Ashmolean Museum, Oxford.

35 *Since I was Twenty-Five* (London: Constable, 1927). The chapter 'The "Allied Artists' Association"', pp.180–99, is the main source for the following summary and quotations.

36 Rutter names Gilman among the artists from Sickert's circle who promised him active support (ibid., p.181). However, in later catalogues Gilman is not asterisked as a founder-member.

37 See the introductory note to the catalogue of Bayes's 1951 exhibition at the Leicester Galleries, in which the catalogue preface written by Sickert for the Leicester Galleries exhibition of Bayes's work in 1918 was reprinted.

38 *Robert Bevan, 1865–1925: A Memoir by his Son* (London: Studio Vista, 1965), p.16.

39 *Art News*, 15 June 1911.

40 Ginner kept notebooks (now in the Archives Department of the Tate Gallery, London) in which he recorded the titles, dates, sizes (usually), exhibition history and sales of his paintings and drawings. Thus details of his works are known, even if the pictures themselves are lost. These two portraits were relatively big works, both done in 1910. Nothing is noted of their history after January 1912.

41 Letter from Manson to Pissarro, now in the Ashmolean Museum archives.

42 *Sunday Times*, 17 July 1910.

43 Ginner records (*Studio*, November 1945, 'The Camden Town Group') that at first Gilman liked Gauguin's work best and did not admire Van Gogh. After renewed study of the pictures Gilman altered the order of his preferences thus: Cézanne, Van Gogh, Gauguin.

44 L & F 1919, p.13.

45 January 1911, 'Post-Impressionists'.

46 1 December 1913.

47 It is unclear whether at this time Manson was an accredited member of the Fitzroy Street Group. In letters to Pissarro principally concerned with his efforts to persuade the *Studio* to accept a series of articles about the group, Manson referred indifferently to 'yr. group of painters at Fitzroy St.' (23 March 1911) and 'our group of painters' (24 March). Nevertheless, the tenor of the letters suggests that Manson was still outside the group and dependent on Pissarro for information and admittance to the group's premises. Manson's tone had changed by May. Then he seemed to be speaking from inside the group when he announced to Pissarro, following a visit to Fitzroy Street by the son of the editor of the *Studio* to select twenty-three paintings to illustrate four articles, that 'It will be a good advertisement to monopolise The Studio for four months.' The scheme came to nothing and the articles never appeared. All these letters from Manson to Pissarro, and vice versa, quoted here and in the text, are in the Pissarro papers in the archives of the Ashmolean Museum, Oxford.

48 This reply exists as a draft, written by Pissarro on Manson's letter to him. It is roughly scribbled, lacks punctuation and some of the verbs are not properly constructed. I have corrected these minor errors in the interests of clarity.

49 *Studio*, November 1945, 'The Camden Town Group'. This article, the fullest factual first-hand account of the birth of the group, is the main source for the following summary and quotations.

50 *Saturday Review*, 25 January 1930, 'The Camden Town Group'.

51 Diana White had met Lucien Pissarro's future wife Esther Bensusan at Crystal Palace Art School at the end of the 1880s. She remained a close friend of Esther and of her husband until their deaths. Both Esther and Lucien highly esteemed her work and her critical opinions. She is now forgotten as an artist.

52 In '"Camden Town" into "London": Some Intimate Glimpses of the Transition and its Artists 1911–1914', appendix to the catalogue of 'Art in Britain 1890–1940', an exhibition held at the University of Hull, 1967, p.66.

53 Letter of December 1913 in the Pissarro papers in the Ashmolean Museum archives, quoted by Dr Easton, ibid., p.68.

54 Catalogue introduction to the exhibition 'English Post-Impressionists, Cubists and Others', held at the Brighton Art Gallery from December 1913 to January 1914.

55 *Outlook*, 25 November 1911, in a review of 'The Goupil Gallery Salon'.

56 *Outlook*, 9 December 1911.

57 *The Times*, 11 December 1911.

58 Ibid., 19 December 1912.

59 *Observer*, 18 June 1911.

60 The full text of this letter is published on p.12 of the Rudolph Ihlee exhibition catalogue, Graves Art Gallery, Sheffield and Belgrave Gallery, London, 1978.

61 3 July 1911.

62 *Observer*, 18 June 1911.

63 Two letters from Manson to Pissarro of 29 and 30 November 1911 (in the Pissarro papers in the archives of the Ashmolean Museum, Oxford) concern Manson's reception of Pissarro's suggestions.

64 The Tate Gallery has one of Gore's studies. The Yale Center for British Art has a study for Gore's *Deer-Hunting* and another for Ginner's *Tiger-hunting* (both illustrated in Anna Gruetzner Robins, *Modern Art in Britain 1910–1914*, catalogue of the exhibition at the Barbican Gallery (London: Merrell Holberton,

1997), p.101). Two further designs by Gore and one by Lewis are reproduced in the catalogue of the exhibition 'Lucien Pissarro et le Post-Impressionisme Anglais', Musée de Pontoise and Château Musée de Dieppe, 1998–9, pp.72–3.

65 Michael Holroyd, *Augustus John*, vol.2: *The Years of Experience* (London: Heinemann, 1975), p.54.

66 Walter Michel, in *Wyndham Lewis: Paintings and Drawings* (London: Thames & Hudson, 1971), p.334, quotes relevant documents, including Lewis's references to the club in his autobiography *Rude Assignment: A Narrative of my Career Up-to-date* (London: Hutchinson, 1950) (pp.124–5).

67 *Queen*, 14 December 1912.

68 *Outlook*, 14 December 1912.

69 10 December 1912.

70 19 December 1912.

71 See n.50, above.

72 Bevan 1965, p.17.

73 6 December 1911.

74 Sandra Jobson Darroch, *Ottoline* (London: Chatto & Windus, 1976), p.129.

75 *Pall Mall Gazette*, 12 December 1912.

76 *Daily Telegraph*, 17 December 1912.

77 Pissarro papers, Ashmolean Museum, Oxford.

78 *Paint and Prejudice* (London: Methuen, 1937), p.29. Richard Shone's article on 'The Friday Club' in the *Burlington Magazine* (May 1975, pp.279–84) contains valuable information about the art and politics of the club.

79 Pissarro papers, Ashmolean Museum, Oxford.

80 A reference to Ginner's inclusion in the Barbazanges show in Paris selected by Roger Fry but his exclusion from the 'English Group' at the Grafton Gallery selected by Clive Bell.

81 For a fuller discussion of the quarrel see Quentin Bell and Stephen Chaplin, 'The Ideal Home Rumpus', *Apollo*, October 1964, pp.284–91.

82 *Daily Graphic*, 13 June 1911.

83 I am deeply indebted to Dr Malcolm Easton for giving me copies of all Manson's minutes of Camden Town Group and Fitzroy Street meetings. He himself drew on these sources for the appendix to his 'Art in Britain 1890–1940' catalogue (see n.52, above).

84 Ibid., p.65.

85 Pissarro papers, Ashmolean Museum, Oxford.

86 *Studio*, November 1945, 'The Camden Town Group'.

87 Manson's mathematics are a little difficult to interpret here. To make up his total of twenty-six members he must have counted the eleven members of Fitzroy Street elected in 1913 together with fifteen Camden Town Group members. Whether Grant or Innes was the member excluded is uncertain. In order to present his case to Pissarro he evidently ranged fourteen of these fifteen Camden Town members on one side and added Ethel Sands, Nan Hudson, Renée Finch, Harald Sund and Harold Squire to their number. The seven in the opposite camp were Lewis, Nevinson, Hamilton, Wadsworth, Etchells, Epstein and perhaps Adeney. In the course of his letter he distorts his numerical case at will. For instance, he wrote that he was in sympathy with Pissarro alone in the NEAC, yet he counts other NEAC members among those belonging to the London Group with whom he was in sympathy.

88 'P. Conway' was the pseudonym of the musician and painter James Brown (1863–1943). His friendship with Pissarro dated from their meeting in 1912. He painted with Pissarro and Manson at Rye in 1913.

89 See Easton, '"Camden Town" into "London"', appendix, p.69.

90 The only other sculptor to contribute to the Brighton exhibition was Mervyn Lawrence, portrayed by Drummond in *The Sculptor's Studio*, a painting admired by Rutter on its exhibition at the AAA in 1910.

91 In the catalogue of the 1974 Arts Council exhibition, 'Vorticism and its Allies', and in Cork's *Vorticism and Abstract Art in the First Machine Age*, vol.1: *Origins and Development*, (London: Gordon Fraser, 1976).

92 Quoted in Easton, '"Camden Town" into "London"', appendix, p.68.

93 30 April 1914.

94 4 June 1914.

95 11 June 1914.

96 18 June 1914.

97 25 June and 2 July 1914.

98 5 March 1914.

99 Letter to Nan Hudson (see n.5, above).

100 9 April 1914.

101 Letter to Nan Hudson (see n.5, above). 'Chivalrous but stupid' was Sickert's comment.

Select bibliography

The following is a selection of the most helpful general literature on the Fitzroy Street and Camden Town Groups. Writings on individual members of the Camden Town Group are listed separately in the biographical notes provided for each artist in the 'Catalogue of paintings in public collections' later in this volume.

Press reviews of exhibitions are perhaps the most useful of all published source material, and publication details of many such reviews are cited in the notes on the plates. Bayes, Manson and Sickert regularly published art criticism. Most of Sickert's contributions at this period are included in the collection *A Free House!* (see below). Manson, under his initials J. B. M., wrote for the *Outlook* in 1911 and 1912. Bayes often wrote for the *Athenaeum* but art criticism in that periodical was published anonymously. It is doubtful whether Bayes was the author of the reviews of the three Camden Town Group exhibitions in the *Athenaeum* (24 June 1911; 9 December 1911; 14 December 1912). These seem to have been written by an outsider, probably from Roger Fry's camp, and although not helpful for the purpose of identifying pictures they are among the most intelligent analytical assessments of Camden Town painting as it appeared to a well-informed outsider. Frank Rutter wrote for *Art News* and for the *Sunday Times*.

Primary source material: published

Bayes, Walter, 'The Camden Town Group', *Saturday Review*, 25 January 1930.

Fry, Roger, *Letters*, ed. Denys Sutton, 2 vols, London: Chatto & Windus, 1972.

Ginner, Charles, 'Neo-Realism', *New Age*, 1 January 1914.

— 'The Camden Town Group', *Studio*, November 1945.

Lewis, Wyndham, catalogue introduction to list of works in the Cubist Room at the Brighton Art Gallery exhibition 'English Post-Impressionists, Cubists and Others', 1913–14.

Manson, James Bolivar, catalogue introduction to list of works in Rooms I and II at the Brighton Art Gallery exhibition 'English Post-Impressionists, Cubists and Others', 1913–14.

Rutherston, Albert, 'From Orpen and Gore to the Camden Town Group', *Burlington Magazine*, LXXX, 1943, pp.201–5.

Rutter, Frank, preface to catalogue 'Post-Impressionist and Futurist Exhibition', Doré Galleries, London, 1913.

— *Some Contemporary Artists*, London: Leonard Parsons, 1922.

— *Since I was Twenty-Five*, London: Constable, 1927.

— *Art in my Time*, London: Rich & Cowan, 1933.

Sickert, Walter Richard, *A Free House! or The Artist as Craftsman*, an anthology of Sickert's writings selected and edited by Osbert Sitwell, London: Macmillan, 1947.

Primary source material: unpublished

Gore, Spencer Frederick, letters to J. Doman Turner (private archive).

Manson, James Bolivar, minutes of Camden Town, Fitzroy Street and London Group meetings. Copies were lent to me by Dr Malcolm Easton who used the material for the appendix to his catalogue 'Art in Britain 1890–1940' (see 'Secondary literature', below).

— correspondence with Pissarro in the Pissarro papers in the archives of the Ashmolean Museum, Oxford.

Pissarro, Lucien, correspondence with Manson, in the Pissarro papers in the archives of the Ashmolean Museum, Oxford.

Rutherston, Albert, letters (family collection), microfiche copies in the Archives Department, Tate Gallery, London.

Sickert, Walter Richard, letters to Nan Hudson and Ethel Sands (Archives Department, Tate Gallery, London; mostly undated). This material, then in a private collection, was used for my 1977 book on Miss Sands (see 'Secondary literature', below).

Secondary literature

Baron, Wendy, *Miss Ethel Sands and her Circle*, London: Peter Owen, 1977.

— *The Camden Town Group*, London: Scolar Press, 1979.

Bell, Quentin, 'The Camden Town Group I: Sickert and the Post Impressionists', *Motif* 10, 1962–3; 'The Camden Town Group II: Opposition and Composition', *Motif* 11, 1963–4.

— 'The Camden Town Group: Sickert among Friends and Heretics', unpublished article lent to me in proof by Professor Bell.

— 'Sickert and the Post Impressionists', chapter in *Victorian Artists*, London: Routledge & Kegan Paul, 1967.

Connett, Maureen, *Walter Sickert and the Camden Town Group*, London: David & Charles, 1992.

Cork, Richard, 'Vorticism and its Allies', catalogue to Arts Council exhibition, London, 1974.

— *Vorticism and Abstract Art in the First Machine Age*, vol.1: *Origins and Development*, London: Gordon Fraser, 1976.

Easton, Malcolm, '"Camden Town" into "London": Some Intimate Glimpses of the Transition and its Artists 1911–1914', appendix to catalogue 'Art in Britain 1890–1940', exhibition held at the University of Hull, 1967.

— 'Lucien Pissarro and his Friends at Rye, 1913', *Gazette des Beaux-Arts*, November 1968.

Farr, Dennis, and Bowness, Alan, 'Historical note', introduction to catalogue 'London Group 1914–1964, Jubilee Exhibition: Fifty Years of British Art', Tate Gallery, London, 1964.

Forge, Andrew, 'Appreciation', introduction to catalogue 'London Group 1914–1964, Jubilee Exhibition: Fifty Years of British Art', Tate Gallery, London, 1964.

Hall, B. Fairfax, *Paintings and Drawings by Harold Gilman and Charles Ginner in the Collection of Edward Le Bas*, London: privately printed in a limited edition, 1965.

Hynes, Samuel, 'Camden Town and its Literary Context', *Arts Magazine*, September 1980, vol.55, no.1.

Owen, Felicity 'Introducing Impressionism: Frank Rutter, Lucien Pissarro and Friends', *Apollo*, vol.138, October 1993.

Robins, Anna Gruetzner, *Modern Art in Britain 1910–1914*, London: Merrell Holberton, 1997. Catalogue of exhibition at the Barbican Art Gallery, London.

Rothenstein, John, *Modern English Painters: Sickert to Smith*, London: Eyre & Spottiswoode, 1952.

— *Modern English Painters: Lewis to Moore*, London: Eyre & Spottiswoode, 1956.

Sausmarez, Maurice de, 'Camden Town Group Pictures in the Leeds Collection', *Leeds Art Calendar*, Spring 1950.

Seabrooke, Eliot, 'The London Group', *Studio*, February 1945.

Shone, Richard, 'The Friday Club', *Burlington Magazine*, cxvii, May 1975.

— *Bloomsbury Portraits*, London: Phaidon, 1976.

— *The Century of Change: British Painting since 1900*, London: Phaidon, 1977.

Sutton, Denys, 'The Camden Town Group', *Country Life Annual*, 1955.

Tate Gallery, London, catalogue of *Modern British Paintings, Drawings and Sculpture*, London: Oldbourne, 1964.

Trumble, Angus, *Bohemian London: Camden Town and Bloomsbury Paintings in Adelaide*, Adelaide, 1997. Catalogue of exhibition at the Art Gallery of South Australia, Adelaide.

Watney, Simon, *English Post-Impressionism*, London: Cassell, 1980.

Wilcox, Denys J., *The London Group 1913–1939: The Artists and their Works*, Aldershot: Scolar Press, 1995.

Catalogues of Camden Town Group exhibitions since 1930

In 1930 the Leicester Galleries mounted an exhibition under the title 'The Camden Town Group: A Review' in which they gathered together a comprehensive selection of paintings executed during the relevant period by members of the group. It was the first retrospective exhibition of work by the group as a group. Frank Rutter wrote the preface to the catalogue, outlining the history. The exhibition itself inspired critical reassessment of the Camden Town Group. T. W. Earp, for example, discussed the group and its painting in the *New Statesman*, 1 February 1930, and the newspapers devoted generous space to the exhibition.

Since 1930 there have been many exhibitions entitled 'The Camden Town Group' but none until 1976 ('Camden Town Recalled') limited the selection to pictures executed during the brief existence of the society or of its forerunner, the Fitzroy Street Group. Several of these exhibitions contained informative catalogue prefaces as noted below. The most important of these exhibitions since 1930 were:

1939. Redfern Gallery, London. 'The Camden Town Group'. Sale exhibition supported by a few loans.

1940. Museum and Art Gallery, Leicester. 'Paintings and Drawings by Members of the Camden Town Group'. Sale exhibition supported by a few loans.

1944. CEMA (Council for the Encouragement of Music and the Arts), London. 'The Camden Town Group'. 36 paintings by Bevan, Gilman, Ginner, Gore and Sickert. Introduction by Lilian Browse.

1950. Lefevre Gallery, London. 'Paintings by some Members of the Camden Town Group'. Preface by Maurice de Sausmarez. Sale exhibition, with two paintings borrowed from Leeds Art Gallery.

1951. Southampton Art Gallery (in association with the Arts Council of Great Britain). 'The Camden Town Group'. Introduced by Eric Westbrook.

1953. The Arts Council of Great Britain. 'The Camden Town Group'.

1961. The Arts Council of Great Britain. 'Drawings of the Camden Town Group'. Introduction by J. Wood Palmer.

1961. The Minories, Colchester. 'Camden Town Group'. Preface by R. A. Bevan.

1965. Hampstead Festival. 'Camden Town Group'. Preface by Frederick Gore.

1967. William Ware Gallery, London. 'The Camden Town Group & English Painting 1900-1930's'.

1969. Cecil Higgins Art Gallery, Bedford. 'The Camden Town Group'.

1974. City Museum and Art Gallery, Plymouth. 'The Camden Town Group and Related Pictures'.

1976. Fine Art Society Ltd., London, and Graves Art Gallery, Sheffield. 'Camden Town Recalled'. Introduction and catalogue notes by Wendy Baron.

1976–7. Norwich Castle Museum, Southampton Art Gallery and Oxford Museum of Modern Art. 'A Terrific Thing: British Art 1910–16', section on the Camden Town Group.

1979. Anthony d'Offay, London. 'Paintings of London by Members of the Camden Town Group'. Anonymous catalogue introduction is both analytical and perceptive.

1980. Yale Center for British Art, New Haven. 'The Camden Town Group'. Catalogue by Wendy Baron with introduction by Malcolm Cormack. Incorporating work by Bevan, Drummond, Gilman, Ginner, Gore, Ratcliffe and Sickert.

1986. Herbert Art Gallery, Coventry, and Plymouth City Museum and Art Gallery. 'Artists at Applehayes: Camden Town Painters at a West Country Farm, 1909–1924'. Catalogue by Rosalind Billingham. Covering work by Bevan, Ginner and Gore.

1988. Christie's, London. 'The Painters of Camden Town, 1905–1920'. Catalogue by Francis Farmar with introduction by Wendy Baron.

1991. Ashmolean Museum, Oxford. 'The Camden Town Group'. Catalogue by Bernadette Nelson.

1997. Barbican Art Gallery, London. 'Modern Art in Britain 1910–1914'. Catalogue by Anna Gruetzner Robins, published by Merrell Holberton, London, 1997.

1997. Art Gallery of South Australia, Adelaide. 'Bohemian London: Camden Town and Bloomsbury Paintings in Adelaide'. Catalogue by Angus Trumble.

1998–9. Aberdeen Art Gallery. 'An Ordinary Life: Camden Town Painters'.

1998–9. Musée de Pontoise and Château Musée de Dieppe. 'Lucien Pissarro et le Post-Impressionisme Anglais', incorporating work by Gilman, Gore, Pissarro and Sickert. Catalogue contributions by Andrew Causey, Frederick Gore, Anne Thorold and Wendy Baron.

The plates

Conventions used in the plate notes

The following plate notes cite medium, support, size (height stated first) and important exhibitions in which the works have appeared. Because inscriptions and provenances are cited in full in the 'Catalogue of paintings in public collections' later in this volume, they are not repeated in plate notes that relate to publicly owned works but are given in plate notes relating to paintings in private ownership and to paintings of unknown whereabouts. The year in which a work was acquired by a public collection is cited in parentheses after the name of the collection.

Exhibition references are divided into three categories: early (group and one-man exhibitions up to 1919); later group; and later one-man shows. The selection of one-man exhibitions, both early and later, echoes the lists incorporated in the relevant biographical sections of the 'Catalogue of paintings in public collections', below. These exhibitions are generally identified by the name of the institution (public or commercial) where they were held, together with the year(s) when they were held. In some cases the institution's name is abbreviated; see the List of abbreviations earlier in this volume. The titles and content of group shows are given more fully in the Select bibliography. Unless otherwise stated, exhibitions were in London. The number in parentheses following each exhibition reference represents the number allocated to the work in the catalogue of that exhibition.

A number in square brackets following the title of a painting by Ginner represents a reference to that work in the artist's notebooks (see the 'Catalogue of paintings in public collections', p.157 below).

A number in square brackets following the title of a painting by Gore represents the number allocated to that painting by Gilman after Gore's death (see the 'Catalogue of paintings in public collections', p.157 below).

See the lists of abbreviations (pp.9–12 above) for other abbreviations used in these notes.

Sickert

1 **The Juvenile Lead: Self-portrait** 1907
Oil on canvas; 51 × 45.8
Collection: City Art Gallery, Southampton (1951)
EXHIBITIONS (EARLY): Paris, *Salon d'automne* 1907 (1535) as *L'Homme au Chapeau Melon*; (LATER ONE-MAN AND GROUP): see RA 1992, no.62 for full list

The 'life-sized head of myself in a cross-light' which Sickert told Nan Hudson he used as 'a punching-ball' when he resolved to paint more considered, elaborated works. Sickert never outgrew his early training on the stage. Ever the player, in each of his self-portraits he became an actor-manager, both directing and executing the part he chose to present. This self-portrait is a searchingly introspective image of the artist in middle age, his air of disillusion tempered with a touch of wry humour. The glasses, which lend the image its quizzical and slightly vulnerable air, were an artificial prop. Many years later Sickert changed the title of the painting. It appeared as *The Juvenile Lead* in the catalogue of Sickert's exhibition at the Savile Gallery in 1928 from where Mrs Wylde (*née* Wendela Boreel), former pupil and close friend of Sickert, probably bought the painting. The new title was perhaps a sardonic comment both on the stage-managed character of the picture and on the actual role Sickert had played as the less than youthful leader of a cast of younger colleagues within Fitzroy Street.

Drummond

2 **19 Fitzroy Street** *c.*1913–14
Oil on canvas; 71 × 50.8
Collection: Laing Art Gallery, Newcastle upon Tyne (1975)
EXHIBITIONS (LATER GROUP): LG 1928, Retrospective (46); FAS 1976 (21);
Christie's 1988 (25)

A valuable document of the Fitzroy Street Group studio. Three men are
examining pictures taken from the stacks. The figures have been variously
identified; I believe they represent (left to right) Manson, Gore and Ginner.
Some of the paintings can also be identified. These include (top left) Gilman's
The Verandah, Sweden (Beaverbrook Art Gallery, Fredericton, New Brunswick,
Canada) of 1912, (top right) a view of Boyne Hill Church by Drummond and
(bottom centre) Ginner's *The Circus* (Leeds Art Gallery) of 1913. Preparatory
studies for the picture (University of Hull Art Collection) and an etching
reveal that the top right space at first depicted Drummond's *At the Piano*
(pl.10). The painting *Boyne Hill Church* in its place is larger than any of the
versions of this subject known today.

It was the practice at Fitzroy Street for each artist to provide an easel and
place his or her paintings on it. However, Drummond has chosen to represent
a wider selection of work by his colleagues on the easels. A preparatory
drawing without the figures points strongly to the identification of the top
centre painting as Gore's *Croft's Lane, Letchworth* (private collection; rep.
d'Offay 1983, pl.24). This drawing and the final painting suggest that the work
exhibited leaning against the bottom of the right-hand easel was Bevan's *Swiss
Cottage* (private collection; rep. Bevan 1965, pl.40). The painting which seems
most readily legible, the landscape behind the chair on the bottom left, has so
far resisted my attempts at identification. The general design of the painting
suggests Pissarro or Manson, but a Swedish view by Ratcliffe cannot be ruled
out.

Sickert

3 Girl at a Window: Little Rachel   1907

Oil on canvas; 50.8 × 40.6

Collection: Tate Gallery, London (accepted by the Commissioners of
Inland Revenue in lieu of tax and allocated 1991)

EXHIBITIONS (LATER ONE-MAN AND GROUP): see RA 1992, no.64 for full list

During the first half of 1907 Sickert rented extra rooms to use as a studio on
the first floor of 6 Mornington Crescent, where he already lodged. Here he
became so 'entangled in a batch of a dozen or so interiors' that he put off his
planned departure for France from July until late August or early September.
The interiors, he told Nan Hudson, were a 'set of Studies of illumination … A
little Jewish girl of 13 or so with red hair and a nude alternate days'. Little
Rachel, the Jewish girl, is identified in the archives of Agnew's as Miss
Siderman who died aged 70 in 1963. She was the model for six oil paintings
(see Baron 1973, p.347) which, together with the series of paintings of the
nude (see pl.26), constitute Sickert's best – and only – claim to be regarded as
an English Impressionist. Their real subject is natural light, filtered through
dusty windows, translated with infinite subtlety in terms of a richly varied
mosaic of stippled paint. However, although light was his subject, Sickert's
method of working, carefully constructing his compositions from drawn
documents and planning his execution in separate stages to allow each coat of
paint to dry before applying the next, was the antithesis of proper
Impressionist practice. His relatively dark palette also set him apart from
Impressionism.

Sickert

4 **The New Home** 1908

Oil on canvas; 50.8 × 40.6 cm

Inscribed: *Sickert* bl

Provenance: Judge William Evans; 1936, bought by City Art Gallery, Leeds; 1938, exchanged for another painting; A. J. L. McDonnell; F. A. Girling; London, Sotheby's, 13 March 1974 (28); Simon Sainsbury Collection: Ivor Braka Limited, London

EXHIBITIONS (EARLY): NEAC summer 1908 (59); Goupil Gallery 1918, 'The Collection of the late Judge William Evans' (105); (LATER ONE-MAN AND GROUP): see RA 1992, no.67 for full list

The New Home is the quintessential Camden Town figure study. More than a portrait of an individual in a particular setting, it represents a whole class and its way of life. Early in 1908, in a letter from Mornington Crescent to Ethel Sands and Nan Hudson, Sickert described his coster-girl models dressed 'in the sumptuous poverty of their class, sham velvet &c. They *always* wearing for everyday dirty, old, worn clothes, but *Sunday* clothes.' The critic of the *Pall Mall Gazette* (3 June 1908) seized on the paraphernalia of the painting in his review of the NEAC exhibition: 'Here is a young woman ill at ease, apparently her hat not yet removed – her head and bust seen large against the mantelshelf – and she taking very unkindly to the second-rate, sordid lodging, to which she is condemned by an unkindly Fate.' Sickert deliberately gave his paintings titles designed to encourage such literary interpretations. But the titles were his final imaginative touch. He did not begin with the illustration of a story in mind. He conjured 'the whole world of pathos, of poetry, of sentiment' by caressing and cajoling the rich and juicy paint into the expression of the image before his eye as a pattern of colour, light and shade. *The New Home* epitomizes Sickert's passionate, visual response to the area of London where he found the raw material of his art.

Gilman

5 **Girl with a Teacup**   *c.*1914–15
Oil on canvas; 62.2 × 52.1
Inscribed *H Gilman* br
Provenance: Murray Urquhart; Edward Le Bas; Christie's, 10 May 1974
(125); B. Fairfax Hall
Collection: Private
EXHIBITIONS (LATER ONE-MAN): probably Reid & Lefevre 1943 (4) as
Portrait of a Girl; AC 1954–5 (28); AC 1981–2 (51); (LATER GROUP): Redfern
1939 (36); Christie's 1988 (147)

There are two portraits of the sitter in identical poses and wearing outdoor
dress and a hat, before a wall clad with a striped, floral paper on which hang
two pictures, that on the left being Ginner's *Wild Duck* (pl.41). The smaller
version (private collection; rep. Baron 1979, pl.43), usually called
Contemplation, Mary L, lacks the table and teacup. 'Mary L', said to be an
Austrian friend of Gilman, is the hatless sitter wearing a headband portrayed
in *The Coral Necklace* (Brighton Art Gallery) and in a profile portrait (private
collection; rep. Christie's, 3 March 1978, lot 115). The hat makes it uncertain
whether the same sitter is shown in all four paintings.

There is an echo of Sickert's *The New Home* (pl.4) in the mood and balance
of Gilman's portrait. However, the compositional device of using a segment of
table in the foreground to set the figure in a more convincing spatial setting
more specifically recalls Sickert's *Ennui* (see pl.6). The teacup, which replaces
Sickert's beer glass, introduces a feature Gilman was to make very much his
own, whether in pure still-life paintings or as a narrative component of his
figure paintings.

Sickert

6 **Ennui** *c.*1914–16
Oil on canvas; 76.2 × 55.9
Collection: Ashmolean Museum, Oxford (1939)
EXHIBITIONS (LATER ONE-MAN); Agnew's 1933 (45); (LATER GROUP): Oxford
1991 (61)

Ennui, Sickert's best-known subject, the culmination of his exploration of the compositional tensions and narrative possibilities of two-figure groups and the vehicle for technical experiment (see Baron 1973, pp.142–4), was conceived during the winter of 1913. The setting is Sickert's Granby Street studio, the models are Hubby and Marie Hayes. The prime version (Tate Gallery, London) was completed in time for its exhibition at the NEAC the following spring. Three other more sketchy renderings, probably all preliminary studies, are in private collections (see note to pl.80, RA 1992). The precise dating of the half-scale version illustrated here has not been established. It is certainly a later reworking and perhaps a deliberate exercise in the manner of Gilman, whose Maple Street interiors, with their characteristic profusion of patterned surfaces, may well have sparked off Sickert's decision to transform all his previously plain areas into busily patterned ones. A comparison with Gilman's *Girl with a Teacup* (pl.5), which in its turn may have been influenced by Sickert's earlier (1913–14) versions of *Ennui*, suggests that the later *Ennui* could be Sickert's acknowledgement of the nature of reciprocity within a collaborative artistic milieu.

Virginia Woolf made this version of *Ennui* the centre point of her brilliant essay (*Walter Sickert: A Conversation* (London: Hogarth Press, 1934)) on the exhibition of Sickert's work at Agnew's in 1933:

You remember the picture of the old publican, with his glass on the table before him and a cigar gone cold at his lips, looking out of his shrewd little pig's eyes at the intolerable waste of desolation in front of him? A fat woman lounges, her arm on a cheap yellow chest of drawers, behind him. It is all over with them, one feels. The accumulated weariness of innumerable days has discharged its burden on them. They are buried under an avalanche of rubbish. In the street beneath, the trams are squeaking, children are shrieking. Even now somebody is tapping his glass impatiently on the bar counter. She will have to bestir herself; to pull her heavy, indolent body together and go and serve him. The grimness of that situation lies in the fact that there is no crisis; dull minutes are mounting, old matches are accumulating and dirty glasses and dead cigars; still on they must go, up they must get.

Gilman

7 **Des Poissons** *c.*1908
Oil on canvas; 25.5 × 30.5
Inscribed *HG* br
Provenance: Sotheby's, 23 May 1984 (90); Fine Art Society
Collection: Private, USA
EXHIBITIONS (EARLY): Paris, *Salon des Indépendants* 1909 (691)

Painted at Snargate Rectory in Romney Marsh, Kent, where Gilman's father
had the living. When finding subjects to paint, Gilman rarely strayed far from
his immediate home environment. Hence, domestic still-life paintings recur
throughout his short career. The silver vegetable dish in front of a mirror in
this example also features in another Snargate still life of about the same date
(Fitzwilliam Museum, Cambridge). Andrew Causey (AC 1981–2, note to
no.15) pointed out that the foreground chair indicates that the Fitzwilliam
painting represents a sideboard still life (not a mantelpiece picture as suggested
in Baron 1979, note to pl.25).

The liquid paint and the subtle rendering of the variety of silver tones in the
dish, salver and fish scales are a virtuoso demonstration of Gilman's ability to
emulate the delicacy of Velasquez.

Manson

8 **Still Life: Tulips in a Blue Jug**   probably 1912
Oil on canvas; 40.8 × 51.5
Collection: Government Art Collection (1982)
EXHIBITIONS (EARLY): possibly one or more of the following: AAA 1912
(96), Goupil Gallery Salon, autumn 1912 (83), CTG 3 (6), Doré 1913 (44),
Brighton 1913–14 (44) and Whitechapel 1914 (398) as *Still Life*

A rare example of a still life with flowers painted before Manson began to
specialize in flower pieces from the 1920s onwards. The extensive list of
exhibitions is suggested because so few still lifes of appropriate date are
known. The *Daily Telegraph* (17 December 1912) described Manson's *Still Life*
as 'a brilliant if somewhat mechanical piece of neo-impressionism', adding that
'Without the aid of the catalogue it would have been difficult to guess that to
the same brush we owe the attractive landscape "Moonlight and Snow".' The
richness of handling and the depth of colour are indeed uncharacteristic of
Manson's work at this early date. These qualities, together with the artificiality
of the arrangement of fancy objects in a shallow space, suggest that Manson
deliberately undertook an exercise in the manner of Ginner (for example
Ginner's *Geranium, Fruit and Flowers* of 1911, rep. Baron 1979, pl.51).

Ratcliffe

9 **Cottage Interior** *c.*1914

Oil on pulpboard; 49.5 × 49.5

Collection: Private

Reproduced courtesy of Phillips Auctioneers

Ratcliffe painted several cottage interiors, some with figures and some without. Many were variations on a theme. The example illustrated here is especially close to the smaller, but more cluttered, cottage interior in the Yale Center for British Art, which incorporates a figure sitting to the right. The table arrangement of flowers in a vase, teapot, cup, saucer and bowl is the whole subject of *Still Life on a Kitchen Table* dated 1914 (private collection, Australia; rep. Sotheby's, 1 May 1991, lot 16). The garden city view outside the square-paned window could be of Letchworth or Hampstead Garden Suburb. The painting propped up against the wall in the background is *Summer Landscape, Sweden* of 1913 (Government Art Collection, London).

Drummond

10 **At the Piano**   *c*.1912
Oil on canvas; 89.8 × 60.8
Collection: Art Gallery of South Australia, Adelaide (South Australia
Government Grant, 1969)
EXHIBITIONS (EARLY): CTG 3 (27); (LATER GROUP): Adelaide 1997 (7)

The pianist here is probably Drummond's first wife (*née* Zina Ogilvie), an
artist best remembered for her book illustrations. They married in 1906; she
died in 1931. Like her husband she was an accomplished musician. The
standing figure may be Mrs Bevan, a close friend of the Drummond family.
Paintings of women playing the piano were popular among members of the
Camden Town Group. Ratcliffe, for example, painted a delightful interior with
a girl at a piano (private collection, Australia; rep. Adelaide 1997, p.36).
Sickert's piano subjects of 1912–14 included drawings and paintings featuring
his models (Hubby and Chicken) as well as his friends such as Ethel Sands.

As in *19 Fitzroy Street* (pl.2), Drummond has represented paintings within
his picture space. The little upright propped up on the left is probably a free
rendering of Ginner's *Neuville Lane* of 1911 (pl.40), given by the artist to Mrs
Drummond. The other two paintings have so far defied identification,
although the colours and layout of the unframed painting propped against the
wall suggest that Bayes could be its creator.

Gilman

11 Le Pont Tournant (The Swing Bridge), Dieppe   1911

Oil on canvas; 30.5 × 40.6
Provenance: 1911, W. R. Sickert and Christine Drummond Angus, to
whom given as a wedding present by the Camden Town Group
Collection: Private
EXHIBITIONS (EARLY): CTG 2 (19); (LATER GROUP): FAS 1976 (33); Christie's
1988 (92); Pontoise 1998–9 (62)

The Camden Town Group must have given this painting to Sickert and his
new wife on or shortly after their marriage, in July 1911. At the December
exhibition, unlike Gilman's other contributions, it was unpriced in the
catalogue and thus, by implication, not for sale. Dieppe, Sickert's second
home, was much visited by his Camden Town Group colleagues. The visit to
Dieppe made by Ginner and Gilman in 1911 on their return from Paris was
so productive that two of Gilman's, and three of Ginner's, four paintings each
at the second Camden Town Group exhibition in December were done in
Dieppe that summer. The direct handling, in a scatter of brightly coloured
marks, and the variety and purity of the colours, of *Le Pont Tournant* show
Gilman moving away from the influence of Sickert towards a style based on
colour contrasts. Sir Claude Phillips (*Daily Telegraph*, 14 December 1911)
classified Gilman as 'a neo-impressionist with a personal accent of his own,
that suffices to make the obvious and everyday interesting. "Le Pont
Tournant" gives this curious type of modern bridge with accuracy as regards
impression, but also with a sense of novelty and wonderment. And this is
enough to give the study a *raison d'être*.'

Ginner

12 **Evening, Dieppe**   1911 [I, p.xli]
   Oil on canvas; 61 × 46.3
   Inscribed *C. Ginner* br
   Provenance: Mrs L. Fox-Pitt; Christies, 18 July 1975 (36)
   Collection: Alan Fortunoff
   EXHIBITIONS (EARLY): CTG 2 (30); (LATER GROUP): FAS 1976 (44)

Two of the three Dieppe scenes Ginner showed with the Camden Town
Group in December 1911, *Evening* and *The Sunlit Quay*, were conceived as a
complementary pair. Together they provide a complete panorama of Dieppe
seen across the harbour with the higgledy-piggledy network of streets hemmed
in behind the arcaded quays. *Evening* is executed in a harmony of gold and
blue; *The Sunlit Quay* has the addition of warmer salmon-pink tones. The
background mass in *Evening* is the cliff which drops down sheer to the sea
below. The silhouette of the château (now the museum) can be seen on the
ridge. The constructive use of small, tight touches of thick paint, the decisive
definition and the rhythmic patterning of both these Dieppe views introduce
Ginner's mature style. Both pictures, but especially the night scene, have a
poetic quality which later in his career was often submerged by Ginner's
obsessional concern with detail.

Ratcliffe

13 Beehives, Sweden 1913
   Oil on canvas; 51.5×41
   Inscribed *W. Ratcliffe* br
   Collection: Private, Adelaide, South Australia
   EXHIBITIONS (EARLY): probably AAA 1913 (90) as *Bee-hives* and Whitechapel
   1914 (430) as *Swedish Beehives*

Perhaps inspired by Gilman's account of his visit in 1912, Ratcliffe spent several months in Sweden during the late winter, spring and possibly early summer of 1913. He travelled with Stanley Parker and his family (Stanley being the brother of Barry Parker who, with Raymond Unwin, planned both Hampstead Garden Suburb and Letchworth Garden City). Their base was in Sundsholm, Färholt, where Ratcliffe enjoyed a period of intense productivity. The crisp outdoor light, which threw the forms of homesteads and domesticated landscape into sharp relief, suited Ratcliffe's natural inclination towards a densely patterned picture surface. He exploited the possibilities of perspective; his colour key tended to become more vivid and high-toned, dominated by purples, turquoise greens and salmon pinks; his handling was often tight, the paint applied in small, stippled touches of thick but dry-textured paint; and his paintings increased in size (most 76 cm wide, 51 or 61 cm high).

Besides the five paintings of Swedish subjects listed in the 'Catalogue of paintings in public collections' later in this volume, there are at least four others in private collections: *Cottages under Snow, Sweden* (rep. Christie's, 4 March 1983, lot 47, closely related to *Winter Scene* in Manchester); *Spring in Sweden* (rep. Christie's 1988, no.131, and Christie's, 11 March 1994, lot 62); *Spring at Sundsholm* (rep. Baron 1979, pl.135); and the painting illustrated here. This painting is closely related to *Beehives in the Snow* (Government Art Collection, London). They are approximately the same (relatively small) size but the version illustrated is vertical instead of horizontal in format and shows the scene in the cool light of spring, with the leaves just bursting, rather than in cold winter. *Beehives in Snow* was exhibited at Brighton in 1913–14 but it is impossible to decide whether the spring or the winter version was submitted to the AAA in 1913 and Whitechapel in 1914.

W. Ratcliffe.

Bevan

14 **The Cabyard, Night**   *c.*1910
Oil on canvas; 63.5 × 69.9
Collection: Brighton Museum and Art Gallery (1913)
EXHIBITIONS (EARLY): CTG 2 (31); Carfax Gallery 1913 (12); Brighton
1913–14 (36); (LATER ONE-MAN): AC 1956 (7); Colnaghi 1965 (24); (LATER
GROUP): FAS 1976 (9); d'Offay 1979 (1); Christie's 1988 (61)

Bevan loved horses. In Tangier in 1891 he had been Master of Fox Hounds
for a season. Horses are the subject of his earliest surviving paintings, done in
Brittany during the early 1890s. On his return to England in 1894 he went to
live at Hawkridge on Exmoor where he could combine painting and hunting.
After he joined the Fitzroy Street Group, Bevan fulfilled Sickert's dictum
about the artist finding subjects ready-made in the everyday life of London, by
painting horses and drivers at work round the clock in the cab-yard at
Ormonde Place, St John's Wood, a short walk from his house near Swiss
Cottage.

In this poetic night-time scene, Bevan's subtle division of tones and colours
models the broad beam of light cast by the oil lamp to throw into relief a
silhouette pattern of strong and simplified shapes. Its inclusion in three major
exhibitions between 1911 and 1913 suggests that Bevan considered it highly. In
his review of the Camden Town Group exhibition, Frank Rutter advised the
Contemporary Art Society to get one of Bevan's masterly cab-scenes for the
nation before more appreciative foreign collectors snapped them up (*Sunday
Times*, 3 December 1911). Two years later Brighton Art Gallery bought the
picture from the show mounted in its own gallery. It remained the only work
by Bevan acquired by a public art gallery during the artist's lifetime.

Ginner

15 **Battersea Park No. 2** 1911 [I, p.xxxvi]
Oil on canvas; 62 x 50
Inscribed *C.GINNER* bl
Provenance: 1936, T.W. Spurr
Last known whereabouts: Sotheby's, 24 November 1993 (71)
EXHIBITIONS (EARLY): CTG I (37); Paris, *Salon des Indépendants* 1912 (1335); Goupil Gallery 1914 (7)

Reproduced courtesy of Sotheby's

When Ginner lived in Chelsea from late 1909 until 1911 he thrice painted nearby Battersea Park. The first version, *Battersea Park No. 1*, painted in 1910, is now in the Art Gallery of South Australia, Adelaide. A year later he painted *Beds of Flowers, Battersea Park* [I, p.xxxiv], a small painting on panel immediately bought by Louis Fergusson (with the Fine Art Society, London, 1999) as well as the painting illustrated here, *Battersea Park No. 2*. A *pochade* study for *Battersea Park No. 2* is listed in the notebooks. Daffodils or narcissi are the main flowers in *Beds of Flowers*; tulips dominate *Battersea Park No. 2*. The contrast of the formality of the round flower beds and the rich riot of spring planting they contained must have appealed to Ginner's aesthetic temperament. The subject allowed him to indulge both his relish for colour and texture and his need to impose a pattern upon wayward nature. The park subjects are thus among his most disciplined paintings of this period.

Gore

16 **Mornington Crescent** 1910 [G.106a]
Oil on canvas; 40.6 × 50.8
Studio stamp br
Provenance: Sir John Mills; Sotheby's, 10 November 1981 (103); Douglas Woolf
Last known whereabouts: Sotheby's, 18 June 1997 (6)
EXHIBITIONS (EARLY): probably Chenil Gallery 1911 (9) as *The Steeple and the Tube*

From 1909 until 1912 Gore rented a front room at 31 Mornington Crescent. In 1910 and 1911, in all seasons and all weathers, he painted the view of the Crescent from his window, its houses, gardens, the tube station and the Camden Theatre. At least a dozen such paintings are known, besides about another ten of the gardens painted from an outdoor vantage spot. In 'A Perfect Modern', published after Gore's death (*New Age*, 9 April 1914), Sickert wrote:

There was a few years ago a month of June which Gore verily seems to have used as if he had known that it was to be for him the last of its particularly fresh and sumptuous kind. He used it to look down on the garden of Mornington Crescent. The trained trees rise and droop in fringes, like fountains, over the little well of greenness and shade where parties of young people are playing at tennis. The backcloth is formed by the tops of the brown houses of the Hampstead Road, and the liver-coloured tiles of the Tube Station.

The 'well of greenness' was replaced in 1926 by the Carreras cigarette factory, but Mornington Crescent remains as a decrepit terrace and the liver-coloured tiles of the tube station also survive. The steeple in the background of this picture belonged to the church of Old St Pancras and St Matthew in Oakley Square. The church, ruined and without its steeple, was finally demolished in 1977.

Because of the number of Gore's Mornington Crescent paintings it is difficult to work out which was exhibited where. However, only three extant paintings incorporate the steeple and the tube named in the Chenil Gallery title (this, the British Council and the sketchier Johannesburg paintings). Only the two latter match the description in *Bazaar* (30 June 1911) of *Mornington Crescent* exhibited in the first Camden Town Group show, 'the Camden Theatre and the very vivid red Tube Station walls heightened by the crescent's acrid green', which, according to a family sales ledger, was bought from the Camden Town Group exhibition by Somerset Maugham. Maugham is not known as the owner of any of the extant versions.

Drummond

17 **St James's Park**   1912
Oil on canvas; 72.5 × 90
Collection: City Art Gallery, Southampton (1953)
EXHIBITIONS (EARLY): CTG 3 (29); Paris, *Salon des Indépendants* 1913 (905);
Brighton 1913–14 (133); (LATER ONE-MAN): AC 1963–4 (6); (LATER GROUP):
Norwich 1976 (24); d'Offay 1979 (8)

Reviewing the 1912 Camden Town Group exhibition, *The Times* (19
December 1912) expressed dislike of the bright colours in Drummond's *St
James's Park*, Bevan's two London horse-sale pictures, Ginner's *Piccadilly
Circus* and Gilman's *The Reapers*: 'the colour is incongruous and imposed
upon the picture for its decorative effect. It is in fact nothing but a new kind
of prettiness, which would tire us as soon as it ceased to surprise.' *The Pall
Mall Gazette* (12 December 1912) found no 'refinement of colour or grace of
drawing' in any of Drummond's pictures at the Carfax Gallery and was
particularly irritated by 'the empty glare of their gaudy tints'. This quarrel with
the use of arbitrary, bright colour must be read within the context of a
rearguard action by the English critics against the pernicious influence of
French Post-Impressionism and indeed Drummond must have found his initial
inspiration in Seurat's *Une Dimanche Après-midi à l'Ile de la Grande Jatte*. In *St
James's Park*, Drummond recaptured Seurat's sense of time suspended at a
moment of pure poetry, using the same means: frozen movement; simplified
silhouettes; heightened colours; wayward accents (with birds in place of
Seurat's dogs and monkeys); a strong sense of pattern; and an austere
compositional structure based on the diagonal division of the picture plane into
a stretch of land and a stretch of water. But Drummond did not plagiarize. He
assimilated the lessons of Seurat to produce an individual masterpiece of
English art.

Bevan

18 **Hay Carts, Cumberland Market**   *c.*1915
   Oil on canvas; 48.3×61
   Inscribed *Robert Bevan* bl
   Provenance: 1961, Edward Le Bas; Christie's, 3 March 1978 (179);
   Mr and Mrs Paul Mellon
   Collection: New Haven, Yale Center for British Art (1999)
   EXHIBITIONS (LATER GROUP): Yale 1980 (9); (LATER ONE-MAN): AC 1956
   (19); Colnaghi 1961 (20)

In 1914 Bevan acquired a first-floor studio at 49 Cumberland Market, one of
the three squares planned in the original development of Camden Town and
the only one – because of its proximity to the Grand Union Canal basin – to
retain its commercial character as a hay market well into the twentieth century.
The studio became the headquarters of the Cumberland Market Group. Five
paintings of 1914–15 and many drawings survive (including a sketchbook in
the Ashmolean Museum, Oxford) to record Bevan's fascination with the life of
the square. The illustrated painting and another closely related version (given
by the artist as a wedding present to his former art tutor, A. E. Pearce, rep.
Sotheby's, 11 March 1981, lot 92) focus on the hay carts and feature the
weigh-house on the north side of the square. Two more related paintings of
the north side, without foreground carts, show a longer stretch of buildings
and a wider expanse of square (one in Southampton City Art Gallery, the
other rep. Christie's, 8 June 1979, lot 38). A fifth painting (rep. Bevan 1965,
pl.50, and Sotheby's, 18 June 1997, lot 7) encompasses the huge space
stretching to the east side of the square in a cold early morning light as seen
from Bevan's window on the west side. Bevan exhibited a work called *The
Market* with the London Group in March 1915 (77) and a *Cumberland Market*
was included in the first Cumberland Market Group exhibition at the Goupil
Gallery in April 1915 (8), but which versions, where and when is not known.

Robert Bevan

Gilman

19 **Nude at a Window**   *c.*1912
Oil on canvas; 61 × 50.8
Inscribed *Gilman* br
Provenance: R. P. Bevan
Collection: Private
EXHIBITIONS (EARLY): possibly Carfax Gallery 1913 (39) as *Nude (No. 4)*;
(LATER GROUP): Yale 1980 (39)

Gilman numbered, rather than described, his nudes. The Camden Town
Group exhibition of December 1911 included nudes numbered *1* and *2*. His
joint exhibition with Gore at the Carfax Gallery in January 1913 included
nudes numbered *1*, *2*, *3* and *4*. It is likely, but not certain, that the same
number, denoting a chronological sequence, remained attached to a specific
picture.

Gilman's interest in the nude as a subject for painting was concentrated
within the years 1911–13. Some ten paintings of this date are known. No
nudes were included in his joint exhibition with Ginner in April 1914. A
contemporary layout plan (see fig. 5, p.57) of the joint Gilman/Gore exhibition
at the Carfax Gallery in 1913 shows *Nude (No. 1)* as a small painting, *Nude
(No. 2)* and *Nude (No. 3)* as slightly larger, upright, paintings and *Nude (No. 4)*
as larger still and of pronounced vertical format. This last was inscribed on the
plan 'Back View' and priced at £20, whereas the other three were £15.

There is not enough evidence to establish which painting was exhibited
where and when. It is possible that the painting in the Yale Center, with its
pointilliste treatment and soft colours indicating a date of around 1911, was one
of the two nudes exhibited with the Camden Town Group in 1911. As one of
the smallest extant examples it could have been *Nude (No. 1)*; as one of the
most charming it could well be *Nude (No. 2)*, described as 'made attractive by a
flicker of fitful sunlight on the undraped body' (*Daily Telegraph*, 14 December
1911). The half-draped nude standing by a mantelpiece in Leeds Art Gallery
might also be *Nude (No. 1)*. If Gilman's numbering remained consistent, *The
Model* (Arts Council Collection), a horizontal-format painting, cannot be any
of the four nudes exhibited in 1913.

Given that there must be other, as yet untraced, nudes by Gilman, the
process of deduction should not be pushed too far. However, the
identification of the back view *Nude (No. 4)* can, on the existing evidence, be
narrowed to two possibilities – the painting in the Fitzwilliam Museum,
Cambridge, and the painting illustrated here. They represent the two extremes
of Gilman's approach to the subject. The Fitzwilliam painting is still close to
Sickert in the unforced naturalism of the nude seated on a metal-framed bed
amid rumpled bedclothes. The firm and delicate modelling, built up to a
crusty surface in rich smears of paint, supports a date of 1911. The *Nude at a
Window* is a more arresting image. The vehement handling in broad, slashed
strokes complements the brazen presentation of the figure in awkward mid-
movement.

Gore

20 'The Mad Pierrot' Ballet at the Alhambra 1911

Oil on canvas; 49.4×51.2

Inscribed *S F Gore* br

Provenance: Given by the artist to his aunt, Mrs Edward Lascelles; her daughter Miss A. L. Lascelles; Sotheby's, 9 December 1970 (49)

Collection: Private, Adelaide, South Australia

EXHIBITION (EARLY): CTG 2 (15); (LATER GROUP): Adelaide 1997 (19)

From 1903 until 1912 Gore painted between thirty and forty theatrical subjects. His first painting on this theme was *The Masked Ball* (a scene from 'The Duel in the Snow', performed at the Empire Music Hall; see d'Offay 1983, pl.1), his last was *A Singer at the Bedford Music Hall* (Tate Gallery, London) in which the angular distortions suited the modernistic setting of the Cabaret Theatre Club for which it was intended. Between 1906 and 1908, when Gore's collaboration with Sickert was closest, they sometimes went together to the Bedford Music Hall in Camden Town where Gore produced drawings almost indistinguishable from Sickert's (see Baron 1979, pl.3). However, by 1909 the Alhambra in Leicester Square was Gore's favourite music hall. Unlike Sickert's shabbier haunts, it mounted spectaculars, specializing in ballets and acrobatic turns rather than bawdy songs. Gore revelled in the riot of colour presented by the luscious backdrops, the ornate costumes and the frenetic animation of the artistes.

Gore's four contributions to the second exhibition of the Camden Town Group in December 1911 included two paintings of 'The Mad Pierrot' ballet staged at the Alhambra for 11 weeks from 13 March 1911 (see Ivor Guest, *Ballet in Leicester Square* (London: Dance Books, 1992), p.151). Both are related compositionally, but *The Promenade* (Johannesburg Art Gallery) is vertical rather than square in format. It encompasses a wider sweep of balcony and a deeper stretch of stage to reveal the big windmill which featured in the set as background to a story involving a miller's wife and a pierrot. In *'The Mad Pierrot' Ballet* Gore has zoomed in on his subject. The closer focus serves to disguise the logic of the space and emphasize the dynamic compositional structure of the painting. In both paintings, the stark division of the picture plane between the darkly silhouetted figures peering over the balcony and the more brightly lit scene below, as well as the skewed vertiginous viewpoint, lead on to the more overtly experimental *The Balcony at the Alhambra* (York Art Gallery), also of 1911.

Gore

21 **Gauguins and Connoisseurs at the Stafford Gallery** 1911–12
   Oil on canvas; 83.8×71.7
   Inscribed *S. F. Gore* br
   Provenance: Sir Michael Sadler
   Collection: Private
   EXHIBITIONS (LATER ONE-MAN): AC 1955 (33); Redfern Gallery 1962 (47);
   (LATER GROUP): Leicester Galleries 1930 (23); Leicester 1940 (27);
   Norwich 1976 (29)

The exhibition portrayed by Gore opened in London in November 1911.
Incorporating paintings by Cézanne and Gauguin, it was one of the series of
stimulating exhibitions of Post-Impressionist European art held in London
between 1910 and 1914. Like the other seminal exhibitions, it was created
through the enthusiasm and initiative of a private individual – in this case
Michael Sadler – and mounted with the co-operation of a discerning
commercial gallery owner – in this case John Neville of the short-lived Stafford
Gallery.

In subject and style, Gore's painting is an explicit gesture of homage to
Gauguin. The high and angled viewpoint, the hot colouring with its heavy
contrasts of red and black, the asymetrical composition, the distorted silhouette
treatment of the figures, all refer directly to Gauguin and in particular to his
The Vision after the Sermon (National Gallery of Scotland), represented on the
right of the impressive wall of paintings by Gauguin portrayed by Gore. The
other two paintings shown are Gauguin's *L'Esprit Veille (Manao Tupapau)*
(Albright Knox Gallery, Buffalo) and *Christ in the Garden of Olives* (Norton
Gallery of Art, West Palm Beach). All three of these paintings belonged to
Sadler, who was also to buy Gore's picture. It may even be that Sadler gave
Gore an informal commission to celebrate the exhibition he inspired as well as
his purchases. Several of the 'connoisseurs' have been identified: Augustus
John is the bearded man in the left foreground; Wilson Steer is the ponderous
central figure, hatless with a stick on his arm; Neville is the diminutive figure
with his hand to his face. If Sadler is also there, he has not yet been
recognized.

Gore

22 The Beanfield, Letchworth   1912 [G.154a]

Oil on canvas; 30.5 × 40.6
Collection: Tate Gallery, London (1974)
EXHIBITIONS (EARLY): Carfax Gallery 1913 (26); (LATER ONE-MAN): Redfern
Gallery 1962 (58); Colchester 1970 (46); d'Offay 1974 (24)

During the summer of 1912, while Gilman was in Sweden, Gore borrowed his
house at 100 Wilbury Road, Letchworth, and produced more than twenty
paintings of the new garden city and its surrounding landscape. The
unparalleled vigour and originality of these paintings represent his response to
the stimulus of European Post-Impressionism as seen in several key exhibitions
recently staged in London, in particular 'Manet and the Post-Impressionists'
(1910–11), Gauguin and Cézanne at the Stafford Gallery (see pl.21) and,
perhaps most crucial to the Letchworth interlude, the Italian Futurist Painters
at the Sackville Gallery in March 1911. In addition a small number of works
by Kandinsky had been included in the annual Allied Artists exhibitions.

The Beanfield was painted from a spot near Wilbury Hills Road, about half a
mile from its junction with Wilbury Road. The chimneys in the distance are
those of a brickyard. A label by Gilman on the back of this picture states: 'The
colour found in natural objects (in the field of beans for instance in the
foreground), is collected into patterns. This was his own explanation.' This
explanation helps our understanding of all Gore's Letchworth pictures. In his
attempt to express the underlying structure of natural objects he not only
grouped the colours into uniform patterns, he also reduced the wayward
shapes of nature, trees, clouds and so on down to their basic geometrical
forms. The resultant stylization may appear exaggerated and conceptual, but it
sprang from intensely concentrated observation of the subject, not from
aesthetic formulae.

Gore

23 **The Icknield Way**   1912 [G.156]
Oil on canvas; 63.5 × 76.2
Collection: Art Gallery of New South Wales, Sydney (1962)
EXHIBITIONS (EARLY): Alpine Club Gallery, 1913, 'Grafton Group' (1);
(LATER ONE-MAN): AC 1955 (35); Redfern Gallery 1962 (61); (LATER
GROUP): Southampton 1951 (63)

The Icknield Way is the ancient track situated close to Wilbury Hills Road
near to the spot from which Gore painted *The Beanfield*. Gore used this
landscape feature, seen from above in plunging recession, to articulate his
composition both in space and on the picture surface. A similar compositional
structure underpins several other Letchworth paintings, notably the two
versions of *The Cinder Path* (Tate Gallery, London, and Ashmolean Museum,
Oxford), *The Road* (Letchworth Art Gallery) and *Letchworth Station* (National
Railway Museum, York). Quentin Bell (unpublished article 'The Camden
Town Group: Sickert among Friends and Heretics' (see the Select
bibliography)) considered *The Icknield Way* 'in which amidst a wide plain of
violent orange and purple fields, a jagged track of acid green plunges towards
the sunset jigsaw of rhomboidal clouds' to be a turning point in Gore's career:
'He had painted a picture which may fairly be termed Cubist or perhaps
Futurist, he had not known his own strength …'

   Gore undoubtedly saw the paintings by Boccioni, Carra, Russolo and
Severini on view in London at the Italian Futurist exhibition in March. This
experience may have been the catalyst which enabled him to identify and
express the dynamic energy of landscape in virtuoso juxtapositions of brilliant
colours assembled into simplified geometric shapes.

Gore

24 **The West Pier, Brighton**   1913 [G.178a]
   Oil on canvas; 63.5 × 76.3
   Studio stamp br
   Collection: Mellon Bank
   EXHIBITIONS (EARLY): possibly Doré 1913 (197); probably Brighton
   1913–14 (54); (LATER ONE-MAN): Leicester Galleries 1928 (78); Colchester
   1970 (59); (LATER GROUP): Lefevre 1950 (28); Southampton 1951 (70)

There are two views of Brighton Pier seen from the first-floor balcony of
Walter Taylor's house in Brunswick Square where Gore stayed for a week
during the summer of 1913 before moving from Camden Town to Richmond.
Both paintings show the same pier but this version is traditionally called *The
West Pier* – the title of the painting shown in the winter exhibition at Brighton
– whereas the version in Southampton City Art Gallery is traditionally known
as *Brighton Pier* – the title of the version shown two months earlier at the Doré
Galleries in October. The inclusion of a triangular section of garden in the
foreground accentuates the bold eccentricity of Gore's construction. His delight
in contemporary life is reflected in the richness of incident.

Sickert

25 Noctes Ambrosianae
1906
Oil on canvas, 63.5 × 76.2
Collection: Castle Museum,
Nottingham (1952)
EXHIBITIONS (EARLY): NEAC
summer 1906 (123); Paris,
Salon d'automne 1906
(1545); (LATER ONE-MAN
AND GROUP): see RA 1992,
no.54 for full list

A view of the gallery of the
Middlesex Music Hall (or
Mogul Tavern, as it was
affectionately known to its
familiars) where Sickert, in
1906, rediscovered music hall
audiences, particularly the eager
boys in the gods, as a subject
for painting. In this picture
Sickert experimented with the
expressive shorthand notation
used in his contemporary
paintings of the nude. Its very
dark tonality (Sickert himself
termed it 'black') is deceptive
in that it has been built up
from many layers of lively
colours, including a strong lilac.
Sickert considered the picture
to be one of his best works and
referred to it with great pride in
letters written to William
Rothenstein in 1906. In 1907
he recommended Nan Hudson
to go and see it hanging in
Walter Taylor's house: 'I
reflect, not without shame, that
it is one of, perhaps, not more
than half a dozen museum-
pieces that I have done in
twenty-seven years.'

Sickert

**26 Mornington Crescent
Nude** 1907
Oil on canvas; 50.8 × 40.6
Inscribed *Sickert* bl
Provenance: 1907, Hugh
Hammersley; Lord
Cottesloe; T. W. Strachan;
the Hon. William Wallace
Collection: Private
EXHIBITIONS (LATER ONE-
MAN): National Gallery
1941 (ex catalogue); Leeds
1942 (163); RBD 1951 (12);
AC Edinburgh 1953 (27);
RBD 1960 (20); AC 1960
(111); Brighton 1962 (32);
FAS 1973 (61); (LATER
GROUP): Yale 1980 (74);
Christie's 1988 (27)

One of three Mornington
Crescent interiors bought by
Hugh Hammersley as soon as
they were painted during the
summer of 1907 (the others
were pl.3 here and a *contre-jour*
nude now in the Art Gallery of
South Australia, Adelaide).
Drawings related to this tender
back view of a seated nude
were developed into a two-
figure man and woman group
which Sickert etched in 1908
and called *The Camden Town
Murder*.

Gore

27 Behind the Blind 1906
[G.34]
Oil on canvas; 50.8 × 40.6
Studio stamp br
Provenance: J. W. Freshfield;
by bequest to his niece
Miss M. Marr-Johnson
Last known whereabouts:
Christie's, 7 March 1986,
lot 220
EXHIBITIONS (EARLY):
Carfax Gallery 1916 (8);
(LATER GROUP): FAS 1976
(48); (LATER ONE-MAN):
Leicester Galleries 1928
(19); Colchester 1970 (4)

Painted in Sickert's first-floor
lodgings at 6 Mornington
Crescent. The setting was the
front room used by Sickert for
many of his paintings of nude
models sitting or lying on a bed
placed parallel to the picture
plane (see pl.26). The
compositional layout and the
furnishings of Gore's *Behind the
Blind* are identical to Sickert's
*Mornington Crescent: Contre-
Jour*, also of 1906 (Christie's, 5
November 1999, lot 222, rep.
in colour). In both a figure is
seated on the near side of the
bed. However, while Gore's
figure is lit from an artificial
source to show off her lilac
skirt and pretty yellow blouse,
Sickert's nude is darkly
silhouetted against the light
filtering through the slats of the
blind behind her which
highlights the summary shape
of a chamber pot beneath the
bed. Gore's touch is feathery;
Sickert's is cursory. These
differences are typical of how,
when he adopted intimate
Sickertian themes, Gore's
sensibility dictated a more
tender approach and a less
harsh treatment.

Gore

28 Some-one waits 1907
[G.65]
Oil on canvas; 51.2 × 41
Collection: City Museum
and Art Gallery, Plymouth
(1958)
EXHIBITIONS (EARLY): NEAC
spring 1908 (62); (LATER
ONE-MAN): AC 1955 (8);
d'Offay 1983 (5); (LATER
GROUP): Redfern 1939 (20);
AC 1953 (28); Plymouth
1974 (15); FAS 1976 (51);
Pontoise 1998–9 (78)

Painted at 15 Granby Street
where Gore lived and worked
until he moved round the
corner to 31 Mornington
Crescent in autumn 1909. The
stretcher label identifies the
little figure glimpsed outside in
the street as Sickert, and gives
the date as 1907. Sickert's
sequence of paintings showing
Little Rachel at the window of
his rooms at 6 Mornington

Crescent (see pl.3) also belong
to 1907. Both artists painted
their models framed by natural
light. The tonality of Sickert's
work is much darker but, like
Gore, he applied the paint in
small, broken touches. Sickert's
pictures are untidier and more
suggestive of mood and
atmosphere. Gore's approach is
more consistently Neo-
Impressionist. His neat
pointillism complements a
strong geometric structure and
a compelling decorative interest
conveyed not only in the linear
patterns but also in his use of
colour; the salmon pinks in the
background, for example, are
echoed in the flowers on the
hat. Gore's constructive,
decorative qualities, as well as
his execution, were probably
encouraged by Lucien
Pissarro's example (compare
this work with *The Turban*,
pl.42 here, of 1907).

25

26

28

27

Gore

29 Interior with Nude Washing 1907 [G.46]
Oil on canvas; 55.8 × 40.6
Collection: City Art Gallery,
Leeds (1932)
EXHIBITION (EARLY):
possibly Chenil Gallery
1911 (22) as *Woman
Washing*; (LATER ONE-MAN):
AC 1955 (9); Colchester
1970 (11); (LATER GROUP):
Southampton 1951 (56);
FAS 1976 (53)

The Gilman label (see the
'Catalogue of paintings in
public collections', below,
p.179) gives 1907 as the date of
this picture, one of the earliest
examples of Gore's intimate
studies of the nude. The
subject-matter was clearly
inspired by Sickert who insisted
that the nude should always be
represented in an appropriate
context. Following Sickert's
example, Gore has shown his
model doing something natural
to her nudity, and he has
provided typically Sickertian
incidental detail in the
washstand, ewer, basin and
chamber pot (see pl.32).
However, Gore's use of colour,
dominated by the brilliant green
of his background wallpaper,
gives this picture a mood of
gaiety totally at variance with
Sickert's renderings of shabby
bed-sitters in Camden Town.

Gore

**30 Morning: The Green
Dress** *c.*1908–9
Oil on canvas; 45.7 × 35.5
Collection: Fitzwilliam
Museum, Cambridge
(1955)
EXHIBITIONS (LATER ONE-
MAN): Leicester Galleries
1928 (7) as *The Green
Petticoat*; Colchester 1970
(17); (LATER GROUP):
Bedford 1969 (19); FAS
1976 (58)

Rutter probably bought this
picture directly from the artist
as it has no Gilman label (see
p.179, below) and no studio
stamp. He lent it to the 1928
exhibition and reproduced it in
his *Modern Masterpieces*
(published in parts in 1935 and
later as a whole (London:
George Newnes, 1940), p.198)
as *The Green Petticoat*. This
title, like the current
modification, is not entirely
appropriate because the model
wears a white petticoat and a
green skirt. The title *The Green
Dress* more properly describes a
smaller painting by Gore (now
in a private collection) of the
same model, by the same
mirror and window, executed in
the same technique, this time
wearing a green dress. A third
picture, entitled *The Mirror*
(formerly in Judge Evans's
collection, now in the Tatham
Art Gallery, Pietermaritzburg),
shows the model, seated and
seen half-length, in the same
setting with the light again
slanting in upon her face and
figure from the window behind.
All three of these paintings by
Gore suggest that he had
looked very closely at Sickert's
Mornington Crescent *contre-jour*
interiors of 1907, for example
the painting illustrated here as
plate 3. The springboard for
Gore's composition may well
have been Sickert's *Little Rachel
at a Mirror* of 1907, now also
in the Fitzwilliam Museum
collection, Cambridge.

Reproduced by permission of the
Syndics of the Fitzwilliam Museum,
Cambridge

Sickert

31 Sally – the Hat *c.*1909
Oil on canvas; 49.5 × 39.4
Inscribed *Sickert* bl
Provenance: Robin
Sanderson; Denys Sutton

29

31

138

Collection: Private
EXHIBITIONS (LATER ONE-
MAN): RBD 1960 (6); LATER
GROUP: probably Lefevre
1950 (50); FAS 1976 (142);
Yale 1980 (81)

The Impressionist-derived
handling developed in his
interiors of the summer of 1907
(see pls 3, 26) never became a
formula for Sickert. He merely
assimilated the use of thicker
paint, applied in broken
touches of lighter and brighter
colour, into his technical
repertoire. In this scintillating
study of a nude, he used the
broken coloured touches to
break down the contours of the
forms and suggest the
shimmering quality of the
natural light as it falls upon the
figure and her immediate
surroundings. The hat
mentioned in the title rests on
the back of the couch. It is
more legible in the preparatory
drawings where it rests on the
arm of the couch. In the
painting, but not in the known
drawings, a dress is thrown
across this arm. The artist has
thus given meaning to the
attitude of the nude: she is
reaching for her clothes.

30

Sickert

32 'What shall we do for the rent?' *c.*1908
Oil on canvas; 51.5×41
Collection: Kirkcaldy Museum and Art Gallery (1964)
EXHIBITIONS (EARLY): probably Paris, *Salon d'automne* 1909 (1582 or 1583) as *L'Affaire de Camden Town*; CTG 1 (10 or 12) as *The Camden Town Murder Series No. 1* or *No. 2*; (LATER ONE-MAN AND GROUP): see RA 1992, no.68 for full list

On 12 September 1907 Emily Dimmock, a blonde prostitute aged 22 known in the pubs and music halls of north London by her working name of Phyllis, was found naked in bed with her throat cut. Her body was discovered at their lodgings at 29 St Paul's Road, Camden Town, by Bertram Shaw, when he returned from his night-shift as a cook on a Midland Railway restaurant car. Robert Wood, a commercial artist, was accused of her murder. During the course of the trial, a vivid portrait of low-life in Camden Town emerged. The evidence against Wood was circumstantial and confused; a week before Christmas he was found not guilty.

With his flair for publicity, Sickert adopted the 'Camden Town Murder' title as an umbrella to encompass several independent series of etchings, paintings and drawings undertaken in 1908–9, each featuring a naked woman and a clothed man. The woman in the Kirkcaldy painting harks back to the *contre-jour* Mornington Crescent nudes of summer 1907. By adding the figure of a clothed man the psychological implications of the work are radically changed;

by focusing upon circumstantial details, such as the high-heeled shoes kicked off under the bed, the dramatic tension is heightened. These were evidently low-life subjects; only a prostitute could be shown naked and shameless together with a fully clothed working man who had not yet removed his cap.

Because the paintings with the *Murder* title have no illustrative relationship to the circumstances of Emily Dimmock's death, Sickert was

able to rename them at will, for example with titles suggestive of everyday domestic problems such as '*What shall we do for the rent?*'. The Kirkcaldy painting is one of a closely related pair of *contre-jour* studies, the other version of which was called *Summer Afternoon* when owned by Sickert's pupil and biographer, Robert Emmons. The critics in June 1911 understandably, if variously, interpreted the time of day as twilight or early morning, never a sunny

afternoon. If these two paintings are the pair exhibited in Paris in 1909, Sickert's earliest choice of title was *L'Affaire de Camden Town.*

All the critics devoted considerable space to Sickert's two pictures, treating them as a pair instead of individually. *The Sunday Times* (18 June 1911) wrote, 'The unclothed figure on the bed and the clothed figure of the man seated at the side afford a contrast which has interested painters for centuries, though Mr. Sickert has given a

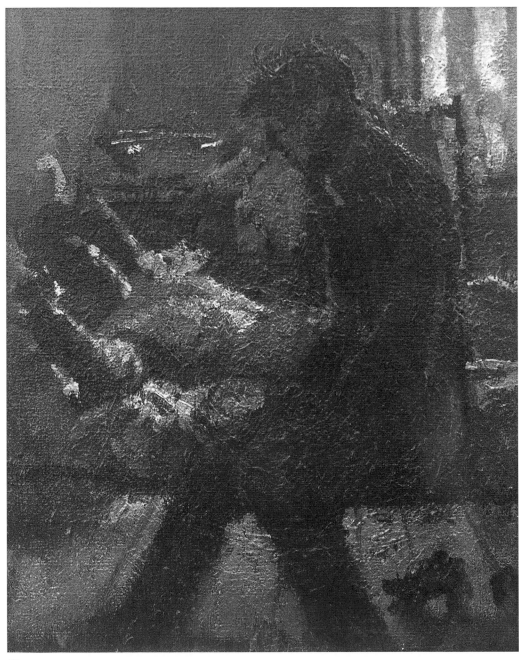

32

novel note to a favourite theme by viewing it in dim twilight through a quivering veil of atmosphere which gives just the sense of mystery and even of impending tragedy to justify the titles.' The *Daily Telegraph* (22 June 1911) noted, 'In both a sinister being sits quietly watching in the dim, struggling light of morning the nude figure of a woman stretched out on a miserable couch.' While most of the critics accepted Sickert's title as descriptive of his subject, dealing with what the *Observer* (18 June 1911) termed 'the utter depravity of a particularly unsavoury phase of life', they also recognized that Sickert's concern was not simply with illustration. The *Daily Telegraph* realized that he 'compasses something that the impressionists very rarely aim at, and still more rarely attain. He combines the dramatic with the merely visual impression.' *Art News* (15 July 1911) explained that 'as Rembrandt found a fine problem of colour in a butcher shop, so Mr. Sickert finds in the sordid surroundings of a tawdry tragedy a fascinating problem of colour, design and suggestion of form'. Desmond MacCarthy (*Eye Witness*, 6 July 1911) wrote:

Mr. Sickert's two studies of the Camden murder owe their impressiveness entirely to this emotional suggestiveness of light and shadow; the way the light from the window falls across the woman's body and under the bed, leaving the figure of the man in sinister obscurity, is aesthetically beautiful, but it is also most expressive. Mr. Sickert has been accused by critics of misusing his talents in painting such a subject. The objection is absurd. His treatment shows no vulgar sensationalism or love of horror, but an imaginative interest well worth sharing.

Sickert

33 **L'Affaire de Camden Town** 1909
Oil on canvas; 61 × 40.6
Inscribed *Sickert* br
Provenance: Paris, Hôtel Drouot, 20 June 1909 where bought by Paul Signac; Fred Uhlman; Sotheby's, 14 March 1973 (25)
Collection: Private
EXHIBITIONS (EARLY): Paris, Bernheim-Jeune 1909 (15); (LATER ONE-MAN AND GROUP): see RA 1992, no.70 for full list

This is the only painting on the Camden Town Murder theme to have no alternative title. However, even this version is not a recreation of the event as it happened (see the note to pl.32, above). Emily Dimmock's naked body was found, in September 1907, lying face downwards; she was blonde and her hair was in curling pins; it was assumed at the inquest, from lack of signs of resistance, that her throat had been cut while she slept: all facts at variance with Sickert's picture. Moreover, the compositional springboard for this disturbing work was a tender drawing of two women, one standing by a bed in much the attitude of the male figure in the painting, the other lying down and looking towards her; it is entitled *Conversation* (Royal College of Art; rep. Baron 1973, fig.189).

33

Pissarro

34 Great Western Railway, Acton 1907

Oil on canvas; 45.5 × 54.5
Collection: Government Art Collection (1964)
EXHIBITIONS (EARLY): NEAC 1908 (83) as *Acton Station GWR*; NEAC 1912 (70) as *Acton, GW Railway*; (LATER ONE-MAN): Leicester Galleries 1963 (6); (LATER GROUP): Southampton 1951 (101); AC 1953 (36); Christie's 1988 (37)

Railway subjects had been a favourite motif of the Impressionists in France. Lucien Pissarro's three railway landscapes of 1907–8 – the painting illustrated here; *Well Farm Bridge, Acton* of 1907 (Leeds Art Gallery; rep. Baron 1979, pl.100); and *Shunting at Acton* of 1908 (private collection; rep. Baron 1979, pl.30) – were directly inspired by his father's 1871 painting of the railway cutting outside Lordship Lane Station, Upper Norwood (Courtauld Institute of Art, London). The *Observer* (18 June 1911) commended Lucien's achievement in extracting 'real beauty from as unpromising a subject as a railway cutting'. However, Pissarro was probably attracted to railway subjects less from a Camden Town bias towards finding beauty in unexpectedly prosaic places than from his liking for the strong constructive elements afforded by their perspectives.

Photograph © Crown Copyright: UK Government Art Collection

Gore

35 Conversation Piece and Self-portrait c.1910

Oil on cardboard; 31.8 × 36.8
Inscribed *S.F.G.* br
Provenance: Mrs R. P. Bevan; R. A. Bevan
Collection: Private
EXHIBITIONS (EARLY): possibly NEAC winter 1910 (137) and Chenil Gallery 1911 (2) as *The Mantelpiece*; (LATER ONE-MAN): AC 1955 (22); Colchester 1970 (30); (LATER GROUP): Colchester 1961 (27) as *The Mantelpiece (with self portrait)*; Ware Gallery 1967 (93)

Mrs Robert Bevan (the painter Stanislawa de Karlowska) bought this painting directly from a viewing at 19 Fitzroy Street. Gore exploited the fact (usually disguised by artists) that he was painting himself reflected in a glass and deliberately emphasized the accidental nature of the image recorded. There are two subjects – one real, one reflected – but the spatial and the imaginative conceptions have been inverted. Part of the artist's head, seen large in the glass, is blotted out by the card stuck in the frame, while the other cards are used to frustrate comprehension of the space in which he is placed. The central subject and the 'real' image, an exceedingly life-like figure group, is in fact false, being made of china. Its small scale, encompassing full-length representations, provides a disturbing contrast to the large scale of the severed portrait head. The painting can be interpreted on different levels. It can be seen either as a demonstration of how the artist can create a painting from his observation of the most casual relationships, or as a sophisticated exercise in picture-making.

Gilman

36 The Blue Blouse: Portrait of Elèni Zompolides c.1910

Oil on canvas; 60.9 × 45.7
Collection: City Art Gallery, Leeds (1943)
EXHIBITIONS (EARLY): NEAC summer 1910 (257); (LATER ONE-MAN): Messrs Tooth 1934 (6); Reid & Lefevre 1943 (9); AC 1954–5 (13); Colchester 1969 (13); AC 1981–2 (16); (LATER GROUP): Redfern 1939 (58); Leicester 1940 (47); Bedford 1969 (12); FAS 1976 (27); Yale 1980 (28)

This is one of the earliest pictures to show Gilman using small, closely juxtaposed and interlocking touches of thick paint in full colour. The background, although not yet a spatial setting, is built up as densely as the figure and thus – in colour and texture – plays an active role. In his later portraits Gilman tended to place his figures within elaborated interiors which, with their patterned surfaces, became an integral part of his pictorial presentation.

In a letter to the *Times Literary Supplement* (16 April 1982) a descendant of the sitter outlined her life. She was an artist and a friend of Gilman. Born in London in 1882 of a Greek father and a Norwegian mother, she studied at the Royal College of Art and specialized in lettering and illumination. She married Charles Francis Townsend and died in Letchworth in 1958.

34

35

Drummond

37 Brompton Oratory

*c.*1910
Oil on canvas; 53.3 × 20.3
Collection: Arts Council
Collection, Hayward Gallery
(1964)
EXHIBITIONS (EARLY):
probably AAA 1910 (33) as
Interior. Oratory of St Philip;
CTG 3 (26) as *The Oratory,
London*; (LATER GROUP): AC
1953 (13); FAS 1976 (14);
(LATER ONE-MAN): AC
1963–4 (3)

Brompton Oratory is dedicated
to St Philip, hence the
assumption that this is the
painting exhibited at the AAA in
1910 and again with the
Camden Town Group in 1912.
 Drummond, the son of
Canon A. H. Drummond,
converted to Catholicism as a
schoolboy. During the 1920s he
received many commissions
from the Church, including
(1926) a set of fourteen
paintings of 'The Stations of
the Cross' for the Church of
the Holy Name at Birkenhead.

Ginner

38 A Corner in Chelsea

1910 [I, p.xv]
Oil on canvas; 96.5 × 134.5
Inscribed *CI Ginner* br
Provenance: 1914, Major
Brody; his son; Sotheby's,
25 May 1983 (92)
Collection: Private
EXHIBITIONS (EARLY): AAA
1910; Goupil Gallery 1914
(1); (LATER ONE-MAN): FAS
1985 (7)

This ambitious painting,
conclusively identified as the
painting exhibited at the AAA in
1910 by Frank Rutter's
description of it as an
atmospheric 'roofscape' (*Sunday
Times*, 17 July 1910), grew out
of little *pochade* sketches
(*Battersea Roofs* and *Whistler
Chimneys*, the latter rep.
Sotheby's, 13 May 1987, lot 97)
made by Ginner soon after his
arrival in England towards the
end of 1909. Ginner had settled
in Chelsea because both his
mother (who had married
Arthur Best following the death
in 1895 of her first husband)
and his sister (a distinguished
dancer) lived there. In 1911 he
moved to Chesterfield Street,
near King's Cross, an address
more convenient for Fitzroy
Street and Camden Town
Group meetings.

37

36

38

Drummond

39 Portrait of Charles Ginner 1911
Oil on fibreboard; 60.3 × 49
Collection: City Art Gallery,
Southampton (1956)
EXHIBITIONS (EARLY): CTG 2
(41); (LATER ONE-MAN): AC
1963–4 (4); (LATER GROUP):
Colchester 1961 (10); FAS
1976 (17); Yale 1980 (20);
Christie's 1988 (3);
Barbican 1997 (31)

One of the most striking images
of Camden Town portraiture,
showing Ginner (not long
arrived in England) looking
wickedly 'French'.

Drummond and Ginner
were in sympathy with each
other from the beginning of
their association. They both
liked strong colours, bold
patterns and emphatic
application of paint. The
handling as well as the
compositional presentation of
this portrait suggests that
Drummond reacted strongly to
the Van Gogh paintings on
view at the Grafton Gallery in
the winter of 1910–11. The
picture on the wall behind the
sitter, painted in thick strips of
gaudily coloured paint, also
refers indirectly to Van Gogh.
Painted in oil on board (31 × 23
cm), it has recently been
rediscovered (with the dealer
Ewan Mundy, 1998). Although
not listed in Ginner's notebooks
(see p.172, below), it is one of
his Van Gogh-inspired works of
around 1908–9, probably a
courtisane subject.

Ginner

40 Neuville Lane 1911
[I, p.xliii]
Oil on board; 28.6 × 17.8
Inscribed *C.GINNER* br
Provenance: Given by the
artist to Mrs Malcolm
Drummond; Sotheby's, 17
March 1976 (33); Christie's,
6 June 1991 (74); Christie's,
6 November 1992 (91)
Collection: Private
EXHIBITIONS (LATER GROUP):
FAS 1976 (45); Barbican
1997 (75)

This painting and *Victoria
Embankment Gardens* of 1912
(Tate Gallery, London)
represent Ginner's explicit
homage to Van Gogh, whose
work he had admired since his
student days in Paris. The
uninhibited verve of their
execution, the swirling forms,
the insistent physical quality of
the paint, the heavy outlines
which stress every convolution
of form, all recall Van Gogh's
late paintings of the garden at
Arles. *Neuville Lane* can be seen
in the background of
Drummond's *At the Piano*
(pl.10).

Photograph courtesy of Richard
Littlewood

Ginner

41 Wild Duck 1912
[I, p.xlvii]
Oil on canvas; 35.6 × 40.6
Inscribed *C GINNER* br
Provenance: 1912, Harold
Gilman
Collection: Private, on loan
to the Whitworth Art
Gallery, Manchester
EXHIBITIONS (EARLY):
Whitechapel 1914 (376);
(LATER GROUP): Lefevre
1950 (20)

Works by friends and
colleagues can often be
identified within Camden Town
Group paintings. Ginner's *Wild
Duck* can be seen hanging on
the wall behind Gilman's *Girl
with a Teacup* (pl.5) and to the
left of the fireplace in his
Maple Street *Interior* (pl.61).
The execution of this still life is
both intricate and opulent; the
surface seems to have been
woven in rich, rough silks. This
handling complements the
choice of subject-matter. The
dead ducks in their gaudy
plumage would be more at
home in seventeenth-century
Holland than in twentieth-
century Camden Town.

39

Pissarro

42 The Turban 1907
Oil on canvas; 44.5 × 36.9
Inscribed *LP07* br
Provenance: Gift from the
artist to J. B. Manson;
F. B. C. Bravington;
Sotheby's, 17 March 1976
(9)
Collection: Private
EXHIBITIONS (EARLY): NEAC
summer 1909 (222); CTG 2
(44); Carfax Gallery 1913
(4); Brighton 1913–14 (63);
(LATER GROUP): FAS 1976
(105)

A portrait of the artist's
daughter, the painter Orovida
Pissarro (1893–1968), aged
about 13. Lucien Pissarro's

experience as a designer of
woodcuts seems to have
influenced the delicate
colouring and the attractive
close-knit decorative patterning
which especially distinguish this
picture. Portraits were rare in
Pissarro's œuvre. Anne Thorold
(Thorold 1983, no.121) quotes
a letter written in 1913 by
Lucien to his wife Esther: 'is it
not funny that everybody is so
much taken by the 'Turban' –
in spite of what you think of it
– after all I perhaps will turn
out to be a figure painter!'
Manson (*Outlook*, 9 December
1911) declared, 'I would rather
possess ... "The Turban", than
any other picture I know.'

40

41

42

Ginner

43 The Café Royal 1911
[I, p.xxvii]
Oil on canvas; 63.5 × 48.3
Collection: Tate Gallery,
London (1939)
EXHIBITIONS (EARLY): AAA
1911(139); CTG 2 (29) as
The Café; Paris, *Salon des
Indépendants* 1912 (1334);
Goupil Gallery 1914 (22);
(LATER ONE-MAN): AC
1953–4 (2); (LATER GROUP):
Redfern 1939 (7)

The Café Royal, opened in
1865, was a favourite haunt of
artists during the early
twentieth century, including
members of the Camden Town
Group who would repair to its
dining-rooms and bars to
continue discussions initiated
earlier in the day at 19 Fitzroy
Street. The most remarkable
records of extensive aspects of
its exuberant interior were
painted between 1911 and
1916. Although the subject-
matter was uncharacteristic of
Ginner, whose relatively few
interiors with figures tended to
represent scenes of work (a
hospital ward, factories and so
on) rather than places of
entertainment, his picture
perhaps sparked off the fashion.
The interior by William Orpen
(Musée d'Art Moderne, Paris),
with its endless reflected vistas
of barley-sugar columns and
moulded ceiling decorations,
complete with easily
recognizable portraits of James
Pryde, Augustus John, George
Moore and William Nicholson,
was painted between 1911 and
1912 and exhibited at the New
English Art Club in the
summer of 1912. In 1912
Gilman painted two versions of
The Café Royal (both included
in his joint exhibition with Gore
at the Carfax Gallery in January
1913; one rep. Baron 1979,
pl.109). Like Ginner, Gilman
peopled his interior with figures
rather than portraits. However,
the character, conception and
planning of his composition,
and even his handling, are
much closer to Orpen's. Later
paintings include William
Strang's eccentric tableau of
1913 and Adrian Allinson's

masterpiece of 1915–16 (now
property of the Café Royal).

Photograph © Tate Gallery,
London 1998

Bayes

44 The Open Door c.1911
Oil on canvas; 69 × 59
Collection: Johannesburg
Art Gallery (1913)
EXHIBITIONS (EARLY): CTG 3
as *Le Petit Casino*

Nearly all the many paintings
produced by Bayes on his
summer holidays feature his
wife Kitty. The original title of
this painting is an example of
his penchant for esoteric titles:
the meaning of 'casino' as a
little summer house had all but
disappeared by the twentieth
century. Proof that it is the
work exhibited in 1912 rests in
a letter of 19 June 1913 from
Sylvia Gosse to Robert Ross
about her gift (Johannesburg
Art Gallery archives) in which
she named it 'le petit Casino'
adding, 'I hope you will like it
as much as I miss it from my
bed-head.' Sylvia Gosse's gift to
Johannesburg in 1913 also
included *The Reapers* by
Gilman, *The Alhambra
Promenade* by Gore and *The
Pork Pie Hat* by Sickert.

Grant

45 Tulips 1911
Oil on panel; 52 × 49
Inscribed *D. Grant 1911* bl
Provenance: 1911, Sir
Edward Marsh, by whom
bequeathed to the
Contemporary Art Society,
by whom allocated
Collection: City Art Gallery,
Southampton (1954)
EXHIBITIONS (EARLY): CTG 2
(53); Whitechapel 1914
(365); (LATER GROUP):
Southampton 1951 (75);
Plymouth 1974 (18); FAS
1976 (71)

This is the only painting Grant
exhibited with the Camden
Town Group, of which he was
little more than a nominal
member. Edward Marsh bought
the picture from the exhibition,
an event of considerable
historical importance. Marsh,
henceforth one of the most

enlightened patrons of
contemporary British artists,
acknowledged that the change
of heart which converted him
from Ancient to Modern
collecting occurred with its
purchase (*A Number of People:
A Book of Reminiscences*
(London: Heinemann, 1939),
p.355). Marsh already owned
paintings by traditional living
artists, including examples by
Neville Lytton who had guided
his early activity as a collector.
As we know from Lytton's
letter to Marsh, *Tulips* was not
his only acquisition from the
exhibition; he also bought *The
Bridge* by Walter Bayes (see
p.159, below). However,
Grant's painting was more
progressive in style than
anything Marsh had previously
owned. Lytton was outraged: 'I
really must protest against the
Tulips. It is a disgraceful

picture. It has neither colour,
drawing, nor composition. Its
technique is atrocious and it is
incompetent beyond measure
… I repeat the Tulips are a
disgrace. I quite understand that
you should give the classic a
rest and buy samples of
romantic artists, but this is not
art at all.' The press was less
discouraging. Sir Claude
Phillips (*Daily Telegraph*, 14
December 1911) thought the
flower-piece was 'beautifully
done, somewhat after the
fashion of Manet, the only
jarring note being the purple
figured cloth on which the vase
of flowers rests'. Marsh himself
was sufficiently proud of his
purchase to lend it to the
Whitechapel exhibition in 1914,
and Lytton ceased to be his
artistic mentor.

© 1978 Estate of Duncan Grant

43

44

46

45

Innes

46 Arenig 1911
Oil on canvas; 36 × 51
Collection: National Gallery
of Canada, Ottawa (Gift of
the Massey Collection of
English Painting, 1946)

Mount Arenig was, for Innes,
the consummation of his
passionate vision of nature. In
1911 he and Augustus John
shared a cottage, overlooked by
the mountain, by a brook called
Nant-Ddu. Innes painted the
mountain in all its moods, in
every light. Arenig became for
him the personification of
Euphemia Lamb, his greatest
love, whose letters he is said to
have buried in a silver casket
on its summit. It is impossible
to say which was the picture of
Arenig exhibited by Innes with
the Camden Town Group.
While the Ottawa painting is a
work of 1911 – rather than one
of the many later pictures of
the same subject – it is
probably not the exhibited
Arenig because Sir Claude
Phillips (*Daily Telegraph*, 14
December 1911) would surely
have noted its low cloud effect
when he described Innes's
painting as 'a beautiful study of
hill and valley, wrapped in the
shadow of deepening evening,
yet still rich in colour'. This
description suggests that the
Arenig at the Carfax Gallery
was closer in its mood to *Sunset
in the Mountains* (private
collection; rep. in colour
Southampton 1977, no.78).

John

47 The Red Feather *c.*1911
Oil on board; 40.2 × 32.4
Inscribed *John* bl
Collection: Ulster Museum,
Belfast (1929)

The model is Dorelia McNeill,
wearing the same hat as in the
picture of the same title
reproduced in Easton and
Holroyd 1974 as plate 53. The
background appears to be
North Wales, where Dorelia
accompanied John in May 1911
(shortly to return without him).
In 1911, inspired by John,
Henry Lamb (for example
Portrait of Edie McNeill – sister
of Dorelia – standing on a cliff
in Brittany, Southampton City
Art Gallery) and Innes (for
example *Girl Standing by a
Lake*, National Museum of
Wales, Cardiff) also painted
romantic girls in poetic
landscapes. The figures,
especially in the work of John
and Innes who often painted
together in Wales, do not so
much inhabit the landscape as
grow out of it, immobile forms
improbably perched in wild and
desolate settings.

Lamb

48 Brittany Peasant Boy
1910
Oil on panel; 35.5 × 25.4
Inscribed *Lamb 1910* bl
Provenance: R. F. Shaw-
Kennedy
Collection: Private
EXHIBITIONS (EARLY): CTG I
(21); (LATER ONE-MAN):
Manchester 1984 (15);
(LATER GROUP): FAS 1976
(86)

This is one of two related
Breton paintings of 1910.
Breton Cowherd was shown at
the NEAC in the winter of 1910,
Brittany Peasant Boy at the
Carfax Gallery in 1911 (a
contemporary catalogue
annotation described the figure
as leaning against a tree). John's
example encouraged the early
development of Lamb's feeling
for pure line and flat colour; it
perhaps also inspired him to
seek ideal beauty and simplicity
in the people and landscape of
rural France. Lamb was the
more conscious artist in his
manipulation of the structure of

his compositions to express the
mood of his subjects, whether
the lyricism of this picture or
the overpowering tragedy of
peasant bereavement illustrated
in *Mort d'une Paysanne*
(Museum of New Zealand,
Wellington), exhibited at the
NEAC in the summer of 1911 (a
version is in the Tate Gallery,
London). Both John and Lamb
drew inspiration from Puvis de
Chavannes. However, Lamb's
response to the art of Puvis
was, on the whole, less
romantic and more analytical
than John's.

Lamb

**49 Portrait of Edie McNeill:
Purple and Gold** *c.*1910
Oil on canvas; 61 × 50.8
Provenance: Judge William
Evans; Wilfrid A. Evill;
Lord Ilford
Collection: A. R. B. Burrows
EXHIBITIONS (EARLY): NEAC
winter 1910 (77) and
probably CTG 2 (5) as
Portrait; Goupil Gallery
1918, 'The Collection of the
late Judge William Evans'
(91) as *Lady, with red
background*; (LATER ONE-
MAN): Leicester Galleries
1961 (41) as *Mrs
McNamara*; (LATER GROUP):
FAS 1976 (87)

Edie McNeill (later Mrs
McNamara), sister of John's
Dorelia (see pl.47), modelled
for Lamb in 1910 and 1911.
The description in the
Manchester Guardian (22
November 1910) – a 'girl in a
mole-coloured dress, which
does not need its strong
crimson background' – strongly
suggests that *Purple and Gold* is
the *Portrait* exhibited at the
NEAC in 1910. During the
summer of 1911 Lamb painted
further portraits of Edie
McNeill, two of her standing
on the cliffs at Douélan in
Brittany (Southampton City Art
Gallery and a smaller study in a
private collection; rep. Baron
1979, pl.70). He exhibited the
Southampton painting at the
NEAC in the winter of 1911 and
a half-length portrait at the
second Camden Town Group
show which was much admired.
The *Daily Telegraph* (14
December 1911) described it as
'an admirably firm and well-

47

48

49

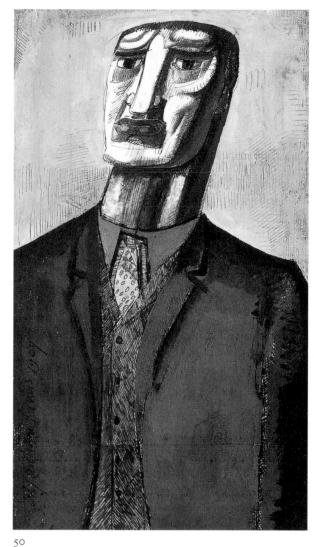

50

characterized study of the same *farouche*, resentful young model who appears in Mr. Lamb's picture at the New English Art Club'. The *Evening Standard and St James's Gazette* (6 December 1911) declared, 'The honours of the exhibition go to Mr. Henry Lamb for his "Portrait" (5) … this head and shoulders of a girl in red has the strange dignity and beauty that come of painting what is felt rather than seen.' This portrait may have been *Purple and Gold*, in which the dominant impression created by the rich ruby red of the background may have caused a false recollection of the colour of the model's dress, or it may have been another portrait altogether, perhaps the half-length he had painted during the summer in Douélan.

Lewis

50 **Architect with Green Tie**
1909
Pen, ink and gouache;
24.1 × 13.3
Inscribed *Wyndham Lewis 1909* bl
Provenance: John Quinn, New York; 1927, his sale where bought by Richard Wyndham
Collection: Private
EXHIBITIONS (EARLY): probably CTG 1 (7 or 8); (LATER ONE-MAN): Tate Gallery 1956 (4); (LATER GROUP): AC 1974 (3); FAS 1976 (91)

The reaction of the *Morning Post* to Lewis's exhibits at the first Camden Town Group show is quoted in the text (see pp.47–8). The *Sunday Times* (18 June 1911) thought that 'A few visitors may be shocked at the elongated noses in the squarely-drawn heads by Mr. Wyndham Lewis … but with the exception of these two pen drawings I can not recall any exhibit which could justly be described as "queer".' The *Observer* (18 June) took more exception to Lewis's 'pen-drawings … executed in an amateurish, laboured method of crosshatching, which is painfully at variance with the artist's grotesque affectation of archaism.' The green gouache used to pick out the tie (colour was not mentioned by the critics) was probably superimposed on the pen hatching at a later date. Lewis frequently altered his work years afterwards and sometimes also altered the dates inscribed. If *Architect with Green Tie* is one of the drawings shown at the Camden Town Group exhibition, it is possible that the other was *Anthony* (Victoria and Albert Museum; rep. Michel 1971, pl.2), a drawing of the same date and probably the same sitter.

Estate of Mrs G. A. Wyndham Lewis. By permission

Lightfoot

51 Mother and Child c.1911
Oil on canvas; tondo,
diameter 58.8
Provenance: Arthur Clifton
Collection: Private
EXHIBITIONS (EARLY): CTG 1
(17); Whitechapel 1914
(352); (LATER ONE-MAN):
WAG 1972 (56); LATER
GROUP: Leicester Galleries
1930 (44); FAS 1976 (97);
Christie's 1988 (88)

Lightfoot was 24 when he
painted *Mother and Child*. Only
one later painting is known,
another *Mother and Child*
(private collection) which, when
exhibited in Belgium in 1921,
was acclaimed as a masterpiece
and bought by the president of
the Beaux-Arts de Liège.
Lightfoot's powerful sense of
design, the exquisite precision
of his drawing, his ability to
render the most subtle nuances
of tone, were precocious gifts.
He seems to have been out of
step with his contemporaries,
although many admired his
work deeply. Both of his
Camden Town Group
paintings, *Frank* and *Mother
and Child*, were included in two
Contemporary Art Society
exhibitions (although not
acquired by the CAS), one in
Manchester in 1911 and the
other at the Goupil Gallery,
London, in 1913. Roger Fry
picked out the tondo in his
catalogue preface to the
Manchester show: '*Mother and
Child* is more than a tentative
effort of a young artist; it is
already a definitive achievement
and serves to show how great a
loss to art his early death has
inflicted.' The mother and child
theme obsessed Lightfoot in
1911. While there may be
symbolist elements in his work,
his art was a passionate
response to nature, perceived
through the emotions as well as
through the eye.

Turner

52 The Joy Wheel, Mitcham
1912
Watercolour and charcoal;
28 × 38.1
Inscribed *J Doman Turner /
The Joy Wheel, Mitcham
7.4.12* br
Provenance: James
Robertson
Collection: City Art Gallery,
Southampton (1996)

The little that is known of
Turner's life is due to the
research of James Robertson
('Spencer Gore & his Circle
with special focus on John
Doman Turner', catalogue of
exhibition at Piano Nobile,
Richmond, 1996, pp.33–40).
Turner lived in Streatham all
his adult life. In 1912 he moved
from 120 Barcombe Avenue,
Streatham Hill, to 63 Downton
Avenue, Streatham. He married
in 1893; he died from
pneumonia in 1938. His work
as a stockbroker's clerk, his
deafness and his unusual
training as an artist through a
sequence of letters from Gore
offering constructive criticism
on the drawings Turner sent to
him, all suggest he was an
amateur. So he was in the
literal sense, but the quality of
his work and his dedication
were professional. It is likely
that his extant drawings of
Ilfracombe, Tenby,
Walberswick, Eastbourne and
Folkestone reflect holidays in
these seaside towns. In London
he studied theatre and music
hall subjects and found
Mitcham – close by Streatham
– with its common and fair on
the green, another fruitful
source of contemporary
subject-matter.

Ratcliffe

53 Clarence Gardens 1912
Oil on canvas; 50.8 × 76.2
Collection: Tate Gallery,
London (1982)
EXHIBITIONS (EARLY): AAA
1912 (187 or 188); CTG 3
(42); Whitechapel 1914
(20); (LATER GROUP):
d'Offay 1979 (29)

Clarence Gardens, the
residential development which
very soon replaced the original
Clarence Market, was painted

51

52

by both Gilman and Ratcliffe in
about 1912. The site is now
occupied by a housing estate.
Ratcliffe exhibited two pictures
of Clarence Gardens at the AAA
in 1912, one (187) priced at 12
guineas and the other (188) at
10 guineas. The latter is
probably the smaller painting
(private collection; rep. FAS
1976, p.10) of the south-east
corner of the square. The larger
painting looks west over the

gardens situated on either side
of Osnaburgh Street.
Commenting on Ratcliffe's
London views, the *Daily
Telegraph* (17 December 1912)
observed: 'Out of two in
themselves fairly prosaic scenes
... Mr. W. Ratcliffe has without
offending against the modesty
of truth, extracted elements of
beauty.'

Photograph © Tate Gallery,
London

53

54

Ginner

54 Piccadilly Circus 1912
[1, p.lxi]
Oil on canvas laid down on
board; 81.3 × 66
Collection: Tate Gallery,
London (1980)
EXHIBITIONS (EARLY): CTG 3
(24); Brighton 1913–14
(35); Goupil Gallery 1914
(19); (LATER GROUP):
d'Offay 1979 (13)

In 1912 Ginner went right into
the heart of London to study
Leicester Square (Brighton
Museum and Art Gallery) and
Piccadilly Circus. He had
executed a poster entitled
Piccadilly Circus for Madame
Strindberg's 'Cave of the
Golden Calf', but whether or
not it was related
compositionally to the painting
is unknown. The extraordinary
concentration of this picture
suggests it might have evolved
from fuller studies, that Ginner
ruthlessly pared away
inessential extensions until he
arrived at his vortical solution.
All sorts of meanings may be
read into the picture. The
market woman left over from
an older age about to be
obliterated by the motorized
machinery of the new could be
seen as a social comment. But
Ginner was an observer rather
than a philosopher and the
power of his picture springs
from his acute eye for detail
and his genius for design. The
Pall Mall Gazette (12
December 1912) judged that
'"Piccadilly Circus", both in its
crude tones and jumbled
composition, happily suggests
the noise and confusion of that
busy thoroughfare.' Other
critics were less pleased with its
effects.

Photograph © Tate Gallery,
London

Gore

55 The Nursery Window, Rowlandson House 1911
[G.136]
Oil on canvas; 40.6 × 50.8
Studio stamp br
Provenance: The artist's family
Collection: Private
EXHIBITIONS (EARLY): CTG 3 (15) as *Euston from the Nursery*; (LATER ONE-MAN): Redfern Gallery 1962 (52); d'Offay 1974 (13); (LATER GROUP): d'Offay 1979 (22)

Gore used the iron bars protecting the window of the nursery as an effective grid to pull his whole design together on the surface and to give interest to the rather amorphous foreground and middle-distance view across the railway tracks at the back of Rowlandson House. This device was not appreciated by the critic of *Queen* (14 December 1912) who accused the artist of being 'more concerned with the bars of the nursery window than with the light and life outside', but this description serves to identify the picture illustrated here as the exhibited painting.

Gore evidently found the approach to Euston of absorbing interest at this period. *Nearing Euston Station* is in the Keynes Collection, King's College Cambridge (on loan to the Fitzwilliam Museum), Cambridge, and a smaller sketch of the view across the railway lines was included in a sale at Sotheby's on 8 November 1989, lot 64.

Pissarro

56 Stamford Brook Green: Sun and Snow 1909
Oil on canvas; 43.8 × 53.3
Collection: Israel Museum, Jerusalem (1981)
EXHIBITIONS (EARLY): NEAC summer 1909 (85); CTG 3 (11)

Pissarro, who lived in Stamford Brook, produced four paintings of Stamford Brook Green under snow, two in 1909 and two in 1927. Both the 1909 paintings, *Snow and Mist* and *Sun and Snow*, were shown at the NEAC in that year. *Snow and Mist*, the bigger painting, was re-exhibited at the Carfax

Gallery in May 1913 (17) where its 120 guineas price-tag was higher than any other picture. Although the atmospheric subtitle of the version of *Stamford Brook Green* at the Camden Town Group show was simply *Snow*, the *Daily Telegraph* (17 December 1912) description of the effect as 'delicately flushed with the rose of sunset', proves that *Sun and Snow* was the painting exhibited. The press all liked this picture better than Pissarro's other contributions. Monet's influence was duly noted. The one quibble was that as a piece of convincing Impressionism the picture suffered from too great an objectivity in front of nature: 'the artist lurks, impassive and effaced, behind his subject, disdainful apparently of anything approaching poetic interpretation' (*Daily Telegraph*, also 17 December 1912).

Gilman

57 Lake Landscape: Kyrksjön, Gladhammer, Sweden 1912
Oil on canvas; 50.8 × 89
Inscribed *H. Gilman* br
Provenance: R. A. Bevan
Collection: Private
EXHIBITIONS (EARLY): CTG 3 (17) and Carfax Gallery 1913 (29) as *Kyrksjön, Gladhammer, Sweden*; (LATER ONE-MAN): (as *Swedish Landscape*) Reid & Lefevre Gallery 1943 (16); Lefevre Gallery 1948 (17); AC 1954–5 (19); Reid 1964 (14); Colchester 1969 (22); AC 1981–2 (38); (LATER GROUP): Lefevre 1950 (11)

The layout plan of the joint Gilman and Gore exhibition at the Carfax Gallery in 1913 (see fig.5, p.57) identifies no.29 as 'Lake' and reveals that it was a relatively big painting of pronounced horizontal format. It was hung centrally on the wall facing the door. Although there are other Swedish lake landscapes, none has the stretched format defined in the 1913 layout sketch.

Gilman's visit to Sweden in 1912 was productive. Three of his four paintings at the Camden Town Group show in December were Swedish subjects; these three and

55

56

another four were shown at the Carfax Gallery in January 1913. They show the town and the landscape around Gladhammer, Sweden. They are not consistent in style and handling but range from the experimental strong drawing and coloured hatching of *The Reapers* to the flat and

simplified representation of *Swedish Village* (National Gallery of Canada, Ottawa). In his pure landscape subjects, Gilman's sure sense of tonal values helped him to capture and give structure to the open expanses of wood, water and land stretching to a distant horizon.

57

58

Bevan

58 The Town Field, Horsgate
1914
Oil on canvas; 50.8 × 61
Collection: Museum of
Reading (1975)

Painted during the late summer
of 1914, the last time that
Bevan painted the fields around
his father's house, Horsgate, in
Cuckfield, Sussex. Another
view of this field, of the same
date but from a different
viewpoint, is in a private
collection (rep. Bevan 1965,
pl.44). Other views of the
Horsgate fields include *Fields at
Cuckfield* of 1909–10 (exhibited
with the Camden Town Group
in June 1911 as *In Sussex*; rep.
Bevan 1965, pl.32) and *The
Front Field, Horsgate* of 1911
(rep. Bevan 1965, pl.39).
Whereas the earlier Sussex
landscapes are painted in
shimmering broken colour, the
two paintings of 1914 are built
up in angular slabs of colour
articulated by schematic
drawing to convey a strong
sense of the underlying
structure and design.

Bevan

59 Under the Hammer
c.1913–14
Oil on canvas; 63.7 × 91.7
Collection: Walker Art
Gallery, Liverpool (1933)
EXHIBITIONS (EARLY): LG
1914 (89); probably
Whitechapel 1914 (404);
probably CMG 1915 (47);
(LATER ONE-MAN): AC 1956
(23)

Bevan painted the horse sales at
Aldridge's in Upper St Martin's
Lane, Wards Repository in
Edgware Road, Barbican in
Aldersgate in the City and
Tattersall's in Knightsbridge
Green. Each auction site had its
own character, with Tattersall's
– where carriage horses and
hunters were sold – at the
upper end of the market. The
site of *Under the Hammer* is not
specified, but the window
design as well as the inclusion
of a woman and a well-turned-
out child among the bidders
suggest it represents
Tattersall's. Two smaller and
less elaborate versions of the
subject are in private
collections.

Under the Hammer, with its
characteristic frieze of figures,
demonstrates how Bevan
expressed the strengthened
overall design of his paintings
through the pattern of
contrasting simplified areas of
colour held together by a fine
sense of tone.

Reproduced by permission of the
National Museums and Galleries on
Merseyside, Walker Art Gallery

Drummond

60 Still Life with Coffee Pot
c.1914
Oil on canvasboard;
49.9 × 38.8
Inscribed *Drummond* br
Provenance: Mrs Margaret
Drummond; Paintings in
Hospitals Collection;
Sotheby's, 9 November
1988 (50)
Collection: Private,
Adelaide, South Australia
EXHIBITIONS (LATER ONE-
MAN): AC 1963–4 (16);
(LATER GROUP): Adelaide
1997 (8)

Returning to the French
tradition exemplified by
Chardin and Manet, domestic
still-life paintings were a
speciality of several Camden
Town Group painters.
Drummond, Ratcliffe, Ginner
and Gilman in particular
perfected the depiction of
everyday objects seen in close
focus. In this example,
Drummond has painted the
components of a breakfast table
– metal espresso coffee pot,
milk jug with its silver lid, two
boiled eggs and a cup and
saucer – with such intensity
that they evoke the smell and
taste of the meal ahead.

Gilman

61 Interior c.1914–15
Oil on canvas; 42.5 × 27.5
Inscribed *H Gilman* br
Provenance: 1916, bought
by T. E. Hulme; David
Auchterlonie; Sotheby's, 27
June 1979 (47)
Collection: Private
EXHIBITIONS (LATER ONE-
MAN): AC 1981–2 (54);
(LATER GROUP): Christie's
1988 (175)

The setting of his rooms at 47
Maple Street inspired Gilman
to paint a sequence of interiors,
some with figures (in particular,
from 1916–17, his landlady,
Mrs Mounter) and a few
without. In the latter, of which
this is a prime example, a
human presence is felt to be
nearby. In *The Washstand* (Art
Gallery of South Australia,
Adelaide) the bucket and ewer
on the floor, the damp towels
on the wall, imply that early-
morning ablutions have only
just finished. In the painting
illustrated here, the free-
standing empty chair pushed
askew in the foreground and
the open door through which
light floods suggest that
someone has popped into the
adjoining room for a moment.
The chair, with its rush seat, is
perhaps a gesture of homage
towards Van Gogh.

59

60

61

62

Gilman
62 **Still Life: Cup and Saucer**
c.1914–15
Oil on canvas; 29×27
Inscribed *H Gilman* br
Provenance: Douglas Fox-
Pitt; Sotheby's 10 June 1981
(104)
Collection: Ivor Braka
Limited, London
EXHIBITIONS (LATER ONE-
MAN): AC 1981–2 (65);
(LATER GROUP): Christie's
1988 (174)

Plain white teacups and saucers
and plain dark round teapots
not only featured in many of
Gilman's figure paintings of
1914 onwards (see also pl.5),
they also stood alone to
compose simple yet joyous still-
life paintings. In this example
the cup and saucer occupy the
foreground and a pair of Indian
figurines the background.
Indian Figurines was the title of
a small painting exhibited by
Gilman in his joint exhibition
with Gore at the Carfax Gallery
in 1913 (41) but this painting,
in which they are accompanied
by a cup and saucer, cannot be
dated earlier than 1914 and
should probably be placed in
1915.

Douglas Fox-Pitt, who lived
in Brighton, was a member of
the Fitzroy Street Group and
elected to the London Group in
January 1914. A watercolourist
and man of means, he collected
work by his colleagues, in
particular by Gilman and
Ginner. Gilman painted his
portrait in 1915 (rep. Christie's,
11 November 1988, lot 314).

Gore

63 Richmond, Winter 1914
[probably G.205]
Oil on canvas; 50.8 × 60.9
Collection: City Art
Galleries, Manchester
(1928)
EXHIBITIONS (LATER ONE-
MAN): AC 1955 (46); (LATER
GROUP): Southampton 1951
(66); Christie's 1988 (162);
Richmond 1996–7

In October 1913 Gore moved
to 6 Cambrian Road,
Richmond. In the final five
months of his life he painted
fourteen or more views of the
trees in Richmond Park. His
resolve to study the park during
bleak March weather led to his
fatal pneumonia. This painting
of water-filled hollows between
the trees is one of his last.
When compared with the
sequence of pure landscape
paintings done in Letchworth in
1912, those in the the
Richmond Park series seem at
first almost insipid. However,
the lack of extravagance
conceals an approach no less
remarkable. Although executed
within a narrow time-frame and
restricted in subject, each
painting is different in
construction and handling.
Quentin Bell (unpublished
article, see note to pl.23, above)
wrote, 'In the Richmond
landscapes there is a return of
tenderness and of atmosphere
and a deeper understanding of
Cézanne, he seems to be
discovering his true self, an
artist neither oversweet nor over
violent, but astonishingly
poetical.'

Photograph © Manchester City Art
Galleries

Gore

64 Blue and Green Bottles and Oranges 1914
[G.211a]
Oil on canvas; 50.8 × 40.6
Collection: New Haven,
Yale Center for British Art,
Paul Mellon Collection
(1993)

The final number – 213 – in
the list of paintings compiled
by Gilman and Mrs Gore after
her husband's death from
pneumonia on 27 March 1914
was but two removed from this
still life. Sickert, telling Ethel
Sands and Nan Hudson of his
last visit to see his friend,
wrote, 'In his delirium it was
paintings and effects. The
bottles were still lifes and then
crowds.'

63

64

Catalogue of paintings in public collections by members of the Camden Town Group

The following is a guide to the locations of oil paintings executed by members of the Camden Town Group that are currently in public ownership throughout the world. It incorporates a summary of the career of each artist (with emphasis on the period up to 1914) and a discussion of the works they showed at the three exhibitions of the Camden Town Group.

For Henry Lamb, Wyndham Lewis, Lucien Pissarro and Walter Sickert, the catalogue includes coverage only of paintings executed between 1906 and 1914, years I regard as the critical period of Camden Town painting. The careers of these artists continued long after the demise of the group, and their work has been much studied and written about elsewhere. On the other hand, I have set aside this time-frame for those Camden Town Group painters whose work has not been extensively written about: Walter Bayes, Robert Bevan, Malcolm Drummond, Harold Gilman, Charles Ginner, Spencer Gore, J. D. Innes, M. G. Lightfoot, J. B. Manson and William Ratcliffe. All their paintings in public collections known to me are included here. The early deaths of three of these artists – Gore, Innes and Lightfoot – in any case forced their productive years to fall within the critical period. Paintings done between 1906 and 1914 by Duncan Grant and Augustus John, who were only marginal members of Camden Town, are listed, but by title only. One member of the group, John Doman Turner, did not paint in oil; I have therefore discussed his contributions to the Camden Town Group exhibitions but not catalogued his work.

The individual sections of this catalogue include a brief outline of the career of each artist, a list of one-man exhibitions, the principal address/es at which he lived during the period 1906–14 and reference to publications (in chronological order) devoted to his life and work. (See also the Select bibliography for works covering more than one of the artists.) The works each artist contributed to the three exhibitions of the Camden Town Group are listed. Those illustrated in this book are more fully discussed in the plate notes; those not illustrated here are discussed in the relevant sections of this catalogue where contemporary press reviews are used to help to identify them.

The general catalogue conventions I have used are as follows:

Sizes	In centimetres, height stated first.
Inscriptions	In italics, locations abbreviated (see the lists of abbreviations, p.9).
Exhibitions	I have listed a selection of one-man and group exhibitions up to 1919 (in London unless otherwise stated). The one-man exhibitions selected are those listed in the biographical section for each artist. The abbreviations for group exhibitions are explained in the 'Exhibitions' section of the lists of abbreviations (pp.9–12).
Provenance	Sale rooms and commercial dealers are in London unless otherwise stated.
Accession numbers	Cited when known to me in square brackets after the accession date.
References	Monographs to which reproduction and/or literary references are made are identified in the notes at the head of the catalogue of works in public collections for each artist. In addition, references will be found to Baron 1979, Watney 1980, Yale 1980, Christie's 1988, Barbican 1997, Adelaide 1997 and Pontoise 1998–9 (see the lists of abbreviations, pp.9–12).

Plate numbers after the titles of works refer to reproductions in this book.

Walter John Bayes
1869–1956

Born in London, son of painter and etcher A. W. Bayes and brother of sculptor Gilbert Bayes. Studied art at evening classes in Finsbury 1886–1900 and briefly full-time at the Westminster School of Art under Frederick Brown c.1902. Exhibited watercolours and oils at the RA from 1890. Married Katherine Teller in 1904. Wrote art criticism for the *Outlook* (late 1890s), the *Athenaeum* (1906–16) and later for the *Saturday Review* and the *Week End Review*. Founder-member AAA (1908), the Camden Town Group (1911) and the London Group (1913), resigning from the last–named in 1915. Member of the Fitzroy Street Group (perhaps from 1908) and the Royal Watercolour Society. Held many teaching posts, was headmaster of the Westminster School of Art 1918–34 and director of painting at the Lancaster School of Arts and Crafts 1944–9. Especial interest in decorative and mural painting. Painted scenery and designed costumes for the 1911 production of Lord Dunsany's play *The Gods of the Mountain*. Author of *The Art of Decorative Painting* (1927). Also wrote *Turner, a Speculative Portrait* (1931) and an autobiographical sketch of a painting trip abroad, *A Painter's Baggage* (1932).

EXHIBITIONS WITHIN HIS LIFETIME

Chenil Gallery 1911; Carfax Gallery 1913; Carfax Gallery 1915; Leicester Galleries 1918; Leicester Galleries 1919; Goupil Gallery 1928; Goupil Gallery 1931; Fine Art Society 1932; Salford Art Gallery 1948; Leicester Galleries 1951.

EXHIBITIONS SINCE HIS DEATH

Parkin Gallery 1978. No loan exhibitions.

LITERATURE

There is no literature specifically on Bayes except Sickert's catalogue preface to the 1918 Leicester Galleries exhibition (reprinted in the 1951 catalogue with a biographical note on the artist), and the preface to the 1978 Parkin Gallery exhibition.

PICTURES SHOWN AT EXHIBITIONS OF THE CAMDEN TOWN GROUP

JUNE 1911
32 *Character Sketches for Lord Dunsany's play 'The Gods of the Mountain'*
33 *Panel for Piano Front*
34 *Classical Landscape*
35 *Design for part of a stage scene for the Haymarket Theatre*
None of these pictures has been found. Lord Dunsany's play was performed at the Haymarket Theatre and it is probable that the stage scene design was also for this production. It was 'a *décor* Hispano-Moorish in character' (*Daily Telegraph*, 22 June 1911), a theme to which Bayes often returned later in his career. Bayes's *Panel for Piano Front* was a 'synthetic rendering of the successive stages of a classic dance, in white on an Indian red ground' (*Observer*, 18 June 1911) and was described as a delightful 'free adaptation of the Pompeian style of decoration' (*Daily Telegraph*, as above).

DECEMBER 1911
50 *The Bridge*
51 *The Glass Door*
52 *Padstow Regatta*
Bayes's exhibits were again much admired by the critics: 'There is something satisfying in the austere modernity of Mr. Walter Bayes, who in the impersonal coldness reveals a certain probity and dignity. He is able to suggest beneath the aerial envelope, beneath the perpetually changing vesture of the earth, something of architectural structure, of permanence' (*Daily Telegraph*, 14 December 1911). A letter written by Neville Lytton to Edward Marsh (quoted by Christopher Hassall in his *Edward Marsh* (London: Longmans, 1959), p.179) suggests that Marsh bought *The Bridge*: 'I went to see your purchases from the Camden Town group and I quite see the point of the picture of the people leaning over the pier (Walter Bayes, is it not?) though it is not my style of picture.' *The Bridge* was 'a bathing scene, reduced to essentials' (*Evening Standard and St James's Gazette*, 6 December 1911); 'an open air scene enwrapped in a half-veiled sunlight' (*Daily Telegraph*, 14 December 1911); and it included a 'bather in the water below' (*Truth*, 13 December 1911). The features described by Lytton and the critics are all found in *The Pier*, sold at Christie's, 3 March 1989, lot 305 (reproduced in the catalogue), a painting of which the early history is unknown. Alternatively, *The Bridge* could be *Low Tide. St Valéry* (see below under Art Gallery of Hamilton, Ontario, Canada), which did once belong to Sir Edward Marsh although the single bather is near rather than in the water. Lytton 'liked even better the picture next to it of a crowd on a shore'. This second picture must be *Padstow Regatta*, described by the *Daily Telegraph* in the article quoted above as having 'an admirable background, and a foreground of fine rhythm, marred, however, by the multitude of small and rather over-defined figures that people the shore'. The *World* (19 December 1911) recorded that it was executed in watercolour. The critic could have been misled by the fact that Bayes often used paper as a support for his paintings in oil at this period.

DECEMBER 1912
35 *Le Petit Casino* (pl.44)
36 *Shade*
37 *Port*
These pictures were well received by the press. '"Shade" ... is a beautiful picture, tender and dignified: green bathing coaches and figures under trees contrasted with the brilliance of a summer sea and sky' (*Pall Mall Gazette*, 12 December 1912). The critics noted that Bayes only allowed himself to paint in flat tones, without any darks. They commended his sense of design. '"Shade" ... and "Le Petit Casino" ... have both a certain largeness and monumental character of design in spite of their general flatness of tint. The larger "Port" ... is even more noble and stately in its effect. It reminds one vaguely of some of Poussin's dignified and reticent compositions. It looks, however, more like a set composition than either of the two other pictures. The sprawling figure of the man in the foreground hardly harmonises with the stately tree and ship or with the charming figures of the women on the right' (*Star*, 10 December 1912). *Port* also reminded the critic of *The Times* (19 December 1912) of Poussin: 'but [it] is not a mere scholastic imitation. There is some incongruity between the homeliness of the background and the majestic figures, but none between the colour and the grandeur of form at which the artist aims. In his other works the colour ... seems to us too bright, or perhaps too pretty for the sharpness of the forms.' Judge Evans bought *Port* and it was included after his death in the Goupil Gallery exhibition of his collection (80). It was sold at Sotheby's, 30 September 1998, lot 75 (reproduced in the catalogue).

PAINTINGS IN PUBLIC COLLECTIONS

Because so little has been written on Bayes, the cut-off date of 1914 I have set for other entries in this catalogue (see p.157) has been set aside here and all his paintings in public collections known to me are listed.

United Kingdom

ABERDEEN: ART GALLERY

Launching the Boat (date unknown but possibly between 1917 and 1924)

Oil on canvas stretched on hardboard; 54.5 × 71.7
Inscribed *Walter Bayes* bl
Purchased from the Art Exhibitions Bureau, 1939

BRADFORD: CARTWRIGHT HALL ART GALLERY

Coast Scene 1911
Oil on paper; 28.6 × 30.8
Inscribed *Walter Bayes/1911* br
Provenance: Arthur Crossland, by whom given, 1947
Ref. Baron 1979, pl.73

Café at Rapallo 1924
Oil on canvas; 35.5 × 53.5
Inscribed *Walter Bayes 24* br
Provenance: Mrs Constance Rea, by whom bequeathed,
1953

BRISTOL: CITY MUSEUM AND ART GALLERY

On the Shore at Clifton, Kent
Oil on paper; 15.9 × 22.9
Inscribed *WB* (in monogram) bl
Provenance: Contemporary Art Society, by whom
allocated, 1952

BURY: ART GALLERY AND MUSEUM

The Blue Pool (possibly 1912–15)
Oil on canvas laid on board; 32 × 50.5
Inscribed *WB* (in monogram) br
Provenance: George and Nellie Clough, by whom
bequeathed, 1941 [BUYGM.475.1941]

Café Scene (possibly 1912–15)
Oil on board; 27.9 × 33.7
Exhibited possibly the Leicester Galleries 1918 (18) as
The Terrace
Provenance: Franklin and Margaret Howarth, by whom
bequeathed, 1939 [BUYGM.452.1939]

HALIFAX: PIECE HALL ART GALLERY

Toulon Shops. 'Aux Dames de la France' 1927
Oil on canvas on board; 32.3 × 37.1
Inscribed *W. Bayes 27* tl
Provenance: Contemporary Art Society, by whom
allocated, 1944

LEICESTER: NEW WALK MUSEUM AND ART GALLERY

The Flanks of Cader or *The Bather* 1917
Oil on canvas; 115.5 × 56
Exhibited Leicester Galleries 1918 (43)
Provenance: Contemporary Art Society, by whom
allocated, 1929

LIVERPOOL: WALKER ART GALLERY

Top o' the Tide c.1899
Oil on canvas; 127 × 165.8
Exhibited RA summer exhibition 1899
Purchased, 1900 [2737]

LONDON: ARTS COUNCIL COLLECTION, HAYWARD
GALLERY

Wine and Fruit 1914–15
Oil on board; 78 × 57.5
Inscribed *WB* br
Exhibited Carfax Gallery 1915 (1); Leicester Galleries
1919 (34)
Purchased from the Leicester Galleries, 1952

LONDON: IMPERIAL WAR MUSEUM

*The Underworld: Taking Cover in a Tube Station during
a London Air Raid* 1918
Oil on canvas; 254 × 548.6
Inscribed *WB* (in monogram)
Exhibited RA summer exhibition 1918 (243), from

where purchased [IVM:ART 935]

Landing Survivors from a Torpedoed Ship 1918
Oil on canvas; 182.8 × 317.5
Commissioned, 1918 [IVM:ART 1234; lost by fire in
1977]

The Road to Peace: Design for Tapestry
Gouache on linen; 396.2 × 236.2
Given by Muirhead Bone, by 1924 [IVM:ART 2753]

*The Armoured Fighting Vehicle School, Bovington: Lunch
on the Driving Grounds* 1941
Oil on canvas; 73.6 × 115.5
Inscribed *W BAYES* br
Commissioned, 1941 [IVM:ART LD 2514]

*Battle of Britain: parachutists from an enemy aircraft
brought down in an apparent attempt to bomb Buckingham
Palace* 1942
Oil on canvas; 119 × 140.9
Inscribed *W.B.* bl
Commissioned, 1942 [IVM:ART LD 1157]

LONDON: TATE GALLERY

The Ford c.1917–20
Oil on canvas; 102.2 × 144.5
Inscribed *Walter Bayes* br
Purchased from the Goupil Gallery, 1928 [N04388]

MANCHESTER: CITY ART GALLERIES

Cornlands 1914
Oil on canvas on board; 26.6 × 35.8
Exhibited Carfax Gallery 1915 (33)
Provenance: 1915, Charles L. Rutherston, by whom
given, 1925 [1925.257]

Oratio Obliqua c.1918
Oil on canvas; 91 × 61.1
Inscribed *WB* (in monogram) tl
Provenance: Howard Bliss, by whom given, 1926
[1926.39]

OLDHAM: ART GALLERY

A Boire (Thirst)
Oil on canvas; 136.2 × 181.6
Provenance: Alderman C. Hardman, by whom given,
1920

OXFORD: ASHMOLEAN MUSEUM

Interior with a Woman Dressing 1932
Oil on canvas laid on board; 35 × 29.8
Inscribed *W.B./32* br
Provenance: Professor Anthony Betts, by whom given,
1967

Two Men seated on a Beach
Oil on canvas laid on board; 26 × 29
Provenance: Professor Anthony Betts, by whom given,
1967

PLYMOUTH: CITY MUSEUM AND ART GALLERY

White Day in Provence 1924
Oil on canvas; 37.5 × 52.3
Inscribed *WB* br
Purchased from the artist, 1954 [1954.44]

READING: MUSEUM OF READING

Smoke of the Fishing Fleet. Boulogne 1928
Oil on board; 45.5 × 54
Inscribed – *WALTER BAYES* – *28* – br
Purchased from the artist, 1937 [1937.13.1]

SHEFFIELD: GRAVES ART GALLERY

The Lemon c.1912
Oil on canvas board; 27.3 × 37

Inscribed *WB* (in monogram) bl
Exhibited Leicester Galleries 1918 (46)
Purchased from the Anthony d'Offay Gallery, 1972
[3891]
Ref. Baron 1979, pl.71

*On the Beach c.*1914–15
Oil on board; 27 × 38.1
Exhibited possibly Carfax Gallery 1915 (2) as *On the
Sands No. 1* or (22) as *On the Sands No. 2* or (6) as
Among the Dunes
Purchased from the Piccadilly Gallery, 1965 [2631]

*Girl on Beach c.*1914–15
Oil on board; 38.1 × 27.6
Inscribed *WB* bl
Exhibition suggestions as for *On the Beach*, with which
it is contemporary
Provenance: E. W. Jenkinson
Acquired, 1965 (painting currently lost)

Canada

HAMILTON, ONTARIO: ART GALLERY OF HAMILTON

*Low Tide. St. Valéry c.*1911–12
Oil on canvas on board; 16.5 × 33.7
Inscribed *WB* bl
Exhibited possibly CTG 2 (50) as *The Bridge*
Provenance: Sir Edward Marsh, bequeathed to
Contemporary Art Society, by whom allocated, 1956

VANCOUVER: ART GALLERY

The End of the Ballet
Oil on board; 78 × 56.5
Inscribed *WB* br
Exhibited possibly Leicester Galleries 1919 (14) as
Finale of Russian ballet "Le vieux noceur"
Provenance: Mrs M. F. Chanter; bequeathed to National
Art Collections Fund, by whom given, 1951

Devonshire Cove
Oil on board; 74.8 × 56.2
Inscribed *Walter Bayes* bl
Provenance: Mrs M. F. Chanter; bequeathed to National

Art Collections Fund, by whom given, 1951

New Zealand

AUCKLAND: ART GALLERY

*Lady with Sunshade c.*1912
Oil on canvas; 35.6 × 31.5
Inscribed *WB* (in monogram) br
Exhibited possibly Carfax Gallery 1913 (4) as *Girl with
Parasol, Plage de la Palud*
Purchased from R. E. Abbott, Barnes, 1956 [1956/4/1]

WANGANUI: SERJEANT GALLERY

Untitled (Seaside Pier) 1925
Oil on board; 67 × 62
Inscribed *WB* (in monogram) *1925* br
Purchased, 1948 [1948/3/4]

South Africa

JOHANNESBURG: ART GALLERY

*The Open Door c.*1911 (pl.44)
Oil on canvas; 69 × 59
Inscribed *WB* (in monogram) bl
Exhibited CTG 3 as *Le Petit Casino*
Provenance: Sylvia Gosse, by whom given, 1913
Ref. Baron 1979, pl.74 (where wrongly identified as
The Glass Door, exhibited with the Camden Town
Group in December 1911)

United States of America

BOSTON: MUSEUM OF FINE ARTS

Interior of a Cinema: Study for Oratio Obliqua
Oil on canvas; 42.7 × 32.5
Provenance: Mr Francis Moore; his sale, Sotheby's, 23
July 1931 (41), from where purchased by Philip Hendy
for the Museum, accessioned 1932

Robert Polhill Bevan
1865–1925

Born in Hove, Sussex. Educated by private tutors at
home in Horsgate, near Cuckfield, Sussex. Studied at
the Westminster School of Art (1888) and at the
Académie Julian in Paris (1889–90). Worked in Pont
Aven, Brittany 1890–91 and again 1893–4 when he met
Gauguin. Visited Madrid 1891 on his way to Tangier
where he worked with Joseph Crawhall in 1892. Lived,
worked and hunted on Exmoor 1894–7. In 1897
married the Polish painter Stanislawa de Karlowska and
visited Poland many times thereafter. Settled in London
1900. Exhibited at the AAA in 1908 and soon afterwards
joined the Fitzroy Street Group. Founder-member of
the Camden Town Group (1911), the London Group
(1913) and the Cumberland Market Group (1914).
Stayed at Applehayes, Clayhidon, in the West Country
as guest of H. B. Harrison in 1912 (with Ginner), 1913
(with Ginner and Gore) and 1915. From 1916 until his
death worked from a number of addresses in Devon.
Member NEAC from 1922.

PRINCIPAL ADDRESS

From 1900: 14 Adamson Road, Swiss Cottage,
London.

EXHIBITIONS WITHIN HIS LIFETIME

Baillie Gallery 1905; Baillie Gallery 1908; Carfax
Gallery 1913.

EXHIBITIONS SINCE HIS DEATH

Memorial exhibitions Goupil Gallery and Brighton Art
Gallery 1926; Lefevre Gallery 1944 (catalogue foreword
by R. A. Bevan, the artist's son); Arts Council 1956
(catalogue introduction by J. Wood Palmer); Colnaghi
1961; Ashmolean Museum, Oxford, and Colnaghi 1965
(centenary exhibition with full catalogue); D'Offay
Couper Gallery 1967 (drawings and watercolours);
Anglo-Polish Society 1968 (with Stanislawa de
Karlowska); D'Offay Couper Gallery 1968 (early
paintings 1895–1908).

LITERATURE

R. A. Bevan, *Robert Bevan 1865–1925: A Memoir by his
Son* (London: Studio Vista, 1965) Frances Stenlake,
*From Cuckfield to Camden Town: the story of artist
Robert Bevan* (Cuckfield Museum, 1999).

PICTURES SHOWN AT EXHIBITIONS OF THE CAMDEN
TOWN GROUP

JUNE 1911
28 *Crocks*
29 *The Cab Horse*
30 *In Sussex*
31 *The Yard Gate*
The original version of *Crocks* was destroyed by the
artist who did, however, paint another version of the

same or a similar composition in 1922 (rep. Bevan 1965, pl.78). *The Cab Horse* is now in the Tate Gallery, London [N05911]. *In Sussex* is the painting now called *Fields at Cuckfield* (private collection; rep. Bevan 1965, pl.32). It represents the landscape around the Bevan family home of Horsgate, in Cuckfield, Sussex. Although *The Yard Gate* is the title of several paintings of the farmyard gate in Mydlow, Poland, where Bevan worked in 1907 and 1908, the painting exhibited with this title in 1911 was an English cab-yard subject. According to Desmond MacCarthy (*Eye Witness*, 6 July 1911) it showed a horse just disappearing into the stable. This was possibly the picture formerly in Judge Evans's collection, reproduced in the short-lived magazine *Colour* in July 1918. The present whereabouts of the painting are unknown.

DECEMBER 1911
31 *The Cabyard, Night* (pl.14)
32 *No. 12612*
33 *Landscape with Cattle*
34 *Morning Sunlight*
No. 12612 was a cab-scene (*Sunday Times*, 3 December 1911), but the painting has not been traced. *Landscape with Cattle* might be any one of a number of Sussex landscapes similar to *Fields at Cuckfield*, discussed above. There is a painting of around 1917 called *Morning Sunlight*, but the work exhibited in 1911 (probably first shown at the AAA in 1910) has not been identified.

DECEMBER 1912
38 *A Devonshire Farm*
39 *'Quiet with all road nuisances'*
40 *In the Blagden Hills*
41 *The Horse Mart*
Bevan showed a painting called *A Devon Farm* at the Carfax Gallery in April 1913 and at the Doré Galleries in October. He showed *The Farm on the Hillside, Devon* at the London Group in March 1914 and at the NEAC in the summer. Whether or not these were all the same picture is unknown. *In the Blagden Hills* may have been a typical Carfax Gallery misprint for *In the Blackdown Hills*, the title of a painting in Bevan's exhibition at the Carfax Gallery in April 1913. Both of these pictures were presumably painted while Bevan was staying with H. B. Harrison at Applehayes in 1912, but neither is now identified. *'Quiet with all road nuisances'* is a horse-sale subject studied at Aldridge's in Upper St Martin's Lane (private collection; rep. Bevan 1965, pl.37). *The Horse Mart* was probably the picture now in the Tate Gallery, London [N04750] as *Horse Sale at the Barbican*. *The Horse Mart* was re-exhibited at the Carfax Gallery in April 1913 and at Brighton 1913–14. The price Bevan asked for *The Horse Mart* at the Camden Town Group (35 guineas as opposed to 20 guineas for *'Quiet with all road nuisances'*) supports the suggestion that it is the Tate Gallery *Horse Sale*, which is larger than average in size, complex in composition and very carefully prepared. It is probable that Bevan decided to change its title to *A Sale at the Barbican* when he re-exhibited it with the Cumberland Market Group in 1915.

PAINTINGS IN PUBLIC COLLECTIONS

The cut-off date of 1914 for listing in this catalogue (see p.157) has again been set aside, as for Bayes, and all the paintings by Bevan in public collections known to me are listed here. Only one painting was bought by a public gallery during Bevan's lifetime. Nor did he sell much to private collectors. Thus, most of the paintings now in galleries throughout the world have come since his death from the artist's family, in particular from the artist's son, R. A. Bevan. The route to public ownership has sometimes been directly by gift or purchase (in which case the family provenance is cited below) and sometimes through the agency of a dealer (in which case the family provenance is not cited).

Plate references are given to R. A. Bevan's book about his father (abbreviated as Bevan 1965).

United Kingdom

ABERDEEN: ART GALLERY

Ploughing on the Downs c.1907
Oil on canvas; 62 × 81.9
Exhibited Baillie Gallery 1908 as *Ploughing the Hillside*
Purchased from the Art Exhibitions Bureau, 1939
Ref. Bevan 1965, pl.21; Connett 1992, p.67 in colour

Grooming Horse c.1909
Oil on canvas; 39 × 44.1
Inscribed *R. B.* bl
Provenance: Frank Rutter
Purchased from Adams Brothers, 1938
Ref. Christie's 1988, no.54

BELFAST: ULSTER MUSEUM

The Yard Gate, Mydlow, Poland c.1907
Oil on canvas; 55.9 × 48.2
Purchased from the Hamet Gallery, 1970
Ref. Christie's 1988, no.21

BIRMINGHAM: CITY ART GALLERY

The Ploughing Team – Dawn c.1905
Oil on canvas; 48.2 × 59.7
Purchased from the Anthony d'Offay Gallery, 1985

BRIGHTON: MUSEUM AND ART GALLERY

The Cabyard, Night c.1910 (pl.14)
Oil on canvas; 63.5 × 69.9
Inscribed *Robert Bevan* br
Exhibited CTG 2 (31); Carfax Gallery 1913 (12); Brighton 1913–14 (36) from where purchased, 1913
Ref. Bevan 1965, col. pl.27; Baron 1979, in colour p.25, pl.77; Watney 1980, pl.48; Yale 1980, no.1; Christie's 1988, no.61

Rosemary. La Vallée c.1916
Oil on canvas; 49.5 × 61
Inscribed *Bevan* bl
Purchased from the Anthony d'Offay Gallery for Hove Museum, 1988

CAMBRIDGE: FITZWILLIAM MUSEUM

The Polish Tavern c.1901
Oil on canvas; 38.3 × 56.2
Purchased from the d'Offay Couper Gallery, 1969
[PD.10–1969]

CARDIFF: NATIONAL MUSEUM OF WALES

Maples at Cuckfield 1914
Oil on canvas; 51.5 × 61.2
Inscribed *Bevan 1914* bl
Provenance: Sir Louis F. Fergusson; 1954, Miss Margaret Davies, by whom bequeathed, 1963 [NMWA 2085]

COVENTRY: HERBERT ART GALLERY AND MUSEUM

Brimley Hill, Devon c.1915
Oil on canvas; 50.7 × 60.4
Inscribed *Bevan* bl
Purchased from the Mayor Gallery, 1982
Ref. Applehayes 1986, no.21

EDINBURGH: SCOTTISH NATIONAL GALLERY OF MODERN ART

The Well at Mydlow No. 2 1922
Oil on canvas; 62.2 × 81.3

Purchased from Agnew's, 1971 [GMA 1244]
Ref. Bevan 1965, pl.25

EXETER: ROYAL ALBERT MEMORIAL MUSEUM AND ART
GALLERY

A Devonshire Valley No. 1 c.1913
Oil on canvas; 50.8×61
Title inscribed on stretcher
Exhibited probably Goupil Gallery Salon, autumn 1913
(147)
Purchased from Agnew's, 1968 [262/1968]
Ref. Christie's 1988, no.156

GLASGOW: ART GALLERY AND MUSEUM

Three Poplars and a Well (Poland) c.1907–8
Oil on canvas on board; 26.7×32.4
Provenance: R. A. Bevan, from whom purchased, 1968
[3255]

HUDDERSFIELD: LIBRARY AND ART GALLERY

Showing the Paces, Aldridge's c.1913–14
Oil on canvas; 51.2×61.5
Provenance: C. E. Mansell
Purchased from the Anthony d'Offay Gallery, 1967
Ref. Bevan 1965, pl.38; Christie's 1988, no.166 in
colour

IPSWICH: CHRISTCHURCH MANSION AND WOLSEY ART
GALLERY

A Small Southdown Farm (Sussex) 1906
Oil on canvas; 37.8×45.1
Inscribed *Robert Bevan* br
Exhibited probably Baillie Gallery 1908 (24)
Provenance: R. A. Bevan, from whom purchased, 1974
[1974-130]

KETTERING: ALFRED EAST GALLERY

Landscape in Blackdown Hills c.1917–18
Oil on canvas; 50.8×61
Inscribed *Bevan* br
Purchased from the Leger Galleries, 1955

LEAMINGTON SPA: ART GALLERY AND MUSEUM

Back of the Farm, Sussex 1906
Oil on canvas; 37×44.5
Purchased from the d'Offay Couper Gallery, 1969
Ref. Christie's 1988, no.22

LEEDS: CITY ART GALLERY

Dunn's Cottage 1915
Oil on canvas; 48.2×55.8
Provenance: Family descent; Anthony Kenman;
Christie's, 6 November 1981 (54)
Purchased from the Mayor Gallery, 1983
Ref. Christie's 1988, no.170; Connett 1992, p.63 in
colour

LEICESTER: NEW WALK MUSEUM AND ART GALLERY

Polish Landscape c.1901
Oil on canvas; 40.6×55.9
Inscribed *R P Bevan* br
Given by Miss Edith Bevan, 1937
Ref. Bevan 1965, pl.15

From the Artist's Window 1916
Oil on canvas; 63.5×76.2
Inscribed *Bevan* bc
Purchased from Reid & Lefevre, 1944
Ref. Bevan 1965, pl.57

LIVERPOOL: WALKER ART GALLERY

Under the Hammer c.1913–14 (pl.59)

Oil on canvas; 63.7×91.7
Inscribed *Robert Bevan* br
Exhibited LG March 1914 (89); probably Whitechapel
1914 (404); probably CMG 1915 (47)
Purchased from the artist's widow, 1933 [112]
Ref. Bevan 1965, pl.45

LONDON: MUSEUM OF LONDON

A Street Scene in Belsize Park 1917
Oil on canvas; 64×92
Inscribed *Bevan* bl
Purchased from Colnaghi, 1961 [61.78]
Ref. Bevan 1965, pl.59; Watney 1980, pl.36; Christie's
1988, no.178

LONDON: NATIONAL PORTRAIT GALLERY

Self Portrait c.1913–14
Oil on canvas; 45.7×35.5
Purchased from the Anthony d'Offay Gallery, 1978
[5201]
Ref. Bevan 1965, colour frontispiece and p.20; Baron
1979, pl.144; Christie's 1988, no.1

LONDON: TATE GALLERY

Morning over the Ploughed Fields c.1901 or 1903
Oil on canvas; 21.9×26.4
Purchased from the d'Offay Couper Gallery, 1969
[T01121]

The Cab Horse c.1910
Oil on canvas; 63.5×76.2
Exhibited NEAC winter 1910 (91); CTG 1 (29); probably
Carfax Gallery 1913 (38) as *Putting To*
Provenance: 1926, purchased from the artist's widow,
through the Goupil Gallery, by the Duveen Paintings
Fund, by whom given, 1949 [N05911]
Ref. Bevan 1965, pl.31; Baron 1979, pl.75

Horse Sale at the Barbican 1912
Oil on canvas; 78.7×121.9
Inscribed *Robert Bevan* bl
Exhibited probably CTG 3 (41), Carfax Gallery 1913
(48), Brighton 1913–14 (32) as *The Horse Mart*;
probably CMG 1915 (19) as *A Sale at the Barbican*
Chantrey Purchase from the artist's widow, 1934
[N04750]
Ref. Bevan 1965, pl.43; Watney 1980, pl.49

Haze over the Valley c.1913
Oil on canvas; 43.2×53.3
Chantrey Purchase from Colnaghi, 1959 [T00282]

MANCHESTER: CITY ART GALLERIES

The Farmhouse 1917
Oil on canvas; 52×66
Provenance: E.C. Gregory, by whom given, 1929
[1929.2]

Horse Dealers (Sale at Ward's Repository No. 1) 1918
Oil on canvas; 48.2×66
Purchased from the Mayor Gallery, 1935 [1935.157]
Ref. Bevan 1965, pl.61

OXFORD: ASHMOLEAN MUSEUM

In the Downs near Lewes 1906
Oil on canvas; 38.1×45.7
Inscribed *Robert Bevan* br
Purchased from Colnaghi, 1961

The Chestnut Tree 1916
Oil on canvas; 50×60
Inscribed *Robert Bevan* bl
Provenance: R. A. Bevan, by whom given, 1957
Ref. Bevan 1965, pl.63

Queen's Road, St John's Wood 1918
Oil on canvas; 50.8×61

Inscribed *Robert Bevan* bl
Provenance: R. A. Bevan, by whom given, 1957
Ref. Bevan 1965, pl.67; Watney 1980, pl.121; Christie's 1988, no.188

Showing at Tattersall's c.1919
Oil on canvas; 58.4 × 71.1
Inscribed *Robert Bevan* bl
Provenance: R. A. Bevan, by whom given, 1957
Ref. Bevan 1965, col. pl.75; Christie's 1988, no.193 in colour

PLYMOUTH: CITY MUSEUM AND ART GALLERY

Green Devon c.1918–19
Oil on canvas; 45 × 55
Inscribed *BEVAN* bl
Provenance: R. A. Bevan, from whom purchased, 1957

READING: MUSEUM OF READING

The Town Field, Horsgate 1914 (pl.58)
Oil on canvas; 50.8 × 61
Provenance: Charles Ginner; Anton Lock
Purchased from Agnew's, 1975 [1976.56.1]
Ref. Baron 1979, pl.143

SHEFFIELD: GRAVES ART GALLERY

Farm Landscape
Oil on canvas; 38.1 × 45.7
Purchased at Christie's, 1968 [3347]

SOUTHAMPTON: CITY ART GALLERY

Mydlow Village, Poland c.1907–8
Oil on canvas; 60 × 79
Inscribed *Robert Bevan* br
Exhibited possibly AAA 1909 (1041) as *A Polish Village*
Provenance: Dennis Peel
Purchased from Reid & Lefevre, 1952

A Sale at Tattersall's c.1911–12
Oil on canvas; 50.8 × 61
Exhibited Carfax Gallery 1913 (24) as *Tattersall's*
Provenance: Miss Horsfall (bought from 1913 exhibition); her son-in-law, Lt. Col. J. K. McConnel, from whom purchased, 1974
Ref. Bevan 1965, col. pl.29

Cumberland Market, North Side c.1914
Oil on canvas; 51.1 × 61
Exhibited possibly CMG 1915 (8)
Provenance: F. A. Girling
Purchased from Agnew's, 1947
Ref. Bevan 1965, pl.47; Baron 1979, pl.146; Watney 1980, pl.120; Barbican 1997, p.145 in colour

STOKE-ON-TRENT: CITY MUSEUM AND ART GALLERY

The Ash Tree c.1911
Oil on canvas; 46.4 × 55.9
Purchased at Sotheby's, 1952

SWINDON: MUSEUM AND ART GALLERY

Back of the Granary, Poland c.1904
Oil on canvas laid on board; 34.3 × 40.6

Provenance: R. A. Bevan, from whom purchased, through the New Grafton Gallery, 1969

Australia

ADELAIDE: ART GALLERY OF SOUTH AUSTRALIA

The Green House, St John's Wood c.1918–19
Oil on canvas; 62.3 × 81
Provenance: R. A. Bevan, from whom purchased, 1969
Ref. Adelaide 1997, p.57 in colour

PERTH: WESTERN AUSTRALIAN ART GALLERY

The Farm Gate in Sunlight (Mydlow) c.1907–8
Oil on canvas laid on board; 49.1 × 40.8
Purchased from the Leva Gallery, 1974

New Zealand

AUCKLAND: ART GALLERY

The Well at Mydlow, Poland, No. 1 1909
Oil on canvas; 60.3 × 80
Provenance: R. A. Bevan, from whom purchased, 1961
Ref. Bevan 1965, pl.24

DUNEDIN: PUBLIC ART GALLERY

West Country Landscape c.1913
Oil on canvas; 56 × 76.3
Inscribed *Robert Bevan* br
Purchased from Agnew's, 1988 [23–1988]

South Africa

PORT ELIZABETH: KING GEORGE VI ART GALLERY

The Little Oak Tree (The Back of Dunn's Cottage) 1915
Oil on canvas; 45.7 × 55.9
Provenance: R. A. Bevan, by whom given, 1958
Ref. Bevan 1965, pl.52

United States of America

BOSTON: MUSEUM OF FINE ARTS

The Parade at Aldridge's 1914
Oil on canvas; 63.4 × 76.3
Provenance: R. A. Bevan, from whom purchased, 1932
Ref. Yale 1980, no.7

Adelaide Road, N.W. 1922
Oil on canvas; 51 × 72
Inscribed *Robert Bevan* bl
Provenance: R. A. Bevan, from whom purchased, 1932
Ref. Bevan 1965, pl.77

NEW HAVEN: YALE CENTER FOR BRITISH ART, PAUL MELLON COLLECTION

Hay Carts, Cumberland Market c.1915 (see pl.18 for details)

Malcolm Cyril Drummond
1880–1945

Born at Boyne Hill, near Maidenhead, Berkshire. Graduated in history from Oxford in 1902. Spent a year in Yorkshire training as an estate agent. Studied at the Slade School from 1903 to 1907 and then joined Sickert's class at the Westminster School of Art 1908–10. Pupil at Sickert's etching class 1909 and founder-pupil at Sickert's Rowlandson House 1910. Lived and worked in Chelsea, for a time at 4 Yeoman's Row. First exhibited at the AAA in 1910. Member

Camden Town Group, founder-member London Group (1913) and its treasurer (1921). Exhibited at the *Salon des Indépendants*, Paris, in 1913. Worked in the War Office during the war. Taught at the Westminster School of Art 1925–31. Following the death of his wife Zina (*née* Oglivie) in 1931, left London and settled in Moulsford, Berkshire. Married Margaret Triquet Browning in 1934. Died in 1945 having been totally blind since 1943.

NO EXHIBITION WITHIN HIS LIFETIME

EXHIBITIONS SINCE HIS DEATH

Redfern Gallery 1946; Grant's Gallery, Edinburgh and
Aberdeen Art Gallery 1948; Municipal Art Gallery,
Reading 1950; Flint House Galleries, Norwich 1955;
Arts Council 1963–4 (catalogue introduction by
Quentin Bell); Maltzahn Gallery 1974 (catalogue
introduction by Charlotte Haenlein).

LITERATURE

No literature except the catalogue introductions for the
exhibitions cited above.

PICTURES SHOWN AT EXHIBITIONS OF THE CAMDEN
TOWN GROUP

JUNE 1911
44 *A Chelsea Garden*
45 *Woman Knitting*
46 *Paddington Station*
47 *Interior*
With one possible exception, the whereabouts of
Drummond's pictures from this first exhibition are
unknown. Few critics paused to comment on works by
such an unfamiliar artist. *A Chelsea Garden* was
described as 'delicately perceived' (*Daily News*, 17 June
1911). I have found no mention of *Woman Knitting*
and only one of *Interior*. This tells us that 'his small
room interior presents very skilfully there figures that
seem the very spirits of that particular place'
(*Manchester Guardian*, 28 June 1911), a description
which could refer to *Interior in Chelsea* (Johannesburg
Art Gallery). Drummond's most important exhibit was
undoubtedly *Paddington Station*. He showed it again at
the Whitechapel exhibition of 'Twentieth Century Art'
in 1914, and it was borrowed from a private collector
in 1928 for the London Group Retrospective exhibition
(inaccurately dated to 1913). It was an original subject.
Composition studies for the painting (now in a private
collection) bear out the description of the painting as
showing 'a handsome decorative use of the girders and
hanging cloths' (*Manchester Guardian*, 28 June 1911). A
contemporary catalogue annotation remarked that the
painting was 'monochromy', while *Art News* (15 July
1911) noted that its chief characteristic was 'Beauty of
colour wedded to a strikingly decorative design ... It is
much lower in key than Mr. Ginner's vivid canvases,
but it has a subdued richness which is most attractive.'

DECEMBER 1911
38 *Viva*
39 *At Dusk*
40 *Portrait of a Lady*
41 *Portrait of Charles Ginner* (pl.39)
I have found no contemporary descriptions to help
identify three of these four exhibits.

DECEMBER 1912
26 *The Oratory, London* (pl.37)
27 *At the Piano* (pl.10)
28 *Chestnut Leaves*
29 *St James's Park* (pl.17)
The title *Chestnut Leaves* is an accurate description of
the painting (now in a private collection), a decorative
and agoraphobic arrangement of chestnut leaves.

PAINTINGS IN PUBLIC COLLECTIONS

Because so little has been written on
Drummond, the cut-off date of 1914 for
inclusion of works in this catalogue (see p.157)
has been set aside here and all the paintings in
public collections known to me are listed. Most
were acquired, either directly or through the
agency of a dealer, from the painter's widow and
second wife, Margaret Drummond.

United Kingdom

ABERDEEN: ART GALLERY

The Tea Party c.1919
Oil on strawboard; 48 × 61.3
Purchased from Agnew's, 1976

BELFAST: ULSTER MUSEUM

Landscape with Trees (Box Hill, near Betchworth) c.1925
Oil on canvas; 51.2 × 34.9
Provenance: K. T. Powell; Christie's, 29 October 1971
(119)
Purchased from the Leicester Galleries, 1974

CARLISLE: TULLIE HOUSE, MUSEUM AND ART GALLERY

Foreshortened Male Nude c.1909
Oil on canvas; 30.4 × 45.9
Purchased, through the agency of Roger de Grey, from
the Arts Council exhibition of 1963–4 (1), 1964

EXETER: ROYAL ALBERT MEMORIAL MUSEUM AND ART
GALLERY

The Park Bench c.1918–19
Oil on canvas; 61.3 × 41
Purchased from Agnew's, 1969 [100/1969]

HUDDERSFIELD: LIBRARY AND ART GALLERY

Hammersmith Bridge 1912–13
Oil on canvas; 71.2 × 45.4
Purchased from the Anthony d'Offay Gallery, 1980

KINGSTON UPON HULL: FERENS ART GALLERY

In the Cinema c.1913
Oil on canvas; 69.5 × 69.5
Inscribed *DRUMMOND* bl
Exhibited probably AAA 1913 (325), Brighton 1913–14
(130) and Whitechapel 1914 (127)
Purchased from Agnew's, 1969
Ref. Baron 1979, pl.140; Christie's 1988, no.139 in
colour

KINGSTON UPON HULL: THE UNIVERSITY OF HULL ART
COLLECTION

Court Scene 1920
Oil on canvas; 45.7 × 40.6
Inscribed *Drummond 1920* br
Exhibited Goupil Gallery Salon 1920 (104 or 132)
Purchased, 1964 [17]
Ref. Christie's 1988, no.194

LEEDS: CITY ART GALLERY

The Coconut Shy c.1920
Oil on canvas; 48.2 × 33
Purchased from the Fine Art Society, 1970
Ref. Watney 1980, pl.112; Christie's 1988, no.196

LEEDS: UNIVERSITY ART COLLECTION

Chelsea Public Library 1920
Oil on canvas; 61 × 50.8
Inscribed *Drummond 1920* br
Provenance: Mrs Margaret Drummond, by whom
given, 1965

LEICESTER: NEW WALK MUSEUM AND ART GALLERY

Chelsea Public Library 1920
Oil on canvas; 39 × 43.2
Inscribed *DRUMMOND 1920* br
Purchased from Monica Kinley, 1981

Seated Nude 1923–5
Oil on canvas; 65.5 × 50.5
Purchased from Monica Kinley, 1981

LONDON: ARTS COUNCIL COLLECTION, HAYWARD GALLERY

Brompton Oratory c.1910 (pl.37)
Oil on canvas; 53.3 × 20.3
Exhibited probably AAA 1910 (33); CTG 3 (26)
Purchased from the artist's widow, 1964
Ref. Baron 1979, pl.119; Watney 1980, pl.54; Yale 1980, no.18

LONDON: TATE GALLERY

Boyne Hill Vicarage, Maidenhead c.1910
Oil on canvas; 50.8 × 40.6
Purchased from the artist's widow, 1963 [T00611]

Girl with Palmettes c.1920
Oil on canvas; 49.8 × 40.3
Purchased from Agnew's, 1966 [T00893]
Ref. Baron 1979, pl.141

NEWCASTLE UPON TYNE: LAING ART GALLERY

19 Fitzroy Street c.1913–14 (pl.2)
Oil on canvas; 71 × 50.8
Purchased from the Anthony d'Offay Gallery, 1975
Ref. Baron 1979, pl.18 and on jacket in colour; Watney 1980, pl.30; Yale 1980, no.26; Christie's 1988, no.25 in colour

OXFORD: ASHMOLEAN MUSEUM

A Chelsea Street c.1912
Oil on canvas; 60.3 × 45
Provenance: R. A. Bevan, by whom given, 1957
Ref. Yale 1980, no.24; Christie's 1988, no.117 in colour

PLYMOUTH: CITY MUSEUM AND ART GALLERY

London Flats. Queen Anne's Mansions 1912
Oil on canvas; 68.5 × 51.7
Inscribed *Drummond* br
Exhibited AAA 1913 (324); Whitechapel 1914 (127)
Provenance: Mrs Margaret Drummond, from whom purchased, 1954 [1954.43]
Ref. Baron 1979, pl.139

Hammersmith Palais de Danse 1920
Oil on canvas; 71 × 51
Provenance: Mrs Margaret Drummond, from whom purchased, 1964 [1964.31]
Ref. Christie's 1988, no.198 in colour

SHEFFIELD: GRAVES ART GALLERY

The Artist's Desk c.1914–15
Oil on canvasboard; 50.8 × 40.8
Inscribed *Drummond* br
Provenance: K. T. Powell
Purchased from the Anthony d'Offay Gallery, 1975 [4134]
Ref. Watney 1980, col. pl.20

Near Beaconsfield, Bucks.
Oil on board; 48.5 × 39.3
Purchased from the Fine Art Society, 1972 [3898]

SOUTHAMPTON: CITY ART GALLERY

Girl Dressing c.1911
Oil on canvas; 45.7 × 35.5
Provenance: Mrs Margaret Drummond; Sotheby's, 21 November 1973 (23)
Purchased from the Leva Gallery, 1975

Portrait of Charles Ginner 1911 (pl.39)
Oil on fibreboard; 60.3 × 49
Inscribed *DRUMMOND* br
Exhibited CTG 2 (41)
Purchased from J. Fairhurst, Flint House Galleries, Norwich, 1956
Ref. Baron 1979, pl.79; Watney 1980, col. pl.19; Yale

1980, no.20; Christie's 1988, no.3; Barbican 1997, p.167 in colour

St James's Park 1912 (pl.17)
Oil on canvas; 72.5 × 90
Inscribed *Drummond* br
Exhibited CTG 3 (29); Paris, *Salon des Indépendants* 1913 (905); Brighton 1913–14 (133)
Provenance: Denys Sutton, from whom purchased, 1953
Ref. Baron 1979, pl.121 and in colour p.47; Watney 1980, col. pl.21; Yale 1980, no.22

Backs of Houses, Chelsea c.1914
Oil on canvas; 65.1 × 57.5
Provenance: Victor Pasmore, from whom purchased, 1952
Ref. Watney 1980, pl.111

Fields and Road, Penn Street, Amersham c.1918
Oil on canvas; 37 × 51
Provenance: Rev. Arthur Browning; by family descent
Purchased, 1998

Wooded Pond, Penn Steet 1918
Oil on canvas; 51 × 37
Inscribed *Drummond/1918* br
Provenance: Rev. Arthur Browning; by family descent
Purchased, 1998

Australia

ADELAIDE: ART GALLERY OF SOUTH AUSTRALIA

At the Piano c.1912 (pl.10)
Oil on canvas; 89.8 × 60.8
Inscribed *Drummond* br
Exhibited probably CTG 3 (27)
Purchased from Agnew's, 1969 [692P11]
Ref. Baron 1979, pl.120; Adelaide 1997, p.37 in colour

New Zealand

HAMILTON: WAIKATO MUSEUM OF ART

Landscape with Church
Oil on canvas; 51 × 40.5
Provenance: J. Wood Palmer
Purchased, 1961

South Africa

JOHANNESBURG: ART GALLERY

Interior in Chelsea
Oil on canvas; 50.8 × 40.6
Inscribed *Drummond* bl
Exhibited possibly CTG 1 (43) as *Interior*
Provenance: St James's Art Group, from whom purchased and donated by the Anglo-American Johannesburg Centenary Trust, 1990

United States of America

NEW HAVEN: YALE CENTER FOR BRITISH ART, PAUL MELLON COLLECTION

The Princess of Wales Pub, Trafalgar Square: Mrs Francis behind the Bar c.1931
Oil on canvas; 66.3 × 43.4
Purchased from Spink, 1984 [B1984.18]

**Harold John Wilde Gilman
1876–1919**

Born at Road, Somerset. Trained at Hastings School of Art 1896, Slade School 1897–1901. Visited Spain 1901–3 where in 1902 he married an American painter, Grace (*née* Candy). Visited America and Canada 1904–5. Exhibited a still life at the NEAC in spring 1904. In 1908 – after some years living with his wife and growing family in his parental home on Romney Marsh, where his father was rector of Snargate with Snave – moved to Letchworth. Founder-member Fitzroy Street Group (1907), Camden Town Group (1911), London Group (1913) and its first president, Cumberland Market Group (1914). Exhibited at *Salon des Indépendants* in Paris 1908, 1909, 1910 and 1912 and from 1908 onwards at the AAA (possibly not a founder-member; see Introduction, note 36). Visited Paris (with Ginner) in 1911, Sweden in 1912 and Norway in 1913. Taught at the Westminster School of Art 1912–15 but displaced when Sickert resumed his post there. Married Sylvia Hardy in 1918. Died during influenza epidemic in London having just completed a picture called *Halifax Harbour*, commissioned by the Canadian Government for the War Memorial at Ottawa.

PRINCIPAL ADDRESSES 1906–16

1908–9: 15 Westholm Green, Letchworth; 1909–12: 100 Wilbury Road, Letchworth; 1914–19: 47 Maple Street, off Tottenham Court Road, London.

EXHIBITIONS WITHIN HIS LIFETIME

(Jointly with Gore) Carfax Gallery 1913; (jointly with Ginner) Goupil Gallery 1914.

EXHIBITIONS SINCE HIS DEATH

Memorial exhibition Leicester Galleries 1919; Messrs Tooth 1934; Reid & Lefevre 1943; Lefevre Gallery 1948; Arts Council 1954–5 (catalogue introduction by J. Wood Palmer); Reid Gallery 1964; The Minories, Colchester (and at Oxford and Sheffield) 1969; Arts Council 1981–2.

LITERATURE

Wyndham Lewis and Louis F. Fergusson, *Harold Gilman: An Appreciation* (London: Chatto & Windus, 1919); Charles Ginner, 'Harold Gilman: an Appreciation', *Art and Letters*, vol.2, no.3, 1919; R. A. Bevan, 'The Pen Drawings of Harold Gilman', *Alphabet and Image*, no.3, December 1946; John Rothenstein, chapter on Gilman (pp.146–59) in *Modern English Painters: Sickert to Smith* (London: Eyre & Spottiswoode, 1952); J. Wood Palmer, 'The Drawings of Harold Gilman', *Connoisseur*, April 1964; B. Fairfax Hall, *Paintings and Drawings by Harold Gilman and Charles Ginner in the Collection of Edward Le Bas* (London: privately printed, 1965); Andrew Causey and Richard Thomson, *Harold Gilman 1876–1919*, catalogue of Arts Council touring exhibition, 1981–2 (with full bibliography); Andrew Causey, chapter on Gilman (pp.54–65), in Pontoise 1998–9.

PICTURES SHOWN AT EXHIBITIONS OF THE CAMDEN TOWN GROUP

JUNE 1911
52 *The Snow Scene*
53 *Portrait*
54 *The Sofa*
55 *Head of an Old Woman*
The Snow Scene, now known as *Washing in the Snow* (private collection; rep. Baron 1979, pl.80) was much admired by critics: 'An oil-painting that has almost the transparency of water-colour, and is an exercise in white, is of laundry hung out' (*Bazaar*, 30 June 1911); 'Frank yet subtle in its light, delicate harmony, moderate and true in its impressionistic rendering of a curious effect' (*Daily Telegraph*, 22 June 1911). *The*

Sofa was either the painting now called *Lady on a Sofa* in the Tate Gallery, London (rep. Baron 1979, pl.81) or a slightly smaller painting from the collection of Edward Le Bas (rep. Christie's, 3 March 1978, lot 181). *Portrait* cannot be readily identified. *Art News* (15 June 1911) noted that 'expressiveness and actuality' together with 'fine characterization distinguish the very personal "Portrait" ... by Mr. Gilman'. *Bazaar* wrote that this portrait was of 'Kaleidoscopic glitter that would be disturbing to live with'. *Head of an Old Woman* was variously called 'vigorous' and 'robust'. On grounds of style, subject and date, *The Old Lady* (Bristol City Art Gallery) is the most likely candidate for identification with this painting.

DECEMBER 1911
19 *Le Pont Tournant* (pl.11)
20 *Nude. No. 1*
21 *Dieppe*
22 *Nude. No. 2*
Dieppe is probably the painting now belonging to the Save and Prosper Group Ltd, an ambitious panoramic view of the town executed in a richly broken technique, rather than the rougher painting from Mrs Hill Clarke's collection, rep. Sotheby's, 14 November 1984 (30). Gilman numbered, rather than described, his nudes (see note to pl.19). If the numbering denoted a chronological sequence, the two nudes shown in 1911 were his first examples in this genre.

DECEMBER 1912
17 *Kyrksjön, Gladhammer, Sweden* (pl.57)
18 *Portrait*
19 *Porch, Sweden*
20 *Reapers, Sweden*
Portrait cannot be identified. *Porch, Sweden* is probably the painting now in a private collection incorrectly known as *Street Scene in Norway* (see catalogue note, AC 1981–2, no.34). *Reapers, Sweden* is now in Johannesburg Art Gallery (Baron 1979, pl.122).

PAINTINGS IN PUBLIC COLLECTIONS

The 1914 cut-off date (see p.157) has been set aside in Gilman's case.

Few paintings by Gilman were sold during his life. Most of the paintings now in public collections worldwide were bought from his widow, Sylvia Gilman, through the agency of a number of trusted dealers (in particular Reid & Lefevre, the Leicester Galleries and Agnew's). Gilman tended to sign paintings he placed in exhibitions, but a number of the paintings he had never exhibited were unsigned at the time of his death. These were subsequently marked with the studio stamp *H. Gilman*, based on his own signature. This stamp is often mistaken for a signature and it must be assumed that some of the paintings cited below as signed were in fact stamped.

Plate references are given below to reproductions in L&F 1919 because of its early publication date, and to the Arts Council 1981–2 catalogue (AC 1981–2) because it is the most comprehensive publication on Gilman to date.

United Kingdom

ABERDEEN: ART GALLERY

Portrait of Grace (née Candy), the artist's first wife
c.1905–6
Oil on canvas; 54.3 × 54.3
Studio stamp
Provenance: Mrs Barbara Duce (daughter of Sylvia, the artist's widow and second wife, by her second marriage to Leofric Gilman, Harold's brother)
Purchased from Agnew's, 1957
Ref. AC 1981–2, no.4

The Artist's Mother at Lecon Hall c.1911
Oil on panel; 24.8 × 34.9
Studio stamp
Purchased from Agnew's, 1955

BIRMINGHAM: CITY ART GALLERY

The Nurse c.1908
Oil on canvas; 61.3 × 51.1
Inscribed *H. Gilman* br
Purchased from Reid & Lefevre, 1947
Ref. AC 1981–2, no.12

Portrait Study of a Woman c.1909–11
Oil on canvas; 50 × 30.5
Provenance: Arthur Crossland; Christie's, 9 March
1956 (133)
Purchased from Agnew's, 1959

BRADFORD: CARTWRIGHT HALL ART GALLERY

Portrait of a Man (said to be Bernhard Sickert) c.1912–14
Oil on canvas; 57.8 × 44.5
Inscribed *H. Gilman* bl
Provenance: Sir John Rothenstein; Sotheby's, 17 July
1963 (38)
Purchased from Agnew's, 1964
Ref. Christie's 1988, no.123

BRIGHTON: MUSEUM AND ART GALLERY

The Coral Necklace 1914
Oil on canvas; 61 × 45.7
Inscribed *H Gilman 1914* bl
Exhibited Goupil Gallery 1914 (40); NEAC summer
1914 (269); CMG 1915 (43)
Provenance: 1915, John Alford; Edward Le Bas,
by whom bequeathed, 1969
Ref. L&F 1919, p.69; Baron 1979, pl.133; AC 1981–2,
no.50; Christie's 1988, no.164

BRISTOL: CITY MUSEUM AND ART GALLERY

The Old Lady c.1911
Oil on canvas; 34.3 × 29.9
Provenance: Hugh Blaker
Exhibited possibly CTG 1(55)
Purchased from the Leicester Galleries, 1948

CAMBRIDGE: FITZWILLIAM MUSEUM

Still Life on a Sideboard c.1908–9
Oil on canvas; 31.4 × 41.6
Studio stamp
Provenance: the artist's mother; Captain S. W. Sykes, by
whom given, 1948 [PD.29–1948]
Ref. Baron 1979, pl.25

Nude on a Bed c.1911–12
Oil on canvas; 61 × 45.7
Exhibited possibly Carfax Gallery 1913 (39) as *Nude
(No. 4)*
Provenance: Edward Le Bas; B. Fairfax Hall, by whom
given in memory of Edward le Bas, 1967 [PD.3–1967]
Ref. Baron 1979, pl.21; Yale 1980, no.34; AC 1981–2,
fig.9

CARDIFF: NATIONAL MUSEUM OF WALES

The Kitchen c.1908
Oil on canvas; 61 × 45.7
Inscribed *H. Gilman* br
Exhibited probably Goupil Gallery 1914 (3) and
Leicester Galleries 1919 (35)
Provenance: Leicester Galleries; 1955, the
Contemporary Art Society for Wales,
by whom allocated, 1957 [NMWA 191]
Ref. Baron 1979, pl.46; AC 1981–2, no.9 (in colour,
p.6)

Mornington Crescent c.1912
Oil on canvas; 51.6 × 61.7

Provenance: 1934, Miss Margaret Davies, by whom
bequeathed, 1963 [NMWA 190]
Ref. Baron 1979, pl.62

EXETER: ROYAL ALBERT MEMORIAL MUSEUM AND ART
GALLERY

Girl combing her Hair c.1911–13
Oil on canvas; 61 × 45.7
Inscribed *H. Gilman* br
Exhibited Brighton 1913–14 (39); Goupil Gallery 1914
(2); Leicester Galleries 1919 (33)
Purchased from Agnew's, 1968
Ref. Yale 1980, no.33; AC 1981–2, no.27; Christie's
1988, no.76; Pontoise 1998–9, no.63, p.56

GLASGOW: ART GALLERY AND MUSEUM

Contemplation c.1914
Oil on canvas; 35.5 × 30.5
Inscribed *H. Gilman* br
Provenance: F.A. Girling; Sotheby's, 13 March 1974
(47)
Purchased from Agnew's, 1974 [3309]
Ref. Baron 1979, pl.43

HUDDERSFIELD: LIBRARY AND ART GALLERY

Tea in the Bed-sitter 1916
Oil on canvas; 71 × 91.5
Inscribed *H. Gilman* br
Exhibited LG June 1916 (72) as *Interior*
Provenance: Lady Alice Shaw-Stewart; Lady Howick of
Glendale
Purchased from the Leicester Galleries, 1965
Ref. L&F 1919, p.61; Watney 1980, pl.117; AC 1981–2,
no.74; Christie's 1988, no.142

IPSWICH: CHRISTCHURCH MANSION AND WOLSEY ART
GALLERY

Seated Girl in Blue c.1912–13
Oil on canvas; 40.6 × 58.1
Provenance: Given by Gilman to Robert Bevan; his
son, R. A. Bevan, from whom purchased, 1974 [1974-
129]

KINGSTON UPON HULL: FERENS ART GALLERY

Clarence Gardens N.W. c.1912
Oil on canvas; 50.8 × 61
Inscribed *H Gilman* br
Exhibited Carfax Gallery 1913 (1) or (18); Goupil
Gallery 1914 (13) or (18); possibly Leicester Galleries
1919 (11)
Provenance: Major R. A. Hornby
Purchased from the Leicester Galleries, 1965
Ref. Watney 1980, pl.58; AC 1981–2, no.31

KINGSTON UPON HULL: UNIVERSITY OF HULL ART
COLLECTION

Orchard 1916
Oil on canvas; 50.8 × 68.6
Studio stamp
Purchased, 1965 [47]
Ref. Christie's 1988, no.171

KIRKCALDY: MUSEUM AND ART GALLERY

The Thames at Battersea c.1907–8
Oil on canvas; 61 × 92
Inscribed *H. Gilman* br
Purchased from Aitken Dott, Edinburgh, 1951
Ref. Baron 1979, pl.47

Romney Marsh c.1909–10
Oil on canvas; 26 × 36.5
Inscribed *H. Gilman* br
Provenance: Reid & Lefevre; 1946, J. W. Blyth
Purchased from his estate, 1964

The White Jumper c.1911
Oil on panel; 35.6 × 25.4
Provenance: Leger Galleries; 1939, J. W. Blyth
Purchased from his estate, 1964

LEEDS: CITY ART GALLERY

Portrait of Spencer Frederick Gore c.1906–7
Oil on canvas; 36.9 × 31.7
Exhibited Leicester Galleries 1919 (1)
Purchased, 1936
Ref. Watney 1980, pl.26

In Sickert's House at Neuville 1907
Oil on canvas; 58.7 × 45.7
Studio stamp
Purchased, 1944
Ref. Christie's 1988, no.24; Pontoise 1998–9, no.61,
p.55

The Blue Blouse. Elèni Zompolides c.1910 (pl.36)
Oil on canvas; 60.9 × 45.7
Inscribed *H. Gilman* bl
Exhibited NEAC summer 1910 (257)
Purchased from Reid & Lefevre, 1943
Ref. Baron 1979, pl.64; Yale 1980, no.28; AC 1981–2,
no.16

Interior with Nude c.1911
Oil on canvas; 50.8 × 40.6
Inscribed *H Gilman* br
Exhibited possibly CTG 2 (20) and Carfax Gallery 1913
(7) as *Nude No. 1*
Provenance: Charles Ginner
Purchased from the Adams Gallery, 1949

In Gloucestershire 1916
Oil on canvas; 59.7 × 46.3
Inscribed *H. Gilman* br
Purchased from Reid & Lefevre, 1944

Portrait of Mrs Mounter c.1916–17
Oil on canvas; 33 × 17.9
Inscribed *H. Gilman* br
Purchased from Messrs Tooth, 1934

LEICESTER: NEW WALK MUSEUM AND ART GALLERY

Meditation 1910–11
Oil on canvas; 62 × 46.5
Provenance: Mr and Mrs Girling
Purchased from Agnew's, 1981
Ref. AC 1981–2, no.18

LIVERPOOL: WALKER ART GALLERY

Interior with Flowers c.1912
Oil on canvas; 61.3 × 71.8
Studio stamp
Purchased from Reid & Lefevre, 1945 [3136]
Ref. Baron 1979, pl.52; Christie's 1988, no.99 in colour

Mrs Mounter at the Breakfast Table 1916
Oil on canvas; 91.8 × 61
Inscribed *H. Gilman* br
Exhibited probably LG November 1916 (109)
Purchased, 1943 [3135]
Ref. Watney 1980, col. pl.27; Barbican 1997, p.124

LONDON: ARTS COUNCIL COLLECTION, HAYWARD
GALLERY

The Model. Reclining Nude c.1911
Oil on canvas; 45.7 × 61
Inscribed *H. Gilman* br
Purchased from the Leicester Galleries, 1958
Ref. Baron 1979, pl.82; Watney 1980, pl.43; AC 1981–2,
no.26

LONDON: BRITISH COUNCIL COLLECTION

Shopping List c.1912

Oil on canvas; 61.5 × 31
Inscribed *H. Gilman* br
Exhibited possibly Carfax Gallery 1913 (42) as *The
Pantry*
Purchased from Reid & Lefevre, 1948
Ref. AC 1981–2, no.36; Christie's 1988, no.134

Interior 1917–18
Oil on canvas; 59.7 × 44.5
Inscribed *Gilman* br
Purchased from Messrs Tooth, 1949
Ref. L&F 1919 (colour frontispiece); AC 1981–2, no.91;
Pontoise 1998–9, no.71, p.59 in colour

The Artist's Mother Reading
Oil on plywood panel; 48.3 × 53.3
Inscribed *H. Gilman* br
Purchased from Reid & Lefevre, 1949

LONDON: GOVERNMENT ART COLLECTION

Norwegian Landscape 1913
Oil on canvas; 51 × 61
Inscribed *H. Gilman* br
Purchased from the Leicester Galleries, 1960 [5218]

LONDON: TATE GALLERY

French Interior c.1906–7
Oil on canvas; 62.2 × 51.4
Exhibited Leicester Galleries 1919 (3)
Provenance: Mrs E. M. Macdonald
Purchased from the Lefevre Gallery, 1947 [N05783]

Edwardian Interior c.1907
Oil on canvas; 53.3 × 54
Inscribed *H. Gilman* br
Provenance: Hubert Wellington, from whom purchased
through the Chantrey Bequest, 1956 [T00096]
Ref. Baron 1979, pl.12

Lady on a Sofa c.1910
Oil on canvas; 30.5 × 40.6
Inscribed *Gilman* br
Exhibited probably NEAC summer 1910 (256); possibly
CTG 1 (54)
Provenance: By 1911, Judge Evans; by 1928, Hugh
Blaker
Purchased from the Leicester Galleries, 1948 [N05831]
Ref. Baron 1979, pl.81

The Artist's Mother c.1913
Oil on canvas; 61 × 50.8
Inscribed *H. Gilman* br
Exhibited Brighton 1913–14 (43); Goupil Gallery 1914
(47); CMG 1915 (20)
Purchased from the artist's widow by the Chantrey
Bequest, 1943 [N05555]

Leeds Market c.1913
Oil on canvas; 50.8 × 61
Inscribed *H. Gilman* br
Exhibited LG November 1915 (61)
Provenance: 1915, Walter Taylor; 1923, the Very
Reverend E. Milner-White, by whom given, 1927
[N04273]
Ref. L&F 1919, p.71; Watney 1980, col.pl.22; AC
1981–2, no.61; Pontoise 1998–9, no.69, p.60 in colour

Canal Bridge, Flekkefjord c.1913–14
Oil on canvas; 45.7 × 61
Inscribed *H. Gilman* br
Exhibited LG March 1915 (26) as *Flekkefjord*
Provenance: 1915, Walter Taylor, from whom
purchased, 1922 [N03684]
Ref. Watney 1980, pl.40; Pontoise 1998–9, no.65, p.61
in colour

Mrs Mounter at the Breakfast Table c.1916–17
Oil on canvas; 61 × 40.6
Inscribed *H. Gilman* br
Exhibited LG April 1917 (41); Leicester Galleries 1919
(9 or 21)

Provenance: By 1928, Hugh Blaker; his sister Miss
Jenny Blaker, from whom purchased, 1942 [N05317]
Ref. L&F 1919, p.65; AC 1981–2, colour cover

MANCHESTER: CITY ART GALLERIES

Portrait of a Lady (possibly Miss Fletcher) 1915–16
Oil on canvas; 61.5 × 51.5
Provenance: Eric C. Gregory, by whom given, 1929
[1929.5]
Ref. AC 1981–2, no.67

Interior with the Artist's Mother 1917–18
Oil on canvas; 51.2 × 61.4
Inscribed *H Gilman* br
Provenance: 1921, Contemporary Art Society, by whom
allocated, 1931 [1931.32]
Ref. L&F 1919, p.89; AC 1981–2, no.88; Pontoise
1998–9, no.70, p.63 in colour

MANCHESTER: WHITWORTH ART GALLERY

Nude seated on a Bed 1911–12
Oil on canvas; 62.2 × 51
Inscribed *H.G.* bl
Exhibited possibly Carfax Gallery 1913 (9 or 21)
Provenance: Arthur Crossland; Sotheby's, 15 November
1978 (67)
Purchased from the Mayor Gallery, 1980

OXFORD: ASHMOLEAN MUSEUM

Cave Dwellers, Dieppe 1907
Oil on canvas; 25.4 × 35.5
Inscribed and indistinctly dated bl
Exhibited AAA 1908 (1386); Carfax Gallery 1913 (38)
Provenance: Sir Louis F. Fergusson; Rex Nan Kivell;
R.A. Bevan, by whom given, 1957
Ref. L&F 1919, p.81; Baron 1979, pl.45

Dieppe from the East c.1911
Oil on canvas; 46 × 61
Provenance: L.H. Gilman (the artist's brother),
from whom purchased, 1961

Interior with Mrs Mounter 1916–17
Oil on canvas; 51 × 76
Exhibited AAA 1917 (164)
Provenance: Hugh Blaker; Edward Le Bas
Given by Benjamin Fairfax Hall in memory of Edward
Le Bas, 1968
Ref. Yale 1980, no.40; AC 1981–2, no.75; Christie's
1988, no.176 in colour; Barbican 1997, p.127 in colour

PLYMOUTH: CITY MUSEUM AND ART GALLERY

The Lane 1915
Oil on canvas; 49.5 × 39.5
Inscribed *H. Gilman* br
Exhibited Leicester Galleries 1919 (22)
Provenance: Mrs Sylvia Gilman, from whom purchased,
1955 [1955.26]
Ref. AC 1981–2, no.55

SHEFFIELD: GRAVES ART GALLERY

An Eating House c.1913
Oil on canvas; 57.2 × 74.9
Exhibited Goupil Gallery 1914 (5) as *An Eating House
(No. 2)*; LG March 1914 (29) or (43); possibly CMG 1915
(49)
Provenance: By 1919, Walter Taylor; Alec G. Walker
Purchased from the Piccadilly Gallery, 1965
Ref. L&F 1919, p.73; Watney 1980, col.pl.23

SOUTHAMPTON: CITY ART GALLERY

Interior c.1907–8
Oil on canvas; 35 × 36
Purchased from Adams Bros, 1937
Ref. Yale 1980, no.27

Portrait of Sylvia Gosse 1913
Oil on canvas; 69.5 × 51.3
Inscribed *H. Gilman* br
Exhibited possibly Goupil Gallery Salon, autumn 1913
(103); Goupil Gallery 1914 (4) or (24); possibly
LG March 1914 (92); possibly Leicester Galleries
1919 (14)
Purchased from the Reid & Lefevre Gallery, 1950
Ref. Watney 1980, col.pl.25; AC 1981–2, no.47;
Barbican 1997, p.95 in colour
NOTE: Another, slightly smaller, portrait of Sylvia Gosse
by Gilman is in the Cleveland Museum of Art (USA).
It is not possible to determine which was exhibited
where between 1913 and 1919. However, both were
included (equally priced at £30) at Gilman's joint
exhibition with Ginner which opened at the Goupil
Gallery in April 1914.

STOKE-ON-TRENT: CITY MUSEUM AND ART GALLERY

Interior. Girl by a Mantelpiece 1911–12
Oil on canvas; 40.6 × 30.2
Exhibited possibly Carfax Gallery 1913 (50) as *The
Mantelpiece*
Provenance: Edward Le Bas
Purchased from Agnew's, 1979

WAKEFIELD: ART GALLERY

Self Portrait c.1909–10
Oil on canvas; 25.4 × 30.5
Inscribed *H. Gilman* br
Provenance: Mr A. A. Haley
Purchased, 1936
Ref. Christie's 1988, no.2

Mrs Victor Sly 1914–15
Oil on canvas; 52 × 41.9
Exhibited LG March 1915 (74); CMG 1915 (15);
Leicester Galleries 1919 (16)
Purchased from Messrs R. Spurr of Bradford, 1938
Ref. L&F 1919, p.95; AC 1981–2, no.53; Christie's 1988,
no.165; Pontoise 1998–9, no.68, p.62 in colour

WORTHING: MUSEUM AND ART GALLERY

The Mountain Bridge, Norway 1913
Oil on canvas; 62 × 80
Inscribed *H. Gilman* br
Exhibited probably Doré Galleries 1913 (52) as *A
Bridge in Norway*; Goupil Gallery 1914 (40); probably
CMG 1915 (6)
Provenance: Hugh Blaker; Miss Jenny Blaker, by whom
given, 1945
Ref. AC 1981–2, no.44; Pontoise 1998–9, no.66, p.65

YORK: CITY ART GALLERY

The Artist's Daughters c.1906–7
Oil on canvas; 61 × 45.7
Inscribed *H. Gilman* br
Provenance: Mrs Sylvia Gilman; Lefevre Gallery; the
Very Reverend E. Milner-White, by whom given, 1950
Ref. Watney 1980, p.44

Nude on a Bed 1911–12
Oil on canvas; 61 × 50.8
Inscribed *H. Gilman* br
Provenance: Private collection; by 1953, Lefevre
Gallery; 1955, the Very Reverend E. Milner-White, by
whom given, 1955
Ref. Watney 1980, pl.41; AC 1981–2, no.24; Christie's
1988, no.75

Beechwood 1916
Oil on canvas; 61.6 × 50.8
Inscribed *H. Gilman* br
Provenance: Mrs Sylvia Gilman; 1948, Lefevre Gallery,
from whom purchased, 1955
Ref. Watney 1980, pl.118; Christie's 1988, no.172

Australia

ADELAIDE: ART GALLERY OF SOUTH AUSTRALIA

The Washstand c.1914
Oil on canvas; 51.6×45.8
Inscribed *H. Gilman* bl
Exhibited CMG 1915 (14)
Purchased from the Leicester Galleries, 1963 [0.1981]
Ref. Adelaide 1997, p.39 in colour

BRISBANE: QUEENSLAND ART GALLERY

Clarissa c.1911
Oil on canvas; 59×44
Inscribed *H Gilman* br
Purchased from the Lefevre Gallery, 1956 [1:0706]

HOBART: TASMANIAN ART GALLERY

The Black Hat c.1911–12
Oil on canvas on board; 45.9×38.2
Purchased from Robert Haines, Sydney, 1961

MELBOURNE: NATIONAL GALLERY OF VICTORIA

Study c.1910–11
Oil on canvas; 35.7×30.6
Inscribed *H. Gilman* br
Purchased, 1946
NOTE: Possibly a study of Madeline Knox.

PERTH: WESTERN AUSTRALIAN ART GALLERY

Norwegian Waterfall 1913
Oil on canvas; 50.8×61
Inscribed *H. Gilman* br
Exhibited LG March 1914 (3) as *Waterfall, Norway*;
Goupil Gallery 1914 (39); CMG 1915 (21); Leicester
Galleries 1919 (37)
Provenance: By 1919, John Alford; Christie's, 2 July
1934 (134); A.J. Carrick-Smith; Christie's, 1 March
1974 (96)
Purchased from the Leva Gallery, 1974
Ref. L&F 1919, p.79; Baron 1979, pl.132

SYDNEY: ART GALLERY OF NEW SOUTH WALES

Self Portrait c.1910–11
Oil on canvas; 35.7×25.7
Purchased from the Leicester Galleries, 1946 [7837]

Canada

FREDERICTON, NEW BRUNSWICK: BEAVERBROOK ART
GALLERY

The Verandah, Sweden 1912
Oil on canvas; 50.8×40.6
Inscribed *H. Gilman* br
Exhibited Carfax Gallery 1913 (8); Doré 1913 (50);
Goupil Gallery 1914 (20 or 29); probably CMG 1915
(28) as *Swedish Veranda*
Purchased from the Redfern Gallery, 1954
Ref. AC 1981–2, no.40

HAMILTON, ONTARIO: ART GALLERY OF HAMILTON

Romney Marsh c.1912
Oil on canvas; 45.7×61
Inscribed *H. Gilman* br
Provenance: Mr and Mrs Murray Proctor, by whom
given, 1967
NOTE: This is probably a Swedish, rather than a
Romney Marsh, landscape.

OTTAWA: NATIONAL GALLERY OF CANADA

Red Houses, Swedish Village 1912

Oil on canvas; 40.9×51.2
Inscribed *H. Gilman* bl
Provenance: Mrs Barbara Duce; Christie's 22 June 1962
Purchased from the Leger Galleries, 1963 [15006]
Ref. Baron 1979, pl.110

Halifax Harbour 1918
Oil on canvas; 198×335.8
Inscribed *Gilman, 1918* bl
Commissioned by the Canadian War Memorials
Committee, by whom transferred, 1921 [8172]

VANCOUVER: ART GALLERY

Study for Halifax Harbour 1918
Oil on canvas; 58.9×144.5
Inscribed *H. Gilman* br
Exhibited Leicester Galleries 1919 (23)
Provenance: Mrs Sylvia Gilman
Purchased, 1931
Ref. AC 1981–2, no.105

New Zealand

AUCKLAND: ART GALLERY

Lake in the Hills c.1913
Oil on canvas; 55.2×66.6
Inscribed *H. Gilman* br
Provenance: Contemporary Art Society, by whom
allocated, 1968 [1968/32]
NOTE: Probably a Norwegian fjord subject. This
painting, or the painting in the Tatham Art Gallery,
Pietermaritzburg, could be *Norwegian Fjord*, exhibited at
the NEAC winter 1914 (112) and at the Leicester
Galleries in 1919 (24).

Mother and Child 1918
Oil on canvas; 69.8×50.7
Inscribed *Gilman* br
Exhibited LG May 1918 (54)
Provenance: By 1919, Sir Augustus Daniel
Purchased, 1952 [1952/2/1]
Ref. L&F 1919, p.75

WELLINGTON: MUSEUM OF NEW ZEALAND

Girl Dressing c.1912–13
Oil on canvas; 59.7×45.7
Exhibited Leicester Galleries 1919 (40) as *Girl putting
on her Jacket*
Purchased from the Leicester Galleries, 1957
Ref. L&F 1919, p.67 as *Girl putting on her Coat*

South Africa

JOHANNESBURG: ART GALLERY

The Reapers, Sweden 1912
Oil on canvas; 50.8×61
Inscribed *H. Gilman* br
Exhibited CTG 3 (20); Carfax Gallery 1913 (11)
Provenance: Sylvia Gosse, by whom given, 1913
Ref. Baron 1979, pl.122; AC 1981–2, no.35 (in colour,
p.15)

PIETERMARITZBURG: TATHAM ART GALLERY

The Lake (A Norwegian Fjord) 1913
Oil on canvas; 43×59
Inscribed *H. Gilman* br
Provenance: Col. Robert H. Whitwell, by whom given,
1926
NOTE: See the note above referring to a painting of a
similar subject in the Art Gallery, Auckland, New
Zealand.

United States of America

BOSTON: MUSEUM OF FINE ARTS

The Beech Wood 1916
Oil on canvas; 61.5×51.3
Inscribed *H. Gilman* br
Exhibited LG, winter 1916 (108) as *Woods*
Provenance: Mrs Sylvia Gilman, from whom
purchased, 1932

CLEVELAND: MUSEUM OF ART

*Sylvia Gosse c.*1913
Oil on canvas; 61×51
Inscribed *H. Gilman* br
Exhibited possibly Goupil Gallery Salon, autumn, 1913
(103); Goupil Gallery 1914 (4) or (24); possibly LG
March 1914 (92); possibly Leicester Galleries 1919 (14)
Provenance: Eustace Calland; Sotheby's, 21 November
1962 (104)
Purchased from the Anthony d'Offay Gallery, 1982
NOTE: Another Gilman portrait of Sylvia Gosse is in the
City Art Gallery, Southampton.

NEW HAVEN: YALE CENTER FOR BRITISH ART, PAUL
MELLON COLLECTION

Nude in an Interior 1911
Oil on canvas; 50.5×35.5
Exhibited possibly CTG 2 (20 or 22) and Carfax Gallery

1913 (7 or 9) as *Nude No. 1* or *Nude No. 2*
Provenance: R. G. Hobbs; Sotheby's, 18 July 1973
(121A); Mr and Mrs Peter Ross
Purchased from the Mayor Gallery, 1982 [B1982.19]
Ref. AC 1981–2, no.21 (in colour, p.10); Barbican 1997,
p.123 in colour

*Interior with Figures at a Meal c.*1912–13
Oil on canvas; 61.3×47
Provenance: Arthur Crossland; F.A.Girling; Sotheby's,
13 March 1974 (46)
Purchased from the Leger Galleries, 1981 [B1981.11]
NOTE: Probably a Scandinavian interior. If Swedish, it
would be a painting of 1912, if Norwegian, one of
1913.

*Mrs Robert Bevan c.*1913
Oil on canvas; 61.8×51.5
Provenance: 1947, R. A. Bevan
Purchased from the Anthony d'Offay Gallery, 1986
[B1986.1.1]
Ref. AC 1981–2, no.45 (in colour p.22)

Sylvia Darning: Interior at Wells 1917
Oil on canvas; 41.3×46.4
Inscribed *H. Gilman* bl
Provenance: Given to Mrs A. R. Hardy (the sitter's
mother); J. W. Freshfield; Christie's, 12 October 1973
(166); Christie's, 13 March 1981 (43)
Given by Agnew's, 1981 [B1981.25.735]
Ref. AC 1981–2, no.87
NOTE: Inscribed on the stretcher *Harold Gilman/Portrait
of his Wife/Interior at Wells/given to ARH by HG 1917*.

Charles Isaac Ginner
1878–1952

Born at Cannes, France, of Anglo-Scottish parents.
Worked in an architect's office in Paris 1899–1904
before studying painting until 1908, first at the
Académie Vitti under Gervais, then at the Ecole des
Beaux-Arts, and again at the Vitti under Anglada y
Camarasa. First exhibited in England at the AAA in
1908. Late 1909 settled in Chelsea, London. In 1910,
exhibited at the AAA and entered the Fitzroy Street
Group. Founder-member Camden Town Group
(1911), London Group (1913) and Cumberland
Market Group (1914). In 1912 painted murals for
Madame Strindberg's 'Cave of the Golden Calf',
exhibited at the *Salon des Indépendants* and was
included in exhibition of contemporary British art
selected by Fry for the Galerie Barbazanges, Paris. Visit
to Dieppe and Paris (with Gilman), 1911; to
Applehayes, Clayhidon on the Devon/Somerset border
(with Bevan), 1912; to Clayhidon (with Bevan and
Gore) and Dieppe, 1913; to Leeds and Cornwall, 1914.
Official war artist both world wars. Member NEAC 1922,
ARA 1942, Royal Watercolour Society 1945. Awarded
CBE 1950. Published 'Neo-Realism', a manifesto of his
aesthetic beliefs, in the *New Age*, 1 January 1914.

PRINCIPAL ADDRESS

1911: 3 Chesterfield Street, near Kings Cross, London.

EXHIBITIONS WITHIN HIS LIFETIME

Salon Costa, Buenos Aires 1909; (jointly with Gilman)
Goupil Gallery 1914; (jointly with John Nash and
Frank Dobson) Birmingham Repertory Theatre 1920
(catalogue foreword by Walter Bayes); Leicester
Galleries 1920 (drawings in colour); Goupil Galley
1922; Goupil Gallery 1924 (watercolours); (jointly with
Randolph Schwabe) St George's Gallery 1926; Godfrey
Phillips Gallery 1929 (catalogue introduction by Hubert
Wellington); (jointly with Ethelbert White) Everyman
Theatre 1931; Leger Galleries 1933; Leger Galleries
1935.

EXHIBITIONS SINCE HIS DEATH

Arts Council 1953–4 (introduction by Hubert

Wellington, extract of 'Neo-Realism' reprinted);
Piccadilly Gallery 1969 (preface by Fairfax Hall); Fine
Art Society 1985 (introduction by Brian Sewell).

LITERATURE

Unpublished: From *c.*1911 until 1947, Ginner kept
manuscript records in notebooks of his pictures, their
dates, measurements, where and when they were
exhibited, to whom they were sold and for how much.
He included as many as he could remember of his
paintings and drawings from 1907 onwards. The four
notebooks are now deposited in the Archives
Department of the Tate Gallery.
Published: John Rothenstein, chapter on Ginner
(pp.188–93) in *Modern English Painters: Sickert to Smith*
(London: Eyre & Spottiswoode, 1952); B. Fairfax Hall,
*Paintings and Drawings by Harold Gilman and Charles
Ginner in the Collection of Edward Le Bas* (London:
privately printed, 1965); Malcolm Easton, 'Charles
Ginner: Viewing and Finding', *Apollo*, March 1970;
Brian Sewell, catalogue introduction, Fine Art Society
1985.

PICTURES SHOWN AT EXHIBITIONS OF THE CAMDEN
TOWN GROUP

JUNE 1911
36 *Sheaves of Corn*
37 *Battersea Park* (pl.15)
38 *Still Life*
39 *The Sunlit Wall*
The Sunlit Wall (private collection; rep. Baron 1979,
pl.84a), identified in his notebooks (I, p.iii) as *Paysage
à Charenton* of 1908, is one of Ginner's earliest extant
paintings. It dominated critical reaction to Ginner's
work at this Camden Town exhibition. The *Observer*
(18 June 1911) considered Ginner to be the most
daring artist of the whole group. Besides mentioning
The Sunlit Wall ('a triumphant song of pure brilliant
colour'), the critic remarked that Ginner's *Still Life* was
'painted with the passionate intensity of a Cézanne, but
with a far better grip of form'. Ginner's notebook
records that this *Still Life* represented fruit and a teapot
and measured 14×18 inches (Ginner was inconsistent

about the convention of stating height before width, so it could have been an upright picture). The artist recorded that the picture, which had appeared in several exhibitions between 1911 and 1914, was subsequently lost. *Sheaves of Corn*, a painting done near Rottingdean in Sussex, is now in a private collection (rep. Baron 1979, pl.84, and Christie's 1988, no.81).

DECEMBER 1911
27 *The Sunlit Quay*
28 *The Wet Street*
29 *The Café* (pl.43)
30 *Evening* (pl.12)
Evening, *The Wet Street* and *The Sunlit Quay* (Walker Art Gallery, Liverpool) are all Dieppe scenes painted in 1911. *The Wet Street* (rep. Sotheby's catalogue, 15 May 1985, lot 90) was bought in 1911 by the watercolourist Douglas Fox-Pitt. The Fox-Pitt family were also the first owners of *Evening* and *The Café*.

DECEMBER 1912
21 *Still Life*
22 *North Devon*
23 *Rain on the Hill*
24 *Piccadilly Circus* (pl.54)
Ginner's notebooks record that the full title of his *Still Life* at the Carfax Gallery was *The Pots and the Carpet*. He had previously exhibited the same picture at the Barbazanges Gallery in Paris in May, and later showed it at the Doré Galleries in the 'Post-Impressionist and Futurist' exhibition (October 1913) and at his joint exhibition with Gilman at the Goupil Gallery (April 1914) as *Pots*. It measured 18 × 14 inches (or vice versa) and was given to Mrs Victor Sly. Its present location is unknown. *North Devon* (private collection; rep. Baron 1979, pl.123) and *Rain on the Hill* (private collection; rep. Baron 1979, pl.116) represent the landscape around Applehayes where Ginner stayed in 1912 as a guest of H. B. Harrison.

PAINTINGS IN PUBLIC COLLECTIONS

Galleries throughout Great Britain are well endowed with paintings by Ginner, who enjoyed a long and productive career. Because so little has been published on his work, my 1906–14 date-bracket (see p.157) has here been set aside in order to list all Ginner paintings in public collections. Collections in the north of England have especially rich holdings, nearly all bought from the energetic dealer T. W. Spurr and Sons of Southport and Bradford, who acquired paintings by Ginner in bulk, at much reduced prices, to sell in the north.

References to Ginner's unpublished notebooks (see 'Literature', above) are given in square brackets after the title, as part of the essential data of each painting. In a few cases it has not been possible to match a painting and its reference, sometimes because original titles have been lost, sometimes because particular subjects were painted so frequently that positive identification of the specific reference is impossible.

Ginner signed nearly all his finished paintings. He incorporated his middle initial 'I' into his earliest works but after 1911 used the form *C. Ginner* in letters of uniform height. It is not always possible to tell whether these are intended to be upper- or lower-case letters; the form quoted below conforms to data presented to me by the galleries.

United Kingdom

ABERDEEN: ART GALLERY

Flask Walk Skyline 1934 [III, p.133]
Oil on canvas; 68.9 × 50.9
Inscribed *C. Ginner* bl
Purchased from the artist, 1939

BELFAST: ULSTER MUSEUM

Clarendon Dock, Belfast 1922 [II, p.72]
Oil on canvas; 106.9 × 83
Inscribed *C. Ginner* br
Provenance: 1922, Richmond Noble
Purchased, 1924

BOLTON: MUSEUM AND ART GALLERY

The Mirror (The French Novel) 1928 [III, p.31]
Oil on canvas; 68.6 × 50.8
Inscribed *C. GINNER* br
Provenance: 1933, T. W. Spurr; R. Scully; Christie's, 11 May 1973 (115)
Purchased from the Crane Kalman Gallery, 1974

Yellow Chrysanthemums 1929 [III, p.62]
Oil on canvas; 76.2 × 55.9
Inscribed *C. GINNER* br
Provenance: 1934, T. W. Spurr; Arthur Crossland
Purchased from the Leger Galleries, 1959

BOURNEMOUTH: RUSSELL-COTES ART GALLERY AND MUSEUM

The Gyrotiller 1943 [III, p.231]
Oil on canvas; 50.8 × 76.2
Inscribed *C. GINNER*
Provenance: Commissioned 1943 by the War Artists' Advisory Committee, by whom allocated, 1948

BRADFORD: CARTWRIGHT HALL ART GALLERY

Roofs and Chimneys
Oil on canvas; 63.5 × 49.5
Provenance: Mrs Arthur Crossland, by whom given, 1947

BRIGHTON: MUSEUM AND ART GALLERY

Leicester Square 1912 [I, p.liii]
Oil on canvas; 64.7 × 55.9
Inscribed *C. GINNER* br
Exhibited AAA 1912 (74)
Provenance: 1912, C. K. Butler; Edward Le Bas, by whom bequeathed, 1969
Ref. Watney 1980, col. pl.28; Christie's 1988, no.120

Lancaster from Castle Hill Terrace 1947 [IV, p.20]
Oil on canvas; 50.5 × 68
Inscribed *C. Ginner* br
Provenance: 1952, given by Mrs Ruby Ginner Dyer (the artist's sister) to Mrs Anton Lock after Ginner's death; Christie's, 9 June 1978 (60)
Purchased from the Mayor Gallery for Hove Museum, 1979

BRISTOL: CITY MUSEUM AND ART GALLERY

Church Farm, Shipley 1933 [III, p.128]
Oil on canvas; 50.8 × 60.9
Inscribed *C. Ginner* br
Provenance: 1934, T. W. Spurr; 1938, the Leger Galleries, from whom purchased, 1958

CAMBRIDGE: FITZWILLIAM MUSEUM

The Church of All Souls, Langham Place 1924 [II, p.128]
Oil on canvas; 76.2 × 55.6
Provenance: 1924, Mrs M. E. L. Brownlow, by whom bequeathed in memory of Goldsworthy Lowes Dickinson and his family, 1972 [PD.75–1972]

Dahlias and Cornflowers 1929 [III, p.60]
Oil on canvas; 50.8 × 61.7
Inscribed *C. GINNER*
Provenance: 1929, Thomas Balston, by whom bequeathed through the National Art Collections Fund, 1968 [PD.9–1968]

The Punt in the Mill Stream 1938 [III, p.184]

Oil on canvas; 60.9×45.7
Inscribed *C. GINNER*
Provenance: 1939, Francis Wormald, by whom given, 1948 [PD.209–1948]

CARLISLE: TULLIE HOUSE MUSEUM AND ART GALLERY

The Cottage Garden, Sussex or *Through a Sussex Window* 1934 [III, p.132]
Oil on canvas; 61.3×45.7
Inscribed *C. GINNER* br
Purchased for Carlisle *c*.1948 by Edward Le Bas

EXETER: ROYAL ALBERT MEMORIAL MUSEUM AND ART GALLERY

Clayhidon 1913 [I, p.lxxii]
Oil on canvas; 38.4×63.9
Inscribed *C. Ginner* bl
Exhibited Brighton 1913–14 (30); Goupil Gallery 1914 (45); NEAC spring 1914; CMG 1915 (16)
Provenance: 1920, given by the artist to Lindsay Wellington; Christie's, 13 March 1981 (42)
Purchased from the Anthony d'Offay Gallery, 1983 [129/1983]
Ref. Christie's 1988, no.138

HUDDERSFIELD: LIBRARY AND ART GALLERY

The Blouse Factory 1917
Oil on canvas; 51×71
Inscribed *C. Ginner* bl
Provenance: Arthur Crossland
Purchased from the Leger Galleries, 1966
NOTE: Not listed in Ginner's notebooks but closely related to the painting of the same title in the Government Art Collection, London (see below). The measurements of the Government Art Collection painting, but not of the Huddersfield painting, match those given in the notebooks.

IPSWICH: CHRISTCHURCH MANSION AND WOLSEY ART GALLERY

The Old Paper Mill – Interior 1941 [III, p.218]
Oil on canvas; 50.8×61
Inscribed *C. GINNER*
Provenance: 1945, Mrs J. A. Wightman Harrison (the artist's cousin); Mrs Ruby Ginner Dyer; Christie's, 21 January 1972 (52)
Purchased from Spink, 1973 [1973-33]

KINGSTON UPON HULL: FERENS ART GALLERY

The Winged Fawn 1926 [III, p.10]
Oil on canvas; 91.5×61
Inscribed *C. Ginner* br
Provenance: 1928, Alec Walker
Purchased from the Piccadilly Gallery, 1969

KINGSTON UPON HULL: THE UNIVERSITY OF HULL ART COLLECTION

The Orchard, Dorset 1920 [II, p.48]
Oil on canvas; 61×50.7
Inscribed *C. Ginner* br
Provenance: Given by the artist to Mrs Ruby Ginner Dyer, from whom purchased, 1967 [71]

Wear Cliffs – Dorset 1922 [II, p.70]
Oil on canvas; 50.8×68.6
Inscribed *C. Ginner* br
Provenance: 1926, Mrs Ruby Ginner Dyer, by whom presented, 1966 [60]

LEEDS: CITY ART GALLERY

The Circus 1913 [I, p.lxiii]
Oil on canvas; 76.6×61.3
Inscribed *C. GINNER* br
Exhibited AAA 1913 (545) as *The Circus, Islington*;

Goupil Gallery 1914 (26)
Provenance: 1920, E. M. O'R. Dickey
Purchased from the Anthony d'Offay Gallery, 1976
Ref. Christie's 1988, no.140 in colour
NOTE: This picture appears on an easel in the background of Drummond's *19 Fitzroy Street* (pl.2).

Leeds Canal 1914 [I, p.lxvii]
Oil on canvas; 73.7×58.4
Inscribed *C. GINNER* br
Exhibited Goupil Gallery Salon, autumn 1914; CMG 1915 (17); AAA 1916
Provenance: E. Forbes; Mrs R. Caldicott, by whom given, 1962

Royal Ordnance Stores 1944 [IV, p.2]
Oil on canvas; 50.8×68.6
Inscribed *C. GINNER* bl
Commissioned 1943 by the War Artists' Advisory Committee, by whom allocated, 1947

LEICESTER: NEW WALK MUSEUM AND ART GALLERY

Brook Green, Isle of Wight 1929 [III, p.53]
Oil on canvas; 50.8×68.9
Inscribed *C. Ginner*
Provenance: 1933, T. W. Spurr; Arthur Crossland
Purchased at Christie's, 3 February 1956 (137)

The Garden in Spring, Standon 1940 [III, p.212]
Oil on canvas; 50.8×40.6
Inscribed *C. Ginner*
Purchased from the artist through Reid & Lefevre, 1944

LIVERPOOL: WALKER ART GALLERY

The Sunlit Quay, Dieppe 1911 [I, p.xl]
Oil on canvas; 64.7×46.7
Exhibited CTG 2 (27); Paris, *Salon des Indépendants* 1912 (1333); Brighton 1913–14 (27); Goupil Gallery 1914 (50)
Provenance: 1916, Carfax Gallery; Contemporary Art Society, by whom allocated 1950 [3137]
Ref. Watney 1980, pl.51; Christie's 1988, no.91 in colour

LONDON: ARTS COUNCIL COLLECTION, HAYWARD GALLERY

The Rib, Standon 1939 [III, p.197]
Oil on canvas; 43.2×53.3
Inscribed *Ginner* br
Purchased from the artist, 1942

Spring Day at Boscastle 1943 [III, p.227]
Oil on canvas; 83.8×53.3
Inscribed *C. Ginner* br
Purchased, 1949

LONDON: BRITISH COUNCIL COLLECTION

The Aqueduct – Bath 1928 [III, p.26]
Oil on canvas; 76×61
Inscribed *C. GINNER* br
Provenance: 1928, Mrs Louis Fergusson
Purchased from the Leicester Galleries, 1948

LONDON: GOVERNMENT ART COLLECTION

The Blouse Factory 1917 [I, p.xci]
Oil on canvas; 61×74
Inscribed *C. GINNER* br
Exhibited AAA 1917
Provenance: 1933, T. W. Spurr
Purchased from the Mayor Gallery, 1965 [6838]
Ref. Christie's 1988, no.186

View of Hampstead
Oil on canvas; 50.5×60.5
Inscribed *C. GINNER* br
Purchased from the Piccadilly Gallery, 1959 [4944]
NOTE: Possibly in notebook II, p.139 as *Hampstead*

Roofs, 1925. *Roof Tops*, in the Harris Museum, Preston, might also be the painting recorded under this reference. The notebook does not list the size of *Hampstead Roofs* which was sold to T. W. Spurr in 1934.

Novar Cottage, Beasley, Warwickshire 1933 [III, p.122]
Oil on canvas; 50.8 × 60.8
Inscribed *C. GINNER* br
Provenance: 1933, T. W. Spurr
Purchased from the Leicester Galleries, 1962 [5799]

Daffodils and Anemones 1935 [III, p.149]
Oil on canvas; 56 × 43.5
Inscribed *C. GINNER* br
Provenance: 1952, given by Mrs Ruby Ginner Dyer to Mrs Anton Lock after Ginner's death; Christie's, 12 July 1974 (262); Christie's, 17 November 1978 (26) where purchased [14313]

Suburb of Harrow-on-the-Hill 1940 [III, p.214]
Oil on canvas; 34.5 × 45
Inscribed *C. GINNER* bl
Provenance: Anton Lock; Christie's, 28 February 1975 (147)
Purchased from the Mayor Gallery, 1980 [14903]

The Kitto Rock, Boscastle, Cornwall 1948 [IV, p.24]
Oil on canvas; 50 × 68.5
Inscribed *C. GINNER* br
Provenance: 1948, Mrs J. A. Wightman Harrison; Mrs Ruby Ginner Dyer; Christie's, 11 May 1973 (125)
Purchased from the Mayor Gallery, 1974 [11025]

LONDON: IMPERIAL WAR MUSEUM

Building of a Warship 1940 [III, p.211]
Oil on canvas; 83.8 × 60.9
Inscribed *C. GINNER* br
Commissioned (for a poster), 1940 [IWM:ART LD 2809]

Machine Tools for Russia 1943 [III, p.226]
Oil on canvas; 76.2 × 60.9
Inscribed *C. GINNER* br
Commissioned by the War Artists' Advisory Committee, 1942 [IWM:ART LD 5693]

The National Physical Laboratory, Teddington 1946 [IV, p.15]
Oil on canvas; 76.2 × 55.8
Inscribed *C. GINNER* br
Commissioned by the War Artists' Advisory Committee, 1945 [IWM:ART LD 6156]

LONDON: MUSEUM OF LONDON

London Bridge: Adelaide House and Fresh Wharf 1913 [I, p.lxv]
Oil on canvas; 76.2 × 48.4
Inscribed *C. Ginner* br
Exhibited AAA 1913 (546); Brighton 1913–14 (31); Goupil Gallery 1914 (30); CMG 1915 (41)
Provenance: 1921, Birmingham Repertory Theatre where bought by R. V. Williams
Purchased from Agnew's, 1968 [68.48]
Ref. Christie's 1988, no.122

LONDON: TATE GALLERY

The Café Royal 1911 [I, p.xxvii] (pl.43)
Oil on canvas; 63.5 × 48.3
Inscribed *C. Ginner* br
Exhibited AAA 1911 (139); CTG 2 (29); Paris, *Salon des Indépendants* 1912 (1334); Goupil Gallery 1914 (22)
Provenance: 1916, Douglas Fox-Pitt; his neice Miss Patience Scott; her husband Sir Henry Holt; 1938, Edward Le Bas, by whom given, 1939 [N05050]
Ref. Baron 1979, pl.85

Victoria Embankment Gardens 1912 [I, p.lvii]
Oil on canvas; 66.4 × 46.1

Inscribed *C. Ginner* br
Exhibited AAA 1912 (75); Goupil Gallery 1914 (57)
Provenance: Anton Lock, by whom sold Christie's, 9 June 1978 (59)
Purchased from the Anthony d'Offay Gallery, 1984 [T03841]
Ref. Yale 1980, no.42

Piccadilly Circus 1912 [I, p.lxi] (pl.54)
Oil on canvas laid down on board; 81.3 × 66
Inscribed *C. GINNER* br
Exhibited CTG 3 (24); Brighton 1913–14 (35); Goupil Gallery 1914 (19)
Provenance: 1934, T. W. Spurr; H. Holdsworth, Halifax, by whom sold Christie's, 15 July 1938 (100), where bought Webberley Gallery, Toronto; 1942, Webberley Gallery, Chicago, by whom sold Christie's, 1 March 1974 (114); Edward Garrett
Purchased from the Anthony d'Offay Gallery, 1980 [T03096]
Ref. Baron 1979, pl.124

Porthleven 1922 [II, p.71]
Oil on canvas; 50.8 × 69.2
Inscribed *C. Ginner* br
Provenance: 1922, Lord Beaverbrook by whom given to the Contemporary Art Society, 1923, by whom allocated, 1924 [N03838]

Flask Walk – 12 May 1937. Coronation Day 1937 [III, p.174]
Oil on canvas; 61 × 50.8
Inscribed *C. Ginner* bl
Purchased from the artist, 1941 [N05276]

Snow in Pimlico 1939 [III, p.196]
Oil on canvas; 40.6 × 35.6
Inscribed *C. Ginner* br
Purchased from the artist, 1941 [N05270]

Hartland Point from Boscastle 1941 [III, p.215]
Oil on canvas; 58.4 × 85.7
Inscribed *C. Ginner* br
Purchased from the artist by the Chantrey Bequest, 1941 [N05306]

Emergency Water Storage Tank 1941–2 [III, p.219 as *Bombed Building for storing Water*]
Oil on canvas; 68.6 × 50.8
Inscribed *C. Ginner* br
Commissioned 1941 by the War Artists' Advisory Committee, by whom allocated, 1946 [N05695]

MANCHESTER: CITY ART GALLERIES

Landscape with Farmhouses c.1912–13 [probably I, p.lx as *Applehayes*]
Oil on canvas; 51.2 × 68.7
Inscribed *C. GINNER* br
Provenance: Eric C. Gregory, by whom given, 1929 [1929.6]
NOTE: The present title is clearly not that given to the painting by Ginner, nor is any painting with the title listed in the notebooks. Stylistically, the work belongs to the 1912–13 period. It has been positively identified as Gollick Park Farm at Clayhidon on the Devon/Somerset border (see R. Billingham's note to no.15, Applehayes 1986). Ginner was a guest at Applehayes, Clayhidon, home of H. B. Harrison, during the summers of 1912 and 1913.

Flask Walk, Hampstead (Snow) 1922 [II, p.73]
Oil on canvas; 61 × 45.7
Inscribed *C. GINNER* bl
Purchased from the artist, 1922 [1922.5]

Allotments at Bethnal Green 1943 [III, p. 230]
Oil on canvas; 55.9 × 76
Inscribed *C. GINNER* br
Commissioned 1943 by the War Artists' Advisory Committee, by whom allocated, 1947 [1947.399]

NEWCASTLE-UPON-TYNE: HATTON GALLERY, UNIVERSITY OF NEWCASTLE

Ripon Cathedral 1934 [III, p.136]
Oil on canvas; 79 × 53
Inscribed *C. GINNER* br
Provenance: 1934, London and North Eastern Railway;
Newcastle Chronicle and Journal Ltd
Purchased from Miller's Saleroom, Newcastle, late
1960s [OP.0058]

OXFORD: ASHMOLEAN MUSEUM

Hampstead Heath – Spring 1932 [III, p.109]
Oil on canvas; 69 × 51
Inscribed *C. GINNER* br
Provenance: 1933, Thomas Balston, by whom
bequeathed through the National Art Collections Fund,
1968

Cornish Cliffs
Oil on canvas; 69 × 51
Inscribed *C. GINNER* bl
Provenance: R. A. Bevan, by whom given, 1957

PLYMOUTH: CITY MUSEUM AND ART GALLERY

Plymouth Pier from the Hoe 1923 [II, p.103]
Oil on canvas; 76.2 × 61
Inscribed *C. GINNER* br
Provenance: 1929, Sir Alexander Park Lyle; Christie's,
6 March 1987 (209)
Purchased from Springfield Fine Arts, Ltd, 1987
[1987.5]
Ref. Connett 1992, p.55 in colour

The Spaniards Corner 1931 [III, p.95]
Oil on canvas; 68.9 × 51.1
Inscribed *C. GINNER* br
Provenance: 1934, Mrs J. A. Du Pontet, by whom given,
1934 [1934.15]

The Red Brick House 1934 [III, p.138 as *Hampstead
Residence*]
Oil on canvas; 69.2 × 51.2
Inscribed *C. Ginner* br
Provenance: 1935, T. W. Spurr; Arthur Crossland
Purchased from the Leger Galleries, 1959 [1959.230]

PRESTON: HARRIS MUSEUM AND ART GALLERY

Roof Tops [probably II, p.139 as *Hampstead Roofs* 1925]
Oil on canvas; 91.4 × 61
Inscribed *C. Ginner*
Purchased from the Modern Art Exhibition Gallery,
1935
NOTE: See *View of Hampstead*, Government Art
Collection, London.

READING: MUSEUM OF READING

The Stonemasons 1921 [II, p.51]
Oil on canvas; 91.5 × 71.2
Inscribed *C. Ginner* br
Provenance: 1921, Eustace Calland; Sotheby's, 3 April
1963 (42); A. J. Martin; Sotheby's, 17 July 1963 (33)
Purchased from Agnew's, 1975 [1976.55.1]

Morning Landscape, Isle of Wight 1929 [III, p.52]
Oil on canvas; 76 × 61.5
Inscribed *C. Ginner* br
Provenance: 1934, T. W. Spurr; A. Zwemmer; 1964,
Peter Rhodes, from whom purchased, 1964
[1964.1727.1]

SALFORD: MUSEUM AND ART GALLERY

Dwarf Sunflowers 1929 [III, p.63]
Oil on canvas; 67.9 × 49.2
Inscribed *C. Ginner* br
Provenance: 1933, T. W. Spurr; R. H. Spurr of Romney
Gallery, Southport, from whom purchased, 1945

SHEFFIELD: GRAVES ART GALLERY

Le Quai Duquesne 1913 [I, p.xi]
Oil on board; 26.5 × 18.3
Provenance: Given by the artist to Mary Godwin
Purchased from the Fine Art Society, 1976 [4228]

St John's Church, Chester 1935 [III, p.150]
Oil on canvas; 69 × 50.8
Provenance: 1936, T. W. Spurr; Mr Booth, from whom
purchased, 1952 [2987]

SOUTHAMPTON: CITY ART GALLERY

The Barges, Leeds 1916 [I, p.lxxxv]
Oil on canvas; 51 × 68.5
Inscribed *C. GINNER* br
Exhibited LG June 1916 (90)
Provenance: Dr E. Wightman Ginner (brother of the
artist)
Purchased from Agnew's, 1974
Ref. Watney 1980, pl.114

Early Morning, Surrey (Oxted) 1917 [I, p.xc]
Oil on canvas; 61.6 × 50.2
Inscribed *C. Ginner* br
Exhibited LG April 1917 (63)
Provenance: R. V. Williams
Purchased from the Piccadilly Gallery, 1969
Ref. Watney 1980, pl.113

Landscape
Oil on canvas; 50.9 × 61.3
Inscribed *C. Ginner* br
Allocated by the Contemporary Art Society, 1964
NOTE: Possibly *The Seaside Residence* of 1921 [II, p.63],
recorded as 'Lost' in the notebooks.

The Albert Memorial 1935 [III, p.155]
Oil on canvas; 81.3 × 61.4
Inscribed *C. Ginner* br
Purchased from the Royal Academy Summer
Exhibition, 1947

SOUTHPORT: ATKINSON ART GALLERY

Victoria Station. The Sunlit Square 1913 [I, p.lxvi]
Oil on canvas; 76.2 × 61
Inscribed *C. GINNER* br
Exhibited AAA 1913 (544); Doré 1913 (49); Goupil
Gallery 1914 (34)
Provenance: 1916, bought from the artist by the
Contemporary Art Society, by whom allocated to Bootle
Art Gallery (now part of Southport Collection), 1924
Ref. Baron 1979, pl.138; Christie's 1988, no.121 in
colour

Chideock in Dorset 1920 [II, p.46]
Oil on canvas; 68.5 × 50.8
Inscribed *C. GINNER* br
Provenance: 1926, Dr E. Wightman Ginner
Purchased, 1963

STOKE-ON-TRENT: CITY MUSEUM AND ART GALLERY

Salisbury Cathedral 1935 [III, p.152]
Oil on canvas; 68.6 × 58
Inscribed *C. GINNER* br
Provenance: 1936, T. W. Spurr, from whom purchased,
1937

SWANSEA: GLYNN VIVIAN ART GALLERY

Penally Hill 1916 [I, p.xcvii]
Oil on canvas; 61 × 50.8
Inscribed *C. Ginner* bl
Exhibited LG November 1916 (65); NEAC 1917
Provenance: Carfax Gallery, by whom given to the
Contemporary Art Society, by whom allocated, 1923

WAKEFIELD: ART GALLERY

Pond Square – Highgate Village 1932 [III, p.108]

Oil on canvas; 50.8 × 61
Inscribed *C. Ginner* br
Provenance: 1933, A. Zwemmer
Purchased from the Piccadilly Gallery, 1961

The River Avon near Salisbury 1935 [III, p.147]
Oil on canvas; 50.8 × 61
Inscribed *C. Ginner* br
Provenance: 1937, T. W. Spurr, from whom purchased,
1937

WORCESTER: CITY MUSEUM AND ART GALLERY

The Malvern Hills c. 1950 [IV, pp.29, 30]
Oil on canvas; 45 × 60
Provenance: Dr E. Wightman Ginner
Purchased from the CCA Galleries, 1996
NOTE: An unfinished (unsigned) work which is almost
certainly one of Ginner's last paintings.

WORTHING: MUSEUM AND ART GALLERY

Rottingdean 1914 [I, p.lxxiii]
Oil on canvas; 64.8 × 81.2
Inscribed *C. GINNER* br
Exhibited LG March 1914 (91); Goupil Gallery 1914
(33)
Provenance: 1921, Frank Rutter, from whom
purchased, 1935
Ref. Christie's 1988, no.157 in colour; Barbican 1997,
p.126 in colour

YORK: CITY ART GALLERY

White Chrysanthemums 1928 [III, p.46]
Oil on canvas; 61 × 50.8
Provenance: 1933, Miss Mabel Wilkinson; Arthur
Coulter, York, from whom purchased, 1955

Australia

ADELAIDE: ART GALLERY OF SOUTH AUSTRALIA

Battersea Park No. 1 1910 [I, p.xviii]
Oil on canvas; 69.4 × 50
Inscribed *C. GINNER* br
Provenance: 1911, Mrs Charles W. Harrison
Purchased from Messrs Tooth, 1958 [0.1820]
Ref. Adelaide 1997, p.43 in colour

PERTH: ART GALLERY OF WESTERN AUSTRALIA

Landscape near Marlborough 1938 [III, p.191]
Oil on canvas; 51 × 68.5
Inscribed *C. GINNER* br
Provenance: Mrs Ruby Ginner Dyer; Mrs Wightman
Harrison
Purchased from the Rutland Gallery, 1972

SYDNEY: ART GALLERY OF NEW SOUTH WALES

The River Lune, Lancaster 1950 [IV, p.27]
Oil on canvas; 60.9 × 91.7
Inscribed *C. Ginner* br
Purchased from the artist, 1951 [8606]

Canada

FREDERICTON, NEW BRUNSWICK: BEAVERBROOK ART
GALLERY

St Joseph, Highgate 1932 [III, p.113]
Oil on canvas; 61 × 50.8
Inscribed *C. Ginner* bl
Provenance: 1932, H. L. Wellington; 1954, Leicester
Galleries, from whom purchased by Lord Beaverbrook
Gift of the Second Beaverbook Foundation, 1960

OTTAWA: NATIONAL GALLERY OF CANADA

No. 14 Filling Factory. Hereford 1918 [I, p.cxx]
Oil on canvas; 304.8 × 365.8
Inscribed *C. GINNER* bl
Commissioned by the Canadian War Memorials
Committee, by whom transferred, 1921 [8173]

South Africa

CAPETOWN: SOUTH AFRICAN NATIONAL GALLERY

Concrete Landing Barges 1944 [IV, p.1]
Oil on canvas; 50.7 × 76.5
Inscribed *C GINNER* br
Commissioned 1943 by the War Artists' Advisory
Committee, by whom allocated, 1947 [1807]

DURBAN: ART GALLERY

Landscape
Oil on canvas; 53.6 × 71.1
Provenance: Contemporary Art Society, by whom
allocated, 1929 [931]

PIETERMARITZBURG: TATHAM ART GALLERY

Woodlane Farm, Beasley 1932 [III, p.115]
Oil on canvas; 60 × 45
Inscribed *C. GINNER* br
Provenance: 1934, T. W. Spurr; Christie's, 12 July 1974
(252)
Purchased through Brian Sewell, 1983

PORT ELIZABETH: KING GEORGE VI ART GALLERY

Leeds Roofs 1915 [I, p.lxxx]
Oil on canvas; 59.6 × 90
Inscribed *C. Ginner* br
Exhibited LG March 1915 (75); CMG 1915 (35)
Provenance: 1922, sold by the artist to unnamed buyer
as *Leeds*; 1956, Leger Gallery
Purchased from the Adler Galleries, Johannesburg,
1961

United States of America

NEW HAVEN: YALE CENTER FOR BRITISH ART, PAUL
MELLON COLLECTION

Design Study for Tiger Hunting (Cave of the Golden Calf)
1912 [I, p.lvi]
Oil and pencil on cardboard; 34 × 57.5
Provenance: Mrs Robert Bevan
Ref. Barbican 1997, p.101

The Fruit Stall, King's Cross 1914 [I, p. lxxv]
Oil on canvas; 65.4 × 55.9
Inscribed *C. GINNER* br
Exhibited Goupil Gallery 1914 (46); AAA 1914; CMG
1915 (2)
Provenance: 1934, T. W. Spurr; Christie's, 30 July 1936
(294) bought by Anton Lock; Christie's, 17 November
1978 (24)
Purchased from the Anthony d'Offay Gallery, 1980
[B1980.18]
Ref. Yale 1980, no.46

Spencer Frederick Gore
1878–1914

Born at Epsom, Surrey. Trained at the Slade School 1896–9. Visited Spain with Wyndham Lewis winter 1902–3 and met Sickert in Dieppe in 1904. Founder-member Fitzroy Street Group (1907), AAA (1908), Camden Town Group (1911) and its president, London Group (1913), but his death from pneumonia in March 1914 meant his works were included only in the first London Group exhibition. Exhibited with the NEAC 1906–11 and 1913–14 (member 1909). Exhibited at the *Salon des Indépendants* in Paris 1906–10 (*sociétaire* 1906). Included in the 'English Group' who contributed to the 'Second Post-Impressionist Exhibition', Grafton Galleries 1912–13. Married Mary Johanna Kerr in January 1912. Supervised decorative scheme and painted (with Ginner and Wyndham Lewis) murals for Madame Strindberg's 'Cave of the Golden Calf' 1912. Principal organizer of 1913–14 exhibition at Brighton of 'English Post-Impressionists, Cubists and Others'. Painting trips out of London during the summers and early autumns: Normandy 1904; Billy, France 1905; Dieppe 1906; Yorkshire and Hertingfordbury 1907; Hertingfordbury 1908; Hertingfordbury and Somerset (at Applehayes as guest of H. B. Harrison) 1909; Somerset (Applehayes) 1910; Letchworth 1912; Somerset (Applehayes with Bevan and Ginner) 1913.

PRINCIPAL LONDON ADDRESSES 1906–14

1909–12: 31 Mornington Crescent, Camden Town; 1912–13: 2 Houghton Place, Camden Town; 1913–14: 6 Cambrian Road, Richmond.

EXHIBITIONS WITHIN HIS LIFETIME

Chenil Gallery 1911; (jointly with Gilman) Carfax Gallery 1913.

EXHIBITIONS SINCE HIS DEATH

Memorial exhibition Carfax Gallery 1916 (catalogue preface by Sickert); Carfax Gallery 1918; Paterson and Carfax Gallery 1920; Leicester Galleries 1928 (prefatory note to catalogue by Manson); Arts Council 1955 (catalogue introduction by J. Wood Palmer); (jointly with his son, Frederick Gore) Redfern Gallery 1962; The Minories, Colchester (and at Oxford and Sheffield) 1970 (catalogue compiled and introduced by John Woodeson); Anthony d'Offay Gallery 1974; Anthony d'Offay Gallery 1983; New York, Davis & Langdale Company, 1990 (drawings and watercolours); Museum of Richmond 1996–7.

LITERATURE

W. R. Sickert, 'A Perfect Modern', *New Age*, 9 April 1914; John Rothenstein, chapter on Gore (pp.194–202) in *Modern English Painters: Sickert to Smith* (London: Eyre & Spottiswoode, 1952); John Woodeson, 'Spencer F. Gore', unpublished MA report, University of London, 1968; Frederick Gore, 'Spencer Gore: a Memoir by his Son', catalogue introduction to 1974 d'Offay Gallery exhibition; John Woodeson, 'Spencer Gore', *Connoisseur*, March 1974; Frederick Gore and Richard Shone, catalogue to 1983 d'Offay Gallery exhibition; Claudio Zambianchi, 'Appunti su Spencer Frederick Gore e la pittura inglese fra il 1908 e il 1910', *Storia dell'Arte*, no.58, 1986; Frederick Gore and Robert Upstone, *Spencer Gore in Richmond*, catalogue of 1996–7 exhibition (Richmond 1996–7); Frederick Gore, chapter on Gore (pp.66–76), in Pontoise 1998–9.

PICTURES SHOWN AT EXHIBITIONS OF THE CAMDEN TOWN GROUP

JUNE 1911
24 *The Bed Sitting Room*
25 *Mornington Crescent*
26 *Scene III*
27 *Stage Sunrise*
A family ledger recording sales made by Gore at the

first show of the Camden Town Group indicates that *The Bed Sitting Room* represented a 'girl on bed'. Under the same reference two paintings called *Mornington Crescent* are listed, one showing the tube station sold to Somerset Maugham (probably the British Council, possibly the Johannesburg, version; see note to pl.16), the other sold to Hugh Hammersley. The latter could be the painting called *Mornington Crescent* (which also shows the tube station) sold by the Hammersley family at Christie's, 12 June 1987 (264). The Hammersley version, however, does not include a view of the Camden Theatre mentioned in press descriptions of the exhibited painting. It is possible that, having sold one painting to Somerset Maugham, Gore substituted the Hammersley version at a later date. This would explain why five paintings are listed in the family ledger rather than the four catalogued. *Scene III* and *Stage Sunrise* were both scenes from the ballet 'Paquita', which ran at the Alhambra Theatre in Leicester Square for 25 weeks from 12 October 1908. Four paintings by Gore of this production are listed in family papers, of which two were sold in 1909 to Mrs Walter Sickert (one probably the painting now in the Government Art Collection, London, the other with the Fine Art Society in 1976). *Scene III* (in a gypsy camp) was bought in 1911 by someone called Hughes (probably the version at Sotheby's, 21 May 1986, lot 101). *Stage Sunrise* is in a private collection (rep. Baron 1979, pl.88).

DECEMBER 1911
15 *The Mad Pierrot Ballet* (pl.20)
16 *The Garden*
17 *Portrait*
18 *The Promenade* (see note to pl.20)
The identification of *The Garden* is problematic. Gore painted garden scenes at most of the places where he worked, especially at Garth House, Hertingfordbury, in 1908 and 1909 and at Rowlandson House in 1911. He exhibited a painting called *The Garden* at the NEAC in 1909, probably a Garth House subject (examples in public collections include pictures in the Walker Art Gallery, Liverpool, and the Harris Museum, Preston). However, press descriptions of *The Garden* at the Carfax Gallery in 1911 indicate this was an urban scene. The *Daily Telegraph* (14 December 1911) noted the artistic rendering of 'the row of typically English houses at the back', while *Truth* (13 December 1911) remarked that the painting might show 'the next-door villa trembling in the misty light'. Several pictures fit these descriptions. Possible candidates include the picture in the Toledo Art Gallery, Ohio; *The Garden, Rowlandson House* (rep. Anthony d'Offay 1974, no.14) which shows the view from the garden staircase railings across the wall to Rutland Street on the opposite side of Hampstead Road; and *The End of the Garden* (also Anthony d'Offay 1974, no.2, not illustrated) painted from a point further to the right, in front of the Hampstead Road façade of Rowlandson House, to show the view over the garden wall straight down Rutland Street as far as Stanhope Street.

DECEMBER 1912
13 *Letchworth Common*
14 *The Broken Fence*
15 *Euston from the Nursery* (pl.55)
16 *The Pond*
Letchworth Common may be *Letchworth* in the Tate Gallery. *The Broken Fence* could be the painting now called *Extensive Landscape* (Yale Center for British Art, New Haven) in which a broken section of fence features on the left. *The Pond* was described by the *Pall Mall Gazette* (12 December 1912) as 'gold and green … rhythmical in design'. This may be the picture in the Worthing Art Gallery unless, as is possible, the Worthing picture represents a Richmond Park scene. On the whole, by the time the critics had commended Bayes, reviled Lewis and discussed Sickert, little space was left for other exhibitors at the Carfax Gallery. Gore's work was mentioned in passing without much enthusiasm (see, for example, *The Times*, 17 December

1912: 'well-considered ... of an accomplished mediocrity'), but seldom described in terms helpful to identification.

PAINTINGS IN PUBLIC COLLECTIONS

The list below covers all paintings by Gore in public collections.

'Gilman labels': in general, Gore signed paintings on their sale. After Gore's sudden death, his widow and Gilman sorted out all the paintings left in his studio. They stamped the artist's name (S. F. GORE within a boxed outline) on the unsigned paintings and placed descriptive handwritten labels on the back. The labels were numbered according to the presumed date of each painting within the chronological sequence of Gore's work. The number is sometimes followed by the letter 'a', denoting that Gilman and Mrs Gore considered the painting especially important. While not necessarily infallible, these numbers provide an excellent guide to the dates of Gore's work. Sadly, many of these labels were removed before their purport was appreciated. Additionally, pictures sold or otherwise dispersed before Gore's death never had Gilman labels. However, some labels survive. Gilman numbers (abbreviated here as G. followed by the number) are quoted below, in square brackets after the title and date, as part of the essential data of a picture. It is not always possible to decipher the numbers. In cases of doubt about a reading, the number is prefixed with a question mark.

Plate references are given to reproductions in the d'Offay Gallery 1983 exhibition catalogue and in the Richmond 1996–7 catalogue (all in colour), as well as to other works.

Provenance: Gore family ownership may be assumed in most cases where no alternative provenance is stated prior to the name of the dealer through whom a purchase was made.

United Kingdom

ABERDEEN: ART GALLERY

Hertingfordbury c.1908
Oil on canvas; 50.8 × 76.2
Purchased, 1967

The Blue Petticoat c.1910
Oil on canvas; 35.3 × 30.1
Purchased from the Redfern Gallery, 1940
Ref. Christie's 1988, no.74

BELFAST: ULSTER MUSEUM

Applehayes c.1909–10
Oil on canvas; 51.1 × 61.1
Inscribed *S. F. Gore* br
Purchased from the Leicester Galleries through the Lloyd Patterson Bequest, 1929

BIRMINGHAM: CITY ART GALLERY

Self Portrait c.1906 [?G.30]
Oil on canvas; 53.3 × 43.2
Studio stamp br
Purchased from the Redfern Gallery, 1962
Ref. Richmond 1996–7, p.10; Pontoise 1998–9, p.67

Portrait of the Artist's Wife 1911 [G.127]
Oil on canvas; 40.5 × 33
Studio stamp br
Purchased from the Anthony d'Offay Gallery, 1983
Ref. d'Offay 1983, pl.14 and in colour

Wood in Richmond Park 1913–14
Oil on canvas; 50.8 × 61
Studio stamp bl
Purchased from the Leicester Galleries, 1928
Ref. Richmond 1996–7, p.36

BRADFORD: CARTWRIGHT HALL ART GALLERY

Panshanger Park c.1908
Oil on canvas; 50.8 × 61
Purchased from the Redfern Gallery, 1962

Suburban Street (Cambrian Road) 1913–14
Oil on canvas; 50.8 × 40.3
Studio stamp br
Provenance: Sir Edward Marsh, bequeathed to the Contemporary Art Society, by whom allocated, 1956
Ref. Christie's 1988, no.160; Richmond 1996–7, p.24

BRISTOL: CITY MUSEUM AND ART GALLERY

Nude on a Bed 1910
Oil on canvas; 30.4 × 40.5
Inscribed *F.G.* and studio stamp br
Purchased from Reid & Lefevre, 1950 [85/1950]
Ref. Baron 1979, pl.20; Watney 1980, pl.44; Yale 1980, no.56; Pontoise 1998–9, p.69

CAMBRIDGE: FITZWILLIAM MUSEUM

Morning: The Green Dress c.1908–9 (pl.30)
Oil on canvas; 45.7 × 35.5
Provenance: Frank Rutter; J.W. Freshfield, by whom bequeathed, 1955 [PD 3–1955]
Ref. Baron 1979, pl.39 and in colour p.21; Yale 1980, no.50

A View from the Window at 6 Cambrian Road, Richmond 1913
Oil on canvas; 50.8 × 40
Studio stamp
Provenance: Robert Bevan and thence by descent in his family
Purchased from Anthony d'Offay, 1983 [PD. 6–1983]

CAMBRIDGE: KING'S COLLEGE, KEYNES COLLECTION

The Toilet c.1910
Oil on canvas; 44.8 × 34.6
Inscribed *S.F. Gore* br
Purchased from the Redfern Gallery by John Maynard (Lord) Keynes, 1943
Ref. Christie's 1988, no.50

Nearing Euston Station 1911
Oil on canvas; 49.8 × 60
Provenance: Sir Michael Sadler; his sale, Christie's, 30 November 1928, lot 133, where bought by John Maynard (Lord) Keynes
Ref. Barbican 1997, p.102 in colour

CARDIFF: NATIONAL MUSEUM OF WALES

Mornington Crescent Gardens c.1911 [G.115]
Oil on canvas; 51 × 61.3
Studio stamp br
Provenance: J. L. Behrend; Leicester Galleries; 1962, Miss Margaret Davies, by whom bequeathed, 1963 [NMWA 2252]

CHICHESTER: PALLANT HOUSE GALLERY

The Garden Path, Garth House c.1910
Oil on canvas; 40.9 × 50.8
Provenance: R. G. Boulton; Walter Hussey, by whom bequeathed, 1985
Ref. Christie's 1988, no.68 in colour

DARLINGTON: BOROUGH OF DARLINGTON ART COLLECTIONS

Yorkshire Landscape 1907 [?G.66]
Oil on canvas; 44.5 × 58.8
Studio stamp br
Exhibited possibly Carfax Gallery 1916 (20); Carfax Gallery 1918 (12)
Provenance: 1918, S. E. Thornton from Carfax Gallery; Contemporary Art Society, by whom allocated, 1943

EXETER: ROYAL ALBERT MEMORIAL MUSEUM AND ART GALLERY

Panshanger Park 1909 [G.84]
Oil on canvas; 50.9×61.1
Studio stamp br
Exhibited possibly Carfax Gallery 1916 (6)
Purchased from the Redfern Gallery, 1968 [263/1968]

HUDDERSFIELD: LIBRARY AND ART GALLERY

The Terrace Gardens c.1912–13
Oil on canvas; 51×61.5
Exhibited Goupil Gallery Salon, autumn 1913 (156)
Purchased from Roland, Browse & Delbanco, 1956

IPSWICH: CHRISTCHURCH MANSION AND WOLSEY ART GALLERY

Interior. Mornington Crescent c.1910 [G.99a]
Oil on canvas; 40.6×50.8
Studio stamp
Purchased from the Fine Art Society, 1968 [1968-38]
Ref. Christie's 1988, no.77
NOTE: Related to *Interior, Fireside Scene*, City Art Gallery, Leeds.

KINGSTON UPON HULL: FERENS ART GALLERY

Still Life with Apples c.1912
Oil on canvas; 38.1×50.8
Inscribed *S F Gore* br
Exhibited Carfax Gallery 1913 (15)
Provenance: E. C. Gregory; David Gibbs; John Russell
Purchased from Agnew's, 1961
Ref. Baron 1979, pl.53; d'Offay 1983, pl.27; Christie's 1988, no.100 in colour; Barbican 1997, p.152

KINGSTON UPON HULL: THE UNIVERSITY OF HULL ART COLLECTION

Somerset Landscape c.1908–9
Oil on canvas; 50.8×61
Purchased from Fred Mayor, 1965 [49]

The Garden of Rowlandson House c.1911
Oil on canvas; 38.1×45.7
Provenance: J. B. Manson; Miss Mary Manson and Mrs Jean Goullet, by whom given, 1963 [6]
Ref. Watney 1980, pl.47
NOTE: Similar to Sickert's painting of this subject in the Tate Gallery, London.

KIRKCALDY: MUSEUM AND ART GALLERY

The Duck Pond 1907 [G.71]
Oil on canvas; 51.5×61
Studio stamp br
Exhibited Chenil Gallery 1911 (8); Carfax Gallery 1916 (31)
Provenance: Scottish Gallery, Edinburgh; 1942, J. W. Blyth, from whom purchased, 1964

The Garden, Hertingfordbury 1909
Oil on canvas; 41×51
Inscribed *SF Gore* br
Provenance: Reid & Lefevre; 1951, J. W. Blyth
Purchased from Blyth's estate, 1964

The Gravel Pit c.1909
Oil on canvas; 51×61.5
Studio stamp bl
Provenance: Scottish Gallery, Edinburgh; 1951, J. W. Blyth
Purchased from Blyth's estate, 1964

Interior
Oil on canvas; 59.5×49.5
Inscribed *SF Gore* br
Exhibited possibly Chenil Gallery 1911 (19)
Provenance: Scottish Gallery, Edinburgh; 1947, J. W. Blyth
Purchased from Blyth's estate, 1964

LEEDS: CITY ART GALLERY

Interior with Nude Washing 1907 [G.46] (pl.29)
Oil on canvas; 55.8×40.6
Studio stamp bl
Exhibited possibly Chenil Gallery 1911 (22)
Purchased from the Leicester Galleries by the Leeds Art Collections Fund and given, 1932
Ref. Baron 1979, pl.19; Yale 1980, no.48

Interior, Fireside Scene c.1910 [G.98a]
Oil on canvas; 50.8×61
Studio stamp br
Exhibited possibly AAA 1911 (121); probably Carfax Gallery 1918 (18)
Purchased from Reid & Lefevre, 1950
Ref. Baron 1979, pl.22

The Balustrade 1911
Oil on canvas; 60.9×50.8
Inscribed *S. F. Gore* br
Exhibited Carfax Gallery 1913 (37)
Purchased from the Redfern Gallery, 1949
Ref. d'Offay 1983, pl.13

Mornington Crescent c.1911
Oil on canvas; 40.6×50.8
Studio stamp br
Purchased from the Leicester Galleries, 1934

Letchworth 1912
Oil on canvas; 25.4×30.5
Studio stamp br
Purchased by the Leeds Art Collections Fund and given, 1936

In Berkshire c.1912
Oil on canvas; 38.1×53.3
Studio stamp br
Purchased 1936
NOTE: Location denoted by title may be mistaken. Painting more probably a Letchworth (Herts.) subject.

LEICESTER: NEW WALK MUSEUM AND ART GALLERY

Harold Gilman's House, Letchworth 1912 [G.142]
Oil on canvas; 63.5×76.2
Studio stamp br
Purchased from the Anthony d'Offay Gallery, 1974
Ref. Pontoise 1998–9, no.86, p.74
NOTE: A view of 100 Wilbury Road where Gilman moved, but seldom lived, after 1909. The Government Art Collection and the Graves Art Gallery, Sheffield have versions of this subject.

LETCHWORTH: GARDEN CITY CORPORATION

The Garden City, Letchworth 1912 [G.160]
Oil on canvas; 61×66
Studio stamp br
Exhibited possibly Carfax Gallery 1913 (32); possibly Whitechapel 1914 (416)
Purchased from the Anthony d'Offay Gallery, 1974
Ref. *Connoisseur*, March 1974, p.178
NOTE: Two pictures with this title were exhibited at Paterson and Carfax in 1920 (as nos.16 and 26). An annotated catalogue described the former as 'showing city & palings in foreground', as does this painting, whereas the latter was annotated 'with cottage & garden & distance'.

LETCHWORTH: MUSEUM AND ART GALLERY

Letchworth, The Road 1912 [G.148a]
Oil on canvas; 40.6×44.5
Inscribed *S. F. Gore* br
Purchased from the Anthony d'Offay Gallery, 1983
Ref. d'Offay 1983, pl.22 and in colour; Christie's 1988, no.125 in colour

LIVERPOOL: WALKER ART GALLERY

The Garden, Garth House 1908 [G.83]
Oil on canvas; 51.4×61

Studio stamp and inscribed *F. Gore* br
Exhibited possibly NEAC winter 1909 (112) as *The Garden*
Purchased from Reid & Lefevre, 1949 [3138]
Ref. AC 1955, pl.IV

LONDON: ARTS COUNCIL COLLECTION, HAYWARD GALLERY

Landscape Somerset c.1909
Oil on canvas; 40.6 × 50.8
Studio stamp br
Purchased from the Redfern Gallery, 1962

Chisholm Road, Richmond 1913–14
Oil on canvas; 40.6 × 50.8
Studio stamp br
Exhibited possibly Carfax Gallery 1916 (21)
Purchased from the Leicester Galleries, 1955
Ref. Richmond 1996–7, p.26 in colour

LONDON: BRITISH COUNCIL COLLECTION

Mornington Crescent c.1911
Oil on canvas; 50.8 × 61
Exhibited possibly Chenil Gallery 1911 (9 or 15); possibly NEAC summer 1911 (211); probably CTG 1 (25)
Provenance: Hugh Blaker
Purchased from the Leicester Galleries, 1948
Ref. Baron 1979, pl.87; Watney 1980, pl.46; Christie's 1988, no.96 in colour; Richmond 1996–7, p.16; Pontoise 1998–9, no.85, p.84 in colour

LONDON: GOVERNMENT ART COLLECTION

Landscape c.1907–8
Oil on canvas; 49 × 39.5
Purchased from the Mayor Gallery, 1957 [3686]

Hertfordshire Landscape 1909
Oil on canvas; 41 × 50.5
Studio stamp br
Purchased from the Mayor Gallery, 1968 [8178]

Somerset Landscape c.1909–10
Oil on canvas; 41.5 × 50
Studio stamp br
Purchased from the Leicester Galleries, 1960 [5219]

Alhambra Music Hall. Ballet 'Paquita' 1909
Oil on canvas; 40.6 × 51
Provenance: Probably 1909, Mrs Walter Sickert
Purchased from the Mayor Gallery, 1961 [5526]

Harold Gilman's House at Letchworth 1912
Oil on panel; 40 × 46.4
Studio stamp bl
Purchased from the Leicester Galleries, 1962 [5928]
Ref. Christie's 1988, no.124
NOTE: See the note to the painting of the same title in the Leicester New Walk Museum and Art Gallery.

LONDON: MUSEUM OF LONDON

Mornington Crescent 1911
Oil on canvas; 40.5 × 50.8
Inscribed *S. F. G* br
Provenance: Edward Le Bas; Christie's, 12 June 1981 (32)
Purchased through the Anthony d'Offay Gallery, 1981 [81.323]

Down the Garden 1912 [G.143a]
Oil on canvas; 51 × 41
Inscribed *S F Gore* br
Purchased from the Anthony d'Offay Gallery, 1983 [83.360]
Ref. d'Offay 1983, pl.18

LONDON: NATIONAL PORTRAIT GALLERY

Self Portrait c.1914 [G.198]

Oil on canvas; 40.6 × 30.5
Studio stamp br
Purchased from the Anthony d'Offay Gallery, 1974 [4981]
Ref. Baron 1979, pl.145; Watney 1980, pl.107; Christie's 1988, no.4 in colour

LONDON: TATE GALLERY

Inez and Taki 1910
Oil on canvas; 40.6 × 50.8
Inscribed *S. F. Gore* bl
Exhibited AAA 1910 (714)
Provenance: 1910, Sir Louis F. Fergusson
Purchased from the Leicester Galleries, 1948 [N05859]
Ref. Watney 1980, pl.38a

Rule Britannia 1910
Oil on canvas; 76.2 × 63.5
Exhibited NEAC summer 1910 (204); Chenil Galleries 1911 (3); Whitechapel 1914 (417)
Purchased from the Anthony d'Offay Gallery by the Patrons of British Art, by whom given through the Tate Gallery Foundation, 1992 [T06521]
Ref. Watney 1980, pl.19; d'Offay 1983, pl.7 and in colour

North London Girl c.1911
Oil on canvas; 76.2 × 61
Studio stamp br
Provenance: 1928, J.W. Freshfield, by whom bequeathed, 1955 [T00027]
Ref. Baron 1979, pl.42

Mornington Crescent c.1911
Oil on canvas; 63.5 × 76.2
Exhibited Carfax Gallery 1916 (3) as *Mornington Crescent Gardens*; Goupil Gallery 1918, 'The Collection of the late Judge William Evans' (70) as *The Tree*
Provenance: 1916, Judge William Evans; 1918, Lord Henry Cavendish-Bentinck
Bequeathed by Lady Henry Cavendish-Bentinck, 1940 [N05099]
Ref. AC 1955, pl.v

A Singer at the Bedford Music Hall 1912 [G.147a]
Oil on canvas; 53.3 × 43.2
Studio stamp br
Provenance: Mr & Mrs Robert Lewin, by whom given through Friends of the Tate Gallery, 1978 [T02260]

Sketch for a Mural Decoration for 'The Cave of the Golden Calf' 1912
Oil on paper mounted on card; 30.5 × 60.3
Provenance: 1912, Mrs Malcolm Drummond; c.1930–5, Redfern Gallery
Purchased Sotheby's, 12 July 1961, lot 242 [T00446]
Ref. Watney 1980, pl.90

Letchworth 1912
Oil on canvas; 50.8 × 61
Studio stamp br
Exhibited possibly CTG 3 (13) as *Letchworth Common*
Provenance: J.W. Freshfield
Purchased from Messrs Tooth, 1933 [N04675]
Ref. Watney 1980, pl.124

The Cinder Path 1912
Oil on canvas, 68.6 × 78.7
Exhibited Grafton Gallery 1912–13, 'Second Post-Impressionist Exhibition' (116)
Provenance: Mme Gerfain; Frank Williams Burford; John Lumley
Purchased from Agnew's, 1975 [T01960]
Ref. Baron 1979, pl.113; Watney 1980, col. pl.3; Barbican 1997, p.103 in colour

The Beanfield, Letchworth 1912 [G.154a] (pl.22)
Oil on canvas; 30.5 × 40.6
Inscribed *S F Gore* br
Exhibited Carfax Gallery 1913 (26)
Purchased from the Anthony d'Offay Gallery, 1974 [T01859]

Ref. *Connoisseur*, March 1974, p.174 in colour; Baron 1979, pl.112; Watney 1980, pl.110

The Fig Tree 1912
Oil on canvas; 63.5 × 76.2
Inscribed *S. F. Gore* br
Exhibited Carfax Gallery 1913 (46); NEAC summer 1913 (151); Brighton 1913–14 (50)
Provenance: 1939, J.W. Freshfield, by whom bequeathed, 1955 [T00028]

Houghton Place 1912
Oil on canvas; 50.8 × 61
Studio stamp br
Provenance: 1916, Contemporary Art Society, by whom allocated, 1927 [N03839]

The Gas Cooker 1913 [G.173]
Oil on canvas; 73 × 36.8
Studio stamp br
Exhibited Brighton 1913–14 (53); Carfax Gallery 1916 (36)
Chantrey Purchase from the artist's widow through the Redfern Gallery, 1962 [T00496]
Ref. Connett 1992, p.37

From a Window in Cambrian Road, Richmond 1913
Oil on canvas; 55.9 × 68.6
Studio stamp br
Given by subscribers, 1920 [N03558]
Ref. Richmond 1996–7, p.22; Pontoise 1998–9, p.75

The Artist's Wife 1913
Oil on canvas; 76.5 × 63.6
Studio stamp br
Given by Frederick Gore, the artist's son, 1983 [T03561]
Ref. Watney 1980, pl.106; Richmond 1996–7, p.20

Richmond Park 1913–14
Oil on canvas; 50.8 × 76.2
Studio stamp br
Exhibited possibly NEAC summer 1914 (181) as *Richmond Park Trees*
Provenance: 1920, Lord Henry Cavendish-Bentinck
Bequeathed by Lady Henry Cavendish-Bentinck, 1940 [N05100]
Ref. Richmond 1996–7, p.38

MANCHESTER: CITY ART GALLERIES

Richmond, Winter 1914 [probably G.205] (pl.63)
Oil on canvas; 50.8 × 60.9
Studio stamp br
Purchased from the Leicester Galleries, 1928 [1928.78]
Ref. Richmond 1996–7, p.36

MANCHESTER: WHITWORTH ART GALLERY

Spring in North London, 2 Houghton Place 1912
Oil on canvas; 50.8 × 40.7
Inscribed *S F Gore* br
Purchased from the Anthony d'Offay Gallery, 1983 [O.1983.4]
Ref. d'Offay 1983, pl.19 and in colour; Christie's 1988, no.136

OXFORD: ASHMOLEAN MUSEUM

Harbour Scene
Oil on canvas; 60 × 50.5
Provenance: Gerald Reitlinger, by whom given, 1972, acquired, 1978

The Cinder Path 1912
Oil on canvas; 34.9 × 40
Studio stamp br
Exhibited Carfax Gallery 1913 (31)
Provenance: R. A. Bevan, by whom given, 1957
Ref. Yale 1980, no.64; d'Offay 1983, pl.25; Christie's 1988, no.126 in colour; Richmond 1996–7, p.18

Richmond Park 1913–14
Oil on canvas; 55 × 74.9
Provenance: R. A. Bevan, by whom given, 1957
Ref. Richmond 1996–7, p.30

PLYMOUTH: CITY MUSEUM AND ART GALLERY

Some-one waits 1907 [G.65] (pl.28)
Oil on canvas; 51.2 × 41
Studio stamp bl
Exhibited NEAC spring 1908 (62)
Purchased from the artist's widow, 1958 [1958.210]
Ref. Baron 1979, pl.33; Watney 1980, pl.24; Christie's 1988, no.35 in colour; Pontoise 1998–9, no.78, p.85 in colour

PRESTON: HARRIS MUSEUM AND ART GALLERY

Garden at Hertingfordbury
Oil on canvas; 40.6 × 50.8
Studio stamp
Provenance: A. B. Clifton; Contemporary Art Society, by whom allocated, 1942

READING: MUSEUM OF READING

The Mimram, Panshanger Park 1908
Oil on canvas; 50.8 × 61
Purchased from Agnew's, 1976 [1976.57.1]
Ref. Christie's 1988, no.47

SHEFFIELD: GRAVES ART GALLERY

Reclining Nude Figure c.1908 [G.73]
Oil on canvas; 46 × 61.2
Studio stamp br
Provenance: Charles Wilfred Janson, from whom purchased, 1935 [1884]

Harold Gilman's House at Letchworth 1912
Oil on canvas; 40.9 × 51
Provenance: E. W. Jenkinson, from whom purchased, 1979 [4472]
NOTE: See the note to the painting of the same title in Leicester New Walk Museum and Art Gallery.

SOUTHAMPTON: CITY ART GALLERY

The Pool, Panshanger Park 1908 [G.80a]
Oil on canvas; 50.8 × 61
Studio stamp br
Purchased, 1933
NOTE: Close to the painting of the same title and size in the Art Gallery of New South Wales, Sydney.

View from a Window c.1908–9
Oil on canvas; 50.8 × 40.3
Provenance: Hugh Blaker
Purchased from the Leicester Galleries, 1938
Ref. Watney 1980, pl.45; d'Offay 1983, pl.6

Brighton Pier 1913
Oil on canvas; 63.5 × 76.3
Exhibited probably Doré 1913 (197); possibly Brighton 1913–14 (54)
Provenance: Mr A. Phillips, from whom purchased, 1956
Ref. d'Offay 1983, pl.32; Barbican 1997, p.151 in colour; Pontoise 1998–9, no.90, p.87 in colour

STOKE-ON-TRENT: CITY MUSEUM AND ART GALLERY

Harrington Square from 2 Houghton Place 1913 [G.164]
Oil on canvas; 40.2 × 50.9
Studio stamp bl
Purchased from the Anthony d'Offay Gallery, 1983
Ref. d'Offay 1983, pl.29

WAKEFIELD: ART GALLERY

The Cricket Match c.1908 [?G.82]

Oil on canvas; 50.8 × 61
Studio stamp br
Exhibited AAA 1911 (120)
Provenance: Probably Mrs Smith Masters; Mr
L. Mallinson, from whom purchased, 1945
Ref. Baron 1979, pl. 57; Christie's 1988, no.48;
Richmond 1996–7, p.12

WORTHING: MUSEUM AND ART GALLERY

*The Pond c.*1912
Oil on canvas; 50.8 × 61
Inscribed *S.F. Gore* br
Exhibited possibly CTG 3 (16); possibly Brighton
1913–14 (51)
Purchased, 1948

YORK: CITY ART GALLERY

*The Balcony at the Alhambra c.*1911–12
Oil on canvas; 48.2 × 35.5
Studio stamp bl
Provenance: Lord Killanin
Purchased from the Anthony d'Offay Gallery, 1983
Ref. Baron 1979, pl.6; Watney 1980, col. pl.4; Yale
1980, no.62; d'Offay 1983, pl.12; Christie's 1988, no.67
in colour

From a Canal Bridge, Chalk Farm Road 1913 [G.165]
Oil on canvas; 48.3 × 68.6
Studio stamp bl
Exhibited probably LG March 1914 as *The Canal*
Provenance: Ernest Gye; Sotheby's, 25 June 1952 (125)
where bought by Leger Galleries; 1952, the Very
Reverend E. Milner-White, by whom given, 1963

YORK: NATIONAL RAILWAY MUSEUM

Letchworth Station 1912
Oil on canvas; 63.5 × 76.2
Exhibited Grafton Gallery 1912–13, 'Second Post-
Impressionist Exhibition' (133); Whitechapel 1914 (418)
Provenance: Hugh Blaker; Peter Cochrane
Purchased from the Anthony d'Offay Gallery, 1983
Ref. Yale 1980, no.66; d'Offay 1983, pl.26 and in
colour; Christie's 1988, no.127 in colour; Barbican
1997, p.103 in colour; Pontoise 1998–9, no.88, p.86 in
colour

Europe

DUBLIN, IRELAND: HUGH LANE MUNICIPAL GALLERY OF
MODERN ART

In Yorkshire 1907
Oil on canvas; 45.7 × 61.6
Studio stamp br
Provenance: Leicester Galleries; 1928, A. E. Anderson,
by whom given, 1931

Australia

ADELAIDE: ART GALLERY OF SOUTH AUSTRALIA

*Autumn Sussex c.*1908–9
Oil on canvas; 46 × 61.3
Studio stamp br
Provenance: Redfern Gallery; 1943, the Hon. Edward
Sackville-West
Purchased from the Piccadilly Gallery, 1967 [0.2121]

BRISBANE: QUEENSLAND ART GALLERY

*English Landscape c.*1907–8
Oil on canvas; 40 × 50
Studio stamp br
Purchased from the Lefevre Gallery, 1956 [1:0707]

MELBOURNE: NATIONAL GALLERY OF VICTORIA

The White Seats, Rowlandson House 1911
Oil on canvas; 61.1 × 50.7
Inscribed *S. F. Gore* br
Exhibited Carfax Gallery 1913 (44) and Brighton
1913–14 (55) as *The White Seats*; Carfax Gallery 1918
(1)
Purchased, 1946

PERTH: WESTERN AUSTRALIAN ART GALLERY

View from the Balcony, 2 Houghton Place 1913 [G.169a]
Oil on canvas; 51 × 40.8
Studio stamp
Purchased from the Anthony d'Offay Gallery, 1976
NOTE: Three paintings called *From a Window in
Houghton Place (Nos. 1, 2 and 3)* were included in an
exhibition at the Paterson and Carfax Gallery in 1920.
Catalogue annotations prove that the Perth version was
neither *No. 2* nor *No. 3*, but it could have been *No. 1*
(annotated 'balcony & houses & trees').

SYDNEY: ART GALLERY OF NEW SOUTH WALES

The Pool, Panshanger Park 1908 [G.79a]
Oil on canvas; 50.9 × 61.1
Studio stamp br
Purchased from Messrs Tooth, 1933 [901]

The Icknield Way 1912 [G.156] (pl.23)
Oil on canvas; 63.5 × 76.2
Studio stamp br
Exhibited Alpine Club Gallery 1913, 'Grafton Group'
(1)
Purchased from the Redfern Gallery, 1962 [OB2.1962]
Ref. Baron 1979, pl.115 and in colour p.51

Canada

FREDERICTON, NEW BRUNSWICK: BEAVERBROOK ART
GALLERY

Woman standing in a Window 1908
Oil on canvas; 50.8 × 35.6
Purchased from the Leicester Galleries, 1955

HAMILTON, ONTARIO: ART GALLERY OF HAMILTON

*The Bedroom c.*1908 [G.76]
Oil on canvas; 50.8 × 40.6
Studio stamp br
Purchased from the Leicester Galleries and given by the
Women's Committee, 1960
Ref. Yale 1980, no.49
NOTE: A woman wearing a shift standing by the same
brass bedstead as in the Bristol *Nude on a Bed*, Baron
1979, pl.20.

OTTAWA: NATIONAL GALLERY OF CANADA

*The Pond, Richmond Park c.*1913 [G.192]
Oil on canvas; 50.8 × 61
Studio stamp br
Provenance: Vincent Massey
Gift of the Massey Collection of English Painting, 1946
[4764]

New Zealand

AUCKLAND: ART GALLERY

Tennis, Mornington Crescent Gardens 1910 [G.101a]
Oil on canvas; 50.8 × 61
Studio stamp br
Purchased from the Redfern Gallery, 1955 [1955/1]

WELLINGTON: MUSEUM OF NEW ZEALAND

Hampstead Road, Camden Town 1910 [?G.113]
Oil on canvas; 46.1×40.8
Studio stamp br
Exhibited probably Carfax Gallery 1916 (14) as *From Wellington House Academy*
Purchased from the Leicester Galleries, 1953
NOTE: The Gilman label states that the picture was painted from the balcony of 247 Hampstead Road (Wellington House Academy in Charles Dickens's day, a name revived by Sickert when he had a studio there). Gore has painted the view looking down Granby Terrace, away from Hampstead Road.

The Window c.1910–11
Oil on canvas; 59.7×49.5
Studio stamp bl
Purchased from Roland, Browse & Delbanco, 1961
NOTE: A figure sits in a window; the view beyond crosses gardens to a terrace of houses in the background. However, the layout and architecture suggest that this is not a view from 31 Mornington Crescent. It possibly represents Harrington Square (where Sickert lived after his marriage in 1911). It is certainly a Camden Town subject.

The Artist's Future Wife. Mornington Crescent 1911 [?G.130]
Oil on canvas; 48×39
Exhibited almost certainly AAA 1911 (121) in place of *Ballet*
Purchased from the Redfern Gallery, 1961

South Africa

JOHANNESBURG: ART GALLERY

Applehayes c.1909
Oil on canvas; 50.8×61
Exhibited NEAC summer 1910 (161)
Provenance: Sir Otto Beit, by whom given, 1910
NOTE: The *Sunday Times*, 19 June 1910, reported the purchase of this painting at the NEAC for Johannesburg.

The Alhambra Promenade 1911
Oil on canvas; 76.2×63
Inscribed *SF Gore* br
Exhibited CTG 2 (18) as *The Promenade*; probably Carfax Gallery 1913 (14) as *The Alhambra*
Provenance: Sylvia Gosse, by whom given, 1913

From a Window in Mornington Crescent 1911 [G.126]
Oil on canvas; 41×51
Inscribed *SFG* bcr
Exhibited NEAC summer 1910 (161)
Purchased from the Leicester Galleries, 1930

PIETERMARITZBURG: TATHAM ART GALLERY

The Mirror. Woman by a Dressing Table c.1908–9
Oil on canvas; 44.6×34.7
Exhibited Goupil Gallery 1918, 'The collection of the late Judge William Evans' (74)
Provenance: Judge William Evans; 1923, Col. Robert H. Whitwell, by whom given, 1924

The Sundial, Garth House c.1908
Oil on canvas; 40×50.8
Provenance: Possibly Judge William Evans; 1923, Col. Robert H. Whitwell, by whom given, 1924
NOTE: No picture with this title was exhibited among those from Judge Evans's collection at the Goupil Gallery in 1918; nor is there a 1918 exhibition label on the back. There is, however, a Goupil Gallery label and R.H. Whitwell bought the picture from the gallery on the same day (11 September 1923) as he bought *The Mirror*. He and the Tatham Art Gallery assumed that both pictures were from Judge Evans's collection.

United States of America

BOSTON: MUSEUM OF FINE ARTS

Mornington Crescent 1911 [G.134a]
Oil on canvas; 40.6×50.8
Studio stamp bl
Provenance: Mrs Spencer Gore, from whom purchased for the Museum 1931, accessioned 1932
NOTE: An exterior view straight into the gardens, in full summer foliage.

Back Gardens from Houghton Place 1913 [G.162a]
Oil on canvas; 61.2×66.5
Studio stamp br
Provenance: Mrs Spencer Gore, from whom purchased for the Museum 1931, accessioned 1932

TOLEDO, OHIO: MUSEUM OF ARTS

From the Garden of Rowlandson House 1911
Oil on canvas; 63.5×76.2
Exhibited possibly CTG 2 (16) as *The Garden*
Provenance: Lady Ottoline Morrell; Wilfred A. Evill; Samuel Carr
Purchased from the Leicester Galleries, 1952
Ref. Baron 1979, pl.59; Yale 1980, no.57

NEW HAVEN: YALE CENTER FOR BRITISH ART, PAUL MELLON COLLECTION

Extensive Landscape (probably Somerset) c.1909
Oil on canvas; 83.8×96.5
Studio stamp br
Provenance: Joseph F. MacCrindle, by whom given, 1983 [B1983.24.1]

Tennis at Hertingfordbury 1910
Oil on canvas; 40.5×50.8
Studio stamp br
Purchased from the Anthony d'Offay Gallery, 1980 [B1980.32]

Ballet Scene from 'On the Sands' 1910
Oil on canvas; 40.6×50.8
Studio stamp bl
Purchased from the Anthony d'Offay Gallery, 1983 [B1983.11.2]
Ref. d'Offay 1983, pl.10 and in colour

Design for Deer Hunting Mural (Cave of the Golden Calf) 1912
Oil and chalk on paper; 28×61
Purchased from the Anthony d'Offay Gallery, 1985 [1985.3.1]
Ref. Baron 1979, pl.117; d'Offay 1983, pl.20 and in colour; Barbican 1997, p.101

Cambrian Road, Richmond 1913–14 [G.201a]
Oil on canvas; 40.6×50.8
Studio stamp bl
Exhibited Carfax Gallery 1916 (17)
Purchased from the Anthony d'Offay Gallery, 1983 [B1983.11.1]
Ref. Baron 1979, pl.142; Watney 1980, pl.108; d'Offay 1983, pl.33 and in colour; Barbican 1997, p.149

Blue and Green Bottles and Oranges 1914 [G.211a] (pl.64)
Oil on canvas; 50.8×40.6
Studio stamp br
Provenance: 1928, Oliver Brown; Mrs Oliver Brown; Christie's, 11 December 1970 (169); Christie's, 9 November 1984 (42); Mr Paul Mellon, by whom given, 1993 [B1993.30.1]

Duncan Grant
1885–1978

Born at Rothiemurchus, Inverness-shire, Scotland. Trained at Westminster School of Art 1902–5, under Jacques-Emile Blanche at the Ecole de la Palette, Paris 1906–7, Slade School 1907 and 1908 but spent much of his time until 1909 in Paris where he met Matisse. Closely associated from 1909 onwards with Roger Fry and Vanessa and Clive Bell. Exhibited at the Friday Club 1910–15. Member of the Camden Town Group after Lightfoot's death, autumn 1911, but only exhibited once with the group, in December 1911. Included in exhibition of contemporary British art at the Galerie Barbazanges, Paris 1912, and in the 'English Group' at the 'Second Post-Impressionist Exhibition' at the Grafton Gallery 1912–13. Co-director with Fry and Vanessa Bell of the Omega Workshops 1913–19. Conscientious objector during First World War. Member London Group 1919. Carried out many decorative schemes in private houses with Vanessa Bell, and executed murals for RMS Queen Mary in 1935. Designed textile patterns, pottery decorations and the decor and costumes for several ballets.

EXHIBITIONS WITHIN HIS LIFETIME

Carfax Gallery 1920; Independent Gallery 1923; London Artists' Association Gallery 1931; Agnew's 1933 (drawings); Agnew's 1937; Leicester Galleries 1945; Leicester Galleries 1957; Tate Gallery 1959 (full retrospective, catalogue introduction by Alan Clutton-Brock); The Minories, Colchester 1963; Wildenstein 1964 ('Duncan Grant and his World', catalogue introduction by Denys Sutton); (jointly with Vanessa Bell) Royal West of England Academy, Bristol (catalogue introduction by Denys Sutton); Arts Council 1969 (portraits, with an introduction by Richard Shone); Anthony d'Offay Gallery 1972 (watercolours and drawings); Fermoy Gallery, King's Lynn 1973 (recent paintings); Anthony d'Offay Gallery 1975 (recent paintings and early paintings); Scottish National Gallery of Modern Art, Edinburgh 1975 (ninetieth birthday exhibition, introduction by David Brown); Fine Art Society, Edinburgh 1975 ('Duncan Grant and Bloomsbury', with an introduction by Richard Shone); Tate Gallery 1975 (ninetieth birthday display, catalogue notes by Richard Morphet); Davis and Long, New York 1975 (drawings and watercolours).

LITERATURE

Roger Fry, *Duncan Grant* (London: Hogarth Press (Living Painters series), 1923); Raymond Mortimer, *Duncan Grant* (London: Penguin Books (Modern Painters series), 1944); John Rothenstein, chapter on Grant (pp.44–62) in *Modern English Painters: Lewis to Moore* (London: Eyre & Spottiswoode, 1956); Richard Shone, *Bloomsbury Portraits* (London: Phaidon, 1976); Frances Spalding, *Duncan Grant: A Biography* (London: Chatto & Windus, 1997).

PICTURE SHOWN AT EXHIBITION OF THE CAMDEN TOWN GROUP

DECEMBER 1911
53 *Tulips* (pl.45)

PAINTINGS IN PUBLIC COLLECTIONS

Duncan Grant exhibited one painting on one occasion with the Camden Town Group and his life and work have been written about extensively. The section below therefore lists only the titles, and dates where known, of a selection of paintings he executed between 1906 and 1914 that are in public collections. Richard Shone illustrates and gives details of many of Grant's publicly and privately owned paintings of this early period; see Shone 1976. Shone's plate numbers are cited below, as are those of Simon Watney (Watney 1980).

United Kingdom

CAMBRIDGE: KING'S COLLEGE, KEYNES COLLECTION

*Detail from Piero della Francesca, National Gallery c.*1906
Still Life 1907
Portrait of John Maynard Keynes 1908
On the Acropolis 1910
King Solomon and the Queen of Sheba 1912
*Portrait of Gerald Shove c.*1912–13
*The Kitchen c.*1914

CARDIFF: NATIONAL MUSEUM OF WALES

Portrait of Ka Cox 1913 [NMWA 2155]

EDINBURGH: SCOTTISH NATIONAL GALLERY OF MODERN ART

Vanessa Bell Painting 1913
John Peter Grant (Ref. Shone 1976, pl.20)

KINGSTON UPON HULL: FERENS ART GALLERY

The Ass 1913 (*The Red Sea*, 1911–12, on verso of *The Ass* and obscured by relining, is reproduced in Shone 1976, pl.37, and Watney 1980, pl.81)

LEEDS: CITY ART GALLERY

The Red House on the Hill, Corfe Castle 1911

LEICESTER: NEW WALK MUSEUM AND ART GALLERY

*Portrait of Lady Ottoline Morrell c.*1914

LONDON: COURTAULD INSTITUTE OF ART

*Peaches c.*1910 (Ref. Shone 1976, pl.30)
Seated Woman. Portrait of Ka Cox 1912 (Ref. Shone 1976, pl.44)
*The Dinner Table c.*1912

LONDON: GOVERNMENT ART COLLECTION

Cader Idris 1913 [8978]
Still Life, Lime Juice 1914 [14378]

LONDON: NATIONAL PORTRAIT GALLERY

*Self Portrait c.*1908 (Ref. Shone 1976, pl.24)

LONDON: TATE GALLERY

*Lytton Strachey c.*1909 [N05764] (Ref. Shone 1976, pl.15)
James Strachey 1910 [N05765] (Ref. Shone 1976, pl.22; Watney 1980, pl.77)
Lemon Gatherers 1910 [N03666] (Ref. Shone 1976, pl.26)
*Dancers c.*1910–11 [N06181] (Ref. Shone 1976, pl.32; Watney 1980, pl.78)
Football 1911 [N04566] (Ref. Shone 1976, pl.36; Watney 1980, pl.83)
Bathing 1911 [N04567] (Ref. Shone 1976, pl.34; Watney 1980, pl.82)
The Queen of Sheba 1912 [N03169] (Ref. Shone 1976, pl.46; Watney 1980, pl.75)
Head of Eve 1913 [T03847]
The Mantelpiece 1914 [T01328] (Ref. Shone 1976, pl.81; Watney 1980, pl.84)
Abstract Kinetic Collage with Sound 1914 [T01744] (Ref. Shone 1976, pl.88)

LONDON: VICTORIA AND ALBERT MUSEUM

Omega Workshops Sign 1913 (Ref. Watney 1980, col. pl.10)

MANCHESTER: CITY ART GALLERIES

*Caryatid c.*1912 but possibly nearer 1917

READING: MUSEUM OF READING

Portrait of Iris Tree 1914

SOUTHAMPTON: CITY ART GALLERY

Tulips 1911 (pl.45; also rep. Baron 1979, pl.89; Watney 1980, col. pl.8; Christie's 1988, no.82)

Australia

ADELAIDE: ART GALLERY OF SOUTH AUSTRALIA

Autumn Landscape 1911

SYDNEY: ART GALLERY OF NEW SOUTH WALES

Still Life with Cyclamen c.1914

South Africa

PIETERMARITZBURG: TATHAM ART GALLERY

Four Cairn Terriers and a Dog Basket c.1912
Vanessa Bell in a Sunhat 1912

United States of America

NEW HAVEN: YALE CENTER FOR BRITISH ART, PAUL MELLON COLLECTION

Two Nudes on a Beach date unknown [B1984.31.1]
Pamela 1911 [B1986.1.2]

NEW YORK: METROPOLITAN MUSEUM OF ART

Virginia Woolf 1911 [1990.236]

James Dickson Innes
1887–1914

Born at Llanelli, Carmarthenshire, Wales. Studied painting at Carmarthen 1904–5 and at the Slade School 1906–8. Occasional visitor to 19 Fitzroy Street 1907–8. Exhibited at NEAC for first time in 1907, member 1911. Exhibited at AAA 1908. Member Camden Town Group but contributed only to second exhibition in December 1911. Travelled extensively in France from 1908 onwards, worked in southern Spain spring 1912 and spent the winter of 1913–14 in North Africa and the Canary Islands. Often worked in Wales from 1910–12, sometimes in the company of Augustus John in North Wales in 1911 and 1912. Died of consumption in August 1914.

EXHIBITIONS WITHIN HIS LIFETIME

Chenil Gallery 1911; Chenil Gallery 1913.

EXHIBITIONS SINCE HIS DEATH

National Gallery 1921; Chenil Galleries 1923 (catalogue containing 'A Short Appreciation' by Augustus John, 'James Dickson Innes' by Fothergill, and a reprint of the anonymous preface to the National Gallery exhibition); Leicester Galleries 1928; (jointly with Augustus John and Derwent Lees) Redfern Gallery 1939; Leicester Galleries 1952; Graves Art Gallery, Sheffield (and at Swansea and Aberystwyth) 1961 (catalogue containing an introduction by Augustus John); Southampton Art Gallery (and at Cardiff, London and Manchester) 1977–8 (a full-scale retrospective).

LITERATURE

John Fothergill, *James Dickson Innes* (London: Faber, 1946; reproductions collected and edited by Lillian Browse); John Rothenstein, chapter on Innes (pp.63–77) in *Modern English Painters: Lewis to Moore* (London: Eyre & Spottiswoode, 1956); Charles Hampton, 'Some of the Sources for the Art of J.D.Innes', unpublished BA thesis, Cambridge University, 1970; A.D.Fraser Jenkins, 'J.D.Innes at the National Museum of Wales' (Cardiff: National Museum of Wales, 1975); John Hoole, *James Dickson Innes*, catalogue of Southampton Art Gallery exhibition 1977–8 containing a chronology, introduction essay, full notes and many illustrations of Innes's work.

PICTURES SHOWN AT EXHIBITIONS OF THE CAMDEN TOWN GROUP

DECEMBER 1911
7 *Arenig* (see pl.46)
8 *Welsh Landscape*
9 *Flowers*
10 *The Mountain Stream*

Welsh Landscape has not been identified. The description of *Flowers* as 'a study of sturdy, juicy, yellow blooms, rising solitary in the foreground of a meadow landscape' (*Daily Telegraph*, 14 December 1911) proves it can only be *Ranunculus* (Walker Art Gallery, Liverpool). *The Mountain Stream* can be identified from the description given by the critic of *Queen* (9 December 1911) who, noting that Innes's work imitated Augustus John, wrote that 'its impossibly elongated figure, measuring about fourteen heads to the body, makes an attractive caricature of one of the exhibits at the Goupil Salon'. The only known picture by Innes to include both the running water indicated in the title and an impossibly elongated figure is *The Green Dress, Arenig* (private collection; rep. Fothergill 1946, pl.40, and Southampton 1977, no.92).

PAINTINGS IN PUBLIC COLLECTIONS

All the oil paintings by Innes known to me in public collections are included in this checklist.

The catalogue prepared by John Hoole for the Innes exhibition first held at Southampton Art Gallery in 1977 collates all the available information on the works. References are given below to this publication and to A. D. Fraser Jenkins's 1975 booklet on the holdings of works by Innes in the National Museum of Wales. The plate numbers from Fothergill's 1946 book on Innes are also quoted.

United Kingdom

ABERDEEN: ART GALLERY

The Little Mother 1909
Oil on canvas; 41.3×33
Exhibited NEAC winter 1912 (182)
Provenance: Horace de Vere Cole
Purchased from the Redfern Gallery, 1938
Ref. Fothergill 1946, pl.12; Southampton 1977 (34)

The Spurs of Arenig c.1911–12
Oil on panel; 24.2×34
Purchased from the Leicester Galleries, 1958

Portrait of a Gypsy c.1912
Oil on canvas; 45.7×35.6
Purchased from Adams Bros, 1960
Ref. Southampton 1977 (88)

BELFAST: ULSTER MUSEUM

Olives at Collioure 1911
Oil on canvas; 30.8×40.9

Inscribed *J. D. Innes 1911* br
Purchased from the Leicester Galleries through the Lloyd Patterson Bequest, 1929

BIRMINGHAM: CITY ART GALLERY

*Provençal Coast, Sunset c.*1912–13
Oil on canvas; 49.5×74.9
Provenance: Mrs Innes (the artist's mother); George Charles Montagu, 9th Earl of Sandwich
Purchased from Roland, Browse & Delbanco, 1948
Ref. Southampton 1977 (113)

Near Collioure – Morning 1913
Oil on board; 30.5×39.4
Inscribed *J.D. Innes 1913* br
Exhibited Whitechapel 1914 (384) as *Banjules – Morning*
Provenance: Julian Lousada; Harcourt Johnstone; Mrs J.B. Priestley
Purchased from Messrs Tooth, 1955
Ref. Fothergill 1946, pl.49; Southampton 1977 (114)

BRADFORD: CARTWRIGHT HALL ART GALLERY

The Town of Collioure 1908
Oil on canvas; 64.1×80
Inscribed *J.D. Innes* br
Provenance: Asa Lingard, by whom given, 1935
Ref. Southampton 1977 (27)

BRIGHTON: MUSEUM AND ART GALLERY

*The Seine at Caudebec c.*1908–9
Oil on canvas; 62.9×81.3
Provenance: Arthur Crossland
Purchased from the Piccadilly Gallery, 1957
Ref. Southampton 1977 (30)

CAMBRIDGE: FITZWILLIAM MUSEUM

*Arenig Fawr, North Wales c.*1911–12
Oil on panel; 30.5×41.9
Lord Ivor Spencer-Churchill; E.M.B. Ingram, by whom bequeathed, 1941, received 1946 [No. 2457]
Ref. Fothergill 1946, pl.16 as *Tan-Y-Griseau*; Southampton 1977 (72)

CARDIFF: NATIONAL MUSEUM OF WALES

The Bead Chain 1910
Oil on canvas; 137.2×97.8
Inscribed *J.D. Innes 1910* br
Provenance: Horace de Vere Cole; Capt. Geoffrey Crawshay
Acquired 1953 [Reg.865]
Ref. Fothergill 1946, pl.13; Jenkins 1975, p.8; Southampton 1977 (44)

*Pembroke Coast c.*1911
Oil on panel; 31.8×38.1
Inscribed *J D Innes* br
Purchased from the Leicester Galleries, 1970 [NMWA 196]
Ref. Jenkins 1975, p.12 in colour

Canigou in Snow 1911
Oil on panel; 22.9×32.4
Inscribed *J.D. Innes 1911* br
Provenance: Horace de Vere Cole
Purchased from the Leicester Galleries, 1935 [NMWA 200]
Ref. Fothergill 1946, pl.24; Jenkins 1975, p.15 in colour; Southampton 1977 (60)

The Cathedral at Elne 1911
Oil on panel; 22.9×33
Inscribed *J.D. Innes 1911* bl
Provenance: Horace de Vere Cole; Miss M.S. Davies, by whom given, 1963 [NMWA 199]
Ref. Jenkins 1975, p.14 in colour; Southampton 1977 (61)

*Arenig c.*1911–12
Oil on panel; 22.9×33
Provenance: Sir Edward Marsh, by whom bequeathed to Contemporary Art Society, by whom allocated, 1954 [NMWA 202]
Ref. Jenkins 1975, p.10; Southampton 1977 (76; not illustrated)

*The Girl in the Cottage c.*1911–12
Oil on panel; 33×22.2
Provenance: Augustus John; Sir Caspar John
Acquired, 1972 [Reg.1508]
Ref. Jenkins 1975, p.17 in colour; Southampton 1977 (79)

*Girl Standing by a Lake c.*1911–12
Oil on panel; 38.1×29.2
Provenance: Augustus John; Sir Caspar John
Acquired, 1972 [NMWA 245]
Ref. Jenkins 1975, p.16; Southampton 1977 (82)

*Vernet (Provençal Landscape) c.*1912
Oil on canvas; 27.9×38.1
Provenance: Sir Henry and Lady Rushbury
Acquired, 1972 [NMWA 198]
Ref. Jenkins 1975, p.20; Southampton 1977 (97)

*French Landscape c.*1912
Oil on panel; 24.1×33
Provenance: Sir Henry and Lady Rushbury
Acquired, 1972 [NMWA 197]
Ref. Jenkins 1975, p.21

*The Pyrenees c.*1912–13
Oil on canvas; 50.8×68.9
Provenance: Sir Michael Sadler
Purchased from the Leicester Galleries, 1944 [NMWA 11440]
Ref. Fothergill 1946, pl.8 as *Mountains*; Jenkins 1975, p.16; Southampton 1977 (116)

KINGSTON UPON HULL: THE UNIVERSITY OF HULL ART COLLECTION

*Sunset in the Pyrenees c.*1912–13
Oil on canvas; 55.9×68.5
Provenance: Frank Roberts; Hugo Pitman; Mrs Reine Pitman
Purchased, 1972 [107]
Ref. Southampton 1977 (117; not illustrated)

LEEDS: CITY ART GALLERY

*In the Pyrenees c.*1911
Oil and pencil on panel; 23.5×33
Provenance: A.E. Anderson, by whom given, 1929
Ref. Fothergill 1946, pl.36; Southampton 1977 (71; not illustrated)

*From 'The White Hart', Guestling, Sussex c.*1911–12
Oil on panel; 30.5×40.6
Provenance: Asa Lingard; Lady George Cholmondeley, by whom bequeathed, 1966
Ref. Fothergill 1946, pl.27; Southampton 1977 (84)

LIVERPOOL: WALKER ART GALLERY

*Ranunculus c.*1911
Oil on canvas; 24.2×33.2
Exhibited CTG 2 (9) as *Flowers*
Provenance: Sir Edward Marsh, by whom bequeathed to Contemporary Art Society, by whom allocated, 1954 [3149]
Ref. Fothergill 1946, pl.43; Baron 1979, pl.91

LLANELLI: PARC HOWARD MUSEUM AND ART GALLERY

*The Furnace Quarry, Llanelli c.*1906
Oil on canvas; 45.7×59.7
Inscribed *J.D. Innes* bl and *J.D.* br
Purchased from the Chenil Gallery, 1923
Ref. Fothergill 1946, pl.1; Southampton 1977 (4; not illustrated)

LONDON: GOVERNMENT ART COLLECTION

*Welsh Landscape c.*1906–7
Oil on canvas; 51.3 × 69
Inscribed *J D I* bl
Purchased from the Leicester Galleries, 1960 [5217]

LONDON: SLADE SCHOOL OF FINE ART

*Composition. A Scene at the Theatre c.*1908
Oil on canvas laid on board; 137.2 × 106.7
Acquired from the artist, 1908
Ref. Southampton 1977 (33)

LONDON: TATE GALLERY

South of France, Bozouls, near Rodez 1908
Oil on canvas; 50.2 × 64.8
Inscribed *J.D. Innes* br
Purchased from the artist's mother, 1919 [N03468]
Ref. Fothergill 1946, pl.3

*Arenig, Sunny Evening c.*1911–12
Oil on wood panel; 22.9 × 32.4
Provenance: Sir Cyril Butler
Purchased from the Redfern Gallery, 1942 [N05367]

Arenig, North Wales 1913
Oil on wood panel; 85.7 × 113.7
Inscribed *J D Innes 1913* br
Exhibited Chenil Gallery 1913 (12)
Provenance: John Quinn, New York; American Art
Association, New York, 11 February 1927 (506) where
bought by W. M. Crane; 1928, sold to Rowland
Burdon-Muller of Boston, Mass., by whom given, 1928
[N04385]
Ref. Fothergill 1946, pl.48; Southampton 1977 (120)

MANCHESTER: CITY ART GALLERIES

*Bala Lake c.*1911
Oil on panel; 32.7 × 40.9
Provenance: the Hon. Jasper Ridley
Purchased from Messrs Tooth, 1934 [1934.194]
Ref. Fothergill 1946, pl.44; Southampton 1977 (59)

*The Prize Fight c.*1912
Oil on canvas; 33.5 × 43.3
Inscribed *J.D. Innes* bl
Provenance: Mrs Evelyn Russell
Purchased from R. H. Jackson, Manchester (dealer),
1934 [1934.528]
Ref. Fothergill 1946, pl.31; Southampton 1977 (86)

SHEFFIELD: GRAVES ART GALLERY

Landscape, Pyrenees 1911
Oil on panel; 30.5 × 40.6
Inscribed *J. D. Innes 1911* br
Provenance: Augustus John; Dorelia John, from whom
purchased, 1964 [2575]
Ref. Southampton 1977 (67)

*Landscape with Figures, Arenig c.*1911–12
Oil on panel; 22.9 × 33
Provenance: Augustus John; Dorelia John, from whom
purchased, 1964 [2574]
Ref. Southampton 1977 (80)

SOUTHAMPTON: CITY ART GALLERY

*The Coast near Collioure c.*1912–13
Oil on canvas; 38.1 × 46.3
Provenance: Lord Howard de Walden
Purchased from Roland, Browse & Delbanco, 1951
Ref. Southampton 1977 (112) in colour; Watney 1980,
pl.35

SWANSEA: GLYNN VIVIAN ART GALLERY

Mount Canigou 1911
Oil on panel; 25.4 × 33.7
Inscribed *J.D. Innes 1911* br
Provenance: Lady Howard Stepney
Purchased from Roland, Browse & Delbanco, 1951
Ref. Southampton 1977 (69)

*Arenig Mountain c.*1911–12
Oil on canvas; 25.4 × 38.4
Provenance: Sir Stafford and Lady Howard Stepney
Purchased from the Trustees of the Stepney Estate,
1953
Ref. Southampton 1977 (75)

Garn Lake 1913
Oil on canvas; 76.8 × 127.1
Inscribed *J.D.I 1913* br
Exhibited probably Chenil Gallery 1913
Provenance: John Quinn, New York; J.H. Johnstone;
Hugo Pitman; Mrs Reine Pitman; Fiore de Henriques
Purchased from the Mayor Gallery, 1982
Ref. Fothergill 1946, pl.47

Australia

ADELAIDE: ART GALLERY OF SOUTH AUSTRALIA

Spanish Landscape 1912
Oil on panel; 32.5 × 40.5
Provenance: Lord Howard de Walden; Oppenheimer
Purchased from Roland, Browse & Delbanco, 1955
[0.1637]
Ref. Adelaide 1997, p.45 in colour
NOTE: Previously called *North African Landscape.*

MELBOURNE: NATIONAL GALLERY OF VICTORIA

Collioure 1911
Oil on canvas; 30.7 × 41
Inscribed *J.D. Innes 1911* br
Provenance: Horace de Vere Cole; Asa Lingard
Purchased from Agnew's for the Felton Bequest, 1949

Canada

OTTAWA: NATIONAL GALLERY OF CANADA

Arenig 1911 (pl.46)
Oil on canvas; 36 × 51
Inscribed *J D Innes 1911* bl
Provenance: Horace de Vere Cole; Lady Kroyer-
Kielberg; Vincent Massey
Gift of the Massey Collection of English Painting, 1946
Ref. Fothergill 1946, pl.17; Baron 1979, pl.90

*South Wales, Evening c.*1911–12
Oil on panel; 30.3 × 40.8
Provenance: Horace de Vere Cole; Lord Ivor Spencer-
Churchill; Maurice Ingram; Vincent Massey
Gift of the Massey Collection of English Painting, 1946

TORONTO: ART GALLERY OF ONTARIO

Afternoon, Ronda, Spain 1913
Oil on canvas; 56.2 × 77.2
Inscribed *J D Innes/1913* br
Provenance: Sir Michael Sadler
Purchased from Messrs Tooth, 1941

VANCOUVER: ART GALLERY

*Pyrénées Orientales c.*1912–13
Oil on panel; 23.5 × 33
Provenance: Possibly Horace de Vere Cole
Acquired 1933

United States of America

Landscape with a Grazing Horse c.1912–13
Oil on panel; 32.4×40
Inscribed *J.D. Innes* br
Provenance: Euphemia Lamb; Christie's 13 March 1981, lot 61

Purchased from Davis and Langdale, New York, 1985 [B1985.8]

Deep Twilight, Pyrenees c.1912–13
Oil on panel; 21.5×31.7
Provenance: Horace de Vere Cole; Lady Kroyer-Kielberg; Mrs Arthur Gibbs; Messrs Tooth
Purchased from Agnew's, 1990 [B1990.2.1]
NOTE: Painted at Collioure. Pendant to painting *Pyrénées Orientales* (Vancouver Art Gallery) which shows the same scene in afternoon instead of evening light.

Augustus John
1878–1961

Born at Tenby, Wales, brother of Gwen John. Trained at the Slade School 1894–8. Taught painting at the University of Liverpool 1901–4. Co-principal with William Orpen of the Chelsea Art School (a private establishment). Travelled and worked in Ireland, Dorset, Wales and France until 1914, often, from 1911, in the company of Derwent Lees or Innes. (In later life he continued to travel abroad frequently, journeying as far afield as Jamaica in 1937.) Began exhibiting with NEAC in 1900, member 1903. Member of Camden Town Group but contributed only to the first exhibition in June 1911. President of National Portrait Society 1914. Elected ARA 1921, RA 1928, resigned 1938, re-elected 1940. Member of London Group 1940. Awarded Order of Merit 1942. Author of *Chiaroscuro, Fragments of Autobiography* (1952) and its sequel *Finishing Touches*, published posthumously (1964).

EXHIBITIONS UNTIL 1914

Carfax Gallery 1899; Carfax Gallery 1903; (jointly with Orpen) Chenil Gallery 1905 (drawings); Chenil Gallery 1906 (etchings); Carfax Gallery 1907 (drawings); Chenil Gallery 1910 (including Provençal studies); Chenil Gallery 1911; Goupil Gallery 1913.

For a complete list of the numerous exhibitions of John's work since 1914 consult the chronology in Easton and Holroyd 1974 (see 'Literature' below).

MAJOR RETROSPECTIVE LOAN EXHIBITIONS

Temple Newsam House, Leeds 1946; Arts Council 1948; Royal Academy Diploma Gallery 1954; Graves Art Gallery, Sheffield 1956; University of Hull 1970 (portraits of the artist's family); Colnaghi 1974 (early drawings and etchings, part sale, part loan); National Portrait Gallery 1975.

LITERATURE

Charles Marriott, *Augustus John* (London: John Lane, 1918); Campbell Dodgson, *A Catalogue of Etchings by Augustus John 1901–1914* (London: Chenil, 1920); A. B.[ertram], *Augustus John* (London: Ernest Benn, 1923); T.W. Earp, *Augustus John* (Edinburgh: Nelson, 1934); Lillian Browse (ed.), *Augustus John: Drawings* (London: Faber, 1941); John Rothenstein, *Augustus John* (London: Phaidon, 1944); Lord David Cecil (ed.), *Augustus John: Fifty-two Drawings* (London: George Rainbird, 1957); John Rothenstein, *Augustus John 1878–1961* (London: Beaverbrook Press, 1962); John Rothenstein, *Augustus John* (The Masters series no.79) (London: Purnell, 1967); Malcolm Easton and Michael Holroyd, *The Art of Augustus John* (London: Secker & Warburg, 1974); Michael Holroyd, *Augustus John: A Biography*, vol.1: *The Years of Innocence* (London: Heinemann, 1974), and vol.2: *The Years of Experience* (London: Heinemann, 1975).

PICTURES SHOWN AT EXHIBITION OF THE CAMDEN TOWN GROUP

JUNE 1911
1 *Llyn Cynlog*
2 *Nant-ddu*

The only pictures John showed with the Camden Town Group. Both were landscape studies in oil of Welsh subjects almost certainly painted during the month before the exhibition. John's reputation was such that nearly every critic noted his work, in spite of its informality, and most wondered what the artist had to do with Camden Town. However, the press descriptions do not serve to identify the pictures with any conviction. They tell us the general character of his offerings which, according to *Queen* (24 June 1911), 'one likes as decorative patches of colour rather than as studies of actual form in landscape'. *Llyn Cynlog* attracted more attention than *Nant-ddu*. The title of the latter is that of the brook by the side of Mount Arenig where Innes and John rented a cottage in May 1911 (and used as their base in North Wales in 1911 and 1912).

PAINTINGS IN PUBLIC COLLECTIONS

John's career was long, productive and publicly recognized from his student days onwards. Thus most of the major galleries in Britain and abroad possess his paintings. However, because he was a peripheral member of the Camden Town Group, the section below lists only the titles, and the dates where known, of a selection of paintings executed between 1906 and 1914 in public collections. Reproductions of a reasonable number of these pictures can be found in the various picture-books on John. Especially useful are Rothenstein 1944 and Easton and Holroyd 1974.

United Kingdom

ABERDEEN: ART GALLERY

The Blue Pool 1911
In the Sandpit 1912

BELFAST: ULSTER MUSEUM

The Red Feather c.1911 (pl.47)

CAMBRIDGE: FITZWILLIAM MUSEUM

Dorelia with a feathered Hat c.1906 [PD. 19–1976]
David and Dorelia in Normandy 1908 [No. 2456]
Sir William Nicholson 1909 [No. 1641]
Portrait of Caspar c.1909 [PD. 23–1976]
Woman with a Daffodil (at Aix) 1910 [No. 1018]
Girl leaning on a Stick 1910 [PD. 24–1961]
The Blue Pool c.1910 [PD. 14–1976]
Dorelia seated, holding Flowers (Martigues) c.1910 [PD. 20–1976]
Dorelia and the Children at Martigues c.1910 [PD. 16–1976]
Dorelia by the Caravan c.1911 [PD. 25–1961]
Dorelia wearing a Turban c.1912 [PD. 18–1976]
David and Caspar c.1912 [PD. 17–1976]
The Yellow Dress ('The top of the mountain') c.1912 [PD. 21–1976]
The Mumper's Daughter c.1912–14 [PD. 22–1976]
The Woman of Ower 1914 [No. 851]

CAMBRIDGE: NEWNHAM COLLEGE

Miss Jane Ellen Harrison 1909

CARDIFF: NATIONAL MUSEUM OF WALES

Study for a Painting of Two Nudes c.1906 [NMWA 155]
Old Ryan 1907 [NMWA 165]
Romany Folk c.1907 [NMWA 166]
Bathers 1908 [NMWA 582]
Printemps 1908 and later [NMWA 2067]
Portrait Study of a Child (Pyramus) c.1909 [NMWA 583]
Study of an Old Man c.1909 [NMWA 249]
Study of Edwin c.1910 [NMWA 161]
Study of Dorelia's Head 1911 [NMWA 162]
Dorelia at Alderney Manor c.1911 [NMWA 163]
The Aran Islands c.1912 [NMWA 157]
Portrait of J. D. Innes c.1912 [NMWA 4908]
Portrait of the Artist 1913 [NMWA 158]

EDINBURGH: SCOTTISH NATIONAL GALLERY
OF MODERN ART

Woman in a Landscape c.1911–12 [GMA 862]

LEEDS: CITY ART GALLERY

Landscape at Chirk c.1911–12

LEEDS: UNIVERSITY ART COLLECTION

Welsh Landscape

LIVERPOOL: UNIVERSITY ART COLLECTION

Sir John Tomlinson Brunner 1906 [FA595]
Edmund Knowles Muspratt 1906 [FA593]

LONDON: TATE GALLERY

W.B. Yeats 1907 [N05218] (Ref. Rothenstein 1944, pl.45)
Woman Smiling 1908–9 [N03171]
Portrait of a Woman 1911 [N03731]
Llyn Treweryn 1911–12 [N04653]
Robin c.1912 [N03523] (Ref. Rothenstein 1944, pl.31)
Dorelia c.1911–12 [N05434]
Lyric Fantasy c.1913–14 [T01540] (Ref. Easton and Holroyd 1974, pl.16 in colour)

MANCHESTER: CITY ART GALLERIES

William Butler Yeats 1907
Dorelia in a Landscape 1910

SOUTHAMPTON: CITY ART GALLERY

Port de Bouc 1910

SWANSEA: GLYNN VIVIAN ART GALLERY

Arenig Mountain c.1910–12
The Tutor c.1914
Irish Coast

Europe

DUBLIN, IRELAND: HUGH LANE MUNICIPAL GALLERY OF
MODERN ART

Decorative Family Group c.1908
Dorelia in a Red Cap 1911 (Ref. Rothenstein 1944, pl.24)
Robin c.1912 (Ref. Rothenstein 1944, pl.30)
Miss Iris Tree
Portrait Study: the Artist's Wife, Ida
Man with a Monocle

DUBLIN: NATIONAL GALLERY OF IRELAND

Dr Kuno Meyer 1911 (Ref. Rothenstein 1944, pl.36)
Francis MacNamara c.1911

Australia

ADELAIDE: ART GALLERY OF SOUTH AUSTRALIA

Caspar John c.1909

ADELAIDE: CARRICK HILL TRUST

The Artist's Children c.1910

BRISBANE: QUEENSLAND ART GALLERY

A Village Girl [1:0766]

MELBOURNE: NATIONAL GALLERY OF VICTORIA

His Hon. H. Chaloner Dowdall, KC, Lord Mayor of Liverpool 1908–9 (Ref. Rothenstein 1944, pl.39)
La Belle Jardinière 1911–12

SYDNEY: ART GALLERY OF NEW SOUTH WALES

Welsh Mountains in Snow c.1911 [8178]
Reverie. The Tired Climber c.1914 [1134] (Ref. Rothenstein 1944, pl.18)

Canada

OTTAWA: NATIONAL GALLERY OF CANADA

An Equihen Fisher Girl 1907 [4775] (Ref. Rothenstein 1944, p.20)
The Red Dress (Dorelia by the Gate) 1910 [15638] (Ref. Rothenstein 1944, pl.12)
A Summer Noon 1911–12 [4776]

New Zealand

DUNEDIN: PUBLIC ART GALLERY

Reading aloud on the Downs 1914

WELLINGTON: MUSEUM OF NEW ZEALAND

Portrait of the Rt Hon. W. F. Massey

South Africa

CAPETOWN: SOUTH AFRICAN NATIONAL GALLERY

Miss Pettigrew [418]
The Woman in Green (Dolly O'Henry) [877]

DURBAN: ART GALLERY

Portrait of Ambrose McEvoy

JOHANNESBURG: ART GALLERY

The Childhood of Pyramus c.1908–9

PIETERMARITZBURG: TATHAM ART GALLERY

Rustic Idyll c.1905–8

United States of America

DETROIT: INSTITUTE OF FINE ART

The Mumpers 1912 (Ref. Rothenstein 1944, pl.77)

NEW HAVEN: YALE UNIVERSITY ART GALLERY

A Woman Reading – Provençal Study 1910
Boy on a Cliff leaning on a Stick 1910

Henry Lamb
1883–1960

Born in Adelaide, Australia, but brought up in
Manchester. Studied medicine until 1904 (and again
1914–16). Trained as a painter at John and Orpen's
Chelsea Art School until 1907, and then at Jacques-
Emile Blanche's Ecole de la Palette, Paris 1907–8.
Closely involved in formation of the Friday Club
1905–6. Worked in Brittany 1908, 1910 and 1911, and
in Ireland 1912–13. First exhibited at the NEAC in 1905
(a portrait of Nina Forrest, henceforth known as
Euphemia, soon to be his first wife and later to be
beloved by Innes and many artists in his circle).
Exhibited regularly at NEAC 1909–14. Contributed to first
AAA show in 1908. Had a studio in Fitzroy Street
1909–11 and probably began to attend Fitzroy Street
Group meetings. Member of Camden Town Group,
founder-member of London Group (1913) but withdrew
his support before the first exhibition in March 1914.
Associated with the Bloomsbury circle of artists and
writers. Medical officer and official war artist 1916–18
(awarded MC). Married Lady Pansy Pakenham, 1928.
Exhibited RA from 1921, elected ARA 1940, RA 1949.
Official war artist 1940–5. Trustee of National Portrait
Gallery 1942–60, and of Tate Gallery 1944–51.

EXHIBITIONS WITHIN HIS LIFETIME

Alpine Club Gallery 1922; Leicester Galleries 1927,
1929, 1931, 1933, 1935, 1938, 1940, 1945, 1949, 1956.

EXHIBITIONS SINCE HIS DEATH

Memorial exhibition Leicester Galleries 1961; New
Grafton Gallery 1973 (part loan); Manchester City Art
Gallery (and Arts Council tour) 1984.

LITERATURE

G. L. K[ennedy], *Henry Lamb* (London: Ernest Benn,
1924); Manchester Art Gallery 1984, catalogue by Keith
Clements and Sandra Martin; Keith Clements, *Henry
Lamb: The Artist and his Friends* (Bristol: Redcliffe
Press, 1985); Suzanne Bardgett, 'Henry Lamb and the
First World War', *Imperial War Museum Review*, no.5,
1990, pp.42–57.

PICTURES SHOWN AT EXHIBITIONS OF THE CAMDEN
TOWN GROUP

JUNE 1911
21 *Brittany Peasant Boy* (pl.48)
22 *Boy's Head*
23 *Man Fishing*
All three of Lamb's pictures were of Breton subjects,
although only the first was thus designated in the title.
Desmond MacCarthy (*Eye Witness*, 6 July 1911) wrote,
'Mr Lamb shows two Breton boys and an admirable
picture of a Breton fisherman with a long pole, at the
base of a cliff.' *Boy's Head* may be either the painting
(now in a private collection) illustrated in
G. L. Kennedy's book on Lamb as pl.3 or *Head of a
Boy* in the Manchester City Art Gallery. The
whereabouts of *Man Fishing* are now unknown; it may
be the *Breton Fisherman* in the 1961 Leicester Galleries
memorial exhibition (66). The *Daily Telegraph* critic Sir
Claude Phillips evidently recognized the debt to Puvis
de Chavannes when he regretted that Lamb's fisherman
lacked 'that pathos which so ennobles the *Pauvre
Pêcheur* of Puvis de Chavannes' (22 June 1911). Frank
Rutter (*Sunday Times*, 18 June 1911), meanwhile,
noting Lamb's use of smooth paint and firm drawing,
defined the artist as a modern classicist 'just as Gauguin
– whom he so discriminately admires – was also
essentially classic'.

DECEMBER 1911
5 *Portrait* (see pl.49)
6 *Drawing*

DECEMBER 1912
30 *Study of a Head*
31 *Study of a Head*

Both studies were 'of young girls of the rustic class'
(*Daily Telegraph*, 17 December 1912). According to the
Pall Mall Gazette (12 December 1912) the 'heads of
children' had 'a Raphaelesque largeness of contour',
were 'phlegmatic and heavy-handed in modelling, with
an impassive, stolid look ... and they are both bare in
texture'. The *Daily Telegraph* noted that 'the execution
has a certain not altogether pleasant "tightness". But
there are manifest, as central and vital qualities, a
breadth and comprehensiveness of vision, a forceful
directness of execution ... Mr. Lamb has the
indefinable quality of style.' A letter from Lamb, written
in Ireland and dated 6 December 1912, to Lytton
Strachey stated that Behrend had paid him £30 for 'one
of the heads I sent to the Carfax Show'. This
provenance supports the suggestion that *Head of an
Irish Girl*, painted in Donegal in 1912, given by
Behrend to the Tate Gallery in 1917, was one of the
exhibited works.

PAINTINGS IN PUBLIC COLLECTIONS

The date-bracket of 1906–1914 for works included in
this catalogue (see p.157) isolates Lamb's early
formative work and excludes the portraits and family
groups in which he later specialized. A notable example
of the latter genre is *The Family of Boris Anrep* of 1920
in the Museum of Fine Arts, Boston. Reproduction
references are given to Kennedy's 1924 book (GLK
1924) and the Manchester exhibition catalogue
(Manchester 1984) (see 'Literature', above).

United Kingdom

CAMBRIDGE: FITZWILLIAM MUSEUM

Lytton Strachey 1913–14
Oil on canvas; 50.8 × 40.6
Provenance: C. K. Ogden; Mrs E. O. Vulliamy; Justin
Vulliamy, by whom given, 1945 [No.2748]

GLASGOW: ART GALLERY AND MUSEUM

Breton Peasant c.1910–11
Oil on canvas; 43.2 × 35.6
Contemporary Art Society, by whom allocated 1928
[1753]

LONDON: GOVERNMENT ART COLLECTION

Thundery Weather, Kennack Sands 1909
Oil on canvas; 54.5 × 39.5
Inscribed *H. Lamb 1909* bl
Purchased from Agnew's, 1979 [14744]

LONDON: NATIONAL PORTRAIT GALLERY

Self Portrait 1914
Oil on panel; 36.8 × 31.8
Inscribed *Henry Lamb/1914/to/Darsie Japp/1924* bcr
Provenance: 1924, given by the artist to Darsie Japp, by
whom given to the National Portrait Gallery, 1965
[4432]
Ref. Manchester 1984, p.44

LONDON: TATE GALLERY

Death of a Peasant (first version) 1911
Oil on canvas; 36.8 × 31.8
Provenance: Sir Michael Sadler (probably bought in
1911 at Fitzroy Street)
Chantrey Purchase from the Leicester Galleries, 1944
[N05630]
Ref. GLK 1924, pl.1; Manchester 1984, p.25

Lamentation 1911
Oil on canvas; 91.4 × 61
Inscribed *Lamb 1911* tl

Exhibited NEAC summer 1911 (209)
Provenance: Hugh Blaker; 1952, Leicester Galleries;
Contemporary Art Society, by whom allocated 1956
[T00102]

Phantasy 1912
Oil on canvas; 86.4×61
Inscribed *Henry Lamb/1912* tl
Exhibited NEAC summer 1912 (152); Whitechapel 1914
(326)
Provenance: 1913, purchased by the Contemporary Art
Society, by whom allocated, 1924 [N03840]
Ref. Manchester 1984, p.37

Irish Girls 1912
Oil on canvas; 74.9×69.2
Exhibited Whitechapel 1914 (340) as *Irish Women*
Provenance: By 1914, Julian Lousada, by whom given,
1939 [N05027]
Ref. Manchester 1984, p.31

Head of an Irish Girl 1912
Oil on canvas; 50.8×40.6
Exhibited probably CTG 3 (30 or 31) as *Study of a Head*
Provenance: 1912, Mr and Mrs J.L.Behrend, by whom
given, 1917 [N03192]

Lytton Strachey 1914
Oil on canvas; 244.5×178.4
Provenance: 1914, J.L.Behrend
Chantrey Purchase from J.L.Behrend, 1957 [T00118]
Ref. GLK 1924, pl.9; Manchester 1984, p.29 in colour

MANCHESTER: CITY ART GALLERIES

Head of a Boy c.1910
Oil on canvas; 50.8×40.6
Exhibited possibly CTG 1 (22) as *Boy's Head*
Provenance: F. Hindley Smith, by whom bequeathed,
1940 [1940.2] (painting currently lost)
NOTE: It is likely that either this painting or the similar
Breton boy (rep. GLK 1924, pl.3) was the work
exhibited with the Camden Town Group.

The Lady with Lizards 1911
Oil on canvas; 51.5×40.9
Provenance: 1930, Sir Edward Marsh by whom
bequeathed to Contemporary Art Society, by whom
allocated, 1954 [1954.1054]
Ref. Manchester 1984, p.31

MANCHESTER: UNIVERSITY OF MANCHESTER

Professor Horace Lamb, FRS, DSA 1913

Oil on canvas; 122×105.4
Commissioned by the University 1912, given 1913
Ref. Manchester 1984, p.41
NOTE: The sitter was Henry Lamb's father, a
distinguished mathematician.

SOUTHAMPTON: CITY ART GALLERY

Portrait of Edie McNeill 1911
Oil on canvas; 127.5×76.2
Inscribed *Lamb/1911* br
Exhibited NEAC winter 1911 (15) as *Portrait*
Provenance: Sir Michael Sadler; J.L.Behrend; by
descent George Behrend
Purchased from the Leicester Galleries, 1938
Ref. GLK 1924, pl.2; Manchester 1984, p.27

Europe

DUBLIN, IRELAND: HUGH LANE MUNICIPAL GALLERY OF
MODERN ART

Landscape in Normandy 1910
Oil on panel; 12.7×20.3
Inscribed *Lamb* bl
Provenance: Leicester Galleries; 1927, Miss Eleanor
Barrington, by whom bequeathed, 1950

New Zealand

WELLINGTON: MUSEUM OF NEW ZEALAND

Death of a Peasant 1911
Oil on canvas; 45.5×42
Exhibited NEAC summer 1911 (198) as *Mort d'une
Paysanne*
Provenance: 1911, Sir Augustus Daniel
Purchased from the Leicester Galleries, 1959

South Africa

PORT ELIZABETH: KING GEORGE VI ART GALLERY

Meadow in Sunlight
Oil on wood; 21×33
Purchased from Adler Fielding Gallery, Johannesburg,
1962

Wyndham Lewis
1882–1957

Born, of an American father and a British mother, on
his father's yacht off Amherst, Nova Scotia. Studied at
the Slade School 1898–1901. Travelled widely in
Europe 1902–8, including a visit to Madrid with Gore
during the winter of 1902–3. Settled in England 1909
and soon afterwards met the poet Ezra Pound. Member
of the Camden Town Group, founder-member of the
London Group (1913). Included in the Galerie
Barbazanges exhibition of contemporary British art in
Paris in 1912, and in the 'English Group' at the
'Second Post-Impressionist Exhibition' at the Grafton
Galleries 1912–13. Involved in decorations and publicity
designs for the 'Cave of the Golden Calf' in 1912.
Exhibited with, and wrote catalogue preface for, the
'Cubist Room' at the 1913–14 Brighton exhibition of
'English Post-Impressionists, Cubists and Others'.
Exhibited with the first Grafton Group exhibition in
1913 and joined the Omega Workshops when they
opened, but quarrelled with Roger Fry and withdrew
from the enterprise three months later. Founded the
Rebel Art Centre in 1914. Contributed to and edited
the Vorticist magazine *Blast* in 1914 and 1915.
Exhibited in Vorticist exhibitions at the Doré Galleries
in 1915 and the Penguin Club, New York in 1917.
Official war artist 1917–18. Founded Group X and
organized their exhibition at Heal's Mansard Gallery

1920. Prolific writer of art criticism, short stories, novels
(the first, *Tarr*, published in 1918) and autobiography.
His writings include *Blasting and Bombardiering* (1937);
*Wyndham Lewis the Artist: from Blast to Burlington
House* (1939); *Rude Assignment: A Narrative of my
Career Up-to-date* (1950) and *The Demon of Progress in
the Arts* (1954).

EXHIBITIONS WITHIN HIS LIFETIME

Goupil Gallery 1919 (war pictures, exhibition entitled
'Guns'); Adelphi Gallery 1920 (drawings); Leicester
Galleries 1921 ('Tyros and Portraits'); Lefevre Galleries
1932 (portrait drawings); Leicester Galleries 1937;
Beaux Arts Gallery 1938; Redfern Gallery 1949
(retrospective); Tate Gallery 1956 ('Wyndham Lewis
and Vorticism', including work of Lewis's artistic
associates during the period under review here).

EXHIBITIONS SINCE HIS DEATH

Zwemmer Gallery 1957; d'Offay Couper Gallery 1969
('Abstract Art in England 1913–15', including works by
Lewis); Arts Council 1974 ('Vorticism and its Allies',
studying the work of Lewis and his associates); Mayor
Gallery 1974.

LITERATURE

Wyndham Lewis's autobiographical books are listed above in his career summary. He also wrote catalogue prefaces for nearly all the exhibitions listed above held during his lifetime. See also Lewis's *Letters*, ed. W.K.Rose (London: Methuen, 1963). The major works on Lewis by other authors are: Charles Handley-Read, *The Art of Wyndham Lewis* (London: Faber, 1951); Walter Michel, *Wyndham Lewis Paintings and Drawings* (London: Thames & Hudson, 1971); Richard Cork, catalogue introduction and notes to Arts Council catalogue of 'Vorticism and its Allies', 1974; Richard Cork, *Vorticism and Abstract Art in the First Machine Age*, 2 vols (London: Gordon Fraser, 1976).

PICTURES SHOWN AT EXHIBITIONS OF THE CAMDEN TOWN GROUP

JUNE 1911
7 *The Architect (No. 1)* (see note to pl.50)
8 *The Architect (No. 2)* (see note to pl.50)

DECEMBER 1911
35 *Port de Mer*
36 *Au Marché*
37 *Virgin and Child*
All three works from the December exhibition are lost. According to Lewis (*Rude Assignment*, p.121), *Port de Mer* was a 'largish' painting representing 'two sprawling figures of Normandy fishermen, in mustard yellows and browns'. On the other hand, Frank Rutter (*Sunday Times*, 3 December 1911) described the picture as 'a blaze of yellow for sunlight, three extraordinarily simplified but cunningly placed figures to symbolise the picturesque loafing of fishermen at rest'. The *Glasgow Herald* (4 December 1911) also read three figures, two of 'slouching gait'. The painting was acquired by Augustus John, but inexplicably disappeared. *Au Marché* and *Virgin and Child* were evidently also paintings. Their price (20 guineas) was the same as *Port de Mer* and the critics did not distinguish between their medium when discussing Lewis's contributions. *The Times* (11 December 1911) called all three 'geometrical experiments'. According to the *Glasgow Herald* the Child in *Virgin and Child* 'consists chiefly in the disproportionately large eye and the bruised look of the face', but he found the Virgin benign. Other critics were outraged and insulted. An inside view, from the extreme right wing of the Camden Town Group, is

given by Manson in the *Outlook* (9 December 1911). He tried, rather clumsily, to pretend that Lewis's style was 'old hat': 'such work has been produced in the gay metropolis [Paris] for the last twenty years'. Manson went on to propose that painting should either be abstract in content as well as design, or if 'they are meant to represent life in some way, they must be built up on a fundamental basis of Nature'. Lewis's drawing was 'untrue and distorted, and therefore bad'. As designs, Manson suggested, they were better fitted for 'a fin-de-siècle carpet'. Having disposed of Lewis, Manson could then go on to write, 'It is from Mr. Lucien Pissarro's work that I derive most satisfaction', and thus proclaim his allegiance to objective perceptual art. Pissarro himself was sufficiently outraged by Lewis's paintings to draft the letter to Gore quoted in the Introduction (p.48).

DECEMBER 1912
25 *Danse*
This picture is lost. Critical comment is quoted in the Introduction to this volume.

PAINTINGS IN PUBLIC COLLECTIONS

All Lewis's early paintings are lost. The only works executed in oil within the period covered by this book are in the Tate Gallery, London. Plate references are given here to Michel 1971.

The Crowd 1914–15
Oil and pencil on canvas; 200.7 × 153.7
Exhibited LG March 1915 (83)
Provenance: Capt. Lionel Guy Baker; Dr Barnet Stross
Given by the Friends of the Tate Gallery, 1964
[T00689]
Ref. Michel 1971, pl.VI in colour

Workshop 1914–15
Oil on canvas; 76.5 × 61
Exhibited LG March 1915 (85); Vorticist Exhibition 1915 (6d, Pictures Section); New York Vorticist Exhibition 1917 (36)
Provenance: John Quinn, New York, by whom sold, 1927: S. Hamilton; 1962, Windsor Galleries, Baltimore; 1963, Edward H. Dwight
Purchased from the Anthony d'Offay Gallery, 1974
[T01931]
Ref. Michel 1971, pl.30

Maxwell Gordon Lightfoot 1886–1911

Born in Liverpool. Studied at Chester Art School *c.*1901–2 until *c.*1905. Apprenticed as a chromolithographer 1905–7 and also attended evening classes at the Sandon Studios Liverpool, under Gerard Chowne and Herbert MacNair. At the Slade School 1907–9. Exhibited at the NEAC in 1910 and with the Friday Club in 1911. Member of the Camden Town Group but resigned after first exhibition. Killed himself September 1911. No exhibition within his lifetime.

EXHIBITION SINCE HIS DEATH

Walker Art Gallery, Liverpool 1972 (catalogue abbreviated below as WAG 1972). The well-illustrated catalogue of this exhibition, by Gail Engert, the only literature on Lightfoot, contains a general introduction and also lists and details all the works by Lightfoot known to the compiler.

PICTURES SHOWN AT EXHIBITION OF THE CAMDEN TOWN GROUP

JUNE 1911
17 *Mother and Child* (pl.51)
18 *Frank*
19 *On Luddery Hill* (drawing)
20 *A Child Playing with a Ball* (drawing)

After Lightfoot's death, all four of the pictures he exhibited with the Camden Town Group remained in the possession of Arthur Clifton, owner of the Carfax Gallery, and are still in a private collection. *Child Playing with a Ball* is reproduced in WAG 1972, pl.19. *On Luddery Hill* is probably a drawing now known as *Cows and Calves in a Field. Frank*, also known as *Boy with a Hoop*, is reproduced in WAG 1972, pl.51, and in Baron 1979, pl.97. The critics wondered at Lightfoot's membership of the Camden Town Group. The *Morning Post* (3 July 1911) pondered Lightfoot's future: his 'powerful drawings suggest that, unlike his fellow "wonders", he is going to compromise with the past. His two oil pictures are carried further in the old-fashioned sense than anything in the gallery. He is obviously not going to remain satisfied with the light, rather precarious, painting of the Camden Town Group. He is a William Orpen in the making.'

PAINTINGS IN PUBLIC COLLECTIONS

The date-bracket of 1906–14 for inclusion of works in this catalogue (see p.157) covers all Lightfoot's oil paintings in public collections. References are given to the 1972 Walker Art Gallery catalogue (WAG 1972) entries, where fuller information is provided.

United Kingdom

LIVERPOOL: WALKER ART GALLERY

Flowers in a Blue and White Vase 1907
Oil on canvas; 39.4 × 31.8
Inscribed *M.G.L. 07* br
Provenance: Herbert Lightfoot, by whom given, 1954
[1124]
Ref. WAG 1972 (8), pl.4

Knapweed, Thistles and other Flowers in a Vase 1907
Oil on canvas; 31.8 × 39.4
Inscribed *M.G.L. 07* br
Provenance: E. Carter Preston; Sandon Studios Society
Purchased, 1970 [7256]
Ref. WAG 1972 (9)

*Landscape, Abergavenny c.*1910
Oil on canvas; 50.8 × 61.6
Provenance: Herbert Lightfoot, by whom given, 1954
[2366]
Ref. WAG 1972 (39)

*Cwmyoy Brest from Llanthony Valley c.*1910
Oil on canvas; 57 × 43
Provenance: Miss M. Morris;
Mrs Poadham, by whom given 1987 [10615]
Ref. WAG 1972 Appendix (54)

*View of Conway c.*1910–11
Oil on canvas; 57.4 × 76.2
Provenance: Herbert Lightfoot, by whom given, 1954
[1720]
Ref. WAG 1972 (41), pl.17

Study of Two Sheep 1911
Oil on canvas; 50.8 × 63.8
Inscribed *M. G. Lightfoot 1911* br
Provenance: Herbert Lightfoot, by whom given, 1954
[1719]
Ref. WAG 1972 (42), pl.24

LONDON: SLADE SCHOOL OF FINE ART

The following works remained in the possession of the
Slade after Lightfoot's training there:

Portrait of a Bearded Man 1908–9
Oil on canvas; 61 × 50.8
Ref. WAG 1972 (13)
NOTE: Awarded a first prize for figure painting by the
Slade for the year 1908–9.

Back View of Seated Male Nude 1908–9
Oil on canvas; 76.2 × 50.8
Ref. WAG 1972 Appendix (27)

Front View of Standing Male Nude 1908–9
Oil on canvas; 91.4 × 61
Ref. WAG 1972 Appendix (28)
NOTE: These two studies of the male nude were
together awarded a first prize for figure painting at the
Slade for the year 1908–9.

Interior of Barn with Figures 1909–10
Oil on canvas; 102.9 × 127
Ref. WAG 1972 (17), pl.6
NOTE: Awarded the Melville Nettleship prize for Figure
Composition at the Slade for the year 1909–10.

James Bolivar Manson
1879–1945

Born in London. Worked in a bank while studying
part-time at Heatherley's School of Art and elsewhere
1896–1903. In 1903, after his marriage to Lilian
Laugher, attended the Académie Julian in Paris where
Jacob Epstein was one of his close friends. Spent
summers painting in Brittany 1905–7, sometimes on
Tom Robertson's sketching parties. Was in Douélan,
Brittany, in 1907. Met Lucien Pissarro late in 1909 and
introduced by him to the Fitzroy Street Group
1910–11. First exhibited at the AAA in 1911. Member of
Camden Town Group and its secretary, founder-
member of London Group (1913) and its first secretary
but resigned in March following the first exhibition,
founder-member of Monarro Group (1919) and its
secretary. First exhibited with the NEAC in 1909,
member 1927. Exhibited at the RA from 1939. Joined
the staff of the Tate Gallery in 1912, assistant keeper
1917–30, director 1930–8. Author of numerous articles
and books on art, including *The Tate Gallery* (1930)
and monographs on Degas, Rembrandt and Sargent.

ADDRESSES 1906–14

1904–08: 184, Adelaide Road, London NW3; 1908–38:
98, Hampstead Way, Hampstead Garden Suburb,
London N2.

EXHIBITIONS WITHIN HIS LIFETIME

Informal show at his home in Adelaide Road, Swiss
Cottage 1904; Dickinson's, New Bond Street 1905;
Leicester Galleries 1923 (flower paintings); Galérie
Balzac, Paris 1924; Reid Gallery, Glasgow 1925;
Wildenstein's 1937; Leicester Galleries 1944.

EXHIBITIONS SINCE HIS DEATH

Memorial exhibition at Wildenstein's 1946; Maltzahn
Gallery 1973 (part loan); New Grafton Gallery 1979.

LITERATURE

Malcolm Easton, 'Lucien Pissarro and his friends at
Rye, 1913', *Gazette des Beaux Arts*, November 1968;

David Buckman, *James Bolivar Manson, An English
Impressionist*, a well-illustrated publication for the
Maltzahn Gallery exhibition 1973, incorporating a
chronology and list of paintings by Manson in public
and some private collections.

PICTURES SHOWN AT EXHIBITIONS OF THE CAMDEN
TOWN GROUP

JUNE 1911
3 *A Corner of the Garden*
4 *The Avenue, St. Valéry-s-Somme*
5 *Child's Head*
6 *In the Garden Suburb*
Manson's work was little noticed in press reviews of the
Camden Town Group exhibition. The possibility that *A
Corner of the Garden* is the painting now known as
Lillian in Miss Odell's Garden is discussed in Baron
1979, note to pl.98. *In the Garden Suburb* was probably
an outdoor scene in Hampstead Garden Suburb where
Manson lived (in Hampstead Way). *Child's Head* was
probably one of his many studies of either Mary or
Jean, the artist's daughters. *Art News* (15 July 1911) tells
us that this 'attractive' picture was 'characterized by
purity of colour'. The same critic described *The Avenue,
St. Valéry-s-Somme* as 'a pleasing study of autumn
foliage'. This painting had previously been exhibited by
Manson at the NEAC in the winter of 1909; thus it
represented Manson's work before he came to know
Lucien Pissarro.

DECEMBER 1911
46 *Evening Sunlight*
47 *The Sussex Downs, Storrington*
48 *Portrait of a Lady*
49 *The Sunlit Valley*
I have discovered no descriptions of any work exhibited
by Manson in December 1911. Nor, with the exception
of the Storrington subject, do his titles aid identification.
Both Pissarro and Manson painted in this Sussex village
in 1911. Pissarro's *Cottage at Storrington* is in Worthing
Art Gallery while one of Manson's Storrington subjects
is reproduced in Baron 1979, pl.99.

DECEMBER 1912
5 *The Cuckmere, Alfriston*
6 *Still Life* (see pl.8)
7 *A little French Harbour*
8 *Moonlight and Snow*

Manson's work was better noticed in this third Camden Town Group exhibition. *The Cuckmere, Alfriston* is probably the freely sketched landscape in blues and greens, executed in oil on panel and inscribed on the back 'Alfriston.../ September 1912', reproduced in the catalogue of Christie's sale on 12 June 1998 (152). The *Pall Mall Gazette* (12 December 1912) noted 'A bright little French harbour in the style of Boudin ... but I prefer a dextrous, short-hand sketch ... "Moonlight and Snow".' I do not know the present whereabouts of either picture. *Moonlight and Snow* was, however, included in the Leicester Gallery Manson exhibition in 1944 (71) and in the memorial show at Wildenstein in 1946 (8), where it was dated 1912.

PAINTINGS IN PUBLIC COLLECTIONS

Because so little has been written on Manson, the cut-off date of 1914 for inclusion of works in this catalogue (see p.157) has been set aside and all his paintings in public collections known to me are listed.

United Kingdom

ABERDEEN: ART GALLERY

A Study of Flowers 1923
Oil on canvas; 51 × 61
Inscribed *J.B. Manson 1923* br
Purchased, 1924

BELFAST: ULSTER MUSEUM

A Freshening Breeze, St Briac c.1907
Oil on panel; 35.3 × 45.7
Purchased from the French Gallery through the Lloyd Patterson Bequest, 1933

BRADFORD: CARTWRIGHT HALL ART GALLERY

Flowerpiece: Vase of Tulips and large Carnations 1940
Oil on canvas; 61 × 50.8
Inscribed *J.B. MANSON 1940* bl
Purchased from the artist 1940

BRIGHTON: MUSEUM AND ART GALLERY

A Breezy Day, Sussex c.1935
Oil on canvas; 50.8 × 61
Provenance: Mrs John Goldsmith, by whom bequeathed, 1970

Evening, Martigues (Bouche-sur-Rhone) c.1935
Oil on canvas; 35.6 × 45.7
Inscribed *J. B. Manson* br
Provenance: Mrs John Goldsmith, by whom bequeathed, 1970

BRISTOL: CITY MUSEUM AND ART GALLERY

Portrait of an Old Woman 1903
Oil on canvas; 52.1 × 41.9
Inscribed *To my father from J.B. Manson 1903* tl
Given by Mrs Goullet, daughter of the artist, 1953

Tulips in a Blue Bowl 1939
Oil on canvas; 91.5 × 76.2
Inscribed *J B Manson 1939* br
Purchased from the artist, 1939 [9670]

DUNDEE: CITY MUSEUM AND ART GALLERY

Mediterranean Landscape
Oil on canvas; 33 × 43.8
Inscribed *J B Manson* br
Provenance: Mrs D. M. Fulford, by whom bequeathed through the National Art Collections Fund, 1946

EASTBOURNE: TOWNER ART GALLERY

Portrait of Edith Matthews (née Meredith) 1904
Oil on canvas; 180 × 84
Inscribed *J.B. Manson 1904* br
Given by Miss Mary Manson, 1973

Portrait of S. E. Markham MP
Oil on canvas; 90.5 × 70.5
Given by Miss Mary Manson, 1973

EXETER: ROYAL ALBERT MEMORIAL MUSEUM AND ART GALLERY

Dartmouth c.1921
Oil on panel; 34.5 × 44.9
Purchased from Agnew's, 1969 [145/1969]

KINGSTON UPON HULL: FERENS ART GALLERY

Portrait of the Artist's Sister, Rhoda 1904
Oil on canvas; 66.2 × 40.7
Inscribed (vertically) *J.B. Manson 1904* tr
Purchased from the Belgrave Gallery, 1985

In Pont Street 1940
Oil on canvas; 71 × 91.4
Inscribed *J.B. Manson 1940* br
Purchased from the artist, 1943

KINGSTON UPON HULL: THE UNIVERSITY OF HULL ART COLLECTION

Portrait of the Artist's Mother c.1900
Oil on canvas; 36.2 × 28.6
Provenance: Mrs Elizabeth Manson; Miss Mary Manson and Mrs Jean Goullet (the artist's daughters), by whom given, 1966 [65]

Night Scene c.1900
Oil on board; 27.9 × 22.9
Given by Miss Mary Manson and Mrs Jean Goullet, 1967 [72]

Portrait of the Artist's Wife 1911
Oil on canvas; 76.2 × 63.5
Provenance: Mrs Elizabeth Manson; Miss Mary Manson and Mrs Jean Goullet, by whom given, 1966 [66]
Ref. Christie's 1988, no.72

Cineraria c.1922
Oil on canvas; 61 × 50.8
Inscribed *J.B. Manson* br
Provenance: J. H. Badcock; Mrs Elizabeth Manson; Miss Mary Manson and Mrs Jean Goullet, by whom given, 1964 [33]

LONDON: GOVERNMENT ART COLLECTION

Still Life: Tulips in a Blue Jug ?1912 (pl.8)
Oil on canvas; 40.8 × 51.5
Inscribed *J B Manson* (date illegible) bcr
Exhibited possibly one or more of the following as *Still Life*: AAA 1912 (96); Goupil Gallery Salon, autumn 1912 (83); CTG 3 (6); Doré 1913 (44); Brighton 1913–14 (44); Whitechapel 1914 (398)
Provenance: Sir Augustus Daniel; John Lumley
Purchased from Christies, 11 June 1982 (28) [16072]
Ref. Baron 1979, pl.126

LONDON: TATE GALLERY

Self Portrait c.1912
Oil on canvas; 50.8 × 39.7
Provenance: D. C. Finchman, by whom given, 1938
[N04929]

Michaelmas Daisies
Oil on canvas; 61 × 50.8
Inscribed *J. B. Manson* br
Purchased by subscribers from an exhibition at the
Leicester Galleries 1923 (61) and given, 1923 [N01355]

Pinks in a Vase c.1940
Oil on canvas; 50.8 × 40.6
Purchased from the artist, 1942

MANCHESTER: CITY ART GALLERIES

Summer Flowers c.1922–3
Oil on canvas; 60.8 × 50.8
Inscribed *J.B. Manson* bl
Provenance: 1923, Charles L. Rutherston, by whom
given, 1925 [1925.315]

Antibes 1928
Oil on panel; 34.9 × 45.8
Inscribed *J.B. Manson* br
Purchased from Messrs Wallis & Sons, 1929 [1929.26]

Lucien Pissarro 1939
Oil on canvas; 60 × 72.6
Inscribed *J. B. Manson 1939* br
Purchased from the artist, 1941 [1941.66]

OXFORD: ASHMOLEAN MUSEUM

Mrs Crump's Garden 1925
Oil on canvas; 50.1 × 60
Inscribed br
Provenance: R. A. Bevan, by whom given, 1957

Lucien Pissarro Reading
Oil on panel; 44.4 × 33.6
Inscribed verso
Given by the artist's daughters, 1963

Portrait of Miss Aylward Lord 1939
Oil on canvas; 90.1 × 70.2
Inscribed on stretcher
Given by the sitter, 1964

SALFORD: MUSEUM AND ART GALLERY

Zinnias at Le Touquet
Oil on canvas; 68.6 × 56.5
Purchased from Charles A. Jackson, Manchester, 1945

SOUTHAMPTON: CITY ART GALLERY

Self Portrait
Oil on panel; 50.8 × 40.6
Purchased from the artist, 1937

The Garden
Oil on canvas; 47 × 36
Purchased, 1934

SWANSEA: GLYNN VIVIAN ART GALLERY

Carreg Cennen Castle, Carmarthenshire 1938
Oil on canvas; 71.1 × 91.4
Inscribed *J.B. Manson* br
Commissioned by local authority Swansea, 1938

WAKEFIELD: ART GALLERY

Flowers
Oil on canvas; 62.2 × 52
Inscribed *J. B. Manson* br
Provenance: Mrs D. M. Fulford, by whom bequeathed
through the National Art Collections Fund, 1946

Europe

BRUSSELS, BELGIUM: MUSÉES ROYAUX DES BEAUX-ARTS DE
BELGIQUE

Mary. The Artist's Daughter c.1912
Oil on canvas; 76.2 × 64.1
Given by the artist, 1928

PARIS, FRANCE: MUSÉE NATIONAL D'ART MODERNE

Flowers 1924
Oil on canvas; 61 × 50.8
Inscribed *J.B. Manson 1924* br
Given by Grace Ellison, 1932 [JP 609 P]

Australia

BRISBANE: QUEENSLAND ART GALLERY

A Summer Bunch
Oil on canvas; 91.4 × 71.4
Inscribed *J.B. Manson* bl
Provenance: Miss Orovida Pissarro, from whom
purchased, 1959 [1: 0806]

South Africa

CAPETOWN: SOUTH AFRICAN NATIONAL GALLERY

Ranunculus
Oil on canvas; 61.1 × 51.1
Inscribed *J B Manson* bl
Given by the artist, 1936 [615]

Lucien Pissarro
1863–1944

Born in Paris, eldest son of Camille Pissarro. Grew up
in France and studied painting at his father's side. His
other mentors included Degas, Cézanne, Seurat and
Signac. Advised on wood-engraving by Auguste Lepère
in Paris. Exhibited at the eighth and last Impressionist
show in Paris 1886, and with the *Salon des Indépendants*,
Paris 1886–94 (serving on Hanging Committee in
1888). Having lived in London during 1883 and early
1884 he settled there in 1890 (naturalized in 1916).
Lectured on 'Impressionism in Art' to the Art Workers'
Guild in 1891 and as a consequence was sought by
Sickert and Steer. Married Esther Bensusan in 1892 and
together they ran the Eragny Press 1894–1914.
Concentrated on wood-engraving, book illustrations and
printing until 1903. Exhibited with the NEAC from 1904,
member 1906. Joined Fitzroy Street Group autumn

1907. Founder-member of Camden Town Group
(1911), London Group (1913) but resigned before first
exhibition, and Monarro Group (1919) which held
exhibitions in 1920 and 1921. Visited France frequently
before and after First World War, often staying at
Eragny where his father had built a studio in 1889.
Exhibited at the RA from 1934. Author of *Rossetti*
(1907) and *Notes on the Eragny Press, and a Letter to
J. B. Manson*, ed. Alan Fern, published posthumously
(1957).

ADDRESS

From 1902: The Brook, Stamford Brook, Chiswick,
London.

EXHIBITIONS IN ENGLAND WITHIN HIS LIFETIME

(Jointly with Ricketts) Ricketts and Hacon's shop 1896 (wood-engravings); Carfax Gallery 1913; Goupil Gallery 1917 (English landscapes); Hampstead Art Gallery 1920; Leicester Galleries 1922, 1924, 1927; Manchester, Jackson's Gallery 1928; Birmingham, Ruskin Gallery 1928; Leicester Galleries 1929, 1934; Birmingham, Ruskin Gallery 1930; Manchester City Art Gallery 1935 (and tour to Lincoln, Birkenhead, Gateshead, Rochdale and Blackpool 1935, Belfast 1936); Leicester Galleries 1936, 1943 (three generations of Pissarro family, Lucien, Camille and Orovida); Yeovil 1941.

EXHIBITIONS SINCE HIS DEATH

Memorial exhibition Leicester Galleries 1946 (catalogue introduction by Raymond Mortimer); Leicester Galleries 1950; O'Hana Gallery 1954 (three generations), 1955; Leicester Galleries 1963 (landscapes); Arts Council 1963 (centenary retrospective, catalogue introduction and chronology by Ronald Pickvance); Lee Malone Gallery, New York 1964; David B. Findlay Galleries, New York 1964; New Grafton Gallery 1977 (Orovida and her ancestors, Lucien and Camille); Anthony d'Offay Gallery 1977 (with introductory essay in catalogue by John Bensusan-Butt, 'Recollections of Lucien Pissarro in his Seventies'); Parkin Gallery 1980 ('Three on Holiday at Rye', Pissarro, Manson and Brown); Anthony d'Offay Gallery 1983; Canterbury Museum 1986 (Anne Thorold on 'Lucien Pissarro: His Influence on English Art 1890–1914'); Spink & Son, 1990 (watercolours, with catalogue introduction and chronology by Christopher Lloyd).

LITERATURE

J. B. Manson, 'Lucien Pissarro's Wood-Engravings', *Imprint*, April 1913; J. B. Manson 'Lucien Pissarro as Painter', *Studio*, 15 November 1916; Clement-Janin, 'Peintres-Graveurs Contemporains – Lucien Pissarro', *Gazette des Beaux-Arts*, November–December 1919; J. Rewald, 'Lucien Pissarro – Letters from London, 1883–91', *Burlington Magazine*, vol. 91, 1949; John Rothenstein, chapter on Pissarro (pp.95–103) in *Modern English Painters: Sickert to Smith* (London: Eyre & Spottiswoode, 1952); W. S. Meadmore, *Lucien Pissarro – Un Coeur Simple* (London: Constable, 1962); Malcolm Easton, 'Lucien Pissarro and his Friends at Rye, 1913', *Gazette des Beaux Arts*, November 1968; Anne Thorold, *Catalogue of Oil Paintings by Lucien Pissarro* (London: Athelney Books, 1983); Anne Thorold, chapter on Pissarro (pp.12–33), in *Pontoise 1998–9*; Anne Thorold, ed., *The Letters from Lucien to Camille Pissarro, 1883–1903* (Cambridge University Press, 1993).

PICTURES SHOWN AT EXHIBITIONS OF THE CAMDEN TOWN GROUP

JUNE 1911

13 *Buttercups, Colchester*
14 *View of Colchester*
15 *Well Farm Bridge, Acton*
16 *A Foot-Path, Colchester*
Pissarro's three-week visit to Colchester in May 1911 produced six paintings, three of which were included in the first Camden Town Group exhibition: *Buttercups, Colchester* (private collection; rep. Thorold 1983, no.148), a view across meadows towards the outskirts of the town; *View of Colchester* from Sheepen Hill (Colchester Public Library; rep. Thorold 1983, no.145); and *A Footpath, Colchester* (private collection; rep. Thorold 1983, no.146). *Well Farm Bridge, Acton* (Leeds Art Gallery; rep. Thorold 1983, no.120) was a work of 1907 which Pissarro had exhibited with the NEAC in that year. The *Daily Telegraph* (22 June 1911) summed him up as 'an impressionist pure and simple, and one of the calmer and more objective order'. The *Morning Post* (3

July 1911), ever facetious, called him a 'Marconigraph between Camden Town and the French battlefields of art', perhaps not realizing that the battle for Impressionism of Pissarro's type had been fought and won years before. Desmond MacCarthy's comments (*Outlook*, 6 July 1911) summed up the more intelligent reactions of the press when he wrote of Pissarro's 'four pictures of patient and admirable honesty. Like his father, he has no wish to embellish anything in Nature and scorns to select her exceptional moods or to avoid the commonplace. They are all taken in bright sunlight. You can feel the touch of the east wind in his view of Colchester. The day he paints is one which everybody would describe on meeting an acquaintance as "very fine"; a perfect day for a coronation or a cricket match, but one on which the epicurean is apt to feel that there is not much that is interesting under the sun.'

DECEMBER 1911

42 *Sunset, Epping*
43 *The Mill, Finchingfield* (sketch)
44 *The Turban* (pl.42)
45 *The Brook, Sunny Weather*
Sunset, Epping dates from the time when Pissarro had a cottage at Epping (1893–7). It is probably the painting of 1894 (present whereabouts unknown; Thorold 1983, no.78) previously exhibited at the *Société des Artistes Indépendants* in Paris (1894) and later at Pissarro's exhibition at the Carfax Gallery (1913). *The Mill, Finchingfield* is a work of 1905. Thorold suggests it is no.103 in her catalogue. *The Brook, Sunny Weather* of 1909 (Thorold 1983, no.133) represented Pissarro's family house at Stamford Brook from 1902 onwards. Whereas in June 1911 Pissarro showed three very recent pictures with the Camden Town Group, in December he presented a selective retrospective.

DECEMBER 1912

9 *Escalier d'Eragny*
10 *An Essex Hall*
11 *Stamford Brook Green (Snow)* (pl.56)
12 *Tomatoes*
Again, Pissarro was not concerned with showing recent pictures. Three of his exhibits in 1912 were very early works. *Tomatoes* is a rare still life of 1893 (rep. Thorold 1983, no.65, sold Sotheby's, 18 June 1997, lot 1); *An Essex Hall*, already shown at the NEAC in winter 1909 (54), is *Coopersale Hall, Essex*, also of 1893 (present whereabouts unknown; rep. Thorold 1983, no.70); *Escalier d'Eragny*, a painting of 1894 (present whereabouts unknown; Thorold 1983, no.86), portrayed the outside staircase – constructed in 1893 – of Camille Pissarro's studio at Eragny.

PAINTINGS IN PUBLIC COLLECTIONS

Paintings by Lucien Pissarro, from all periods of his long and prolific career, are in public galleries throughout Great Britain. The Ashmolean Museum, Oxford, and the City Art Gallery, Manchester, have particularly fine and extensive collections of his paintings, although only two in each gallery fall within the 1906–14 date-bracket governing the selection below (see p.157).

Inscriptions: Pissarro's initials (*LP*) were formed as a monogram.

References are given to Thorold's illustrated and fully documented *catalogue raisonné*.

United Kingdom

COLCHESTER: COUNTY LIBRARY, ESSEX COUNTY COUNCIL

View of Colchester from Sheepen 1911
Oil on canvas; 53.7 × 65
Inscribed *LP 1911* br

Exhibited CTG I (14)
Provenance: Ruth Bensusan-Butt, by whom given to the
County Library, Essex County Council, 1949
Ref. Thorold 1983, no.145; Christie's 1988, no.95

EDINBURGH: CITY ART CENTRE

Blackpool Valley 1913
Oil on canvas; 54.6×65.4
Inscribed *LP 1913* br
Exhibited Carfax Gallery 1913 (9); NEAC summer 1913
(254)
Provenance: S. L. Bensusan; Contemporary Art Society,
by whom given, 1923, to the Scottish Modern Arts
Association, by whom allocated, 1964
Ref. Thorold 1983, no.161

EDINBURGH: SCOTTISH NATIONAL GALLERY
OF MODERN ART

The Mill House, Blackpool, Devon 1913
Oil on canvas; 36.3×31
Provenance: Dr R. A. Lillie, by whom bequeathed, 1977
[GMA 1954]

KINGSTON UPON HULL: THE UNIVERSITY OF HULL ART
COLLECTION

Blossom, Sun and Mist: Chipperfield 1914
Oil on canvas; 53.3×65.4
Inscribed *LP 1914* br
Exhibited NEAC summer 1914 (184)
Purchased from Messrs G. M. Lotinga, 1960 [1]
Ref. Thorold 1983, no.177

LEEDS: CITY ART GALLERY

Well Farm Bridge, Acton 1907
Oil on canvas; 45.7×54.5
Inscribed *LP 1907* br
Exhibited NEAC winter 1907 (110); CTG I (15); Carfax
Gallery 1913 (8)
Provenance: 1913, Frank Rutter, from whom
purchased, 1925
Ref. Baron 1979, pl.100; Watney 1980, pl.37; Thorold
1983, no.120; Barbican 1997, p.102 in colour

LONDON: THE BOROUGH OF EALING, LIBRARY SERVICE

Acton: Morning; Temps Gris 1906
Oil on canvas; 38.4×45.7
Inscribed *LP 1906* br
Exhibited NEAC spring 1906 (6); NEAC winter 1912
(184)
Provenance: J. B. Manson; Sotheby's, 19 July 1967 (17)
Purchased from the Leger Galleries, 1967
Ref. Baron 1979, pl.31; Thorold 1983, no.108;
Christie's 1988, no.33 in colour; Pontoise 1998–9,
no.11, p.25 in colour

LONDON: GOVERNMENT ART COLLECTION

Great Western Railway, Acton 1907 (pl.34)
Oil on canvas; 45.5×54.5
Inscribed *LP 07* bl
Exhibited NEAC spring 1908 (83) as *Acton Station GWR*;
NEAC summer 1912 (70) as *Acton, GW Railway*
Purchased from the Mayor Gallery, 1964 [6681]
Ref. Thorold 1983, no.118; Christie's 1988, no.37

Rye from Cadborough Cliff – Grey Morning 1913
Oil on canvas; 54×64.5
Inscribed *LP 1913* bl
Purchased from the Leicester Galleries, 1963 [6055]
Ref. Thorold 1983, no.165

MANCHESTER: CITY ART GALLERIES

The Hills from Cadborough 1913
Oil on canvas; 54×65
Inscribed *LP 1913* bl

Exhibited NEAC winter 1913 (84)
Provenance: Charles L. Rutherston, by whom given,
1925 [1925.309]
Ref. Thorold 1983, no.171

Wild Boar Fell, Brough 1914
Oil on canvas; 59.6×73
Inscribed *LP 1914* bl
Exhibited NEAC winter 1914 (132); Goupil Gallery 1917
(39)
Provenance: Charles L. Rutherston, by whom given,
1925 [1925.306]
Ref. Thorold 1983, no.191

OXFORD: ASHMOLEAN MUSEUM

Gelée Blanche, Chiswick 1906
Oil on canvas; 39×45.7
Inscribed *LP 1906* bl
Exhibited NEAC summer 1912 (198)
Given by the artist's family, 1952
Ref. Thorold 1983, no.107

Poulfenc à Riec 1910
Oil on canvas; 54×65
Inscribed *LP 1910* br
Exhibited NEAC summer 1910 (230)
Given by the artist's family, 1952
Ref. Thorold 1983, no.134; Christie's 1988, no.70

PRESTON: HARRIS MUSEUM AND ART GALLERY

Eden Valley 1914
Oil on canvas; 53.3×64.8
Inscribed *LP 1914* bl
Provenance: 1916, Sir Michael Sadler for the
Contemporary Art Society, by whom allocated, 1924
Ref. Thorold 1983, no.186; Christie's 1988, no.185

WORTHING: MUSEUM AND ART GALLERY

Cottage at Storrington 1911
Oil on canvas; 40.5×60
Inscribed *LP 11* br
Provenance: Orovida Pissarro; E. Hilton Ltd; Christie's,
30 October 1970 (124)
Purchased from Agnew's, 1975
Ref. Thorold 1983, no.149

Europe

JERUSALEM, ISRAEL: ISRAEL MUSEUM

Stamford Brook Green: Sun and Snow 1909 (pl.56)
Oil on canvas; 43.8×53.3
Inscribed *LP 09* br
Exhibited NEAC summer 1909 (85); probably CTG 3 (11)
Provenance: Sotheby's, 13 December 1967, lot 23;
Edith Porjes, by whom bequeathed, 1981
Ref. Baron 1979, pl.127; Thorold 1983, no.131

TEL AVIV, ISRAEL: MUSEUM OF ART

The Mill, Blackpool 1913
Oil on canvas; 65×54.5
Inscribed *LP 1913* bl
Exhibited NEAC summer 1913 (157)
Provenance: Esther Pissarro, by whom given to Mr and
Mrs H. D. Meyer, by whom given, 1963
Ref. Thorold 1983, no.155

South Africa

JOHANNESBURG: ART GALLERY

Matin, Soleil, Riec 1910
Oil on canvas; 43.8×53.5
Inscribed *LP 1910* bl

Exhibited NEAC winter 1910 (83) as *Matinée Soleil à Riec*; Carfax Gallery 1913 (1)
Purchased from the Goupil Gallery, 1930
Ref. Thorold 1983, no.137

United States of America

INDIANAPOLIS: MUSEUM OF ART

Rye from Cadborough 1913
Oil on canvas; 53.5 × 64.5
Inscribed *LP 1913* br

William Whitehead Ratcliffe 1870–1955

Born near King's Lynn, Norfolk. Studied design at Manchester School of Art under Walter Crane. From 1894 to 1906 worked as a wallpaper designer in London. Moved to Letchworth in 1906 and worked there as a commercial artist. Gilman, who moved to Letchworth in 1908, encouraged Ratcliffe to devote himself to painting. Moved to London around 1910, living at various addresses in north London, especially in Hampstead Garden Suburb. Studied at the Slade School, part-time for one term, in 1910 and attended Fitzroy Street meetings c.1910–11. Member of the Camden Town Group, founder-member of London Group (1913) with whom he regularly exhibited until 1926 (resigned membership, 1930). First exhibited at the AAA in 1911. Paid a long visit to Sweden in 1913, followed by a visit to Dieppe. Returned to Letchworth during the 1930s, moved to Baldock 1937–46 and back to Letchworth from 1946 until his death.

PRINCIPAL ADDRESSES 1906–14

10 Westholm Green (1906–9) and 18 Westholm Green (1909–10), Letchworth; Willifield Green, Hampstead Garden Suburb.

EXHIBITIONS WITHIN HIS LIFETIME

Roland, Browse & Delbanco 1946; Letchworth Art Gallery 1954.

EXHIBITION SINCE HIS DEATH

Letchworth Museum and Art Gallery 1982, with catalogue introductory text by John Marjoram (the most complete account of Ratcliffe's life and work to date).

PICTURES SHOWN AT EXHIBITIONS OF THE CAMDEN TOWN GROUP

JUNE 1911
48 *The Window Seat*
49 *Haystacks*
50 *The Dressing Table*
51 *Graven Images*
Ratcliffe's career as an exhibitor began in the summer of 1911 with the Camden Town Group in June and the Allied Artists' Association in July. Next to Doman Turner (who also launched himself on the public for the first time this summer, and whose contributions were all drawings), Ratcliffe's pictures at the Carfax Gallery were the most modestly priced. Those critics who noted his pictures treated the artist with respect, and grouped him together with Drummond and Gilman (*Morning Post*, 3 July 1911) or with Manson (*Truth*, 28 June 1911; *Sunday Times*, 3 December 1911). The only descriptive comment noted on an individual picture noted that *The Window Seat* gave a 'view of waste common with a gypsy van' (*Bazaar*, 30 June 1911). *Haystacks* is almost certainly *Haystacks in a Field* (private collection), an agricultural landscape measuring 25.4 × 35.6 sold at Sotheby's, 6 February 1985, lot 286 (reproduced in the catalogue).

Provenance: S. L. Bensusan; Mrs M. Hodson; Christie's, 21 May 1965 (179); W. J. Holliday, USA, by whom given, 1979
Ref. Thorold 1983, no.167

SEATTLE: ART MUSEUM

The Thames at Lambeth 1914
Oil on canvas; 54 × 65.5
Inscribed *LP 1914* br
Provenance: 1914, Charles Rutherston; 1924, Dr MacNish; 1956, Norman Davis, by whom given
Ref. Thorold 1983, no.175

DECEMBER 1911
23 *Cottage Window Seat*
24 *Sunshine*
25 *Still Life*
26 *The Veranda*
It is probable that *In the Sun* (Walker Art Gallery, Liverpool) is *Sunshine*, shown with the Camden Town Group in December 1911, at Brighton in 1913–14 and with the London Group in 1914 (see Baron 1979, note to pl.103). The other paintings have not yet been identified.

DECEMBER 1912
42 *Clarence Gardens* (pl.53)
43 *Hotel Cecil from Hungerford Bridge*
44 *Still Life*
45 *Landscape*
Neither *Still Life* nor *Landscape* can be identified. They were not described in the press. Critics concentrated on Ratcliffe's two London views. A pen-and-ink drawing of *Hotel Cecil from Hungerford Bridge* is in the Letchworth Art Gallery but the oil remains of unknown whereabouts. Like *Clarence Gardens*, it was priced at 15 guineas, whereas the other two works were 10 guineas apiece.

PAINTINGS IN PUBLIC COLLECTIONS

Because so little has been written about Ratcliffe, the 1906–14 date-bracket for inclusion of works in this catalogue (see p.157) has been set aside in favour of listing below all his oil paintings known to me in public collections.

United Kingdom

ABERDEEN: ART GALLERY

Dieppe c.1913–14
Oil on canvas; 50.8 × 61
Purchased from the Leicester Galleries, 1963
Ref. Christie's 1988, no.144

LEEDS: CITY ART GALLERY

Landscape with Cow 1917
Oil on canvas; 50.8 × 61
Inscribed *W. Ratcliffe 1917* br
Purchased, 1964
Ref. Watney 1980, pl.57

LETCHWORTH: MUSEUM AND ART GALLERY

Manor Farm, Norton c.1912
Oil on canvas; 60 × 80
Inscribed *W. Ratcliffe* br
Given by the artist, 1954
Ref. Christie's 1988, no. 132; Connett 1992, p.78 in colour

Temple Church c.1914
Oil on canvas; 50.8 × 40.6
Given by the artist's executors, 1955

Regents Canal at Hammersmith 1910–20
Oil on canvas; 60 × 50
Inscribed *W. Ratcliffe* br
Given by the artist's executors, 1955

Cottage Interior c.1920
Oil on canvas; 49.5 × 59.7
Given by the artist's executors, 1955

Old Cottage at Worth, Sussex c.1920
Oil on canvas; 52.1 × 55.9
Given by the artist's executors, 1955

The Warped Table 1921
Oil on canvas board; 56.5 × 60
Inscribed *W. Ratcliffe* bl
Exhibited LG April 1924 (47)
Given by the artist's executors, 1955

Still Life 1910–30
Oil on board; 60 × 50
Given by the artist's executors, 1955

Totnes 1931
Oil on canvas; 51 × 61
Given by the artist's executors, 1955

Lower Wilbury Farm
Oil on board; 50 × 60
Given by the artist's executors, 1955

Ickleford Farm 1910–50 (unfinished)
Oil on canvas board; 40 × 50
Given by the artist's executors, 1955

Still Life 1910–50
Oil on board; 51 × 40.5
Given by the artist's executors, 1955

Back Yard 1910–50
Oil on canvas board; 50.6 × 75.8
Given by the artist's executors, 1955

Baldock High Street 1930–50
Oil on canvas board; 50.3 × 60
Given by the artist's executors, 1955

Still Life
Oil on canvas; 48 × 38.5
Given by the artist's executors, 1955

LIVERPOOL: WALKER ART GALLERY

In the Sun c.1911
Oil on canvas; 45.7 × 35.6
Inscribed *W. Ratcliffe* bl
Exhibited probably CTG 2 (24), Brighton 1913–14 (127)
and London Group 1914 (102) as *Sunshine*
Provenance: S. K. Ratcliffe, the artist's brother, by
whom given, 1956 [1112]
Ref. Baron 1979, pl.103

LLANELLI: PARC HOWARD MUSEUM AND ART GALLERY

Hertford Landscape
Oil on board; 49.5 × 61
Provenance: Theodore Nicholl, by whom bequeathed,
1975

LONDON: GOVERNMENT ART COLLECTION

Beehives in the Snow, Sweden 1913
Oil on canvas; 42.5 × 51
Inscribed *W. Ratcliffe/1913* bl
Exhibited possibly AAA 1913 (90) as *Bee-hives*; Brighton
1913–14 (126) as *Beehives in Snow*; possibly
Whitechapel 1914 (430) as *Swedish Beehives*
Purchased from the Leicester Galleries, 1962 [5929]
Ref. Baron 1979, pl.136

Summer Landscape, Sweden 1913
Oil on canvas; 51 × 75.6

Inscribed *W. Ratcliffe 1913* bl
Purchased from the Leicester Galleries, 1960 [5220]
Ref. Baron 1979, pl.134

LONDON: HAMPSTEAD GARDEN SUBURB INSTITUTE

From the Club Tower, Hampstead Garden Suburb c.1913
Oil on canvas; 49.5 × 74.9
Inscribed *W. Ratcliffe* br
Exhibited LG March 1914 (103)
Provenance: S. K. Ratcliffe
Given by the artist's executors, 1956 (on loan to the
Tate Gallery)

LONDON: TATE GALLERY

Clarence Gardens 1912 (pl.53)
Oil on canvas; 50.8 × 76.2
Inscribed *W. Ratcliffe 1912* bl
Exhibited AAA 1912 (187 or 188); CTG 3 (42);
Whitechapel 1914 (20)
Provenance: Contemporary Art Society; 1945, allocated
to Russell-Cotes Art Gallery and Museum,
Bournemouth, by whom sold at auction; Mr and Mrs
D. Drown
Purchased from the Anthony d'Offay Gallery, 1982
[T03359]
Ref. Baron 1979, pl.128

The Attic Room 1918
Oil on wood; 50.8 × 50.8
Inscribed *W. Ratcliffe* bl
Exhibited LG April 1919 (8)
Bequeathed by Miss Eveline Annie Dear, 1980 [T03167]

The Artist's Room, Letchworth 1932
Oil on board; 45.7 × 55.2
Inscribed *W. Ratcliffe* bl
Given by S. K. Ratcliffe, the artist's brother, 1955
[T00062]

MANCHESTER: CITY ART GALLERIES

Swedish Farm 1913
Oil on canvas; 61 × 76.4
Inscribed *W. Ratcliffe* br
Exhibited possibly AAA 1913 (89) as *A Swedish
Homestead*; possibly Brighton 1913–14 (124) as *A
Swedish Homestead* or (125) as *Spring, Sweden*
Provenance: S. K. Ratcliffe, by whom given, 1955
[1955.350]

Winter Scene, Sweden 1913
Oil on canvas; 61.6 × 76.7
Inscribed *W. Ratcliffe* bl
Exhibited probably Doré 1913 (55) and Whitechapel
1914 (413) as *Snow Scene, Sweden*
Provenance: E. C. Gregory, by whom given, 1946
[1946.44]
NOTE: An almost identical, but smaller, version is in a
private collection (rep. Christie's, 4 March 1983, lot
47).

PLYMOUTH: CITY MUSEUM AND ART GALLERY

Bodinnick Ferry, Fowey c.1920
Oil on canvas; 51 × 61.4
Inscribed *W. Ratcliffe* br
Purchased from the Piccadilly Gallery, 1978 [1978.20]
NOTE: *Terminus ante quam* provided by exhibition of
painting with the London Group in 1920.

SOUTHAMPTON: CITY ART GALLERY

The Coffee House, East Finchley 1914
Oil on canvas; 51 × 61.3
Inscribed *W. Ratcliffe* br
Exhibited LG April 1919 (35)
Purchased from the artist, 1953
Ref. Baron 1979, pl.137; Watney 1980, pl.56; Yale
1980, no.69

Canada

Landscape with Gate, Sweden 1913
Oil on canvas; 43.2×63.5
Inscribed *W. Ratcliffe/1913* br
Provenance: William Townsend, by whom given, 1965
Ref. Yale 1980, no.68

United States of America

*Cottage Interior c.*1913–14
Oil on board; 38×51
Inscribed *W. Ratcliffe* bl
Provenance: Sotheby's, 11 November 1987, lot 51
Purchased from Agnew's, 1990 [B1990.10]

Walter Richard Sickert
1860–1942

Born in Munich, eldest son of Oswald Adalbert Sickert, painter and illustrator of Danish descent, and of an Anglo-Irish mother. The Sickert family settled in England 1868 and Oswald later acquired his wife's British nationality. From 1877 to 1881 worked as an actor in repertory companies. Studied at the Slade School 1881–2 and then became Whistler's assistant and pupil. Independent of Whistler by 1888. Met Degas in Paris 1883 and again in Dieppe 1885. Exhibited with *Les XX* in Brussels 1887. Member (Royal) Society of British Artists 1884–8, and its president 1927–9. Member NEAC 1888, thereafter frequently resigning and re-joining until final resignation in 1917. Membership of other societies included Society of Twelve (1912), National Portrait Society (1914). Organized and wrote catalogue preface for 'London Impressionists' exhibition at the Goupil Gallery 1889. Founder of Fitzroy Street Group (1907), founder-member of AAA (1908), of Camden Town Group (1911) and of London Group (1913) but resigned before the first exhibition. Re-joined London Group 1916 and (with periodic resignations) remained a member until 1936. Occasionally exhibited with the *Salon* and the *Salon des Indépendants*, Paris, and 1905–9 with the *Salon d'automne* (*sociétaire* 1907). 1885–1922 spent part of each year (except 1915–18) in Dieppe, living there permanently (with visits to Venice) 1898–1905, and (with visits to London) 1919–22. Prolific writer of art criticism. Teacher at numerous private schools 1893–1928, the most important in the present context being Rowlandson House at 140 Hampstead Road 1910–14. Also taught at local government-sponsored schools until 1939, the most notable being the Westminster School of Art 1908–12 and 1915–18. Elected ARA 1924, RA 1934 but resigned 1935. Hon.LL.D. Manchester University 1932, Hon.D.Litt. Reading University 1938. Left London 1934 to live in Thanet until 1938, then in Bathampton until his death. Sickert married three times: Ellen Cobden (1885 until divorce 1899); Christine Angus (1911 until her death 1920); and the painter Thérèse Lessore (1926 until his death).

PRINCIPAL ADDRESSES 1906–14

Until 1912 had a house in France at Neuville-lès-Dieppe; 1913 acquired Villa d'Aumale, Envermeu, near Dieppe.
    From 1905: 6, Mornington Crescent, Camden Town (lodgings and studio); 1905–6: 8, Fitzroy Street (studio); 1908 onwards: 247 Hampstead Road, Camden Town (studio); 1909 onwards: 31, Augustus Street, Camden Town (etching studio); *c.*1909 onwards: Brecknock Road, Tufnell Park (studio); 1909: 64, Grosvenor Road, Pimlico; 209, Hampstead Road (etching school); 1910–14: 140, Hampstead Road (art school); 1911–12: Harrington Square, Camden Town (lodgings); 1912–15: 68, Gloucester Crescent, Camden Town (lodgings); 1914: 24, Red Lion Square, Holborn (studio).

EXHIBITIONS UNTIL 1914

Dowdeswell's Gallery 1886; (jointly with his brother Bernhard Sickert) Dutch Gallery 1895; Durand-Ruel, Paris 1900; Bernheim-Jeune, Paris 1904, 1907, 1909 (the last being a preview of a sale of the pictures at the

Hôtel Drouot); Carfax Gallery 1911; Stafford Gallery 1911; Carfax Gallery 1912, 1913 (studies and etchings), 1914.
    For a complete list of the numerous exhibitions of Sickert's work from 1914 until his death and thereafter, consult the exhibitions list published in the catalogue to 'Sickert Paintings', RA 1992. A selection of the most important exhibitions follows.

MAJOR RETROSPECTIVE LOAN EXHIBITIONS

National Gallery 1941; Temple Newsam House, Leeds 1942; Arts Council 1949 ('Notes and Sketches' from the collection of Sickert's work acquired by the Walker Art Gallery, Liverpool from the Sickert Trust, catalogue compiled by Gabriel White); Arts Council, Edinburgh 1953; (jointly with Jacques-Emile Blanche) Musée de Dieppe 1954 (from local public and private collections); Roland, Browse & Delbanco 1957; Graves Art Gallery, Sheffield 1957; Agnew 1960 (all borrowed from private collections); Arts Council 1960; Roland, Browse & Delbanco 1960; Royal Pavilion, Brighton 1962; Arts Council 1964 (Midlands Tour); Hirschl & Adler Gallery, New York 1967 (part sale, part loans from public and private collections in the USA); Art Gallery of South Australia, Adelaide 1968; University of Hull 1968 ('Sickert in the North', work borrowed from Northern English collections, essay by Malcolm Easton published as catalogue appendix); Islington Town Hall 1970 ('Our Own Sickerts', the collection of Sickert's work belonging to the Islington collection); Fine Art Society, London and Edinburgh 1973 (catalogue incorporates a biography of Sickert and notes on the pictures by Wendy Baron); Towner Art Gallery, Eastbourne and Guildford 1975 ('Sickert in Dieppe', catalogue introduction and notes by Wendy Baron); Arts Council touring exhibition 1977–8 (catalogue includes essays by Wendy Baron and Gabriel White and a reprint of Gabriel White's article on Sickert's drawings, first published *Image*, no.7, 1952); New Haven, Yale Center for British Art, 1979 ('Walter Sickert as Printmaker', catalogue by Aimee Troyen); The Art Gallery of Western Australia, Perth, and tour in Australia ('The Drawings of Walter Richard Sickert', catalogue by Lou Klepac); Arts Council tour 1981–2 ('Late Sickert: Paintings 1927–42'); Liverpool, Tate Gallery 1989–90; Victoria Art Gallery, Bath 1990 (Sickert portraits, catalogue by Richard Shone); London, Royal Academy and Amsterdam, Van Gogh Museum, 1992–3 ('Sickert Paintings', catalogue by Wendy Baron and Richard Shone with contributions by Patrick O'Connor and Anna Gruetzner Robins); (with Whistler) Fundación "la Caixa" Madrid and Museo de Bellas Artes de Bilbao, 1998 (catalogue essay by Wendy Baron).

LITERATURE

(A more complete bibliography is published in *Sickert Paintings*, ed. Wendy Baron and Richard Shone (New Haven and London: Yale University Press, 1992) (RA 1992).)
Virginia Woolf, *Walter Sickert: A Conversation* (London: Hogarth Press, 1934); W.H. Stephenson, *Sickert the Man; and his Art: Random Reminiscences* (Southport: Johnson, 1940); Robert Emmons, *The Life and Opinions*

of *Walter Richard Sickert* (London: Faber, 1941); Lillian Browse (with an essay on Sickert's art by R. H. Wilenski), *Sickert* (London: Faber, 1943); Walter Richard Sickert, *A Free House! or The Artist as Craftsman being the Writings of Walter Richard Sickert* (ed. Osbert Sitwell who also contributed the introduction, 'A Short Character of Walter Richard Sickert') (London: Macmillan, 1947); Anthony Bertram, *Sickert* (London and New York: Studio Publications, 1955); Lillian Browse, *Sickert* (London: Rupert Hart-Davis, 1960); Sir John Rothenstein, *Sickert* (London: Beaverbrook Newspapers, 1961); Ronald Pickvance, *Sickert* (The Masters series no.86) (London: Purnell, 1967); Marjorie Lilly, *Sickert: The Painter and his Circle* (London: Elek, 1971); Wendy Baron, *Sickert* (London: Phaidon, 1973); Denys Sutton, *Walter Sickert* (London: Michael Joseph, 1976); Richard Shone, *Walter Sickert* (Oxford: Phaidon, 1988); Wendy Baron and Richard Shone, eds, *Sickert Paintings* (catalogue to Royal Academy and Van Gogh Museum exhibition of 1992–3; published London: Yale University Press, 1992); Anna Gruetzner Robins, *Walter Sickert: Drawings* (Aldershot: Scolar Press), 1996; Wendy Baron, chapter on Sickert (pp.34–52), in Pontoise 1998–9.

PICTURES SHOWN AT EXHIBITIONS OF THE CAMDEN TOWN GROUP

JUNE 1911
9 *'Chicken'*
10 *The Camden Town Murder Series, No. 1* (see pl.32)
11 *Lena*
12 *The Camden Town Murder Series, No. 2* (see pl.32)
The critics concentrated entirely on Sickert's *Camden Town Murder* pictures, leaving the remaining two paintings unreported. *'Chicken'* is a vibrant study in oil on panel of around 1908 showing the back view of a young girl at a mantelpiece (Fine Art Society, 1999; rep. Baron 1979, pl.105). Jean McIntyre, who lent this painting to the exhibition, was one of Sickert's most talented pupils at Rowlandson House. I have not been able to identify *Lena*.

DECEMBER 1911
11 *Louie*
12 *Mother and Daughter*
13 *The Old Hôtel Royal*
14 *Carolina dell'Acqua*
Louie, 'a powerful, living study of slatternly humanity' (*Daily Telegraph*, 14 December 1911) is a bust portrait study of a coster-girl painted *c*.1906 (private collection; unpublished and unreproduced). It is not possible to identify which of Sickert's many paintings of *The Old Hôtel Royal* (demolished 1900), or which painting featuring *Carolina dell'Acqua*, one of his favourite models in Venice in 1903–4, were exhibited. *Mother and Daughter* (rep. Browse 1960, pl.64), the only recent painting Sickert showed at this exhibition, showed two coster-women wearing boater hats and coats with fur shawl collars, sitting on opposite sides of a bed apparently oblivious to each other's existence. Sickert also studied this composition in an intricate pen and ink drawing of 1911 (published *New Age*, 6 July 1911, under the title *Lou! Lou! I Love You*; rep. Baron 1979, pl.107) and published an etching in 1915.

DECEMBER 1912
32 *Past and Present*
33 *Chicken*
34 *Summer in Naples*
The whereabouts of *Past and Present* are unknown. The painting showed 'a mature wench and another younger – both equally objectionable' (*Daily Telegraph*, 17 December 1912); the girl possessed 'a bright impertinent eye' and 'plaited hair' (*Outlook*, 14 December 1912). This suggests that Sickert's younger model was the girl represented in a drawing, *My Awful Dad* (Ashmolean Museum, Oxford; rep. Baron 1973, fig.235).

The *Chicken* exhibited in December 1912 was not the painting shown in June 1911, although it is likely that the same model sat for both paintings. 'Chicken' was Sickert's nickname for Emily Powell, who lived with her parents in a house where Sickert rented a studio. She was training to be a singer and by 1914 had joined the chorus of the Royal Opera House. When Sickert painted her by a mantelpiece *c*.1908 she was about eleven years old. She modelled most frequently during the first winter of the war, playing the piano in his Red Lion Square studio. The *Chicken* exhibited in 1912 must have portrayed her as 15 or younger. Press descriptions are helpful, but not conclusive, as regards identification: 'A study of a child ... in an impulsive and wayward mood, but the instinct for selection has not slept, and so life is captured in a masterly ellipsis' (*Pall Mall Gazette*, 12 December 1912); 'a pretty portrait of a girl' (*Yorkshire Observer*, 7 December 1912). Pre-war portraits of 'Chicken' include the head and shoulders portrait of her wearing a felt hat and smiling broadly (private collection; rep. RA 1992, pl.81); a vivid study of her seated on a bed (present whereabouts unknown, rep. Browse 1960, pl.66); and perhaps *The Blue Hat* (Manchester Art Gallery; rep. RA 1992, pl.76) in which the model is traditionally identified as 'Emily'. The first of these paintings is probably a work of early 1914, but the last two paintings could be works of around 1912. The case is not yet proven.

Sickert's main contribution to the third Camden Town Group exhibition, *Summer in Naples*, attracted distaste and admiration (sometimes together) in equal measure. Every critic rose to the bait presented by Sickert's exceptionally perverse choice of title, and many provided full descriptions of the painting to prove their point. Thus the painting, in spite of its present title *Dawn, Camden Town* (private collection; rep. Baron 1979, pl.129) can be identified beyond any doubt. The *Star* (10 December 1912) told its readers that the painting 'represents a hideous middle-aged woman in a state of nature seated on a bed in a wretched attic. Seated on the bed beside her is an ordinary street-corner loafer fully dressed. His attitude suggests that he is suffering from some kind of internal discomfort. But there is no evident relation between the two figures. They seem unaware of each other's existence, and they appear to belong to two different realms of thought. The colour of the picture is a discord in dirty mud – the colour Mr. Sickert has made peculiarly his own.' *The Times* (19 December 1912), on the other hand, remarked that if Sickert's colour 'is a little grimy ... so is his mood'. The *Daily Telegraph* (date as above) found the 'unstimulating realism' of the 'masterly, sordid, unemotional study' depressing: 'As to the bravura and withal the subtlety of the execution, as to the consummate ability of the artist, there can hardly be two opinions ... Is Mr. Sickert cynical, is he flouting the conventional proprieties, or is he really content with these musty, flabby realities – three ugly motives upon which he plays skilful, but still ugly variations?' The *Pall Mall Gazette* (date as above) judged Sickert 'serenely (and very consciously) contemptuous of popular opinion'. It is probable that Sickert's choice of subject was deliberately calculated to remind the critics, perhaps even to remind his fellow-exhibitors, of themes developed in Fitzroy Street under his guidance. His were the only typically 'Camden Town' figure pictures left in an exhibition dominated by landscapes. Apart from *Danse* by Lewis, *Summer in Naples* was the only provocative painting at the Carfax Gallery.

PAINTINGS IN PUBLIC COLLECTIONS

The date-bracket for inclusion of works in this catalogue (see p.157) separates Sickert's work of the Camden Town period from his vast production between 1882 and 1942. Lillian Browse, in her book on

Sickert published in 1960, included a comprehensive list of Sickert's drawings and paintings in public collections throughout the world. There have, of course, been many acquisitions since that date but her list still provides an excellent guide to Sickert's work in public ownership. Most galleries in Great Britain, and many in the English-speaking world, own examples of Sickert's work of all periods.

Catalogue and reproduction references are given to my monograph (Baron 1973) and to Baron and Shone (RA 1992). In the latter the plates (but not the figures) are all in colour and the accompanying text is informative. Reproduction references are given to Richard Shone's monograph (Shone 1988).

United Kingdom

ABERDEEN: ART GALLERY

La Gaîté Rochechouart 1906
Oil on canvas; 61 × 50.8
Inscribed *Sickert* bl
Exhibited Paris, Bernheim-Jeune 1907 (50) and 1909 (64)
Provenance: Lord Cottesloe
Purchased from Alex Reid & Lefevre, 1950
Ref. Baron 1973, cat. no.234, fig.156; Christie's 1988, no.31; Shone 1988, pl.27 in colour; RA 1992, fig.140

The Basket Shop, Rue St Jean, Dieppe c.1911–12
Oil on canvas; 50.2 × 60.9
Inscribed *Sickert* bl
Provenance: Mrs Wemyss Honeyman, from whose estate purchased, through Christie's, 1979
Ref. Baron 1973, cat. no. 293

Hampstead c.1914
Oil on canvas; 51.1 × 61.8
Purchased from Agnew's, 1937

BATH: VICTORIA ART GALLERY

Celia Brunel, Lady Noble (d.1962) c.1905–6
Oil on canvas; 50.8 × 40.6
Inscribed *Sickert* tr
Provenance: Lady Noble, by whom given, 1948 [1948.269]
Ref. Baron 1973, cat.no.204, fig.138

BIRMINGHAM: BARBER INSTITUTE

The Eldorado, Paris c.1906
Oil on canvas; 48.3 × 59
Provenance: Madame de Gandarillas; Charles E. Eastman
Acquired 1968
Ref. Baron 1973, cat.no.235, fig.163; Christie's 1988, no.30

BIRMINGHAM: CITY ART GALLERY

Noctes Ambrosianae c.1906
Oil on canvas; 63.5 × 76.2
Inscribed *Sickert* br
Provenance: Miss E. D. Trevelyan
Purchased from Roland, Browse & Delbanco, 1949
Ref. Baron 1973, under cat. no.230

BRISTOL: CITY MUSEUM AND ART GALLERY

Army and Navy 1914
Oil on canvas; 50.8 × 40.6
Inscribed *Sickert* br
Exhibited Carfax Gallery 1914 (21)
Provenance: 1914, Contemporary Art Society, by whom allocated, 1935
Ref. Baron 1973, cat.no.311, fig.219; Watney 1980, pl.100

CAMBRIDGE: FITZWILLIAM MUSEUM

Mrs Swinton c.1906
Oil on canvas; 76.2 × 63.5
Provenance: The Hon. Mrs Maurice Glyn; J.W. Freshfield, by whom bequeathed, 1955 [PD. 2-1955]
Ref. Baron 1973, cat. no.223, fig.157; RA 1992, pl.53

Little Rachel at a Mirror 1907
Oil on canvas; 50.8 × 40.6
Inscribed *Sickert* bl
Provenance: L. G. Hoare; Keith Baynes, by whom given, 1974 [PD. 91-1974]
Ref. Baron 1973, under cat.no.263; Yale 1980, no.73

Mornington Crescent Nude 1907
Oil on canvas; 45.7 × 50.8
Inscribed *Sickert* bl
Provenance: O. Sainsière; Norton Simon; Parke Bernet, New York, 5 May 1971 (50); Mrs Maurice Hill, by whom given, 1990 [PD. 103-1990]
Ref. Baron 1973, cat.no.261, fig.177; Christie's 1988, no.38 in colour

Woman with Ringlets c.1911
Oil on canvas; 35.6 × 30.5
Inscribed *Sickert* br
Provenance: F. Hindley-Smith, by whom bequeathed, 1939 [No. 2411]
Ref. Baron 1973, cat.no.317

L'Oeuillade c.1911
Oil on canvas; 38.1 × 30.5
Inscribed *Sickert* bl
Exhibited Carfax Gallery 1912 (18); Brighton 1913–14 (58)
Provenance: Howard Bliss, by whom given, 1946 [No.2727]
Ref. Baron 1973, cat.no.316; Shone 1988, pl.35; Barbican 1997, p.119 in colour

CAMBRIDGE: KING'S COLLEGE, KEYNES COLLECTION

Théâtre de Montmartre 1906
Oil on canvas; 48.9 × 61
Inscribed *Sickert* bl
Exhibited probably Paris, Bernheim-Jeune 1907 (35) and 1909 (63)
Provenance: Goupil Gallery; 1924, John Maynard (Lord) Keynes
Ref. Baron 1973, cat.no.233, fig.162; RA 1992, pl.58

CHICHESTER: PALLANT HOUSE GALLERY

Hubby and Wilson Steer c.1914
Oil on canvas; 37.8 × 30.5
Inscribed *Sickert* br
Provenance: Charles Kearley, by whom bequeathed through the National Art Collections Fund, 1989

DUNDEE: ART GALLERY AND MUSEUM

La Scierie de Torqueville or *Le Vieux Colombier* 1913
Oil on canvas; 66 × 105.4
Inscribed *Sickert* br
Exhibited Carfax Gallery 1914 (22)
Provenance: W. Rees Jeffreys
Purchased from Messrs Tooth, 1955
Ref. Baron 1973, cat.no.342, fig.236; Christie's 1988, no.145 in colour

EASTBOURNE: TOWNER ART GALLERY

The Poet and his Muse or *Collaboration* c.1906
Oil on canvas; 45.7 × 22.9
Inscribed *Sickert* br
Exhibited probably Paris, Bernheim-Jeune 1907 (72)
Provenance: Sylvia Gosse, by whom given, 1955
Ref. Baron 1973, cat.no.256, fig.173

EDINBURGH: SCOTTISH NATIONAL GALLERY
OF MODERN ART

La Rue Pecquet c.1906–8
Oil on canvas; 32.4×24.5
Provenance: Sir Hugh Walpole
Bequeathed by Dorothea Walpole and Mr
R.H.Walpole, 1963 [GMA 863]
Ref. Baron 1973, under cat.no.287

EXETER: ROYAL ALBERT MEMORIAL MUSEUM AND ART
GALLERY

Le Lit de Cuivre c.1906
Oil on canvas; 40.9×50.9
Inscribed *Sickert* bl
Exhibited possibly Paris, Bernheim-Jeune 1907 (55) and
1909 (40)
Provenance: c.1925, Paul Fleming, Copenhagen;
Sotheby's, 12 April 1967 (62)
Purchased from Agnew's, 1968 [121/1968]
Ref. Baron 1973, under cat.no.209; Yale 1980, no.71;
Shone 1988, pl.28

KINGSTON UPON HULL: THE UNIVERSITY OF HULL ART
COLLECTION

Mornington Crescent Nude 1907
Oil on canvas; 40.5×51
Provenance: Helen Lessore; Lawrence Harvey
Purchased, 1979 [121]
Ref. Christie's 1988, no.39 in colour; RA 1992, fig.6

KIRKCALDY: MUSEUM AND ART GALLERY

'What shall we do for the rent?' c.1908 (pl.32)
Oil on canvas; 51.5×41
Exhibited probably Paris, *Salon d'automne* 1909 (1582
or 1583) as *L'Affaire de Camden Town*; CTG I (10 or
12) as *The Camden Town Murder Series No. 1* or *No. 2*
Provenance: Dr Alastair Hunter; 1953, J.W.Blyth
Purchased from his estate, 1964
Ref. Baron 1973, cat.no.275, fig.193 as *Summer
Afternoon*; Baron 1979, pl.106; Christie's 1988, no.51;
RA 1992, pl.68

Wellington House Academy 1914
Oil on canvas; 41×51
Inscribed *To W.H.Davies/ Walter Sickert /Wellington
House Academy* bl
Provenance: Scottish Gallery, Edinburgh; 1948,
J.W.Blyth
Purchased from his estate, 1964
Ref. Christie's 1988, no.150

LEEDS: CITY ART GALLERY

Off to the Pub (The Weekend) c.1912
Oil on canvas; 49.5×30.5
Inscribed *Sickert* tr
Provenance: Capt. A.K.Charlesworth; his widow, Lady
George Cholmondeley,
by whom bequeathed, 1966
Ref. Baron 1973, cat.no.303, fig.212; RA 1992, pl.72

Café des Arcades, Dieppe or *Café Suisse* c.1914
Oil on canvas; 53.3×38.1
Provenance: Mrs M.Clifton
Purchased from Agnew's, 1942
Ref. Baron 1973, under cat.no.347; RA 1992, pl.78;
Pontoise 1998–9, no.47, p.51 in colour

LINCOLN: USHER ART GALLERY

Reclining Nude c.1906
Oil on canvas; 38.1×50.8
Inscribed *Sickert* br
Provenance: Contemporary Art Society, by whom
allocated, 1936
Ref. Baron 1973, under cat.no.209

LIVERPOOL: WALKER ART GALLERY

Fancy Dress, Miss Beerbohm 1906
Oil on canvas; 50.8×40.6
Inscribed *Sickert* bl
Provenance: Walter Taylor; Mark Oliver; Mrs
D.M.Fulford, by whom given through the National Art
Collections Fund, 1945 [2263]
Ref. Baron 1973, cat.no.215, fig.149
NOTE: The British Council owns a version of this
subject painted c.1916.

LONDON: ARTS COUNCIL COLLECTION, HAYWARD
GALLERY

The Belgian Cocotte 1906
Oil on canvas; 49.3×39.3
Inscribed *Sickert* bl
Purchased from Roland, Browse & Delbanco, 1953
Ref. Baron 1973, cat.no.220, fig.154

Woman seated on a Bed 1907
Oil on canvas; 66×78.7
Inscribed *Sickert Dieppe 1907* bl
Exhibited possibly NEAC summer 1911 (195) as *The
Ebony Bed*
Purchased from the Leicester Galleries, 1955
Ref. Baron 1973, cat.no.255, fig.176

LONDON: COURTAULD INSTITUTE OF ART

Mrs Barrett 1906
Oil on canvas; 50.2×40
Inscribed *R^d St A.R.A./Sickert* bl
Provenance: Roger Fry, by whom bequeathed, 1934
Ref. Baron 1973, cat.no.219, fig.153

LONDON: GOVERNMENT ART COLLECTION

Two Coster Girls c.1908
Oil on panel; 35.5×26
Provenance: Vanessa Bell; Mrs A.V.Garnett
Purchased from the Fine Art Society, 1979 [14531]
Ref. Baron 1979, pl.23

The Integrity of Belgium 1914
Oil on canvas; 92.5×71.3
Inscribed *Sickert – 1914 –* bl
Exhibited RA January 1915, 'War Relief Exhibition'
(210)
Provenance: J.L.Rayner; by descent
Purchased from Phillips, 5 November 1991 (29) as *The
Belgian Soldier* [16778]
Ref. Baron 1973, under cat.no.351; RA 1992, pl.83

LONDON: MUSEUM OF LONDON

Gallery Box at the New Bedford Music Hall c.1906–7
Oil on canvas; 50.7×41
Inscribed *Sickert* bl
Provenance: Edward Le Bas
Purchased from Christie's, 3 March 1978 (118)
[78.155]
Ref. Baron 1973, cat.no.247

LONDON: TATE GALLERY

La Hollandaise c.1906
Oil on canvas; 51.1×40.6
Inscribed *Sickert* br
Exhibited Paris, Bernheim-Jeune 1907 (33) and 1909
(54)
Provenance: Mark Oliver; Hart Massey; 1960, Peter
Shand-Kydd; Mrs Janet Shand-Kydd, from whom
purchased, through Browse and Darby, 1983 [T03548]
Ref. Baron 1973, cat.no.211, fig.144; Baron 1979, pl.7;
Shone 1988, pl.25; RA 1992, pl.49

Woman Washing her Hair 1906
Oil on canvas; 45.7×38.1

Inscribed *Sickert* tl
Exhibited possibly Paris, Bernheim-Jeune 1907 (21) as
La Toilette
Provenance: By 1927, Lord Henry Cavendish-Bentinck
Bequeathed by Lady Henry Cavendish-Bentinck, 1940
[N05091]
Ref. Baron 1973, cat.no.248, fig.170; Watney 1980,
pl.17; RA 1992, fig.138

Girl at a Window: Little Rachel 1907 (pl.3)
Oil on canvas; 50.8 × 40.6
Inscribed *Sickert* br
Provenance: 1907, Hugh Hammersley; Dr Robert
Emmons; T. W. Strachan; William Wallace; Executors
of the Hon. Mrs E. A. Wallace
Accepted by H M Government in lieu of tax and
allocated to the Tate Gallery, 1991 [T06447]
Ref. Baron 1973, cat.no.263, fig.182; Baron 1979, pl.34;
Christie's 1988, no.40; RA 1992, pl.64

L'Américaine 1908
Oil on canvas; 50.8 × 40.6
Inscribed *Sickert – 1908* br
Exhibited Paris, Bernheim-Jeune 1909 (4) as *The
American Sailor Hat*
Provenance: By 1925, Lord Henry Cavendish-Bentinck
Bequeathed by Lady Henry Cavendish-Bentinck, 1940
[N05090]
Ref. Baron 1973, cat.no.266, fig.185; RA 1992, fig.146

Jacques-Emile Blanche c.1910
Oil on canvas; 61 × 50.8
Exhibited NEAC summer 1912 (163)
Provenance: Miss Hilda Trevelyan, from whom
purchased, 1932 (N04912)
Ref. Baron 1973, cat.no.294, fig.204

The Garden of Rowlandson House – Sunset c.1910–11
Oil on canvas; 61 × 50.2
Inscribed *Sickert* bl
Exhibited Whitechapel 1914 (434)
Provenance: By 1914, Lord Henry Cavendish-Bentinck
Bequeathed by Lady Henry Cavendish-Bentinck, 1940
[N05088]
Ref. Baron 1973, cat.no.290, fig.200; Baron 1979, pl.61

Off to the Pub c.1911
Oil on canvas; 50.8 × 40.6
Inscribed *Sickert* br
Given by Howard Bliss, 1943 [N05430]
Ref. Baron 1973, cat.no.296, fig.205; Watney 1980,
pl.73

Harold Gilman c.1912
Oil on canvas; 61 × 45.7
Chantrey Purchase from Mrs Sylvia Gilman, the sitter's
widow, 1957 [T00164]
Ref. Baron 1973, cat.no.299, fig.207; Baron 1979,
frontispiece in colour; Watney 1980, pl.39; Yale 1980,
no.86

Ennui c.1914
Oil on canvas; 152.4 × 112.4
Inscribed *Sickert* br
Exhibited NEAC summer 1914 (164)
Provenance: 1914, purchased by the Contemporary Art
Society, by whom allocated, 1924 [N03846]
Ref. Baron 1973, cat.no.313, fig.223; Watney 1980,
pl.14; RA 1992, pl.80, rep. facing catalogue 79

Tipperary 1914
Oil on canvas; 50.8 × 40.6
Provenance: 1914, Lord Henry Cavendish-Bentinck
Bequeathed by Lady Henry Cavendish-Bentinck, 1940
[N05092]
Ref. Baron 1973, under cat.no.352; RA 1992, pl.84

MANCHESTER: CITY ART GALLERIES

The Blue Hat, Emily c.1911–12
Oil on canvas; 50.8 × 40.6
Exhibited possibly CTG 3 (33) as *Chicken*

Provenance: Charles L. Rutherston, by whom given,
1925 [1925.265]
Ref. RA 1992, pl.76

Hubby and Marie 1914
Oil on canvas; 51 × 40.7
Inscribed *Sickert* br
Provenance: Charles L. Rutherston, by whom given,
1925 [1925.576]
Ref. Baron 1973, under cat.no.309

Nude seated on a Couch 1914
Oil on canvas; 50.8 × 40.8
Inscribed *Sickert* br
Provenance: Charles L. Rutherston, by whom given,
1925 [1925.578]
Ref. Baron 1973, cat.no.310, fig.220; Baron 1979,
pl.147; Shone 1988, pl.52

NEWCASTLE UPON TYNE: LAING ART GALLERY

The Piazzetta, Venice with La Giuseppina. c.1906
Oil on canvas; 40.7 × 50.8
Inscribed *Sickert* bl
Acquired, 1932
Ref. Baron 1973, under cat.no.130
NOTE: A later reworking, on an English canvas, of a
subject Sickert studied in Venice in 1900.

NOTTINGHAM: CASTLE MUSEUM

Noctes Ambrosianae 1906 (pl.25)
Oil on canvas; 63.5 × 76.2
Inscribed *Sickert* br
Exhibited NEAC summer 1906 (123); Paris, *Salon
d'automne* 1906 (1545)
Provenance: Walter Taylor; J. B. Priestley
Purchased, 1952
Ref. Baron 1973, cat.no.230, fig. 159; Baron 1979, pl.1;
Shone 1988, pl.32; RA 1992, pl.54

OXFORD: ASHMOLEAN MUSEUM

Rue Aguado 1914
Oil on canvas; 33 × 41
Inscribed *Sickert* br
Provenance: J. E. Bullard, by whom bequeathed, 1961

Ennui c.1914–16 (pl.6)
Oil on canvas; 76.2 × 55.9
Inscribed *Sickert* br
Provenance: F. Hindley-Smith, by whom bequeathed,
1939
Ref. Baron 1973, under cat.no.313; Shone 1988, pl.46
in colour

PLYMOUTH: CITY MUSEUM AND ART GALLERY

Little Rachel 1907
Oil on canvas; 42.3 × 35
Inscribed *Sickert* tl and bl
Provenance: Sotheby's, 12 July 1961 (165)
Purchased from Agnew's, 1961 [1961.117]
Ref. Baron 1973, cat.no.264, fig.184

PORTSMOUTH: CITY MUSEUM AND ART GALLERY

Belgian Cocottes. The Map of London 1906
Oil on canvas; 50.8 × 40.6
Inscribed *Sickert* br
Exhibited probably Paris, Bernheim-Jeune 1907 (67)
Provenance: Sir Augustus Daniel; J. W. Blyth
Purchased, 1973
Ref. Baron 1973, cat.no.227

PRESTON: HARRIS MUSEUM AND ART GALLERY

Two Women c.1911
Oil on canvas; 50.8 × 40.6
Inscribed *Sickert* bl
Provenance: Contemporary Art Society, by whom
allocated, 1938

Ref. Baron 1973, cat.no.295, fig.203; Christie's 1988, no.73

SALFORD: ART GALLERY

Reflected Ornaments c.1909
Oil on canvas; 29 × 39.4
Inscribed *Sickert* bl
Purchased from the Tib Lane Gallery, Manchester, 1964
Ref. Baron 1973, cat.no.279

SHEFFIELD: GRAVES ART GALLERY

The Soldiers of King Albert the Ready 1914
Oil on canvas; 196.2 × 152.4
Inscribed *Sickert–1914* tl
Exhibited NEAC winter 1914 (151)
Provenance: L. G. Wylde; his sale, Christie's, 14 December 1932 (111); G. P. Dudley Wallis; his sale, Christie's, 21 May 1943 (71); Christie's, 17 July 1959 (64); Christie's, 5 July 1963 (22)
Purchased Sotheby's, 9 July 1969 (22) [3530]
Ref. Baron 1973, cat.no.351, fig.245; Shone 1988, pl.51 in colour; RA 1992, pl.82

SOUTHAMPTON: CITY ART GALLERY

The Mantelpiece c.1906–7
Oil on canvas; 76.2 × 50.8
Exhibited Paris, Bernheim-Jeune 1907 (48) and 1909 (3)
Purchased, 1932
Ref. Baron 1973, cat.no.298, fig.210; RA 1992, fig.136

The Juvenile Lead: Self-portrait 1907 (pl.1)
Oil on canvas; 51 × 45.8
Inscribed *Sickert* bl
Exhibited Paris, *Salon d'automne* 1907 (1535) as *L'Homme au Chapeau Melon*
Provenance: Mrs L. G. Wylde; David Niven, from whom purchased, 1951
Ref. Baron 1973, cat.no.257, fig.174; Baron 1979, pl.35; RA 1992, pl.62

Europe

FRANCE, ROANNE: MUSÉE JOSEPH DECHELETTE

Reclining Nude 1906
Oil on canvas; 50 × 61
Inscribed *Sickert* bl
Exhibited probably Paris, Bernheim-Jeune 1907 (53) and 1909 (31) as *La belle Rousse*
Provenance: Paris, Bernheim-Jeune 1909: Paul Jamot, by whom bequeathed, 1942 [2584]
Ref. Pontoise 1998–9, no.41, p.46

FRANCE, ROUEN: MUSÉE DES BEAUX-ARTS

The South Façade of St Jacques 1907–8
Oil on canvas; 76 × 63
Inscribed *Sickert* bl
Provenance: Jacques-Emile Blanche, by whom given, 1923
Ref. Baron 1973, cat.no.288, fig.198; Pontoise 1998–9, no.44, p.47 in colour

Australia

ADELAIDE: ART GALLERY OF SOUTH AUSTRALIA

Mornington Crescent Nude, Contre-Jour 1907
Oil on canvas; 50.8 × 61.1
Inscribed *Sickert* bl
Provenance: 1907, Hugh Hammersley
Purchased from Agnew's, 1963 [0.1977]

Ref. Baron 1973, cat.no.260, fig.179; Baron 1979, pl.38; RA 1992, pl.65; Adelaide 1997, p.21 in colour

ADELAIDE: CARRICK HILL TRUST

The Red Blouse (Mrs Barrett) c.1908
Oil on canvas; 50.9 × 40.4
Inscribed *Sickert* bl
Provenance: 1952, Mr and Mrs E. W. Hayward, by whom bequeathed, 1983
Ref. Baron 1973, under cat.no.265

BRISBANE: QUEENSLAND ART GALLERY

Little Rachel 1907
Oil on canvas; 61 × 50.8
Inscribed *Sickert* bl
Exhibited Eldar Gallery 1919 (1)
Provenance: Mrs Rayner; Robert Emmons
Purchased from the Adams Gallery, 1956 [1: 0727]
Ref. Baron 1973, under cat.no.263

Canada

FREDERICTON, NEW BRUNSWICK: BEAVERBROOK ART GALLERY

Bonne Fille c.1905–6
Oil on canvas; 46 × 38.1
Inscribed *Sickert* br
Provenance: Bernard Falk
Purchased by Lord Beaverbrook from Christie's, 18 November 1955, lot 62

The Old Middlesex c.1906–7
Oil on canvas; 63.5 × 76.2
Inscribed *Sickert* br
Exhibited possibly Paris, Bernheim-Jeune 1907 (38)
Provenance: L. G. Wylde; Sir Geoffrey Hutchinson (Lord Ilford); 1954, Lord Beaverbrook
Given by the Second Beaverbrook Foundation, 1960
Ref. Baron 1973, cat.no.231, fig.160

Sunday Afternoon c.1912–13
Oil on canvas; 50.8 × 25.4
Inscribed *Sickert* bl
Provenance: Bernard Falk
Purchased by Lord Beaverbrook from Christie's, 18 November 1955, lot 61
Ref. Baron 1973, cat.no.305, fig.214; Yale 1980, no.87; Shone 1988, pl.39 in colour; RA 1992, pl.74

HAMILTON, ONTARIO: ART GALLERY OF HAMILTON

The Painter in his Studio 1907
Oil on canvas; 50.8 × 61
Inscribed *Sickert* bl
Exhibited NEAC spring 1907 (73) as *The Parlour Mantelpiece*
Provenance: 1907, Hugh Hammersley; Christie's 25 April 1930 (125); Dr Robert Emmons; Mrs George Swinton
Purchased from Roland, Browse & Delbanco and given by the Women's Committee, 1970
Ref. Baron 1973, cat.no.258, fig.178; Baron 1979, pl.36; Yale 1980, no.72; RA 1992, pl.63

Hubby and Marie 1914
Oil on canvas; 47 × 38.1
Inscribed *Sickert* br
Provenance: J. Stanley-Clarke, from whom purchased through Agnew's and given by the Women's Committee, 1960
Ref. Baron 1973, cat.no.309, fig.218
NOTE: Close to the composition sketched by Sickert in his letter to Nan Hudson of February 1914. The picture of the same title in Manchester is related to this Hamilton picture.

MONTREAL: MUSEUM OF FINE ARTS

Landscape
Oil on panel; 13.7×23.8
Inscribed *R. St* bl
Provenance: Mrs Maud Morgan, by whom given, 1961

TORONTO: ART GALLERY OF ONTARIO

*St Jacques c.*1914
Oil on canvas; 67.3×50.2
Inscribed *Sickert* br
Provenance: E.M.B. Ingram; Contemporary Art Society,
by whom allocated, 1946
Ref. Baron 1973, cat. no.349, fig.244

New Zealand

WELLINGTON: MUSEUM OF NEW ZEALAND

The Blue Hat 1914
Oil on canvas; 46.5×38.4
Inscribed *Sickert* br
Purchased through the British Council, 1951
Ref. Baron 1973, cat. no.320
NOTE: Another of the 'direct little pictures' sketched in
Sickert's letter to Nan Hudson of February 1914.
Sickert altered his proposed dimensions a little.

South Africa

JOHANNESBURG: ART GALLERY

La Rue Ste Catherine and the Vieux Arcades 1910
Oil on canvas; 56.5×49.5
Inscribed *Sickert* bl
Provenance: 1910, commissioned by Sir Hugh Lane for
Sir Otto Beit, by whom given, 1910
Ref. Baron 1973, under cat. no.155

United States of America

BOSTON: MUSEUM OF FINE ARTS

Les Petites Belges 1906
Oil on canvas; 50.8×40.6
Exhibited probably Paris, Bernheim-Jeune 1907 (43)
Provenance: Mrs Montgomery Sears; Mrs
J.D. Cameron Bradley, by whom given, 1938
Ref. Baron 1973, cat. no.216, fig.150; Yale 1980, no.70;
RA 1992, pl.50

CLEVELAND: MUSEUM OF ART

Easter Monday. Hélène Daurmont 1906
Oil on canvas; 51×40.5
Inscribed *Sickert* bl
Provenance: Mrs Wemyss Honeyman; Sotheby's, 25
June 1980 (51)
Purchased from the Fine Art Society, 1982
Ref. Baron 1973, cat. no.217, fig.151

COLUMBUS: GALLERY OF FINE ARTS

*Farmhouse, Dieppe c.*1913
Oil on canvas; 21×25.4
Inscribed *R. St* bl
Provenance: Miss Marjorie Lilly
Purchased from Agnew's, 1956
NOTE: Probably inscribed many years after its execution.

NEW HAVEN: YALE CENTER FOR BRITISH ART, PAUL
MELLON COLLECTION

*La Rue Pecquet c.*1907
Oil on canvas; 40.6×33
Inscribed *Sickert* bl
Provenance: Lord Croft; Sotheby's, 21 November 1973
(35)
Purchased from Browse & Darby, 1982 [B1982.5.1]
Ref. Baron 1973, under cat. no.287

Camden Town Murder or *What shall we do for the Rent?*
*c.*1908
Oil on canvas; 25.6×35.5
Inscribed *Sickert* br
Provenance: R.M. Coode; Sotheby's, 21 November
1973 (32); Sotheby's, 14 November 1979 (39)
Purchased from the Anthony d'Offay Gallery, 1979
[B1979.37.1]
Ref. Baron 1973, cat. no.269, fig.192; Shone 1988,
pl.38; RA 1992, pl.69

NEW YORK: METROPOLITAN MUSEUM

Jeanne Daurmont, La Cigarette 1906
Oil on canvas; 50.8×40.6
Inscribed *Sickert* br
Exhibited Paris, Bernheim-Jeune 1907 (81) and 1909
(62)
Provenance: Vincent Astor; Mr and Mrs James
Fosburgh; Mary Cushing Fosburgh, by whom
bequeathed, 1978 [1979.135.17]
Ref. Baron 1973, cat. no.221, fig.155; RA 1992, pl.51

La Maigre Adeline 1906
Oil on canvas; 45.7×38.1
Inscribed *Sickert* bl
Exhibited Paris, Bernheim-Jeune 1907 (16)
Provenance: Adolphe Tavernier; Scofield Thayer,
by whom bequeathed, 1982 [1984.433.24]
Ref. RA 1992, pl.57

NEW YORK: MUSEUM OF MODERN ART

*La Gaieté Montparnasse c.*1907
Oil on canvas; 61×50.8
Inscribed *Sickert* br
Exhibited possibly NEAC summer 1909 (169)
Provenance: G.P. Dudley Wallis; Lord Cottesloe
Purchased from the Mayor Gallery, 1960 [422.60]
Ref. Baron 1973, cat. no.236, fig.164

WASHINGTON: PHILLIPS COLLECTION

*Miss Hudson at Rowlandson House c.*1910
Oil on canvas; 91.4×50.8
Inscribed *Sickert* br
Provenance: Anne Hope Hudson; Miss Ethel Sands, by
whom bequeathed, 1966 [1740]
Ref. Baron 1973, cat. no.318

John Doman Turner
c.1870–1938

A stockbroker's clerk and amateur artist who worked in
pencil, charcoal, chalk and watercolour, but not in oils.
Pupil of Gore, to whom he was introduced by Frank
Rutter. Because Turner was deaf, Gore's tuition took
the form of thirty letters over the period 1908–13
offering constructive comments on the drawings Turner
sent to him by post from his home in Streatham. A
drawing of the nude by Turner done *c.*1908–9,
scattered with criticism and advice in Sickert's hand,

suggests that he also attended classes taken by Sickert at
the Westminster School of Art. Member of the Camden
Town Group. First exhibited at the AAA in 1911.
Founder-member of the London Group but resigned
almost immediately and did not contribute to the
1913–14 exhibition in Brighton, 'English Post-
Impressionists, Cubists and Others', arranged by the
Camden Town Group. Exhibited one drawing in the
summer of 1918 with the London Group.

DOMAN TURNER

EXHIBITIONS SINCE HIS DEATH

Piano Nobile, Richmond 1996–7, 'Spencer Gore & his Circle with special focus on John Doman Turner' (introduction and catalogue notes by James W. Robertson); Michael Parkin, 1997 (introduction by Frederick Gore).

PICTURES SHOWN AT EXHIBITIONS OF THE CAMDEN TOWN GROUP

JUNE 1911
40 *Duncan and Godfrey in 'The Coster's Courtship'* (pastel)
41 *Elizabeth II at Brighton* (watercolour)
42 *In the Grand Circle* (drawing)
43 *Brighton Shelters*
The fullest review of Doman Turner's work was given in the *Sunday Times* (18 June 1911): 'we may possibly find a future recruit to classicism in Mr. J. Doman Turner, whose watercolours show a tendency to ascetic composition though his drawing "In the Grand Circle" … reveals a touch of Sickertian romanticism'.

During the past twenty years, largely due to the researches of Mr James Robertson, many of Turner's works on paper have been discovered. These include several drawings of Gore's favourite music hall, the Alhambra, which might well have been the location of *In the Grand Circle* (although a positive identification is not possible). The two Brighton titles suggest that Turner visited Walter Taylor, friend and patron of Sickert and other Camden Town Group painters, who had a house there. Some of Turner's work, for example *Interior* of 1909 (rep. Richmond 1996–7, p.38), reveals a distinct affinity with Taylor – whose preferred medium was watercolour. Both artists had an instinct for design expressed in the bold deployment of bright, clean colours confined within crisp lines of drawing.

DECEMBER 1911
1 *Walberswick*
2 *H.M.S. '–' Sheerness*
3 *St. Valéry-s-Somme*
4 *The Sound of Kerrera and Kerrera Island, Oban*
Two of Turner's extant drawings of 1911 are of St Valéry-s-Somme. The date 8 July 1911 on one of the drawings, *Rue des Pilotes, St. Valéry-s-Somme* (rep. Richmond 1996–7, p.36), proves that Turner visited France during the summer of 1911. He may have travelled with Manson. Traditionally the other St Valéry drawing (from Gore's collection and now in the collection of the University of Hull) is believed to be the work exhibited with the Camden Town Group. Executed in soft pencil, pen and ink and watercolour, with the planes of colour and tone clearly defined, it again has something of the quality of a drawing by Walter Taylor. A drawing, *Walberswick*, was exhibited at the Parkin Gallery in 1997 (13).

DECEMBER 1912
1 *Eastbourne*
2 *Canal Boats*
3 *The Fair Green, Mitcham* (see pl.52)
4 *Mitcham Common* (watercolour)
It is possible that *Canal Boats* is the drawing now known as *Bargees, Kingston upon Thames* and that *Eastbourne* could be *Burlington Hotel, Eastbourne* (both exhibited in the Parkin Gallery in 1997, nos.21 and 30 respectively).

WORKS IN PUBLIC COLLECTIONS

Turner did not paint in oil. Therefore his works are not catalogued in this list of paintings in public collections. Works on paper by Turner are in the Southampton City Art Gallery (pl.52) and the University of Hull Collection (*Montvilliers, near le Havre*, 5 August 1912, and *St. Valéry-sur-Somme*, 1911; see Baron 1979, pp.283–4, pl.108).

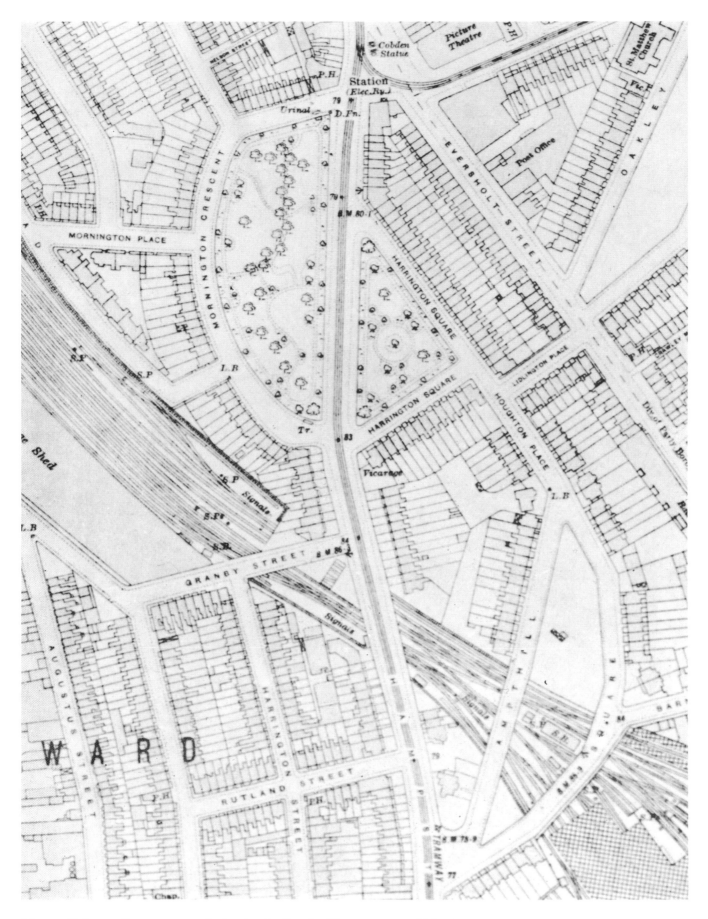

Map 1 Ordnance Survey map, 1916, showing the Camden Town area around Mornington
Crescent, Hampstead Road (with Rowlandson House) and the great railway tracks behind

General index

The general index covers all sections of the book, including the catalogue section (pp.154–208). Indexing of the catalogue section is selective. Information in the catalogue which might enhance the use of the book as an aid to further research on the period 1906–14 has been incorporated in the index. Thus references to significant early patrons and owners, and to key exhibitions up to 1920, are collated and cross-referenced in the index. Career summaries are likewise cross-referenced, but notes on membership of the Fitzroy Street and Camden Town groups (covered in the introductory text) and on the later careers of Camden Town Group members are omitted. Plate numbers are in brackets, printed in **bold**.

Abbreviations of institutions and exhibitions follow the conventions used elsewhere in the book. In addition the following abbreviations are used in the index:
CTG   Camden Town Group
FSG   Fitzroy Street Group
n.   note
p.   page

217

Index of works
by Camden Town Group members

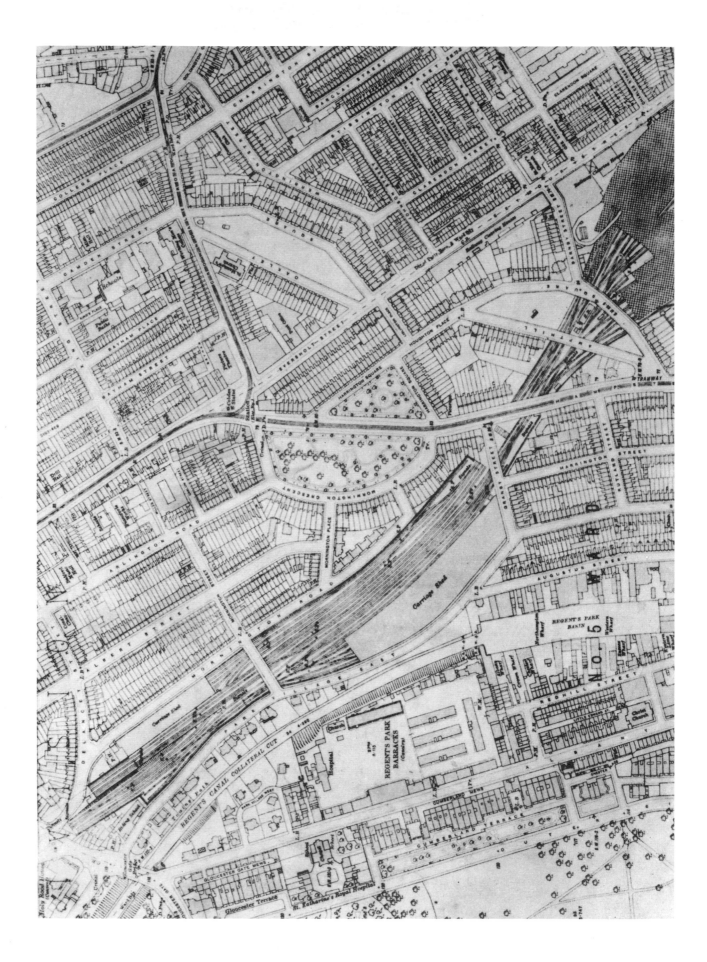